Mother's
Revenge

Mother's Revenge

A DARK AND BIZARRE ANTHOLOGY OF GLOBAL PROPORTIONS

Scary Dairy Press

MOTHER'S REVENGE
Copyright © 2017 Scary Dairy Press
Cover artwork by Logo Design Team © Scary Dairy Press LLC
Stories Copyright © 2017 Their individual authors. All rights reserved.

Library of Congress Control Number: 2017905497
Scary Dairy Press LLC, Palmyra, VA

ISBN: 0996052739
ISBN-13: 9780996052733

Dedication

To all mothers, everywhere.

Contents

Acknowledgments ix
Introduction xi

Water
Bottom Trawler 3
The Food Chain 12
Rusalka 25
It Wants to be a Swamp 43
Bride of the Deep 54
Snickerdoodle Bunkum 64
From the Bluff 78
Sleet Teeth 85
Miracle Material 96
Downpour 110

Air
Midwives 131
A Choice in Exile 148
Swarms 163
Earth Mother 178
She Had a Lot of Problems 196

Fire

b.E.L.F.r.y. 213
Mean Green 226
A New Kind of Eden 237

Earth

Don't Fool with an Earth Witch 259
A Mother's Fury 280
Nature's Promise 302
The Path 315
Stones are Breathing Tonight 325
A Cautionary Tale 336
Annals of the Allred Clan 349
Ursus Horribilis 373
Mud Babies 385
Acquired Taste 396
Voice of the Mountian 406
Plat 7 417

Hope

Scientific Mothers 429
Last Natural Woman 439
About the Editors 455
Affirmation of Copyrights 457

Acknowledgments

A PROJECT SUCH AS THIS requires many people contributing in a team-work effort to foster and grow the concept into reality. Many thanks to Broos Campbell and Cin Ferguson for organizing and editing the stories in this piece of work. The Logo Team in the U.K. provided their artistry and excellence in the development of the *Mother's Revenge* book cover. Each of the thirty-two writers were amazing to work with. Without their artistic contributions, their ability to collaborate with the editors, and dedication to this project, this anthology would have remained simply a dream. Many thanks to the beta readers who included their thoughts and suggestions to help this book become the best it could be. And finally, we thank our conscientious readers who we are certain care about the Earth just as much as we do.
—Scary Dairy Press

Introduction

THERE ARE THIRTY-TWO TALES IN this global anthology. Thirty-two (32). The number was not arbitrarily selected. In numerology, the number thirty-two is that of personal freedom and creative expression. It exudes the qualities of curiosity and optimism, as well as adventure and inspiration. In science, the number 32 is the freezing point of water at sea level on the Fahrenheit temperature scale. There are thirty-two teeth in the adult human mouth, including wisdom teeth, which for some reason have failed to make us collectively wise.

This anthology was conceived with the element of hope. Hope that it would encourage readers to seriously commit to becoming active caretakers and watchdogs for our Earth. Together we can drink water from the tap instead of investing in so many plastic water bottles. We can turn off lights when we leave the the room, reduce water consumption and waste, and grow organic vegetables and fruits instead of using harmful pesticides.

Together, we can save our dying oceans. Right now, over 14 billion pounds of garbage is dumped into the ocean every year, and a large part of that is composed of plastic. Over a trillion gallons of untreated sewage and industrial waste is dumped into U.S. waters every year. There are over one hundred pesticides on and in our fruits and vegetables as well as in our air and water. These pesticides are known to contribute to birth defects, gene mutations and cancer. By purchasing organic foods, and demanding pesticide free environments, we can change the world by voting with our wallets.

Our combined pollution kills an average of three million children under the age of five, one million seabirds and a hundred million mammals each year, and yet most of our population does nothing about it. Our children can no longer swim in rivers and lakes because of toxic water pollution.

The Scary Dairy Press team reaches out to you, dear readers, as we ask you to help us heal the Earth and stop the destruction done to her every day. If we all work together, we become part of the solution that will last for lifetimes. In a show of support, Scary Dairy Press has made a commitment to donate funds to four groups that work desperately toward making our world a better place. Ten percent of profits made every year from the sale of this book will go to the following well-respected organizations: Union of Concerned Scientists; the Clean Air Task Force; Water is Life; and the Sierra club.

Our team is constantly making changes to improve the Earth, and we are grateful for anything our readers do to help improve the state of the world. Each Earth-saving action we all take goes a long way toward making change for the better. Finally, we hope you enjoy reading these fantastic tales born from very talented and creative minds. Just reading shows you care. Read on!

—Cin Ferguson

I had no idea what to expect when Q invited me aboard this project, except that the stories would be much like the good doctor herself—quirky, intelligent, and exuberant, with a dark side to keep things interesting.

I wasn't disappointed. The tales in *Mother's Revenge* come in a variety of flavors, from classic gothic to '50s pulp to modern gonzo, with a few detours into speculative fiction and the paranormal. Some build slowly from sweetness and light to bloody frenzy. Others are creepy from the get-go.

While editing these little monsters, I leaped onto their backs with a sledgehammer in one hand and a chainsaw in the other, in some cases, and left well enough alone in others. We've made certain style choices for the sake of cohesiveness, but left British usage intact in stories from Commonwealth countries. Regardless, the stories were born of the hard work and talent of those who created them, not those who straightened their ties and sent them out into the world. The authors were free to accept or reject suggestions, and these tales are their own. —Broos Campbell

Water

Bottom Trawler

by

David Agranoff

THE MESH MOVED SILENTLY THROUGH the ocean's depth. Sound, as humans know it, didn't exist there. The network of tightly woven ropes created a wall of sand and debris as it scraped slowly across the ocean floor. This wall hid the approaching death. Out of the dark blue, two eyes stared at him. A cod swam alone, eyes blinking at him, innocent, unknowing of the destruction that was coming.

It hit him from behind. He felt the wall of sand and the net gripped him like a suffocating hug. It felt like a hand, crushing him.

Rowtta opened his eyes to see Doctor Ross standing over him, gripping Rowtta's shoulder. Ross shook him again.

"Captain?"

Rowtta sat up in his rack and tried to shake off the nightmare. The balding scientist was not what he wanted to see when he woke up, but Rowtta was glad to have awakened.

"Captain, you need to get on the bridge."

"Miller?"

Ross nodded.

3

Rowtta swung his leg out of the rack; he had never taken his boots off. He had been so tired, he barely remembered going below deck. He took a deep breath and ascended the steps to the deck of his ship. The cold air made him shiver. Grossman, one of the scientists, stood on the deck with a flashlight, looking into the dense fog.

Rowtta extended his arm and could barely see his hand.

"Any signs of the city?"

Grossman shook his head. "We must be getting close. Miller is freaking out again."

The ship pulled hard to the left. Grossman would've slid across the deck if Rowtta hadn't grabbed his arm. Rowtta looked up at the bridge and saw Miller's silhouette over the helm. The ship was turning quickly.

Rowtta ran the steps to the bridge and pushed the door open, and Miller jumped back. Rowtta gripped the wheel tightly as he turned it. The useless radar droned on across the bridge. First Officer Miller dropped to the floor and lay in a lump crying, as he did any time they came close to shore. The captain gritted his teeth as he maneuvered the ship through the intense fog. He watched Grossman go below, most likely to pray. That praying was a habit the scientists had developed recently.

"Captain, please, take us back," Miller wept.

Rowtta hated watching a grown man cry, but he had to do this. Their water supply was gone and their food had run out days ago.

Miller crawled across the floor and hugged Rowtta's legs. "I can catch us some dinner, just get back out to sea."

Rowtta spared Miller a glance. The first officer no longer looked like a man in his thirties. He had always seemed like a brave kid, and Rowtta had hired him as a favor to his dad, who'd given him his first job in the fishing fleet. Miller had been a hell of a trawler. Now Rowtta just wanted the kid to shut up. The fog started to break and Rowtta felt the urge to pray—for a skyline, lights, helicopters, any sign that New York was where it was supposed to be.

"Goddamn it, Captain! Stop!"

Rowtta kicked at Miller. "Get a hold of yourself, son."

He grabbed the kid. Burkin, another of the scientists, stepped onto the bridge and helped him lift. The two men held Miller up as he screamed.

"He did this in Boston," Burkin said.

"Not as bad."

A wave rocked the ship. The three men fell over as the vessel's parts rattled. A boom echoed from the shore. It sounded like a blast from a tuba, but loud enough to move the earth. They'd heard this sound hourly for weeks now, but they had never been this close. The sounds were increasing in numbers and intensity with each day.

Miller wept again before laughing like a maniac.

"No!" Burkin said as he stood.

Rowtta looked up reluctantly as the fog drifted away from the city, following the wave. Now, seemingly in an instant, the night became as clear as glass. Under the glow of the moon, the building turned to ash before them. Miller laughed like a maniac.

Burkin fell back and put his hands in his face. "No, no!"

There were no lights in the skyline. Only a few flames burning among the shadows of the empty skyscrapers. Another boom, and the buildings waved like stalks in a wheat field. Several crumbled, and the sounds of destruction became a chorus. Another wave from the bay rushed toward the boat.

"Impossible." The captain grabbed onto something to steady himself. "Hold on!"

The ship shook and bounded over the wave. Papers flew, gauges and alarms went crazy.

Miller grabbed Rowtta's collar. "You've seen it. Now, go! Get us out of here."

Ross stood in the doorway, allowing the frigid air into the bridge. "We can't leave," he said.

Miller rolled onto his back and laughed, kicking his feet like a two-year-old having a tantrum.

Burkin leaned his head against the wall. "Look at it, Ross; it's dead, just like Boston."

"We need food, we need answers."

Rowtta held Miller down.

"This is my ship," Rowtta said to Ross, "and you're getting pretty goddamn close to giving me an order. On my fucking ship."

Rowtta could tell that Ross was biting his tongue. From the moment the radios had gone dead, any respect or trust the head scientist had had for Rowtta was gone. He was a *scientist* after all, and thought he knew better than some washed-up, divorced, drunk sea captain. Miller suddenly became still, whispering something over and over. Rowtta couldn't understand him.

"Yog Saggoth. Yog Saggoth," Miller said.

"What is he saying?" Ross asked.

Miller's eyes grew wide and didn't blink. Rowtta waved Ross inside, but Ross didn't move from the doorway.

"In or out. You're letting in the cold."

Miller suddenly stopped his chanting.

"Cap'n." Miller sounded like a little boy. "It's July."

Rowtta stared into Miller's eyes. The life had all but drained out of him, and it was like Rowtta was watching his own sanity drain away. Miller's eyes danced left to right. And when Miller's body relaxed, Rowtta let go of him and stood up.

"We're turning around."

Rowtta cranked the wheel and felt the nets rise up out of the ocean. The sky was blue, and the sun felt warm. The crank turned quickly and the motor assist would not engage; the trawling net rose from the surface with a whoosh. Rowtta waited until the water strained from it and turned the net over the deck. It was empty. He'd trawled the floor for hours, maybe days, maybe weeks. He felt woozy.

The net hung in front of him dripping on the deck. One fish flopped in the net, her mouth gaping and closing repeatedly—a single silver-skinned cod. Rowtta looked away, not wanting to see the fish's struggle. He turned his back on the net, but felt the two eyes on him. The ship rocked.

The distant booming horn had sounded for weeks. But today it was deeper, more urgent, as the wave rocked the ship enough to wake Rowtta at his table in the galley. He was actually thankful for this wave. He didn't need the nightmares when he slept; he was living one.

Two days since New York. Rowtta sat staring at his empty coffee cup. His body ached for caffeine, his head pounded. Miller sat across the galley from him. He hadn't said much since New York. The scientists were on the deck trying to figure out a way to remove the salt from the ocean water so they could drink it.

Rowtta studied Miller. His first officer, once a fine young man, just smiled at him. Insanity had taken over. Miller kept smiling like he was sitting in a park, watching children play. Rowtta slammed his empty cup down on the table and stood up. He went up to the deck and left Miller laughing like a maniac.

The sky was a dark purple, and it had been weeks since they had really seen the sun. It burned dull in the sky, behind the curtain of dark haze. Burkin had called this a nuclear winter, but they had seen no sign of any bombs having been detonated. Rowtta stood on the deck, feeling the cool breeze. The ocean didn't have the same fresh, salty smell anymore. Now an unsettling metallic odor drifted about under the gloomy sky.

Ross was on a laptop and the other three scientists stood over him arguing. Rowtta never wanted to deal with these scientists, but without a single paying cod season in years, he didn't have much choice. His father had made over a million dollars a year back in the 1970s selling cod, but now they were like the buffalo of the Great Plains. The scientists on board the trawler claimed that their research might bring the cod back.

That was a lie, of course; they were watching them die.

Rowtta stood over Ross, who was looking at a bunch of numbers on his computer screen. Burkin pulled a tube out of the water and dropped it like a dead snake on the deck.

"Where is our water, Ross?"

Ross closed his laptop.

"We're doing the best we can given that we're not hydro engineers."

Rowtta turned to head back to the bridge and then stopped.

"Well, but you were supposed to watch fish. Why don't you find us something to eat?"

Ross stood and stomped towards the captain.

"We need to go ashore," Ross said.

Rowtta looked past him at Burkin. He was the reasonable one.

"You want to go ashore?"

"No, but I think we have to."

Then there was laughter; crazy, intense laughter. Miller walked out onto the deck.

"We having a little debate without me?"

Rowtta stepped closer to Miller and placed a hand on his shoulder. Miller's skin was oddly cold. Rowtta stepped back.

Ross tapped his fist on a railing. "Damn it, Miller, let's be rational," he said.

Miller looked all around at the dark afternoon sky. The frigid air caused the water in the rain buckets on deck to freeze at night. When they still had water.

No, Rowtta thought. *There wasn't anything rational happening.*

"So, Ross, tell me," he said. "Have you found any rational explanation for what is happening?"

Ross nodded. "Chemical biological attack. Terrorist dirty bombs. For all we know, Europe, Asia, and Africa are unaffected. We go ashore, refuel, stock our food and water supplies, and we head east to Africa."

"Why aren't the satellites still working?"

Ross thought about Miller's question.

"EMP?" Burkin said.

"I'm not sure what did it, but something wiped the whole god-damn slate clean," Miller said, and pointed at the sky. "It took out the fucking sun."

Rowtta walked up the first two steps to the bridge and turned around. "I'll find a small port."

Miller ran at him but Burkin blocked his path. "To what? Throw us at it?"

Rowtta stopped at the door. "At what, Miller?"

Miller walked back towards the galley. "I'm not going to stop you this time. I'll let you drive us into the belly of beast."

They broke through the fog line and hit choppy waves. Burkin and Ross walked in and looked surprised to see Miller sitting calmly behind Captain Rowtta. Rowtta ignored them, intent on directing the ship. Burkin was the first to gasp.

They had no idea which city it was. Some place along the shore of New Jersey, or Delaware. But for the first time they saw the source of the screams. Legs the size of buildings, and a body the shape of a giant spider. Its skin crawled with tentacles.

Rowtta slowed the ship as the horrible thing opened its mouth. It hadn't been a horn that they were hearing; that booming sound was a howl. The earth shook and the ocean sloshed. Rowtta hung onto the helm. Miller stood up and smiled at it. Burkin's sanity snapped like a rubber band.

Ross screamed. "Turn around!"

"He can't!" Miller laughed.

The earth rumbled under the pressure as the creature walked, destroying the city in its way. The buildings collapsed under its feet. Rowtta cut the engine and ran around pushing buttons. The ship stopped and everyone was quiet. Burkin cried, prone on the floor, and Ross stepped out onto the deck. He didn't want to believe his eyes.

Rowtta joined him. The air was colder than ever. Miller laughed hysterically, lying on the floor of the bridge. Beyond the enormous monster eating the skyline, something hung in the sky. At this distance it didn't look bigger than a carousel. It was a void, spinning in the sky and growing larger by the second. Rowtta put his hands up and felt a great rush of air.

Miller walked up behind him.

"I don't think we're meant to understand."

The creature howled, shaking the ground. Buildings crumbled and the whole city turned to dust under force of the creature. The ocean air pushed toward the spinning void, which sucked the wreckage of humanity up into its swirling vortex. The ocean chopped under the ship, pulling it slowly toward the shoreline.

Ross held onto the railing. "It can't be!"

Rowtta fell to the deck and couldn't bring himself to struggle. What would remaining upright do at this point? He thought about Erin. His ex-wife was the only person left in the world he had cared about. Even if she *had* hated him, he still loved her. Did she make it out of Boston? Did her new husband die with her? The air roared over them like a wind tunnel.

It was impossible, unimaginable, and a thousand other words that all meant insane. There was nothing left to do but scream. Rowtta opened his mouth, but nothing came into his lungs. He rolled onto his back. The night was silent and still. He had never heard such an empty quiet. He couldn't hear his breath.

Scream!

Nothing. He heard nothing. His chest seethed in pain, and he felt pressure inside his skull. He felt like he might very well explode. He kicked and punched the deck, but heard nothing. Ross sat slumped on the deck of the ship, already dead. Miller sat up dead with a smile on his face. Rowtta felt his eyes get heavy. Slowly they closed.

Rowtta stood on the deck of his ship. A single blue-skinned cod lay on the deck, her body stretched in a U, her mouth and gills flapping, searching for water. Suddenly the cod's eyes found him. Rowtta turned and flipped a switch. The net unfurled, dumping thousands of cod onto the deck.

David Agranoff is the author of four published novels, and two short-story collections. His novels include *The Vegan Revolution...With Zombies, Hunting the Moon Tribe, Boot Boys of the Wolf Reich* and *Punk Rock Ghost Story.* His first short story collection, *Screams from a Dying World,* was nominated for the Wonderland Book award. His short-stories have appeared in *Dark Discoveries, The Magazine of Bizarro Fiction,* and his story "Punkupine Moshers of the Apocalypse" appeared in the *Best Bizarro Fiction of the Decade* anthology.

He writes primarily horror but in summer 2017 is releasing his first science fiction novel, *Flesh Trade,* co-written with Edward R. Morris. He lives in San Diego with his wife and their brood of cute non-humans. He loves kung fu movies, Torrey Pines State Park, vintage sci-fi paperbacks, the Portland Trailblazers, IU basketball and vegan cookies. Follow him on Twitter @Dagranoffauthor

The Food Chain

by

Edward Ahern

WALTER PEAKED FISHED THROUGH THE dawn without a hookup. At seven a.m. he set down his rod and picked up his paddle, his kayak's bow spinning toward shore and sliding in a familiar surge-slow pattern toward the beach. At a hundred yards from shore he noticed silver glints in the water beneath him. *Bait school*, he thought. But just then a shiny ten-pound fish split the surface and arced over the bow.

It was a ranging shot. Bluefish leapt out of the water from both sides, snapping at anything their jaws encountered. As the blues slammed into him they sheared off apple-sized mouthfuls of skin and muscle. He screamed and began paddling as fast as he could get his muscles to coordinate. The relentless blues bit into his chest, back, and head. Two flopped into the kayak's foot-well and began biting off calf and thigh muscle.

His screams went unheard by the few people on the shore. Muscle cramps and blood loss slowed his progress, and the feeding frenzy of open-jawed fish intensified. He felt a twinge in his left hand and glanced down to see that his pinky finger had been nipped off.

Walter lost consciousness fifteen yards from shore and the kayak slowly coasted onto the sand. Two orange-suited lifeguards ran down toward him.

The schooling blues veered off to run along the beach. Mary Perillo was the only person in the water, wading in water just over her hips. It took the fish four seconds to reach her.

The swarm cut through calves and thighs. People on the beach saw a middle-aged, overweight woman staggering in frothing water and screaming, "Help! Help! My God, help me!"

She toppled over backward, water filling her mouth and stopping her screaming. One of the lifeguards ran down the beach and into the surf in front of Mary, and then screamed and jumped back out of the water, blood gushing from three large bites.

There were perhaps two hundred blues. Mary died from blood loss and asphyxia less than a minute after they hit.

"Dr. Charpentier? Larry Westcott from the Connecticut Department of Energy and Environmental Protection. Thanks for getting here so quickly. Everyone else is already in the conference room."

Westcott had the slender build and earnest, bifocaled stare that Laura Charpentier associated with environmentalists. She turned to him as they walked. "Have there been other attacks since yesterday?"

"Yes, three on the New York side of the sound, two more each in Connecticut and Rhode Island. You'll get the details in the briefing." Westcott raised his voice as they entered the conference room. "Everyone, this is Dr. Laura Charpentier, the marine biologist from Woods Hole. Please introduce yourselves."

The room smelled of stale coffee and aftershave. Fifteen men of varying ages sat around the table. *Don't get academic on them,* she thought.

Laura braced herself for the evaluating stares. At forty-three she was still attractively trim, but was confident that the men's' eroto-meters wouldn't spike.

Two of the men were state troopers, and Laura's mouth twitched when she imagined them trying to handcuff and interrogate a fish.

The junior trooper presented capsule reports—the attacks had occurred at seven different locations at apparently random times, two women and one man dead, seventeen others wounded, three dead fish available for dissection. While the trooper was speaking, Laura hooked up her laptop to the AV system in the room. When the trooper finished, sixteen pairs of eyes focused on her.

"Good afternoon," she said. "I study our bluefish population, which is why I'm here. I know a lot about bluefish taxonomy and biology, but a commercial fisherman can probably tell you as much about bluefish behavior in Long Island Sound as I can."

Laura fired up a picture of an open-jawed bluefish, its scalpel teeth glinting.

"How many of you are fishermen?" she asked. About eight hands went up. "And have any of you seen a bluefish act like this?"

Larry spoke up. "When they're in a feeding frenzy they strike at anything, even a beer can. But the only people I know who got bit put their fingers too close to those teeth."

Laura nodded. "And that's what we know about them too. Bluefish eat fish, not people. And it's a good thing they do eat other fish, because they forage along the same beaches that we wade and swim in. But the only suspected bluefish attack on a human was in Spain, on a seven-year-old girl. Have any of you heard of other blues attacking a human?"

The heads swayed from side to side. "Not before this," the older cop said.

Laura offered more projections. "Bluefish teeth are extremely sharp, and they'll frequently bite off the tail of another fish so they can turn around and chop up the cripple. That often includes their own young. They're quite aggressive, and travel in loose schools.

"Their formal name is *Pomatomus saltatrix*. Streamlined, high-speed predators, often reaching fifteen to twenty pounds and occasionally up to forty pounds. The only surviving species of the family *Pomatomidae*, so not closely related to any other fish. They feed in huge numbers in most temperate and subtropical waters, but almost nothing is known about how and where they reproduce.

"While in a feeding frenzy, blues will snap at anything shiny or quickly moving. In short bursts they can outrun a boat, and are as common as clams everywhere from Maine down through Florida. Some people even eat them."

That comment got Laura the expected laugh. Most people who fished for bluefish just threw them back because they didn't like their oily taste. She put up her final picture, a photo of beachgoers lined up along the water's edge looking at frothing water a few yards offshore.

"This is a frenzy of bluefish feeding on menhaden. We know that by last month commercial trawlers had taken out over half of the menhaden in the sound, forcing the blues to feed opportunistically on any other fish they could find. A predator population like the bluefish declines one breeding cycle after the decline in the prey population, but that's a year away. My best immediate advice is what you're already doing. Keep instructing the lifeguards to quickly get the people out of the water if they see a feeding frenzy close to shore. I believe that this is a one-time aberration, but I'm giving you all my contact information in case anything else happens."

Laura got back to her condo that evening, sat at her kitchen table, and ate take-out Chinese. She'd lived with three men over the last fifteen years, but had eventually cut them all loose. At 10:30 she stripped down for a shower.

As the warm water flushed over Laura, a man named Pete Grosswald, also naked, was wading into the surf at Penfield Beach in Fairfield, Connecticut. He'd filled and drained his plastic beer cup several times before staggering down the beach slope away from the party.

He stripped and shivered his way out until the water was up to his nipples, and then dove under. He barely felt the first shearing bite on his cold-deadened skin, but then he screamed as jaws attacked him from neck to ankle. He sucked in air and screamed again when he saw his intestines spill out into the water. The rock music from the party blared in tempo with his screams, swallowing them up.

By the time Laura stepped out of the shower, Pete's body had settled onto the sand in six feet of water, left to be further shredded by crabs. The jumbled pile of clothes and shoes was found the next morning, a half hour before low tide revealed his head and bones.

Pete's body was laid out on a metal examining table. "Bluefish?" the trooper asked.

Laura's stomach churn held below the level at which she'd vomit. She'd been helicoptered back down to view what was left of Pete's body after the fish and crabs had dined.

"Hard to tell, but I'm guessing yes. The crabs have also been nibbling, but the bite radii are that of adult bluefish, and the bite edges are sharp, like a blue would cause. Is he the only fatality like this?"

The trooper shrugged. "So far. But not many people go swimming in the sound after dark. We're scanning the missing-persons reports to see if we have other possible victims."

She used a magnifying glass to examine the remains more closely. Getting within inches of the dead flesh and bone was somehow more clinical and less repulsive. "Ah," she muttered.

"Something?"

She used tweezers to extract a broken tooth from Pete's shinbone. "I won't know for sure until tests are done, but this looks like a fragment of a bluefish tooth. It's weird, though—bluefish are sight feeders, usually a lot less active at night. Do we know who this man is?"

"The ID in the pants on the beach was for a Fairfield U. student, Pete Grosswald." The trooper's voice had risen an octave. "Bluefish don't do this, doc."

"Not in my experience, no."

Laura knew her tone wasn't reassuring. She walked up one flight of stairs and into a teleconference room. Twenty-seven state police and government officials waited for her.

"Are we online for this meeting?"

"Yes, doctor. There's about forty people listening in. You'll have the list later. I'll mike you up now. What've you discovered?"

"Initial examination indicates that Mr. Grosswald was also attacked by bluefish—"

An overbearing voice interrupted her. "What the hell is going on here, doc? Our beaches are on lockdown, and we have no idea what's up. Our shorefront residents are screaming about the danger and the damage to property values—"

Another voice overrode the first. "Another time, a different meeting, Arthur. Dr. Charpentier, I'm Fred Malone. I head up the U.S. Office of Emergency Management. That was Arthur Lillard, who handles the dirtier jobs for Connecticut governor Malloy."

"I thought this was a regional concern. wasn't aware this was a national concern."

"Dr. Charpentier, we're missing a bunch of people up and down the Atlantic coast, and while the reports we've gotten aren't as precise as yours, it looks like they were attacked by bluefish."

"I haven't heard anything about these other attacks."

"You weren't meant to. Nobody seems to have given much of a damn up till now about bluefish, except maybe you, and we want you to take a point position on this. Dragoon whoever you like out of Woods Hole, or wherever else you need them from. But we need answers quickly. We seem to have already lost more people than this year's murders in Chicago."

Laura nodded, and then realized that he couldn't see her. Her ideas churned like chunks of fish in boiling chowder. "Okay, sure. I assume I can use a contact at your organization to clear away obstacles?"

"Of course, but we'll try and clear a path for you ahead of time. Right, Arthur?"

"Uh, yeah, sure."

Laura continued. "A lot of the talent I'll need is right here in this room, and I'd like to focus the meeting on identifying alternatives and deciding on emergency first steps. For now, we need to keep people and bluefish apart. And I'm going to need data. As much as you all can gather, no matter how insignificant it seems."

Five hours later the meeting broke for dinner. Laura used the time to make a call.

"Frank?"

"Yeah, who's this? Laura? I thought you'd consigned me to the lowest level of hell."

"I did. I do. But now I need to use the devil I know. You're going out on a charter for me tomorrow."

"Laura, I've already got a charter. In fact, I'm booked for the week. Tuna and shark."

"You can keep the sports on board, but you're going bluefishing tomorrow."

"I may be a devil, but you're sure as hell not God. Go play with yourself, little lady."

"Frank, I don't have time to piss back and forth through the phone line. In ten or fifteen minutes you're going to get a call from the Rhode Island State Police. If you don't do as I ask they're going to shut your ass down. Hard. You'll get paid, and your sports will get to fish for free. But you're going to fish for bluefish for the rest of the week in several locations I'll provide, keeping the fish intact and on ice."

"I'll believe it when I see their uniforms."

"Just call me back when you get the confirmation. And Frank . . ."

"Yeah?"

"I want you to bait half the hooks with raw pork."

Two mornings later, Laura pushed herself out of bed at five a.m., microwaved a cup of yesterday's coffee and sat down at her desktop computer. The in-boxes were bloated with reports, frequently conflicting, but only one fatal attack was logged in. The regional beaches had been closed to swimmers and waders.

A week, maybe, and we can begin to figure this out. She hoped her task force hadn't forgotten anything.

Victor Sudvoy had been surf fishing Long Island Sound for over twenty years. He moved out and back in the water with the tide, in an isolated spot where he wouldn't have to deal with lifeguards or security. His waders had been patched with sealant so often that they glittered in the morning sun. He was fishing the ebb, working his way out to Penfield Reef as the water level dropped.

The blues swam against the rip until they found the source of the smell. The first few bites were tentative, but soon the teeth were poking through the unappetizing wader skin deeply enough to draw blood. Once it swirled into the water the feeding frenzy began. He screamed, but was a quarter mile from shore, just a knobby bump on the reef to anyone watching from land. He stumbled and fell, bluefish tearing at his upper body. By the time he could stand up, seawater had filled his waders up to his thighs.

He threw away his surf rod and began slogging toward the shallows, but the fifty pounds of water in his waders held him back, making him easy pickings for the churning fish. Before he had gained ten yards toward shore, he passed out and fell under the water. The blues shredded him from neck to waist, and then burrowed into the waders to rip off flesh down to his knees. The tidal rip pushed his remains into deeper water. His sealed tackle bag and shreds of his waders washed onto shore.

"Talk to me, Frank."

His voice crackled on the ship-to-shore phone. "It's weird. We're painting big schools of fish, blues and stripers. The stripers took both jigs and fish bait, but we couldn't get a blue hooked up. Not until we switched to Porky Pig. The blues hammered the meat baits. We've got forty of them at least, and need to get them back on shore before they go bad. Why pork?"

"Because it's the closest to how we taste. Have you got a live well?"

"Yes."

"Before you come back, put one or two blues into the well and try to keep them alive until I can get my hands on them."

"It's your money. Sure."

Laura spent the next three days farming out data research, and dissecting and running tests on dead bluefish. Her live blues shunned baitfish, but bit each other trying to get at morsels of beef or pork. She scheduled a teleconference for the fourth day.

God help me, she thought, *for what I'm about to recommend.*

After clipping on a microphone, Laura began. "Please hold your questions until after I've briefed you. I gather from the data that the beach closures have almost eliminated incidents to swimmers, but that we've had two dozen cases of shore fishermen who've been attacked or gone missing. We need to notify the public that shore fishing is also prohibited.."

Laura continued. "We've examined the stomach contents from one hundred thirty-five blues and found flesh from seals, humans, and in two separate instances a dog and a sea gull. But no fish. The blues have apparently changed their feeding habits, something corroborated by the fifty percent decline in the observed seal population, and the discovery of seal remains washed up at over twenty sites.

"In short, we've become a prey species for the blues, a danger that needs to be, if not eliminated, reduced to a manageable risk.

"We've already agreed to use Long Island Sound as the initial focus because of its contained nature. What I'm going to propose is related to the sound and not the open waters along the Atlantic coast.

"I . . . I'm reluctant to recommend these emergency first steps, but the alternatives would leave the blues in control of the sound. In order to reopen the beaches we need to greatly reduce the number of bluefish. This could be done in two steps. First, commence sustained commercial fishing targeting the bluefish. Use trotlines with thousands of hooks baited with mammalian byproducts. That would largely spare the striped bass.

"Second, use shallow-water commercial netting for immature bluefish, the snappers. The immature fish seem to still be targeting smaller baitfish, which would realistically have to be removed with the snappers. This should greatly reduce the number of adult bluefish next year.

"The health of marine life in the sound will be changed greatly for the worse, and changed in ways we can't foresee yet, but we would hopefully have regained the sound for recreational use. The costs would be borne by commercial fishermen, supplemented by the federal government and the contiguous states of New York, Connecticut, and Rhode Island in some equitable way, perhaps calculated on shoreline miles.

"While this is going on we can make plans to attack the bluefish menace along open seafronts. It's mid-June. If we begin immediately we may be able to get back into the sound in late August."

Laura had barely stopped when verbal bedlam erupted, replaced ten seconds later with an eerie silence.

A voice spoke through the speaker system. "This is Fred Malone. I've temporarily shut down your outgoing sound. The one thing we can't do is nothing. We can argue deficiencies and consequences while we proceed. If you have better first steps than what Dr. Charpentier has proposed, send me an email right now. We'll take a day to winnow through suggestions and if there's not a better one then we're going to proceed with her plan. I will now accept your oral comments on why her proposals are impossible to implement."

The eerie silence resumed. What Laura had proposed was environmentally brutal but relatively easy to perform. The teleconference concluded an hour later. Taiwanese and Chinese commercial fishing ships already illegally netting in the Atlantic were granted permission to operate in the sound to target bluefish. Over the next few weeks, thirty-seven tons of fish were taken out of the sound.

On July 19, fishing operations were expanded to include the entire Atlantic seaboard, and on August 13, Long Island Sound was declared open for swimming and water sports.

Larry Westcott was one of the first to call and congratulate Laura. "I still think what we did was ecologically dangerous, Laura, but I can't argue with its results. Incidentally, you did a great job selling the gutting of the bluefish population on *Good Morning Americans*."

"It was a bad choice, Larry, but we didn't have any better ones. Are your Connecticut beachgoers getting back into the water?"

"Slowly. We've got a week of hot weather forecast and I expect to see many more folks in up to their necks."

Laura hesitated. "I wonder if God knew what he was doing when he gave us dominion over the animals."

The third day of hot weather brought thousands to the beaches and into the water. And something else as well. From the deeper pockets and trenches of the sound, tens of thousands of snakelike, four-foot-long shapes rose up, schooled, and swam toward the shallows. The spiny dogfish, deprived of their usual food, were on the move.

Helen McDonald was the first victim. The raspy snouts bumped into her thighs, sniffing out that the fourteen-year-old was mammalian. The teeth, more widely spaced than a bluefish's, sank into her legs. The dogfish then spun and twisted until chunks were torn off her body. She dragged herself by her arms halfway onto the shore but died there as the dogfish slithered through inches of water to continue eating her legs. Four hundred attacks followed hers.

Laura was frozen out of the task force, not being a shark expert, and being held somehow responsible for the new attacks. As she watched the news she worried that the sharks, having released themselves from bottom feeding on dark nights, would find a way to proliferate and survive. They wouldn't easily relinquish their place in the sun. She pondered the domino effect that occurred when mankind intervened in life and tried to control nature. It usually took years to discover the impact. Now, it seemed, nature was tired of waiting. Tired of hoping humans would recognize their errors and set things right. First the bluefish. Now the dogfish. She had no doubt the government was forming new task forces designed to destroy this next problem.

And after that, what will follow?

Ed Ahern resumed writing after forty-odd years in foreign intelligence and international sales. He's had a hundred forty stories and poems published so far. His collected fairy and folk tales, *The Witch Made Me Do It,* was published by Gypsy Shadow Press. His novella *The Witches' Bane* was published by World Castle Publishing, and his collected fantasy and horror stories, *Capricious Visions,* was published by Gnome on Pig Press. Ed's currently working on a paranormal/thriller novel tentatively titled *The Rule of Chaos.* He works the other side of writing at Bewildering Stories, where he sits on the review board and manages a posse of five review editors.

Rusalka

by

Neil Davidson

Look at the girl: Her feet don't quite touch the ground. Earlier in the day a road crew with jackhammers dug away the cement underneath her. They left only the ravaged and grassless dirt. The patch of earth looks naked and strange even in the green cityscape of Portland, where, usually, the gray and green of plants and civilization are neatly segregated. But still stranger is that the girl is afloat, and that only one man sees her. As she hovers, water drips from her, slowly making muddy splotches on the ground. The rest of the city is dry, and a man in a dark gray suit gawks across the street. *This is impossible,* he thinks, but no one else notices.

Her head hangs back as though she had been knocked unconscious by some accident or, in a certain light, it could almost seem as if she were being held aloft by some hook caught in her mouth, but there is no indication of this other than her mouth being slightly agape.

A middle-aged woman with a bag of groceries in one arm and a tight grip on the hand of her child passes the man, bumping against him. He doesn't notice.

The floating woman is young, and looks barely old enough to drive. Her features are soft, except for her nose, which, though rather sharp, has a jagged crook to it in the center of the bridge. Her red hair hangs heavy, clumped together in bunches like seaweed just pulled

25

from the tide. She wears a black dress, so thin that it seems to melt from her tired, emaciated body.

The man approaches her, walking as in a trance, and she stirs for the first time. Her head rises up to gaze at him. Her eyes look as though they can't decide whether to be green or blue, and still she drips onto the naked earth below. Under her sharply defined jawbone, a bruise stretches across the front of her neck. When she moves her head up, he can see the subtle shifting of free-floating cartilage where her larynx collapsed as she hung from the rafters of her home far from this city, but he doesn't know this. He sees the shifting fragments of throat as only a strange trick of the light, giving rise to the vague sense that she might be able to turn her head in any direction, that she can always see him.

"Who are you?" he says slowly, not quite believing what he sees.

She rests a hand on his shoulder, and comes in to kiss his cheek.

"No," he says, trying to step away. The suit underneath her hand soaks through. "Who—? I don't know you."

Her grip hardens on his shoulders, until he fears she could break his bones with her hands. Her kiss, however, is gentle, and he finds himself leaning into it though he could not explain why. Her miraculous appearance feels suddenly inevitable. How else could this day have happened? An angel has come to me, he thinks without question. A gift from God.

"You remind me of a man I knew back home," she says. The words have only the slightest trace of a lilting accent, a gentle push given to each word that gives a rhythm just shy of normal. "I will have to come and see you again." She kisses him once more, and stares at him, admiringly. "Yes. I'll have to come back for you."

He cowers, obediently, beneath her, coming up only to her breast despite her being a great deal shorter than he, and then, in an instant, she is gone. The ground between the two slabs of sidewalk is soaked and muddy. He steps out of the mud with a loud squelch and almost loses the shoe, but doesn't notice. How bizarre a sight this must be for anyone standing witness among the daily May lunch rush.

The man, Matthew Bunin, returns home from a long day at the law firm. It is just after seven. The girl's appearance earlier that afternoon, though, lies somehow dormant, clouding the back recesses of his mind. His wife, Lena, sits in the kitchen, holding a cup of coffee and already wearing the sea-foam green scrubs of the downtown hospital where she works the graveyard shift.

She looks incredible, one leg crossed over the other as though mimicking relaxation. Her posture hides a latent energy. She sits perched on the edge of the chair as if ready to throw the cup across the room and sprint in any direction. There's something particularly beautiful about that starched cloth; something about her always seems more alive with the promise of an emergency. The green knows this, can sense it, and responds accordingly whenever she wears it. Other pastels lack the same vitality.

The light of the setting sun drapes the counter in a warm orange.

"Morning," Lena says. "How did the day go?"

Matthew doesn't answer. Instead he circles the room in a wobbling ellipsis, feeling there is something important he has forgotten. His eyes wander, but nothing here reminds him of the girl.

"Losing it already?" she says. "A little young for dementia, aren't you?"

Matthew laughs. "Yeah. A bit." But still the sense something is missing lingers—an empty place that should be filled at the table, a noise or smell he can't quite place. Lena takes two plates out of the cupboard and serves herself amid a sudden cloud of steam from the pot on the stovetop. Matthew, no longer circling, examines a blank space on the wall below the cupboard and next to the switch for the garbage disposal.

"Seriously?" Each syllable is enunciated with crisp aggression. "Matthew, honey, can you sit with me before I have to go to work?" Her eyebrows rise, as though the answer should be obvious.

"Of course," he says. "I didn't realize it was so late."

"Seven o'clock happens at the same time every night," Lena says, but continues in a softer voice: "Sorry. It must have been a rough day at the office?"

He knows he should say something, but he sits there, staring into his plate of stir-fry as it loses heat. It really hadn't been that bad. Just another day.

He is a divorce lawyer in the financial district of downtown Portland, but their firm also has corporate accounts. He rarely sees a client in something other than a three-piece because of this, despite not working directly for the companies. His caseload, though, has been piling up lately.

"All right. Good talk, Matt," she says, putting her mug and empty plate in the sink. "I'm really glad we had such a meaningful connection tonight. It feels like it's a turning point." She gives a quick shake of her head and leaves. The front door slams a second later.

They've been married for just under seven years, and dated for several years before that. They met when he lived in the Bay Area as a law student. Mostly, he's happy.

In the morning, he goes downstairs to make coffee. The hardwood floor is cold under his bare feet. He grinds the coffee beans, dumping them onto the filter paper, and pours the water in the coffeemaker, mindlessly lulled into the rhythm by muscle memory. He starts the machine and it begins to percolate with a happy gurgle, full-throated and hearty, like the sound of someone laughing despite their lungs being filled with liquid. A bizarre way to listen to the brewing coffee, to be sure, but it seems, in that moment, stranger that he had never heard it before, like there was something in the laughing burble that had always been waiting for him to discover it.

He pours, and takes a bitter sip. It had been years since he'd last gone without at least one cup, though he rarely enjoys the almost-ritual. The silence is what most appeals to him, but even this pleasure is born of loneliness. It's the same delight one would get from pressing against a bruise.

At some point, Lena must have noticed his growing detachment and volunteered to work graveyard shifts, despite that they hadn't needed the money in years. Matthew never mustered the courage to suggest she quit, though he anticipated she would once he got established at a good firm. Wasn't that the way things went?

He wants to tell Lena that this wasn't his idea. None of it: being a lawyer, their empty, clockwork life, even the modest home in a nice neighborhood. This is what they're supposed to be happy with, and he can't see why that isn't enough for her. What more did most people get?

He refills the cup and walks outside. The cement under his bare feet bites softly into his soles. Their little house sits at the top of a hill near the edge of downtown Portland. He crests the summit only to be dwarfed by another, larger hill to the left. He picks his way to a bridge stretching over the I-5, just as he has every day since they moved into the house a year ago. The bridge railing is enshrouded by a chain-link fence, seven or eight feet high that curls back on itself to prevent jumpers from climbing over it. Every few feet there are signs advertising suicide hotlines. Matthew shivers, but doesn't particularly mind the cold.

As far as the eye can see, the world is gray. The clouds are hanging low over the city, but benign—content to only block out the sun, where on another day they would shower. The buildings, which seem so colorful up close, covered as they are in murals and the occasional bit of graffiti, are just steel and concrete from this distance. Pretty, sure, but with a sort of endearing dirtiness to them, as though they used to shine but calmed down once they came to Portland.

He walks back to his house and goes upstairs. The second story is nothing more than a master bedroom, neatly furnished, and a door by their bed that leads to a little uncovered ledge with an iron railing patterned after some kind of vine, rising to Matthew's hip. The balcony, they called it, though it can barely fit Matthew and Lena at the same time. He walks to the balcony, and she is there below him.

"Kolya," she says. The daze of the previous afternoon lifts, and he remembers. He can't tell whether her feet are touching the ground. She laughs. "I knew I'd find you again, my little Nikolai. I made a promise, didn't I?"

"The other day," he says. "I saw—"

"Yes," she says. "You saw me. Why don't you come down? Come to me before Lena comes home. We have so little time."

It doesn't strike him as strange that she knows both Lena's name and schedule. Of course she would. This angel sees the entirety of him with those blue eyes, so bright that they seem to glow in the morning sun. A slight wind rustles against her limp black dress, and she smiles at him.

Before he realizes what he is doing, he sprints downstairs, feet slamming with each step. The clamor echoes through their narrow halls. Along her back and shoulders are the thin, crisscrossed lines of white and red, scars alongside welts that seem as fresh as the day they were struck. Matthew fumbles with the latch to the sliding glass door, wishing he could caress the wounds from her back, and looks up as the door opens. She looks back boldly before breaking eye contact, suddenly demure, with an embarrassed laugh. It is the gesture of another era, and Matthew feels a century older.

The front door opens, and the girl is gone again.

"Matthew," Lena calls, walking into the living room. "You home?"

He steps into the backyard, without answering, but still holds onto the door handle, fearful of leaving his portal back to a world of sense and reason, a world where there are no red-haired women carrying the scent of foreign oceans with them everywhere they go. The air feels like a thick fog, and smells like kelp decaying on the sand, though his backyard looks just as it did before she left. His lips taste salty.

When he was in San Francisco the coastline smelled the same. The air was heavy and moist, and there was always that dead smell of decay underlying everything. The Pacific rose and fell as the water pulled back into itself with every break and recess. The tides, he heard, came from the moon's gravity, but this never made sense. He didn't see how something so far away, so otherworldly, could have such a powerful influence on the earth, which always seemed to be spinning with such benign predictability.

A hand touches his shoulder.

"Are you okay?" Lena says. "I wanted to remind you we have guests coming over tonight. A couple from the hospital."

He nods a weak acknowledgement, not knowing what he could possibly say. He tries to ignore the smell of the sea, but now that he has caught it, the scent lingers, unshakable, as though he carries the red-haired girl with him.

Lena stands in the kitchen, her hand extended to him. It hangs in the air uselessly, as though failing to reach across an inexplicably long distance. "Matthew?" she says.

He says nothing, staring back at her.

"Never mind," she says, finally turning away. "Just, please don't be late tonight."

"Of course," he says, but he'll be forty minutes late. He'll start home as soon as he gets Lena's text saying only: *8:13. where are you?* He won't say much all night.

The moon will have just begun to wane as they eat, and the spring tide will start to lose its strength. Along the coast, the sand will have at last pushed back the encroaching water, but it cannot last.

Matthew wakes one night, and Lena is there, sitting at the edge of their bed. He knows that she has been thinking of waking him.

"How long have you been sitting there?" he says.

She shrugs. "Long enough," she says, and then after a pause: "I worry. These were supposed to be our best years. Before kids. This is the time we are supposed to be together, alone, but we're in our thirties now. It doesn't feel real, I guess. I thought I'd—we'd be different, but everything seems the same, except for being surprised how long ago things were. Like we should be more than . . ."

"More than what?" he says, but immediately regrets it. He shouldn't play into her constant discontentment.

"I don't know," she says. "It's stupid. I keep having these dreams that you've died. I always see your body afterwards. It's stupid. But you make these horrible faces, and I can't stop . . . I just—the idea of everything ending like this, us like we are, is so frustrating."

He knows what he should say: He should sit up, pull her to him, and offer the kindness of an empty promise to be there for her no matter what, and he almost does. But he thinks of sea salt on his lips, and a red-haired stranger caressing him, the palm of her hand softly crashing against his chest with the inevitability of the tide. He is certain that, should he move to kiss her, Lena would taste the stranger on his lips, so he lies there, rigid, and prays he were a different man, a stronger man, who could stop the dreams from coming to them because he, too, has been dreaming.

"Matthew," she says. "Are you still awake?"

He curls into the thick warmth of the comforter, feigning sleep. For a moment, he almost believes that everything will be all right, as though cotton and this little deception are enough to protect him.

Matthew dreams of the Old Country, a time and world that he has never known. In these dreams, his name is Nikolai Petrovich, an officer in the Great Northern War, serving under Tsar Pyotr Alexeyevich, Peter the Great. As reward for his service, he is offered an administrative position in the new capital, Petersburg. He accepts. He has a wife and a child, and very little means of supporting them. As a military man, he is often far from them, and has no guarantee that he will be able to continue to provide for them should he die. A desk in Petersburg, though dull and tedious, is a far better option. He offers his sincere thanks to the Tsar, but the Great War refuses to leave him. Matthew knows that Nikolai is plagued by dreams of his own, waking each morning to the memory of the war that he wishes he could forget, but is able to see Nikolai's dreaming only once.

A Swedish man, dirty blond hair spattered with blood that bubbles up from his mouth, stares up blankly. His eyes glaze over as they struggle to move, to dart back and forth, but they can do so only sluggishly. The Swede's left eye is bloodshot. He mouths words that seem, even if only in Nikolai's mind, to accuse the very streets of Petersburg of shedding his blood.

Then Nikolai wakes, carrying Matthew's consciousness with him, with a sudden thrash. His fist, clenched still from the nightmare war, breaks his wife's nose. Matthew feels the collapse of bone and cartilage under Nikolai's knuckles, and the sudden warmth of her blood, staining the rough, woolen blanket. They have no money. The only treatment she receives is the hastily thrust-out scrap of Nikolai's shirt to staunch the bleeding. Her nose will heal crooked.

She rises, naked, from the bed. The cloth, already dripping and bloody, is clutched tightly to her nose. Her long red hair covers her breasts. She isn't as pale as Matthew remembers her being when she first appeared to him on the streets of downtown Portland. Though he can't see them clearly, Matthew knows there are only two or three of the whip marks, marring her back and shoulders from past beatings. In the coming years, something in Nikolai will snap, some psychosis, and the whip marks will checker her entire back, though Matthew can't say how he knows this. Nikolai will sometimes tell himself that it was the war, but Matthew knows that Nikolai will never be fully convinced of this. There was always something in Nikolai, something dead, that was desperately searching for some kind of feeling, and it only got worse as he spent those endless hours behind that Petersburg desk. He strikes her to relieve his own hollowness.

Their child wails in the background, and it is this that most disturbs Matthew when he wakes.

The air feels claustrophobic. He steps out to the balcony, hoping for a breeze, just a little fresh air to offer some reprieve.

She waits for him. They are both naked, but, like it was in the dream, this seems to Matthew normal, inevitable. He goes down to her. The moon is out, only half of its glowing fullness, but the sky is clear. She appears in its light, a luminous gray.

"Kolya," she says. "You came to me."

"Why?" His voice is weak. "Why me? I shouldn't be dreaming these things. I don't know any Niko . . . My name is Matthew." He looks at the grass tickling the edges of his bare feet.

"Of course, my dear Nikolai. Call yourself whatever you'd like." She looks up at the moon. "Isn't she beautiful? I wanted to visit you much sooner, but she wouldn't let me." A laugh. "She gets so jealous. You must know. She wants to keep an eye on us." With every word, she steps closer, deftly sidestepping the cement circles that form a path to the little planters along the thick brush that wall the two of them in. She looks so young.

She touches him on the arm. Her hand feels clammy and dead.

"This is—I'm still dreaming, aren't I?" Matthew says.

"If that's what you'd like to tell Lena," the girl says, looking up at him. She kisses him on the collarbone and then on the neck. Her eyes are a light green, soft. She whispers in his ear, her breath warm against his ear: "I know a nice spot on the river we could go. I could show you where, and we could meet there tomorrow night. It's a beautiful little piece of shore. Far from the lights. Just us and the river and the roots of trees." He can't help but see the spot. The two of them, bodies tangled together, and surrounded by only earth and trees and some small river that feeds into the Willamette. He hears the water hit the rocks with the sound of a slap. The girl traces the contour of his spine gently with the blade of a finger. "The dirt would be soft against our backs."

The drip of the water where her finger ran itches slightly as though suddenly infected, and he draws away from her. She glares, the green of her eyes suddenly gone, leaving only a hard gray.

"What is it now, Nikolai? It's so soon, and already you draw back from me. Does your eye wander so easily?" She laughs, but it sounds hollow. Her eyes have the same disinterested glaze one would see in the eyes of a child deciding whether or not she wants to crush an insect into the ground. "Silly me, but of course it does. How could it not? I've known so many men like you. Stoic men. Day after day, stuck in the same little circle. Whose eye wouldn't wander? Who wouldn't kill for something new?"

Not like that, he wants to say. Not like Nikolai, whose routine served only to hide from the blue eyes of that Swede, accusing him from the grave. Matthew had known no wars, had spilled no blood.

"Are you so sure, *solnitsa?*" she replies, though he said nothing. She presses against him. He tries to ignore the feeling of her closeness brushing against his ribs. It seems so much easier to go away with this stranger than to remain with Lena, who, he must admit, never did anything to rescue the two of them from the deadness of their life together. The fantasy of life with this girl seems to hover, palpably, before him. One of her hands rests on his chest, a trickle of water dripping from underneath her palm.

But she looks so young, so impossibly young in the moonlight, as though that weak, gray light somehow keeps her perpetually frozen in a single moment.

He wishes he had never seen her on the street that day—that he had continued on in the endless repetitions that compose his life. Nothing upended.

But it is almost dawn, and the sun's light threatens to spill out onto the sky, drowning out the moon as she hangs low over the trees and high-rise buildings. The girl rises to the tips of her toes, and kisses him once. "You should come with me for a swim, Kolya. Soon. Monotony has never been good for you," she says. "It brings out the worst." And then she is gone. He gasps for air, realizing he was holding his breath. His pulse pounds against the edge of his throat so fast he thinks he might vomit. The ground is flooded where she stood, and his naked soles sink into the muck.

After that night, Matthew sees her everywhere he goes. She hides in a tree, carefully balanced on the thin, gray-brown branches, but the arms seem not to move under her weight. He walks past homes, and she moves delicately at his side, each mincing step precisely placed in the grass, until she comes to a stop at the sidewalk. She calls to him. Her voice pleads like a child's, as though she were at the edge of a cement sea in which she could not swim. At the sound of a call, Matthew's vision blurs: the cement sidewalks and asphalt melt and shift, until he is convinced that he walks, instead, on the cobbled street and dirt paths of Old Petersburg.

He runs from her, deeper into the ocean of gray steel and cement, but still it becomes harder to know where he is with every passing moment. Burnside becomes Nevsky Prospect, with its bustling crowds, the Columbia and Willamette sing the same as the Neva, and the gray steel of downtown Portland blends with the stone and wood and brick of ancient streets and houses. He runs, but she returns moments later in a different tree, on a path of beaten earth, or standing in a flower-bed, the dirt between her bare toes. He imagines how it must feel to touch only grass and dirt and water. How soft it all must be. He shakes his head, but the thought remains.

Matthew can't say anymore how long this is has been going on. Three days? Four? A week?

"Kolya," she will say. "Come with me. We can swim until night, and then . . ."

He will see it in lurid detail. The cries she will make, how it will feel to hold her too tightly to himself as she presses her nakedness against him, the wash of silver light against the slowly rustling river next to them, and he will never want to leave that magic hollow, as though it were the paradise of God himself.

Matthew, in these moments, forgets his own place in the decisions that brought him into this caged life, and Lena takes on a more sinister light. She seems to Matthew nothing more than a seductress, luring him into the godless repetition that his life has become. It was never his idea to watch the shattering of marriage after marriage, destroying his faith in the institution, and the red-haired girl, whose green eyes bore into his, seems the perfect salve to help forget everything that Lena has done to him.

But the moment ends, and Matthew looks away, remembering the sound of Lena's breathy laugh, barely louder than a sigh. The quiet sound shakes her whole body, as though to compensate for the lack of volume. On one of their first dates, he had said something, forgotten almost immediately after, followed by a long silence. He quickly drank his beer to hide his embarrassment, when she laughed with a glass of red wine in hand. Her hand shook, even though her laughter could barely be heard, until she spilled the wine on herself. That night was the first that they had gone home together, and that laugh had, in retrospect, seemed especially significant, as though every previous interaction had possessed a certain coldness, an awkwardness, and it was this wine-stained night, more than anything else, that had set the continued tone of their time together, though that playful quality had grown quite neglected.

When Matthew looks up again, the girl is gone, and he can't remember why he had been so angry with Lena.

The dreams of Nikolai grow worse, more violent every night, and Matthew resists the urge to sleep for as long as he can, until his body, pushed beyond the point of reason, collapses, and Matthew is forced to become Nikolai.

Matthew sees the tedium of Nikolai's birchwood desk, not so very distant from his own hundreds of years later. An endless tide of bureaucratic shuffling as papers stacked at the desk's edge rise and ebb predictably. In some of the dreams, their lives blend together. Nikolai, in Matthew's Portland office, puts his hand on a weeping husband's shoulder, and mumbles his condolences in Russian. He feels the starched shirt under the blue cloth of Nikolai's imperial dress uniform tight against his chest and neck, and a pin pricking lightly against his breast where he wears three medals for his services in the Great Northern War.

But the dreams always end the same: the dry heaviness of a leather horsewhip in his hand, and the red-haired girl staring at him with the same accusation that was in the dying eyes of the Swede. Matthew wants to scream, to drown out the relentless cracking of the whip, but Nikolai's mouth never opens from its determined grimace. He wants to scream because he knows that she isn't looking at Nikolai, who has lain in a distant grave for centuries.

"There have been others, *solnitsa*," she says. "I have known more men than you can imagine. You all come to me, call me to yourselves, and I obey." She smiles slowly.

Nikolai screams at her to stop telling lies. He accuses her of unfaithfulness. Matthew wishes Nikolai would stop. It is so strange a feeling to be at the precipice of another man's rage, trapped in a body not your own.

"Eventually, they all swim with me," she says. "And that's the end of it."

Matthew wakes, shaking and covered in sweat. He resists the urge to vomit, but still drags himself to the toilet. He clings to it weakly.

"It's not me," he whispers, though he no longer quite believes it. "It's not me."

When the shaking finally stops, he goes back to his bedroom.

"Lena?" he says. It sounds thunderous in the stillness of their room. "Lena, are you awake?"

Her body stirs under the covers, but she offers no other response, and he collapses at the foot of their bed. It seems impossible that his life should come to this. That he would be guilt-wracked and brought to the brink of confession in the middle of the night, though he had done nothing. He never asked for any of this, but he knows, somehow, it will all go away if he wakes Lena and tells her everything.

Since they had settled in Portland, neither Lena nor Matthew drank often, but tucked into the back of a cupboard they have a nice bottle of vodka that someone has given them. It is almost untouched.

Matthew goes downstairs. He pours himself a glass, and then another, and listens to the unmoving night. He could still wake her, tell her about the girl. Get help or, maybe, a padded cell smelling of spilled bleach and sedatives. A younger version of himself wouldn't have hesitated. He was naive enough to still believe that life gave back when people put in enough effort.

He drinks until his whole world spins, and stumbles up to the suicide-fence at the edge of the bridge. His eyes drag shut only to snap open again, and his fingers are locked into the chain link. What if he climbed it? The metal beneath his hand is warm and inviting. There is no one around on the street, no one who would try and stop him. How many cars would he end up bouncing between before actually touching cement? His ragdoll body surrounded by cars flying past at sixty-plus.

He remembers reading of underworlds. Sheol. Hades. After the river of the dead and meeting Charon, they really don't have much going for them. The dead just disappear, growing ghostlier, until someone makes a sacrifice to them. The blood, the ancients said, gives the soul a taste of the life that it used to have, and the soul becomes, if only for a moment, more substantial in that gray, hollow world.

It all seems too familiar to Matthew. What if he did go with the girl? Let someone else make the decision for him as to which gray world he would live in. The air tastes salty again like drinking seawater with every breath. Maybe she wants to punish him for some unremembered sin, an adulterous thought or a moment of cruelty to Lena.

Or, maybe, he has never been good to his wife.

The bottle of vodka is almost empty by the time Lena wakes, and Matthew sits there, one hand still on the clear glass neck. His head wobbles as he looks up, hearing Lena's shuffling steps on the floor, which stop suddenly as she looks at Matthew's dirty clothes and the empty bottle in his hand.

"What the hell happened to you?" she says.

"I quit my job," he says. He speaks slowly, trying to enunciate, but the words are still slurred, caught somewhere in the back of his throat. He laughs.

She squints at him, head tilted slightly, as though trying to make sure she heard correctly. Matthew looks down at the bottle, suddenly embarrassed.

"I thought this is what you wanted," he says. "I thought you wanted me around more."

"Matthew, what have you done?" she says.

"What have I done?" He slams a hand against the table, and almost falls from his seat. "I never asked for any of this. This isn't the kind of life I wanted." The walls of their house suddenly feel confining, like a drywall prison made by the devil himself, surrounded by an ocean of steel, cement, and stone. He longs for birch and pine as far as the eye can see. He longs for the Old Country.

It had been a mistake to come to these ghostly streets, this Sheol, where the blood dries in the veins, and nothing is real. One movement follows another, and every action seems to mean less than it did in the last repetition. He has had enough of this gray world.

Matthew looks at Lena. She used to be so beautiful, but the last seven years have been hard on her. Her hair, though she is only thirty-two, has grayed at the roots, and her skin hangs more loosely from her bone and muscle, which are still hard and strong.

"I need to leave," Matthew says, and Lena tries to stop him. He pushes her out of his way, as though realizing for the first time that some things have to be fought for.

He makes his way to the Willamette River. The Rusalka waits for him, past the dirt and tree roots, ankle-deep in the water. She extends a hand to him with the openness of a preacher welcoming the repentant to a baptismal service.

They kiss, and the water rushes past, unseeing.

Nikolai gets home, and his small Petersburg house is quiet. The usual sounds of the knife battering the chopping block or borsht bubbling and simmering on the grate in the corner of their fireplace are gone. There isn't even the crackle of a fire. He hears only a faint creaking from their bedroom.

"Nastya, you lazy dog," he yells. "Where are you?"

The only answer is another creak of wood.

He drops the horsewhip, and walks into the room. In his moments of honesty and lucidity, Nikolai knew this was coming, predicted it, but was also shamed by his powerlessness to stop himself from bringing her to this point.

She hangs from a noose slung over a rafter and tied to their back bedpost. A stool lies overturned on the floor next to her. The creaking of the wood follows her slowly swinging form like a groaning metronome.

Nastya Mikhailovna died at the age of nineteen after five years of marriage to Nikolai Petrovich, aged forty-two. The year was 1723. Before her suicide, the Rusalka had led her first man to the grave when she drowned Nikolai's son in a soup pot.

Neil Davidson is a graduate from the University of Oregon and will be starting at the University of California, Davis in the fall, where he will be getting his M.A. in creative writing. He has a friendly obsession with myth of all varieties, but an especial love of Russian and Slavic folklore. When not reading or writing, Neil can generally be found at punk shows, drinking coffee somewhere, or cooking. He also has a weakness for campy horror movies, especially those from the eighties.

It Wants to be a Swamp

by

C. S. Malerich

THE WORST PART ABOUT THE nights I closed was riding home on the metro. Past midnight, and I'd be bone-tired and shuffling, with no patience left, and half the time there were delays because one or another track was shorting. The announcement would come scratching over the PA, apologizing for the inconvenience. Then I'd drop my head against the seat and hear Hector's voice in my head: *"It's the climate here. Water's always getting into the tunnels."* He liked explaining things—book smart, the boy was—and then he'd shake his head like I was acting foolish just for expecting things to work like they were supposed to. *Well, don't look at me, hombre. I didn't build the city in a swamp.*

Even if the train did run smoothly, there were always people around, no matter how late it was, all ready to work my last nerve. Like, for instance, someone would block the escalator off the platform. Two hundred feet long and slow as molasses, and somebody was always standing on it, like it's an amusement park ride. Right in the middle too, where no one could get around them to walk up. I mean, if you're going to stand, at least stand to the side and let people by. Some of us want to get home and watch a half hour of TV before we pass out on the couch and put a crick in our neck.

I would never push someone, but I would get to the step right behind them, tap my foot, and cough—loud—in their ear. Most people, they got the hint and scooched over. Then I'd slide past with a sarcastic "*Thank you*" and stomp the rest of the way up the stairs.

But as soon as I saw the hulking figure ten steps above me, I knew I was stuck. She—I figured it was a she because of the round hips—was standing in the exact center of the escalator, surrounded by plastic shopping bags, which, so far as I could tell, were stuffed full of more shopping bags. Her head was down, or else pulled inside that grimy knit sweater like a turtle's, but I could see strings of long gray hair. A pale, flowery skirt covered her rear, ending just above the back of the knees. From there the legs were thick as tree stumps, gnarled with bulging veins and cellulite. The feet disappeared into unlaced work boots. It was a hot night in the middle of the summer, and I knew if I got any closer the B.O. would just get stronger and sharper. If I did try my usual trick—if I coughed or sighed or snorted—I couldn't imagine this person caring enough to move aside.

As the woman stood there on the escalator, she rocked from side to side in her boots, slowly and slightly. I heard a soft moaning. "Oh . . . oh . . . oh . . . uh-oh . . . oh . . .oh," she went, the sound rising in pitch step-by-step until she kind of hiccupped and it dropped again. Then the pattern repeated, seven notes in all.

What's that about? I wondered. Did she even know she was making a sound? Maybe it was some kind of tic, or a chant. My jaw clenched. I was polite to customers all day at work, even the rude ones and the crazy ones, and the rude, crazy ones; I didn't have the energy for it after hours.

Two wiry teenagers passed me, laughing and hollering. They weren't afraid, and they weren't stopping. So what the hell? I began to climb the ten stairs that separated me from the bag lady.

The kids reached her before I did. The first one squeezed past and cleared the shopping bags with the grace of a gymnast. He turned around three steps above, looking for his friend.

Instead he got an eyeful of the bag lady's face. Whatever it was he saw there, it turned him three shades paler and froze him to the step.

Meanwhile, the second kid tripped on his untied shoelaces and fell into the woman's left side, where she had another bag balanced on the crook of her hip, under her sweater.

At least I thought it was another bag. So did the kid, I think. But as he sprang away, he must have realized the same thing I did: The bulge under the woman's sweater was part of her. An extra appendage or an ulcer. I'd have sworn I heard a *splish-splish*, the same noise my cousin's waterbed made when you sat on it.

"Jesus Christ!" shouted the kid who'd fallen. It was enough to startle his buddy into motion, to run back down and yank him to his feet. They took off, racing back up the steps.

In this system, the escalators were no better than the train rails: Half the time they broke down into nothing but stairs with teeth. And ours picked that moment to grind to a halt. The two kids ran, whooping and laughing in relief when they made it to the top.

Me, I was stuck. *Crap.* I wasn't brave enough now to climb the last five steps between me and the bag lady. I *definitely* wasn't brave enough to press past her. What if she looked at me? What if I touched that fleshy bulge?

But the escalator wasn't moving. Neither was she. I'd just decided to walk back down and take the elevator instead when she turned around.

Her eyes were streaming water. I don't mean she was crying, I mean her eye sockets were open faucets and water was pouring out. Two streams ran down her cheeks and off her jaws, into the collar of her sweater, which was already soaked through in the front. And she was coming toward me.

It didn't take me a second: I spun around and hightailed it back down the motionless escalator. The steps were damn slippery, more slippery than usual—damp, I realized, and I squeezed the rubber handrail harder. As soon as my sneakers hit the platform I changed direction for the elevator, but the soles squeaked and went sailing off the opposite way. I crashed into the concrete on my shoulder.

A train was just leaving the platform, its few passengers approaching the escalator. At the sight of my wipeout, I heard gasps.

"Are you all right, miss?" asked a middle-aged man in a gray suit.

"Wait a minute," said a woman in a turquoise hijab as I struggled to pull myself up. "Make sure you haven't broken anything first."

Good advice. The kind of thing I might have said if somebody had fallen in front of me. But these people didn't have a demon bag lady coming down the stairs after them. As soon as I got to my feet, I pushed away the helping hands and bolted for the elevator. The button lit at my push, but the doors didn't open. I hit the button again. And again.

Behind me, I could hear screams and gasps as the other people caught sight of the crying woman. Above it all rang that same seven-note moan. "Oh . . . oh . . . oh . . ." Getting nearer. I hit the elevator button again.

Finally the car reached the platform level and the door slid back. Laughing with relief, I stepped into the elevator and slapped the button to take me to street level. Then I went to the far corner of the little space and turned. The door hadn't slid closed yet. Hadn't even begun to . . .

Are you kidding me? Nothing *works in this system?*

On the platform, the woman had passed the startled knot of passengers where I'd slipped. Her eyes were still streaming as she ambled toward me with her bags, leaving a smear of water behind her. Her gaze—I know this sounds strange, because with her eyes just open holes gushing water the whole time, how could I tell?—but her gaze was fixed on me. "Oh . . . oh . . . oh . . uh-oh . . ."

Could anyone help me? Did I *need* help? I couldn't even make my lips form the words.

Now the woman had crossed the threshold into the elevator car. She looked at me with her spigots-for-eyes, blinked once—for a split second the twin rivulets went dry—and then turned around. She set down one set of plastic bags and pushed the button.

Her action relaxed me, unexpectedly. It made sense. As impossibly strange as this person was, she'd had the same idea I did, to walk back to the platform and take the elevator when the escalator went kaput. I didn't blame her. I didn't want to climb all those stairs either.

The elevator door slid closed and the car began to rise.

As we rode, the woman didn't face me again, and I tried to concentrate on catching my breath and not looking at the steady trickle running down the inside of each leg into her boots, or thinking about that unnatural bulge below the left side of her sweater. Not my business, not my problem. But with every little motion she made in the elevator, I could hear a gurgle.

All at once, the car came to a stop. The door did not open.

After a moment, the woman took a step forward and hit the "Door Open" button, but nothing happened. Frustrated, she did it again, repeatedly.

"We aren't at street level yet," I said, looking through the grimy glass walls at nothing but black.

The woman half-turned toward me, and I flinched again at the sight of her face, her empty eyes.

"I think we're stuck," I said.

She turned back toward the elevator buttons and then stood motionless. If it wasn't my imagination, the water flow was even greater now, like someone had opened a faucet full blast.

"Okay, ma'am," I said after a moment, "I'm going to call for help." She didn't move. To reach the red emergency button, I had to step over her bags and press myself against the wall. I did it. I didn't even hesitate when my sneaker filled with water in the cold puddle she'd made.

The dispatcher at the other end of the speaker told me to sit tight. "An engineer is on the scene, and the fire department is coming. We'll get you out soon."

"Oh . . . oh . . . oh," chanted the woman. I didn't dare change positions, because the dispatcher might come back with instructions for our rescue, and the woman didn't give me an extra inch. I looked anywhere but her eye sockets. Her face was plump but wrinkled, and her neck was covered in liver spots. She ignored me and went on with her moaning and gurgling and spilling.

It was probably her fault the elevator had stopped. Maybe the escalator too. Sure, breakdowns happened pretty often—but both the escalator and the elevator on the same night?

Water's always getting in, I remembered Hector telling me. Was *this* the reason, standing in front of me? A demon haunting our metro system.

"Oh . . . oh . . . oh . . . uh-oh . . . oh . . . oh," went the woman. The rhythm seemed to match the thought that occurred to me then: *This place wants to be a swamp.*

"Do you have to keep doing that?" I snapped.

"Oh . . . oh . . . oh . . ."

"What is it, anyway? What are you crying for?"

The noise stopped. The only sound in the elevator became the tinkle of pouring water. The woman turned her head toward me, the stream of her right eye socket soaking her shoulder.

Her lips parted, and a mouthful of water ran out there too. With it came a voice that sounded like a gurgling fountain. "I cannot feed my children."

I would have bet you anything she wasn't going to reply, bet you my flat-screen or three months' tips—whatever you wanted. And even less than that, I wouldn't have expected words that made sense.

Once she spoke, I was mesmerized. "Oh," I said, as if this were a normal, make-nice conversation, "how many children do you have?"

Her mouth opened again, spilling more water to the floor—now I was standing in a good six inches—and she said, "Too many to count." She cocked her streaming head for a moment, like she was deciding whether to trust me or not, and her arms folded over her sweater protectively. "I could show you."

"Okay, yeah," I said, daring myself more than her. "Show me."

She unfolded her arms and pulled open her sodden sweater. Underneath, she was naked. I could handle that. I could handle seeing her skin, pale and slick and liver-spotted, her breasts and stomach drooping over the waistband of her skirt.

But on her left side, the extra bulge that had frightened the boy on the escalator came rolling over her hip. It was a pocket of flesh, stuffed full as a turkey carcass at Thanksgiving. She reached one hand inside; with the other, she beckoned me closer.

My hand went to my mouth.

"Look! Look!" she gurgled, as she drew something from the pouch. A live fish. She clutched it where the tail met the body, while it flopped this way and that—a river fish, with bluish-brown body and spots along the belly, eight or nine inches long. Hector would have known what kind it was.

I stared as she dropped it into the water. It landed with a splash and jackknifed its body back and forth furiously, attempting to swim away. I was standing in water up to my ankles, but it wasn't enough for the animal.

I turned my attention away from the flopping fish as the woman cupped both hands into her pocket of flesh and showed me the contents as she scooped them out. A school of silver minnows. A water bug. A dragonfly. Two frogs. More fish. They all went into the water. A slimy body brushed my calf before swimming away, and I felt heebie-jeebies crawl up my spine. The water kept rising and the elevator was becoming—

"Here, look, you'll like him." The woman was pulling out something fuzzy now, yellow and brown. A duckling? Yes. She had it by the neck, but didn't hold onto the duckling any longer than the others. It landed in the water too, but had more luck paddling around the elevator than the first fish did swimming. She was right: My heart warmed at the sight of the downy baby like it hadn't to the fish or frogs.

Another duckling came from the woman's pouch then, and another and another after that, until I could only think of a magician pulling scarves from his sleeve. Finally came a mother duck, gray and brown, with a flare of indigo on one hind feather, who quacked to her babies. They paddled into formation behind her in a neat line. Meanwhile, the large fish had disappeared below the surface of the water, and five frogs sat ribbetting back and forth on the bag lady's floating bags.

"They look fine to me," I said. I was anything but. The water was nearly at my waist, and I was feeling desperate to get out before it got any higher. Before she pulled a hungry alligator out of that pouch.

"No," she said sharply, shaking her head and releasing another gush from her mouth. "All dying." Gush. "Starving. Choking." Gush, gush. "Smothered. Poisoned—"

"I see your point!" I said. If I could stop her from talking, maybe I could buy myself enough time for the fire department to get me out. I hit the emergency button again, waiting for the dispatcher to answer, but all I got was static. "And I'm very sorry about your . . . children," I said.

"No you aren't," she gushed back, and reached for one of her plastic bags full of plastic bags, shooing a frog off of it. The frog hopped into the water with a plop and came swimming toward me. I splashed to keep it away.

Meanwhile, she'd separated one bag out, and before I could understand what she meant to do with it, she'd seized a fish again with her free hand and dropped it into the bag. "Starved. Choked. Smothered . . ." she chanted, while the fish thrashed inside the bag. She tied the handles and strung it over her wrist.

"What—?"

She grabbed the smallest duckling around the neck and started to put it inside another bag.

"Don't!" I shouted now, lunging through the chest-high water to cup the fuzzy little body in my hands instead. "You'll suffocate him," I scolded—stupidly, for someone who was about to drown. But I released the duckling again to the water. The tiny webbed feet paddled frantically to get away, as if it understood the danger.

I dove for the bag hanging from the woman's wrist and managed to tear open a hole large enough for the poor fish to slip through. It flopped back to the water with a swell of its gills that I imagined must have been relief.

In turn, the woman caught my wrist in her clammy hand. It didn't matter, I was already soaked through and the phone in my pocket I'm sure was ruined, and I'd already been exposed to whatever bacteria must be swimming in this soup with us. She gave me a hard stare, difficult while her eyes were still open sockets filling our glass tank, and I stared back, like they were deep, deep pools that I very much wanted to get to the bottom of.

And Hector says I never show any curiosity.

For a moment I could imagine this place, years and years ago. Before the city, before plantations, maybe even before people, there'd been a wetland stretching to the horizon, with sharp, tall grasses I didn't know the name of, and trees in clusters on the high ground. Frogs singing. Dragonfly wings buzzing. And birds everywhere, in the air and wading in the water and perching on branches. A mama duck settling on her nest in the middle of the tall, tall grass.

"You care?" the woman gurgled at me, wondering. Her hand felt squishier now—less firm.

I didn't get a chance to answer, but I would have said yes.

Metal screeched and creaked above our heads, a worse whine than the woman's moaning. Half of the elevator's ceiling swung back, revealing human faces staring down at us.

The elevator had an emergency door in the ceiling. I should have thought of that.

"What the hell?" asked one man, a headlamp beaming above his broad, sweaty face. He looked tired. "Where'd all this water come from?"

"Is that a duck?" asked another.

"Miss, can you put your foot through this loop? We'll pull you up." They were lowering a cord.

"Jeezus, there's more! Should I call animal control?"

Instead of responding, I clutched the weeping woman. She felt less solid by the second, like paper dissolving in the rain. And all I knew was, the second I was out of this flood—and even worse, the second I was home in dry pajamas and with a cup of hot tea—I would stop feeling curious. I'd stop caring why she kept crying. Tomorrow I'd probably even complain about a train delay.

"What about her?" I called to my rescuer. The crying woman was melting all away, leaving nothing but old clothes and plastic bags stuffed into plastic bags.

"Who?" asked the men above me.

I couldn't begin to explain. As the woman became water, I closed my eyes. I shut my mouth and leaned my head back, letting her saturate my hair. The minnows swam through it like reeds. For once I didn't mind.

"Come on, miss! Let's go!"

I heard them, recognized the weariness in their voices, but I couldn't feel it. My limbs were numb.

"This place wants to be a swamp," I moaned, before I dipped below the surface.

"This place wants to be a swamp," I told Hector, when he picked me up from the back of the ambulance. I couldn't see a thing, but I could feel the tears gushing down my face.

C.S. Malerich lives and works near the District of Columbia. Her speculative fiction has appeared previously in *Ares Magazine*, *The Again*, and the anthologies *Among Animals* and *Among Animals 2* from Ashland Creek Press. Her short story "Phoenix Cross" was nominated for a

2017 Pushcart Prize. She is also a founding member of the collective DC Stampede, supporting grassroots organizing on behalf of animals, people, and the planet.

Bride of the Deep

by

Karissamae Masters

MARISSA STEVENS STOOD IN SHOCK on the edge of the shore as she surveyed the devastation around her. The tsunami had struck her island home with little warning. Like many of her neighbors, she had clambered onto her rooftop as the waters rushed upon her. For countless hours she had held onto the laboratory's chimney, watching as wave upon wave rushed through the streets and homes of her friends and neighbors. Panic had put her body in shock. With no food or water throughout the night, she simply watched and waited as the sea erased everything she cared about.

The tide had receded hours ago, but the townsfolk remained weeping and praying on their rooftops, afraid of the tsunami's return. Ever the scientist, Marissa had overcome her shock from the disaster and scrambled to the beach to assess the damage and plan the recovery efforts.

Standing on the remains of a dune and staring out at the treacherous horizon, Marissa surveyed miles of land and sea littered with mingled fish and flesh. She walked without destination yet with purpose; each step drew her nearer to understanding the extent of the damage.

She came upon the body of one of her neighbors. Kneeling beside him, Marissa recognized him as a local fisherman. He had always smiled at her whenever they met in line for coffee. She struggled to recall his name, but failed. Instead, she recalled the grandfatherly affection in his voice as he innocently asked her one time when she would settle down with a nice boy and trade in her white lab coat for a veil. She remembered giving him a sad smile along with her polite response: that her quest for a bride, not a groom, was on hold during the current crisis.

She placed a hand on the shrunken frame of the drowned fisherman, closing the jaundiced eyes that looked up lifelessly at the turquoise sky. She cursed in regret, knowing that the man was dead long before the tsunami had struck. As the town's ecologist, it was Marissa's job to maintain the purity of the water supply—an impossible task since the river of sludge from the nearby factory had broken through its retaining wall and poisoned the island's freshwater months ago. The townsfolk were dying, and everything Marissa was trying to do to counteract the contamination had been futile. She had devised a system of cisterns for collecting rainwater and dew, but now that too was destroyed. She realized that, just like the bucket nestled neatly in the dead man's hands, what little drinkable water remaining in the cisterns on the island was contaminated by seawater as well.

"I'm so sorry," Marissa murmured, hoping his fate was not an omen for the rest of the town. She placed her hat over his face in a sign of respect, despite the pain of her sunburned neck and shoulders. Her pixie-short brown hair gave no protection from the sun, but she felt the sacrifice of her hat was the least she could do for the dead man that lay at her feet. She turned away in shame and regret. Her eyes began to mist, but now was not the time for tears. His loss would be mourned later, after the living could be assured that they would overcome the ravages of this new disaster.

As she walked closer to the water's edge, she saw the remains of strange fish and creatures unused to daylight's touch. These were deep-sea fishes, many species unknown to her. Marissa picked up a lifeless body, admiring the novelty of the creature despite the death and destruction around her. As she looked at the strange fish, she cursed again, knowing that, like it, the townsfolk would die without water.

Suddenly, the animal thrashed in her hand in one last desperate push for survival. Marissa gently deposited the creature in the waves, hoping the animal had the strength it needed to return to its underwater home and heal. She gave a quick prayer of thanksgiving that one life had been saved when so many other souls around her had not.

With it came a new prayer. Marissa began to sing an old ballad in honor of the dead, recalling the shanties of her superstitious fishermen neighbors. Her song became a melody of the prayers they would sing, asking for full nets, calm seas, and safe passage home. She sang until her throat felt raw, and then fell silent once more.

She pulled off her dirty clothes, stripping to her underwear. Leaving her sweat-soaked T-shirt and denim overalls just out of the ocean's reach in the cleanest spot of sand that she could find, she hurried out several paces into the water and knelt down as a wave crested around her. Squatting in the knee-high water, she used the gently lapping waves to bathe her tired limbs and form; she knew that this was likely the only opportunity she would have to feel clean in the grueling recovery efforts ahead. She stumbled back to her clothes and put them on. Wetness quickly soaked through her clothes at chest and crotch, revealing a rough outline of her damp underwear. She awkwardly adjusted her squishy panties, but could do little but accept the discomfort.

Morning had broken, and the tide was returning to its normal swell. Scanning the horizon for additional signs of life, Marissa spotted a swimmer heading to shore. At first she gave a shout, waving her arms in a futile act meant to encourage the swimmer to safety. But as the stranger approached, Marissa watched in wonder as each graceful thrust of a fish tail propelled the woman onwards.

"A mermaid!" she whispered in awe as she watched the creature. Its tail and scales receded, and two pale legs emerged to boldly stride ashore.

A diaphanous skirt made of a jellyfish bell and tentacles rhythmically slapped at the backs of her legs with each step. A sea star hung casually across the woman's hips, two arms clasping each side, with its fifth arm stringing between her legs as a protective thong. A diadem was draped across the luminescent antennae on the mermaid's green-haired brow.

"Greetings," Marissa offered with a bow, stunned by the woman's beauty. She quickly shook off the overwhelming urge to embrace the enchanted creature. Her own exhaustion and dehydration were making her giddy. *Beware the siren's song*, she thought, recalling the superstitions of her nautical neighbors.

The mermaid received the gesture with a nod, a frown of disdain clearly etched upon her brow.

"Have you come to investigate the devastation, too?" Marissa inquired.

"I have come," the mermaid began in an imperious voice, and after a long pause continued, "to see what has survived the wave."

They stood together in silence for a long while, gauging each other and the situation. Finally, lost to the overwhelming weight of it all, Marissa muttered, "Gods! This world is a mess."

The mermaid's gray eyes flared, startled. "I know, little human, but the balance toppled years ago."

"So much destruction," Marissa mourned, "so much waste of life and innocence."

"So much pollution," the mermaid replied angrily, kicking debris from beneath her feet. "Orange rivers of poison flowing through my seas!"

Marissa flinched, unable to repress her feelings of incompetence. "Are your people safe?" she inquired, concerned.

"Thank you for asking," the woman replied, clearly not expecting empathy from the human at her side. "But what good is there in asking? What can you do?"

"Nothing," Marissa admitted, looking down at her hands in regret. "I have tried, but . . ."

"How have you tried? What can you do?"

"I am an ecologist. I have been trying to find a chemical to undo the pollution from the spill, but everything I have tried has failed. My people were dying even before the tsunami hit."

The mermaid gave a wry grin of satisfaction. "You can move," she suggested. "Far from this place."

"Move? We can't move. This is our home. Can you move away from this place?"

"I suppose not, little human." The mermaid cast her gaze out to the sea for a moment.

"My name is Marissa," the scientist offered, surprised that she had not yet introduced herself.

"I am Tethys."

Marissa's eyes widened in alarm, and she bowed in deference. "That is an old name of power. We worship Tethys as the goddess of the depths in the temples of our ancestors. Are you . . .?"

"I have not been worshipped in a long time." The mermaid smiled at the memory. "But no, I am no goddess. I am merely a visitor—albeit an immortal one—on your shore, little human."

"I am sorry that you visit to see only the bad. There is good in this town—good people. There are good people here who don't deserve such suffering."

Tethys shrugged. "I am concerned only with the poison that is in our waters."

"Me, too. But I am concerned with the water because of the people. Now the sea is in our wells." Marissa sighed. "First the sludge, now the tsunami. We cannot drink what little we had left."

"Poisoned by your own hands! Fitting punishment," Tethys scoffed, the antennae upon her brow twinkling in satisfaction.

Stung by her words, Marissa shot back, "You know, they say that when the gods punished mortals with the Flood, they punished themselves as well. Neptune's seals swam in the trees, salt washed over

Demeter's fields. Even Hades' dead could not find their way home. Perhaps the answer isn't punishment, but life."

"Life?"

"Life!" Marissa exclaimed, inspired by her own words. "Life could save our waters! Living beings from the seas in our waters, used to filter out the pollution by consuming it and transforming it to neutral byproducts! Diatoms! Algae! Plankton! The smallest change can make the biggest impact!"

Tethys arched an eyebrow, swept up by Marissa's passionate outburst. "The salt sea will not heal the water, but the bacteria that live in the depths could," she agreed. She collected a drop of the glowing substance upon her antennae and offered it to Marissa. Marissa wiped a drop onto her fingertip, marveling at the liquid.

A tear of relief descended from Marissa's cheek. Tethys collected it on her finger and brought it to her lips. She smiled as she savored its salty taste.

"Thank you," Marissa breathed.

"Do not thank me," Tethys laughed. "I brought the tsunami to wipe this island clean, not to heal your people."

Marissa's eyes widened and then she calmed herself. "I guess the outcome is the same," she replied. "The best punishment for us is life."

"Indeed." Tethys smiled, appearing amused. The tentacles of her jellyfish skirt brushed against Marissa's leg, teasing her through her clothes. Her antennae glimmered in the daylight, undulating alluringly.

"Tethys," Marissa said in wonder, "The antennae at your temples— do they glow from the bacterium that can heal our water?"

"Indeed."

"Is it healthy? Does it harm you? Why do you paint yourself in it?" Marissa inquired, daring to touch the moving tendrils of flesh that sprang like antlers from Tethys' brow.

"It is natural. In the depths, we use our light to attract a mate and to mesmerize our prey."

"Does it work?" Marissa asked in wonder.

"Unfortunately, not on you."

Marissa thought she saw hunger in the mermaid's eyes. Her breath caught and she felt her cheeks blush. "Oh? I am prey to you?"

"Little human, you could be so if you choose."

With a mischievous smile, Marissa reached up to pull Tethys into a kiss. She smelled and tasted of fresh ocean air, salt, and some kind of sweet fruit.

Tethys chuckled and seemed pleased by her boldness. Her delicate hands, surprisingly warm, cupped Marissa's face.

Tethys lowered herself onto the sand, drawing Marissa into an embrace. Together they sat in silence as the sound of the waves crashing further down the beach drowned out the sounds of suffering around them.

This simple act of comfort was like a soothing balm to Marissa' soul. Suddenly the death and suffering around them faded away. Although she knew that sorrow would always exist, for this brief moment in time the joy and tenderness between them drowned out the pain of the world.

"Wow," Marissa said after, resting her head on Tethys' breast. She closed her eyes and savored the feel of Tethys' fingers running through her short brown hair.

"You have seal fur for hair, it is so short," she laughed as she stroked Marissa's head.

"Yours is the color of seaweed," Marissa mused, rising to capture the mermaid's mouth with a kiss.

Tethys chuckled, fingering the strap of Marissa's denim overalls. "You wear the strangest clothes. The last time I was among mortals, only the *menfolk* wore such attire." She gave a sneer as she said the term.

"Three generations have passed since women joined the workforce wearing pants," Marissa explained as she continued to fumble with a button, "It is comfortable and safe to wear when I work in the lab. Your attire," she faltered as she watched the jellyfish skirt sway in the sand beside her, "has a mind of its own. Is it uncomfortable to have it hold onto you in such a way?"

"It is not uncomfortable," Tethys said with laughter in her eyes. "It is part of me."

"Are you a mermaid or a selkie?" Marissa couldn't help but giggle a moment later, when she was tickled by the tentacles that wove patterns around her calves at Tethys' command.

"I am neither," the mermaid smiled knowingly as she felt Marissa's legs jump and twitch from her teasing.

"So you *are* a goddess, then?"

"When I have to be," Tethys said seductively, and captured Marissa's lips with her own.

When both women lay panting on the shore in utter satisfaction, Marissa smiled and said, "Thank you, my goddess."

"Thank you, my little human." Tethys placed a finger on Marissa's glowing lips. "Now you glow with emotion, too, dear one."

Intrigued, Marissa wiped her lips with her hand to see the change. "My lips are glowing," she announced, confused.

"Aye. It is my blessing. You have my ichor within you now. Use it as you will."

"I don't understand."

"Try to summon the living ones into your hand."

Marissa closed her eyes, and as she focused her mind into one single thought, her right hand began to tingle. She opened her eyes to find a luminescent glow pooling in her palm.

"Did I . . ." she stammered, trying to understand what had just happened. "Did I just summon the healing . . .?"

"Yes." Tethys nodded.

Still flabbergasted, Marissa dared to ask, "Why? Why did you give me such a gift?"

Tethys sighed, "I came here to destroy this place. To wipe clean the wrong. I swam ashore to gloat at what I'd done. But then I met you . . ."

"Tethys, your act of destruction was also an act of redemption." Marissa kissed Tethys' breast. "It has given us a chance to save what is left of my people. You have healed our water. But you have taken my heart."

"So choose," Tethys spoke. "Use the ichor within you to create the bacteria that will heal the water completely, or use it to become immortal and live forever in a world beyond your imagination. Choose your paltry humans ... or join me in the Deep."

Marissa's breath caught, but suddenly the weight of the world returned upon her. The prospect of a new lover, the new world of discoveries in a biome totally unfamiliar to her beckoned her, encouraged her to enter a world of endless opportunities and learning.

Yet as her heart raced for new adventure, her vision cleared once more. She contemplated the devastation and the rotting corpses around her. The wails of parents and children, and the smell the fish and flesh beginning to rot in the heat of the midday sun, plagued her. This was the effect of leaving the land unhealed. The suffering from the sludge and tsunami was the result of the wrath of a goddess who must be appeased.

"Tethys, I wish to join you," she said carefully. "But not yet. Let me heal my people. Let me give them hope, as you have given it to me."

With a wry smile, the goddess nodded. "May it be so, little human. Be well, Marissa."

"Be well, Tethys."

With a final kiss, Tethys returned to the sea and disappeared into the waves.

KarissaMae Masters writes tales of fantasy inspired by Greek myths. Born in the Sunshine State, she enjoys traveling the world in search for her next inspiration. When she isn't traveling, she likes to snuggle on the couch with her two cats, Diamond and Boo. Her latest novel, *Afterglow of Dawn*, was published in 2016 by Torquere Press.

Snickerdoodle Bunkum

by

J.C. Raye

SNICKERDOODLE BUNKUM HAD COME TO be much the same way as any Codswallop might, in a medley of miscellany and human discard. The pieces of him, painstakingly selected at his mother's hand, were swirled into life by her pleading and lonely invocations to the sea, and the shifting will of the Cape May winds. For as all rubbish creatures well know, on the last day of any October, and only on southernmost sands, when the sea heaps up white with foam, and the waves break into vapor over the jutting craggles of jetty rock, a sticky wrapper and a rotten gull feather, a clench of hair tangled with the carcasses of a thousand tiny biting flies, the broken end of a plastic spoon and a flayed frond of seaweed, might very well become a thing to love.

And so it was with Snickerdoodle, and all Codswallop kind which came before him, when the sea finally decided to not only spit back the spoils of the humans and reject the waste wantonly plunked into her gullet, but to bestow upon this refuse the gift of life, for some larger purpose as yet to them unknown.

Codswallop children—*Tosh*, as they were lovingly called by their elders—were in constant peril in their first few years of life. Those were the curious days, before maturity and fear set in. A time before complacency, and before the horrible realization that their rubbish lives served little purpose except to grow in number and ingeniously hide from the humans that walked on *legs* and were unlovingly called Wegs.

The Tosh, so terribly soon after their nativity, quickly discovered that hurts did not pain them, and that their parents could easily replace their broken or torn parts from the generous and daily leavings of litter returned by the sea. With no need for food, water, air, or sleep, and with their speedily expert skills in managing any space, crevice, branch, or board, Tosh set on a path of rash adventure that could often mean their untimely doom. More than a quarter of Tosh did not survive their first year. Some were carried off by orange-beaks or canine hairies. Some were impaled on the end of a trash spike and thrust into a murky bag of screaming friends to be seen no more. And many were swept too far away to recover by the seemingly innocent yet iron grasp of a stormy gale. Codswallops usually weighed no more than a pickleball, so their aptitude in reading the skies for signs of squall was imperative.

Snickerdoodle, in his second year, was no less a burden for his own mother, Drivel, from the moment she decided it was time to unwrap his Band-Aid arms from round her ragged egg carton shoulders and set him down free, onto his red coffee stirrer and blue barrette limbs. As any Tosh, he loved to climb and scramble, hop and swim, catch seawater in his plastic cap crown, and crinkle his chip bag body in a thousand ways, quite enjoying the serenade it provided. Crease. Wrinkle. Ruffle. Crunch. His mother scrutinized these noisy exertions with no little worry, bemoaning her impatience to craft a child.

Her husband had rushed her. He said they were behind, and by now should have had two or three Tosh as others of their kind did. Him and his comparisons. His lofty allocutions of purpose and consequence. As if the reason for children had a higher purpose beyond love. Why had she listened to him and not simply waited for the appearance of some eelgrass or plastic wear with which to cobble together her son's torso, as opposed to making him a dinner bell for the orange-beaks?

Perhaps a few more trips to the sea, a week's waiting at the most, and she could have provided her son a less acoustic, more clandestine life. But then, of course, she might have missed October altogether and would then need to wait an entire year to try again. Another *year.* A forlorn and solitary existence, now that her husband was mostly off with the others, travelling great distances to take the yearly count. *No.* Trouble and tribulation though Snickerdoodle might be, she was right in the making of him and loved him with a fire-woven Codswallop fervor that no Weg mother could ever hope to feel or even understand.

Snickerdoodle lived with his mother and father in a place called The Nine Sticks, quietly nestled into the marshiest part of the inlet at Linger Point. Mostly though, he had only his mother for company, as his father had been away from home almost six months now. "Preparing for his silly war," Drivel would say, and stare off into the distance, inland. It seemed to him that whenever she mentioned his father, her carton body would sag and wheeze, just a bit, and her twist-tie arms would fold together tightly.

Unlike the other places his parents had taken him on rare occasion to meet Codswallop kinfolk, such as Preserve or Lighthouse or Meadows, Nine Sticks was exactly as its name implied. Nine wooden sticks, dense, round, and tall, half underwater, driven deep into the thick sand, and half towering to the sky. Strangely hard and smooth, the sticks were far too wide for Snickerdoodle to climb by wrapping his Band-Aid limbs round them fully, but enjoyably large enough to easily tuck his whole body behind in endless afternoons of playing the underwater hiding game with his mother. Drivel, however, whether upside-down, right-side up, or sideways, could never fully hide all her body parts (carton, watchband walking limbs, lipstick cap head) behind a Stick, and Snickerdoodle found delicious joy in prolonging the hunt by pretending he could not find her at all.

Except for a splintered and decaying dock, half-drowning in the squelchy bay, there were no structures near their home. Beach heather and ninebark thickly cascaded over the dunes, which were a major highway for all Codswallop travel at the Cape. Mother said The Sticks were made of something called "piling," and that, years before she was made, it was a place where Wegs would tie up their boats and step off onto a dock so as not to get wet. Snickerdoodle could not imagine why a Weg would fear the water in this way, but knew better than to press her on the subject. Mother would always become impatient when he asked even the smallest of questions about the Wegs. He'd wait and ask his father, who was only too happy to impart the juicy, forbidden details of the creatures, with very little prodding, to his mother's dismay.

Occasionally, orange-beaks came to rest atop The Sticks, but not often, for as his mother explained, the winged creatures mostly stayed in groups and followed each to places where Wegs left food behind. This was another peculiarity. *Food.* Snickerdoodle could not seem to comprehend what food was, and why all other creatures but Codswallops sought it, fought for it, or left it behind. A year ago, he had found a piece of it just lying on the sand. It was long and yellow, and sculpted into the shape of a twig. The pokes of his coffee stirrer limb made deep impressions in the soft outer skin of it. His mother screamed when she saw him, and hurried him away to hide under the water until well past daylight. She would not tell him why they could no longer play that day.

On some late evenings when tides were tranquil, and the sounds of inland places became still, Snickerdoodle and Drivel judiciously marched under the water and emerged on the long beach. Once on land, they stayed just inside the final stretch of beach heather for cover. For hours, she'd keep him busy and nearby, enticing him with various treasure hunts of sorts, saying things like, "We'll each gather what might be good findings for a future sister and then share our gems!"

Drivel knew he loved proposals such as this, which made him feel useful and needed. He would immediately and energetically begin digging up cigarette stubs, pop-tops, and pieces of colored brown and green glass. After a good long while, they amassed quite a collection of potential sister thingamajigs, which now included an empty thread spool, a brown shoelace, a pencil top, and one white silk flower petal. They also had a small pile of glass bits, which Drivel kept separate from the other items, expertly bundling them into short stacks, tied with lashes of burnt grass.

Once, after Snickerdoodle tired of the game and before Drivel could protest, he scrambled up into a high bough of a bayberry and grandly dove downward into a thick cluster of its leaves. A very surprised winged seed-eater exploded from the bush. It powerfully grabbed at one of Snickerdoodle's Band-Aids in self-defense, and tore it from his body entirely. Snickerdoodle immediately lost his balance and tumbled to the rocky sand, while Drivel lunged at the seed-eater and repeatedly whapped it with her carton, until it dropped the appendage, screeched painfully, took wing, and headed far down the beach.

"You see there," his mother said, her face sadly following the creature as it turned west and flew inland to the towns, "if that thing had decided to carry you off rather than simply peck at you, I would have very well lost you forever."

Drivel used her cap head to swiftly iron out the severed Band-Aid, and broke off a small piece of her own twist-tie to help refasten the limb to her son's torso. "You must stay near. You must be careful. Never be seen by animals or by humans." She dipped one of her arms into a slit gap of bayberry root and pulled out a bead of dark brown goo, which she generously slathered on Snickerdoodle's new joint.

"Oh, but Mother, I know very well you would make yourself wings from Popsicle paper and fly to rescue me!" Snickerdoodle teased, testing his healed limb by slapping it against a peach-colored pebble. Drivel could only sigh, and make preparations to drag some of their treasures home. At times like these, she questioned her choice to keep Snickerdoodle isolated from other Tosh. He knew so very little about the world they lived in. Perhaps playing with the others, learning from their example, might be more of a boon than she had first divined.

One November day, about an hour before sunset, and well after the orange-beaks had departed from the beaches, Drivel announced to her son that they were travelling to visit his friend Pocky, whose family lived far away in an area frequented by Wegs, called Congress. They would depart in a week, and they would *practice* their travelling every day before that.

Up until then, Snickerdoodle had only known the *direction* of Pocky's home. He'd climb atop a bush and peer out over the salted marshland for a brief glimpse of the massive yellow Weg structure in the distance, away from the waves, easily stretching the length of twenty docks along one side. This feat was always followed by his mother crossly yanking him down, and making him promise to not repeat such a wholly unsafe action ever again, to which he did promise in earnest.

Snickerdoodle only ever saw Pocky when his family came to visit The Nine Sticks, and he would often overhear Pocky's mother, Debri, quietly scolding his own mother about it when they thought he was distracted. Mother held firm to her convictions whenever this happened, saying the excursion was too dangerous without her husband along, and she was not yet willing to take the risk.

For though Codswallops never tired, and could walk and run just as they pleased, whenever traveling in the open they were forced to wait for a manageable wind, and then merely tumble to and fro to their desired destination. This was the way they had learned to conceal themselves from Wegs, by simply acting as they looked. Acting like trash. Tumbling took much longer, of course. And should a wind maliciously cease, then so unfortunately did the journey, leaving the rubbish creature defenseless and exposed to an open sky of things with beaks and claws, or possibly the curious, destructive clutches of unsupervised Weg children, as they waited patiently for another gust to help them along.

For a whole week, Drivel made Snickerdoodle practice his tumbles over and again. Catching the breeze, lurching in a certain way so as not to look forced, and then falling flat as could be when the wind died down. She taught him how to sail, roll, and spin through the air, as well as how to plunge, and even skate along the sand. And, as if the whole world were put on pause the day they finally left for Congress, their journey was resplendent with favorable winds and miraculously without incident or intruders. They reached Pocky's home in less than thirty minutes.

Pocky had a mother, father, and three sisters. This was rare bounty for a Codswallop family, and it gave them some prestige amongst the others. Pocky himself had been fashioned by his father using a considerable amount of actual Weg hair (also a kind of honor), woven through irregular shards of driftwood, which the child would boast about unremittingly.

"My father says someday I will take the lead when we march on the Wegs. For I am a symbol of his purpose."

Pocky was Snickerdoodle's closest friend, and understandably so, as the only other Tosh that Snickerdoodle had ever actually met. And, never wanting to irritate his only friend, Snickerdoodle would agree with whatever Pocky said, and acquiesce to every suggestion Pocky made, silly or no, whether it was digging up broken shell bits to make him a crown, having to hunt for him all afternoon in the heather, or dressing in a gull feather and pretending to be an orange-beak he'd slaughter in conquest.

But all day, this day, Pocky had been trying his hardest to convince Snickerdoodle to sneak away with him and see the Cobblestone Road in a place called Washington. Certainly it was not the first time Pocky suggested they leave the safety of their mothers, the scrubs, and the white chairs of Congress, and travel to this mystical place where rocks, the color of sunset, were all the same. But now he seemed more serious than ever before. There was something in his tone that frightened Snickerdoodle. It was a tone that seemed to threaten the end of friendship should he not comply.

"Don't be a newborn," Pocky said. "You are well past two years of life and need to see the world! How else will you be a help to your father when the war comes?"

"But how far is it?" Snickerdoodle asked, shuffling some broken shell bits with his red stirrer limb.

"Not far," Pocky said, "I told you I have been there four times. I know my way." Reaching up with his purple broccoli-band limbs, Pocky grabbed onto a branch of heather, lifted his hairy, driftwood body from the sand, and vigorously swung back and forth, stewing in disappointment. "We'll be there and back before your mother calls for you to travel home, silly."

By the time Snickerdoodle and Pocky had crossed the mountainous sand yard beyond the white chairs at Congress, dodging a few Wegs and a hairless canine that was thankfully lashed by rope to a railing, the wind had picked up considerably. Not more than once that hour did they find themselves pitched in the wrong direction, or into each other for that matter, and grasping at any immediate clumps of undergrowth for momentary anchorage. Snickerdoodle heard the sea winds growling low in the distance, and felt a few tiny droplets of water bounce off his plastic cap and roll down his back. When he finally looked back toward the shadowy beach, white splashes of light in a black sky illuminated a murderously churning ocean. A terrible storm was making its way inland.

The both of them whirled through streets teeming with Wegs. Bouncing off curbs, flattening against walls, and billowing under benches as the merciless gale intensified. It was terrifying for Snickerdoodle. Surely by now his mother would have noticed the change in weather, and protectively called for him to come to her. She would be steeped in worry. He knew he should turn back. But now Snickerdoodle could only desperately hurry after Pocky, no longer because he cared to see the sights of Washington, but because he knew that should he lose his friend, he would never find his way home.

But when then they finally arrived, the Cobblestone Street was certainly the most beautiful place Snickerdoodle had ever beheld in his very short life. It now seemed well worth the trip and disobeying his mother just this one time. A flickering dance of shadow and color, glitter and wind. It was just as his friend had promised, and more. Crusty orange-brown stones, shaped all the same, coated the ground for as far as he could see and shimmered like buttery glass in the mix of dark azure sky, drizzling rain, and bright lights that shone down from all the mysterious structures. Pocky had called these *stores*, but Snickerdoodle scarcely knew what he meant, and only nodded, mesmerized by how the Wegs lived.

Each store had an opening made of wood and glass with a large jewel-cut stone in the center. The Wegs would tug upon this stone with some effort, and each yank was followed by the sound of divine twinkles, surely meant to advertise their arrival. A string of nimble illuminations, much like the comforting stars, which dappled the sky at The Nine Sticks, were delicately wrapped in the branches of tall flappy green trees lining the walkway on either side of the cobblestones. Each tree did not grow from the ground, but was stuffed into a box of dirt, lined with gray dock wood.

But the most amazing of all the sights appeared in the very center of the cobblestones. A strange green pool of water was raised into the air and dribbled in arcs around its base to a lower pool, filled with flat brown circles. The circles had pictures carved into them. Snickerdoodle wanted very much to see the pictures, but the water was in motion, thus making it difficult to see down into the lower pool clearly. Without knowing he was doing so, Snickerdoodle drew nearer to the dribbling water and stepped right into the path of a Weg.

Then Snickerdoodle was airborne, trapped in the claw of the beast who had unwittingly stepped on his barrette. Snickerdoodle had never seen a human's face before, only their long bristly legs, while hiding between craggles of rock or bushy undergrowth with his mother. Yet he knew, in the twinkles of the tree lights, in the whir of the storm, his body held fast by the creature's pressings, that this was one of them, and it was more terrifying than he ever could have imagined. Rows of flat dirty brown rocks snapped open and shut in the center of its face, and beyond them a dreadful cavernous black hole contracted. Atop its head, a thousand black fronds, moving as one in the wind, snaked over Snickerdoodle's chip bag and wound round his cap head.

The Weg then stretched its terrible black hole even wider and screeled at him so loudly his whole chip bag body vibrated and crackled. Then using both its claws, the Weg crumpled him into a ball and tossed him high into the air over its shoulder. Spiraling through the sky faster than he had ever tumbled in the wind, Snickerdoodle bounced off another human's head before hitting the ground with a short pop! It was then he knew he'd lost the blue barrette limb altogether. It took him just a moment to uncurl his crunched-up torso, before a vicious breeze caught him just right, and sent him sweeping across the cobblestone, cap over coffee stirrer. This time, he blew right into the opening of a store filled with Wegs.

Petrified, Snickerdoodle could not think what to do next, for there was no wind to catch here on the inside, and one of his limbs was now gone. Surely he had only seconds before another Weg reached down and did him further harm. But then, between the cage of shifting legs, he caught sight of one of the illuminated trees not ten feet away, and decided the very next time he heard the twinkling of the store opening up, he'd roll along the floor until he reached it. Perhaps the Wegs might think the same wind that had blown him into the store would also pull him out. He waited, heard the sounds, and rolled quickly.

With each turn of his bag, he kept his focus on the tree. And just when he was sure he was out of the store, he hit something. Something hard. Something he could not see at first. For he had not blown out of the store at all, but into an area that faced the Cobblestone yet was surrounded entirely by glass. No matter which way he rolled away from the store, he would strike the glass. Glass, much like the bits his mother collected, but not green or brown. This was clear. And not bits, but a *wall* of glass. It towered far higher than the length of a Nine Stick, and was the like of which he had never seen, and in his heart he knew it to be an obstacle that rubbish creatures the weight of a pickleball could never penetrate.

Realizing his fate, and that more movement would certainly attract the Wegs lumbering past the glass on the outside, Snickerdoodle Bunkum tucked himself low into a corner of the enclosure and did not move for many hours. All this time, he could do nothing but watch the Cobblestone Street and berate himself for ever letting Pocky convince him to come here.

This was a terrible place. Large, noisy, confusing, and dangerous. Wegs, hauling strange items back and forth, which made no sense. Their children, howling freakishly, until food stuffed into their jaws made them quiet again. There was a little comfort for him in the sound of the rain. It hit the glass in a way that reminded him of droplets rebounding off the splintered dock at home.

Time passed. There were a fewer Wegs on the street now, and those that remained snapped open brightly colored wings to lift over their horrid heads. Did the water pain them? Would it dissolve them over time? Snickerdoodle had almost forgotten his fear, watching the Wegs shout to each other and slip on the walk. They acted as if this was the first rainstorm they had ever experienced. It was quite funny. A few flashes of lightning more, and it sent the Wegs into even more of a scurry up and down the street.

In a particularly bright wash of lighting, movement at the base of a tree caught his attention. It was his mother. And it was also his father. Without thinking, Snickerdoodle, who could not stand, rolled over to the panel of glass closest to where they were hiding outside. His father swiftly lifted his syringe extremity, as if to warn his son to stay still. It was too late. A Weg stepped into the glass enclosure, picked him up, and tore Snickerdoodle into three pieces. It carried him to the outside and carelessly tossed his parts into the street. Instinctively, Snickerdoodle dragged what was left of his functioning cap head, a third of his torso, and one limb closer to a wall where he might be safer. Perhaps his father could help him recover his other parts, if only he could find his parents now.

But something stopped Snickerdoodle from looking for his father. The Wegs were screaming. All of them. Every Weg. Those on the street and those in the stores. It was the first moment Snickerdoodle knew something was wrong on the Cobblestone Street.

Hundreds of his kind. From all directions. Codswallops. Leaping out from the branches of flappy trees. Clambering out from between sprays of sea grass planted in dirt boxes. Plunging down from Weg rooftops. He even saw one rubbish creature inventively wriggle up from a crevice in the cobblestone, where it must have been hiding for half a day.

Snickerdoodle was utterly astonished. Perhaps even more shocking than the appearance of so many of his kind all in one place was the fact that they no longer tumbled to and fro, nor caught the wind to fashion their travel, but were instead *chasing* the Wegs. This time, they *wanted* the humans to see them and know they were there.

And though he never knew what the word *war* meant when his father would accidently mention it in his presence at home, only to be sourly hushed by his wife, Snickerdoodle was convinced that he was seeing one now. Seeing a war. And the Codswallops, with boundless intention, were hurting the Wegs very badly. Poking Weg eyes with their pointed plastic limbs, slicing Weg necks with razor sharp can tops, and stuffing up Weg mouths and ear holes with the very bundles of glass bits he had seen his mother tie up so many times.

The urge to move, to stand, to find his father in the chaos and help the others was very strong, and Snickerdoodle used what was left of his ripped bag to push himself away from the wall and into the action. But a Weg who seemed as large as the sky spotted his movements. Its face twisting with hate, it lunged at him. Another flash of light and a deafening crack of thunder, and Snickerdoodle saw his father trip the

Weg by throwing himself under its feet. Snickerdoodle never felt so much love for his father as in that moment.

The Weg fell forward, landing only a foot from Snickerdoodle's mangled torso. The creature's pointed chin struck the cobblestone first, exploding in spray of shattered bone and gummy red liquid. Using his head and only limb, in a series of eruptive jerks and drags, Snickerdoodle heaved himself closer to the fallen Weg's hideous, momentarily lifeless face.

All, around them, he heard the frenzied shouts of the Wegs and saw explosions of red light. Though he could not discern their language, he could detect their broadcasts of panic and pain to each other; clearly the sound of beings unhappily comprehending their end. The flickers of firelight danced across his chip bag body now, and a new wave of Codswallops scuttled past him in a fury, their low shadows blackening the stone.

But Snickerdoodle would not be distracted from his enterprise. Finally reaching the Weg's face, Snickerdoodle wormed up a nostril, contracting and contorting, expertly revolving his body so the coffee stirrer took the vanguard. With full knowledge that this was a journey from which there would be no return, and fueled with his newfound sense of true Codswallop purpose, Snickerdoodle Bunkum pushed on until he reached the Weg's soft brain.

J.C. Raye is a professor of communication at a small community college in the Garden State. For seventeen years she has been teaching the most feared course on the planet: public speaking. Witnessing grown people cry, beg, freak out, and pass out is just another delightful day on the job for her, so she does know a little something about real terror. J.C. has won numerous artistic and academic awards over the years for her projects in the field of Communication and Media, some at the national level. Seats in her classes fill quicker than tickets to a Rolling Stones concert. Her most notable lectures include How Not to Be Awkward in Public and Practically Painless Speaking. When not teaching or writing horror, Ms. Raye creates disturbing short films for her friends using found family footage. She also loves goats of any kind.

From the Bluff

by

Jan Rittmer

BACK IN THE '60S IN my big house at the top of Clay Street hill, I would stand in the bay window of our bedroom, coffee cup in hand, looking out over the tops of the oak trees in the park, over the white-veined church steeples to the river beyond, never wishing to live anyplace else. On sunny days the river glittered like the sequins on my blue satin formal; on cloudy days it lay in its valley, gray, flat, remote. But always at night, looking over the thousands of lights of the cities, I saw it as a magnetic black hole, a sinuous absence defined by the lights along its shores. Car lights whizzed nervously across its four shadowy bridges like tightrope walkers running the last few feet to safety.

The river's magnetism is obvious. Towns grow long beside its bank, unwilling to expand over the bluff. People try to keep the river in sight, building houses that stare blankly at the prairie but open wide in every possible way to the river on the other side. My friend, a contractor, built his home so that each room overlooked the river, even installing an interior window between the master bath and the bedroom so he could see the river as he stepped from the shower.

Those who grow up with the Mississippi sliding past their door have trouble leaving its valley. When they do, they do it like suppliants to an oriental court with their heads bowed. When they return, they approach on their knees, forelock to the ground. In the '60s, I met young Chris, who, as part of a cliché for the '60s, despised every-thing his wealthy parents represented. He had fled our valley for the Ganges, and with help from Indian and Tibetan wise men, searched for peace and balance. I first met him after he returned home. He became a deckhand on our company's towboats. "I was happy over there for a while," he said, "But I became obsessed with a need to come home. It wasn't until the plane circled over the Mississippi, and I felt a pull downward, like pulling extra g's, that I realized it was *my* river that had been calling me back." For two years Chris brought his newly serene personality to the raucous, dirty work of tow boating; he made his considerably less-centered mates uncomfortable. Oh, Chris was nice enough, but they felt as if he knew something they didn't, and he never bothered to explain. Then there was my neighbor, Richard, who moved from the town of Clinton, just upriver, to live on my bluff. When he was a boy he would head for the Clinton riverfront to walk the railroad bridge and spit in the water. He swam the slough across to Beaver Island, where he built a hideaway and learned how to smoke a pipe. On the river he ran into old Gus, who taught him about boats and fishing and eventually gave him a green jon boat and motor of his own. As a kid Richard explored every turn of the local backwa-ters in that little boat. Later, after med school and a stint in the Navy that took him around the world, he married and opened a practice in Tucson. Eventually, though, he gave it up and came home. Years later (when he was somewhat mellow one night) he admitted why: "It was those damn Arizona aquifers," he said, looking out his living room window towards the Mississippi, "Real estate agents kept talking about aquifers like they were invisible underground rivers. I needed to come home to a *real* river."

Looking downstream from my window on Clay Street, beyond the most distant bridge, downstream below Smith Island, in my mind's eye I could see the stretch of river I remember most vividly, the five miles or so between the Illinois shore and the main navigational channel that the river charts call Andalusia Island. That one name encompasses dozens of small, unnamed islands, laced by sloughs and backwater, forming miles of secluded, quiet places. I've seen those gray-green waters so smooth they seemed two dimensional, mirroring willows drooping from the bank, clouds scudding across the flat surface, and filtering blue sky to a murky green. But I knew that beneath the surface, catfish curled in a gnarl of tree roots, and ancient sturgeons slid stealthily along the bottom.

At other times these same waters vibrated with life. Dragonflies darted and hovered like tiny cobalt drones. Catfish leaped from their hiding places; a frog belly-flopped smack in front of a turtle that was up on a log, sniffing the sunshine. At these times the surface of the water was ragged with comings and goings, landings and departures, concentric circles bumping into each other, interrupting the wake of a mallard hen and her ducklings.

On the other side of the islands, out on the main channel, is a different river, less natural but also crowded and vital. On a summer day these stretches were very busy, and even more congested on weekends. Pleasure boats ranged from pontoons slogging along to cruisers with sleeping quarters for eight, from canoes to flat little speedboats snarling and splatting by. All vied for space, dodging each other. I knew this river because it was there where much of my family's life took place. Out there on the main channel was where the giant towboats pushing fifteen barges rumbled by, and our smaller harbor boats skated around to help them, all of us hoping to make a living while struggling to avoid the foolhardy water-skiers who played there, believing their bravado would keep them safe.

On the Iowa bank there was a mixture of summer cabins and short stretches of trees that were interrupted by occasional boat-launching ramps with cars and trailers clustered around them.

There were also factories and barge terminals transacting the serious, hard work of the river. Lining the Iowa side of the islands were trees with fleets of huge steel barges tied to them, sharing space with beaches lined by pleasure boats. Frequent visitors to those beaches furnished their favorite island playgrounds with tire swings, picnic tables, and even an occasional two-hole outhouse. During the day, families picnicked and swam; at night, campfires blazed and radios blared. The crisscrossing searchlights of passing towboats strobe-lit these all night parties.

Upstream from there, closer to my home, the river divided the Quad Cities in ways mere state boundaries could not have done. Chambers of Commerce slogans not withstanding, there are two sets of cities on opposite shores. People measure each other like feisty kids on opposite sides of a toe drawn line. Even men fishing in the turbulence below the dam—one in the shadow of the Davenport Bank Building, the other in the lee of Rock Island's Modern Woodman's office—eye each other suspiciously across the water. When a towboat or an excursion boat distracts the fishermen by pushing out of the lock, the disruption reinforces a sense that the river makes strangers of the two groups.

During the summer, competing cities call periodic truces: They give homage to the Mississippi by convening with others to bring tribute. There is a jazz festival, fireworks, a cardboard raft race, Catfish Days, Steamboat Days, River City Days. The towns of Port Byron and Le Claire act out old rivalries by stretching a rope across the river in a hotly contested tug-of-war. There was a Crappiethon, now abandoned (possibly because people pronounced the name in embarrassing ways), and a lighted boat parade. One upriver community actually celebrated the plague of short-lived insects that regularly infests all river cities with an annual Shad Fly Festival. But when the summer hoopla is over, all go their separate ways.

The river towns on both banks exist because of the Mississippi. Early settlers came because of the valley's fertile soil, and many of them arrived by riverboat, at first settling almost arbitrarily on one bank or the other. The towns needed a reliable water supply and an easy way to swap farm produce and minerals for manufactured goods. Early settlers mined the river for sand and gravel and its banks for lime to make cement. Later, lumber from the logging off of the great Minnesota and Wisconsin forests floated downriver in acre-sized rafts to become buildings, and houses like the one I lived in, as well as mansions for great lumber barons like Young, Lamb, and Weyerhaeuser.

Many fortunes have been made on the river, but the boom and bust of logging and the dramatic rise and demise of gilded steamboats illustrate a pattern: Only hard, dirty work on the Mississippi has yielded a lasting living. The oldest companies still move sand and gravel. But the river always seems to encourage schemes for making easy money. Those schemes have been like the shadflies: numerous, succeeding briefly, but born and dead in an instant.

Even today the Mississippi sustains the Quad Cities. At night, searchlights still bounce off the windows of the Clay Street house. During the season, the view from there still includes several big tows bringing coal, fertilizer, and petroleum to exchange for barge after barge of local grain, each fifteen-barge tow carrying the year's work of more than a dozen farm families.

And recently the old song of the calliope is again floating up the hill on the night air. A flock of new excursion boats is bringing a new generation of pilgrims from around the world to pay homage to our river.

Those who could afford it, like doctor Richard and the wealthy Petersen family of department store fame who built our Clay Street house in the early 1900s, built safely, high on the edge of the bluffs. From there they easily overlooked the river's excesses. But even those who lived down below did the same, strangely blind to flooding, merely cleaning up the mess with little complaint. From the early 1800s the federal government tried to make the Mississippi dependable for navigation, and in the '30s the Corps of Engineers hired thousands of depression-weary men to soften its cycle of flood and drought. The men constructed the twenty-six navigational locks and dams between Cairo, Illinois, and St. Paul, Minnesota. This plan succeeded just well enough to encourage unjustified complacency.

Responding to some primordial schedule, the foaming, mindless river still periodically reverts, erupting in a flood both relentless and insidious. The murmur of our supposedly tame river becomes the chest-rattling roar of the Mississippi as it used to be, relentlessly re-leveling its flood plain, eroding whatever is not completely solid. And even miles away, manholes pop open as the river snakes through storm sewers and into basements, seeking its own level.

The flood of 1965 is the one I remember best. They foolishly called it a hundred-year flood. All of our cities banded together against the river-turned-enemy. Old and young frantically shoveled sand and piled sandbags. Our company towboats were running on River Drive, rescuing and ferrying people past Petersen's Department Store, and delivering sandbags where needed. From the pilothouse of the *Jay Hawk* I saw rows of television antennas poking up from rooftops like periscopes peering above the rushing water. I saw deer, raccoons, foxes, a horse. I saw a cow struggling, trying to swim against the current, her eyes rolling with fear. And once I saw the body of a man in a T-shirt and flowered shorts come swirling downstream facedown, knees and arms bent like a fetus.

For weeks, like everyone else, I stared in vacant-eyed disbelief, feeling betrayed.

Jan Williams Rittmer is an ex-harbor boat dispatcher who has been related by marriage or birth to twelve licensed Mississippi riverboat pilots. From experience she knows that when families challenge Mother Nature, their victories come at a price. Jan's grandson was licensed this year, and became the sixth generation of river pilots in the Williams family. In addition to having sold and dispatched for the family business, Jan holds a BA in English from Augustana College in Illinois and an MA in expository writing from Iowa University. She taught technical writing, and has been the go-to writer for numerous volunteer organizations. Now, as a *very* latecomer to writing creative nonfiction and fiction, she has begun to share her experiences with the working Mississippi River from an anti-Twain perspective. Jan and her husband are retired in Davenport, Iowa.

Sleet Teeth

by

Goran Sedler

I DIDN'T BRING MY GLOVES, Christian Clark realized as he gave his snow-covered driveway a hard look.

What had seemed like a fun little exercise was turning into a terrible idea.

He buried the blade of the shovel in the snow and started his chore, cursing Diane with every swing for talking him into abandoning their penthouse in the city and moving down here to the suburbs. In his old life, he would've been sitting in front of his big-screen TV right now, working on increasing his carbon footprint and dismissing the vicarious news reports for hyping a case of falling flurries into an overblown natural disaster. In his new life, he was destined to freeze. And down here, snowfalls came in no flurries; the flakes were as fat as cherubs.

Back in the house, while putting on his winter clothing, he'd had the confidence of a wooly mammoth, but standing in the driveway, up to his elbows in his least favorite state of water, he felt more like a plucked penguin. The cold was hurting his face, his hands, and his neck.

After a dozen swings of the shovel, his back started reminding him of his poor shape and a lifetime of unhealthy choices. Christian was forced to give his forty-year-old heart a short pause.

He found himself thinking about the Program and wishing he wasn't on Step Seven. But giving up now would be a disaster. He was so close to the Twelfth Step he could almost, in a clumsy way of putting it, taste it.

The air felt like liquid destined to turn to ice, yet Christian's body was somehow able to perspire. As he wiped his forehead with the back of his hand, the friction scratched him like sandpaper. This body was falling apart as efficiently as his life was.

A sound not unlike something peeing in the snow pricked his ears. Christian looked down his relaxed arm, his wiping hand.

Where there had been skin, he was now staring at proof of his mortality. The flesh on his hand was glittering like a split grapefruit. The knuckles were peeled to the bone and the snow under his fingers was a bloody mire.

Christian ran.

Where are you running to? And from what?

His heavy clothing tripped his legs, and Christian, a middle-aged lawyer who had spent his career warming up the world to the agendas of big corporations, landed facedown in the snow.

He pushed himself up and stared at the impression his face had left behind. The imprint was a creamy tomato soup.

Christian's scream turned to steam.

He went for the fence, trying to bring himself up, but instead of a fleshy hand, he shoved a set of bloody bones against the iron rail. Whatever was eating him, it was doing it fast. God knows what it was doing to his face.

He felt the fiery cold on his cheeks burrow inside, deeper and deeper, well beyond his eyes, deep enough to cut the cord that enabled him to see the world and plunge him into eternal darkness.

The fall on his ass was as undignified as it felt.

Christian's breathing slowed while his mind drowned in a hive of questions that would forever remain unanswered.

In another reality he was drinking scotch, watching TV, and hugging his ex-wife like their marriage had never fallen apart.

Here and now, Christian Clark was a bag of winter clothing filled with an oozing paste of meat and blood.

I should've gone back for the gloves, was the last thing that crossed his mind before it too was finally devoured.

"I think Clark is drunk again," said George Reed to no one in particular.

He knew Martha wouldn't be listening (well, definitely not on this day) but he had to satisfy his need for gossip.

The tip of his nose touched his upper lip as he pressed his wrinkled face against the window.

"How can anyone drink liquor this early in the day? The man should be locked away."

George's neighbor was on his ass, back against the iron fence, while the angry snowfall was turning him into a snowman. The headline on the newspaper in George's hand promised (and delivered) the worst winter in thirty years, which meant the most he'd get out of his life in the next couple of days would be spying on his neighbors.

And this was a promising start.

"He's not moving," said George, disappointed the show was already nearing an end. "Just sitting there, in the snow. How cold d'ya think it is outside?"

His wife didn't say a word. She was kneeling in front of the living room couch, her clasped hands bound by a rosary, murmuring prayers as old as sin. George had decided a long time ago that these fits of hers were insane. A normal person would've let go of the pain, and embraced the rest of their life for whatever it was. In other words, moved on. But not Martha. Not his damn wife.

"He fell down," said George. There were still some surprises left in the old drunk. "He probably passed out. Should I call someone?" But before he reached for the phone he remembered. "Oh yeah, the lines are out."

This got Martha's attention. She left her religious trinkets on the living room table and joined him by the window.

"See?" asked George, worried her old eyes might miss the show. Clark was all the way across the street, and the heavy blizzard didn't help the resolution. "I bet you he's vomiting."

She turned away from the window and went for her coat in the hallway.

"I'm going out there," she said. Whenever Martha wasn't sure about her actions, she announced them out loud to the world, as if the sound of her own voice was a good enough reassurance.

"Don't be crazy," shouted her husband, "this is between him and his hangover!"

If this were any other day, his remark would've led them to an argument—but not today. There would've been a fight, and later on, who knows, maybe even some good old sex to amend the wounds of exchanged verbal missiles, but—you sure as hell know it, George—not today.

She slammed the door behind her as she stormed out. He could hear her on the other side putting on her boots and stomping them on the welcome mat. Crazy old woman. She could've put them on inside.

George went back to spying on his passed-out neighbor when he noticed something fall on their snow-covered lawn. It was bigger, faster, and blacker than a snowflake. And it made a nice little crater in all that whipped cream.

Standing on his toes, he saw it was a bird. A raven.

Or was it?

He could've sworn he had seen a lump of black feathers; now the thing looked more like a small red ball.

There was that cramped feeling of misdiagnosis in his gut again. The fear of getting things wrong forever looming over all of his actions.

George grabbed his glasses from the living room table. He was sure as hell, once he put them on, that everything would be clear; the world would return to normal.

But as he focused, trying to make sense of what he saw, he realized that thing inside the hole was not a bird but the contents of a meat grinder. Immediately, armed with crystal vision, his eyes went to Clark. His neighbor wasn't lying down and vomiting; his neighbor was nothing but vomit of blood and pieces of meat, all wrapped up in winter clothing.

And Martha was out there.

Out there!

He could see her fighting her way through the deep snow, trying to reach the leftovers of Christian Clark.

Jesus Christ...

The old man ran to the front door and found it locked. Locked? Why would she lock the damn door?

He fumbled through the hallway cabinet and found the keys. Hitting the lock proved to be more of a challenge. George cursed his arthritis. It had cost him his career; would it now cost him his wife?

When he unlocked the door, cold air greeted his pajama-clad body. The snowfall was so furious the outside world looked like bad TV reception.

"Martha!" he screamed. "Martha!"

His wife, the love of his life, the woman he hadn't told nearly enough how much he loved her, was standing at the end of their driveway. She still hadn't crossed the street. She was just standing there, frozen. A bundle of a hirsute coat and boots buried in the snow.

Why wasn't he rushing after her?

A gust of wind swept through the street and blew her body away. All her flesh and skin turned to glittering confetti. The coat fell down on the snow; an empty shell of a dead animal.

Where Martha had been standing, a red rain colored the white snow into a cute shade of pink.

This was it. This was the "until death do us part" of their magnificent love story.

While George's brain was still processing his new widowhood, a snowflake landed on his palm.

The pain was short and convincing. George yelped, grabbed his hand, and watched as the trickle of blood ran down his palm and under his wrist.

Has the world gone mad? Has he?

He walked back into the living room and stood before the window, where, just minutes ago, the day had promised bad things would be happening to someone else.

The spot where Clark leftovers had been sprawled was evenly covered with a blanket salmon-colored snow. Even his clothes were gone. The same was happening with Martha's resting place. A minute later and you wouldn't be able to tell that anyone had died there.

It was only then that it occurred to him how unnaturally quiet the street was. Sure, the heavy snowfall always brought its own kind of silence, but this was like pressing an ear to a coffin.

The street hadn't been cleared (where the hell were the snowplows, anyway?), and wasn't that little Steven's winter hat across the street, on old man Henderson's white lawn? No footsteps around it. Nothing that would indicate the boy had dropped it while delivering the morning papers.

All traces of death, carpeted by snow.

Over at Stewart's place, wasn't that Julia behind the window, crying and pleading for help? Her face whipped with open wounds (she hardly looked like a teenager now), her hands as red as used surgical gloves. She was dressed for a winter walk, but most of her clothing had been soaked in blood and ripped to shreds. She wouldn't stop crying. Crying and slapping the glass window with her tortured hands.

It was then George remembered the front door of their house. He had left it wide open and inviting.

The snow was already inside. It was crawling through the entrance and spilling in the hallway; a billion white ants riding a white wave. Piling higher and higher ...

How could he accept this? He was looking at nothing more than crystals of frozen water. How could he, in his right mind, stare at it and be scared shitless?

Unless he wasn't. Unless this was him losing his mind.

The creature didn't care about the state of his sanity. It was prodding the inside of the house like a fat white tongue in search of food.

Where are you, old man? No use in hiding.

There was a room in this house George Reed had promised himself he would never enter. A shrine that had been built in memory of a future that had never materialized. A temple raised up and sanctified with tears and wounds that had never healed.

There couldn't have been a more fitting place to hide.

If this white monstrosity were of his own making, he would go to the place where even his insanity would be terrified to follow.

The house creaked under thc wcight of snow.

It was like being trapped inside the hull of a ship, all that force of destruction just a squeaking layer of protection away.

George had barricaded the door with all the furniture he could move. He had shut the blinds and covered the only window with blankets. Now, George was holding his breath.

Something crashed upstairs. Just another victim of the snow's deadly embrace. He could imagine the white powder of death slowly filling every corner of the house. Searching. Hunting.

Except in this one room.

This was Jonathan's room. This was the room Martha had given all her care and attention to, to make it look as though it were being lived in. George could trace his finger down the kid-sized work desk (which he had used to block the door) and there wouldn't be a single speck of dust on it. The pictures in frames had been updated with memories of George's and Martha's latest safaris. The blankets he had stripped from the bed smelled as fresh as morning.

The place tried to be everything but a room-sized memorial, yet the weight of its purpose was undeniable: This would always be the room Jonathan would have lived in.

Plaster from the ceiling snowed on top of George's head as the house sighed under the deadly squeeze. These walls wouldn't be able to take much more of it.

Why? Why is this thing so bent on eating him? Why can't it move on to someone else? There is a whole town out there teaming with sin; what gives his own such a coveted flavor?

Yes, George, what else could it be.

It wasn't just a piece of trivia that thirty years ago today this area had one of the heaviest snowfalls the town had ever seen.

Thirty years today? On the anniversary of your wife's miscarriage?

He thought he had managed to build a wall around that memory but, without breaking a wrinkle, George recalled the vivid details of the evening like it had been yesterday.

Martha had been in another room, celebrating over the fake ultrasound photo that was showing all was fine with their unborn baby boy. George was in his study, brooding over the original he had decided no one ever needed to find out about. Outside, the world had been engulfed in a heavy snowfall. Inside, George kept staring at the black and white ultrasound that, if you blurred your focus enough, looked exactly like another blizzard.

But if you looked at it with the eyes trained to recognize abnormalities and deformities, you'd have felt kicked in the stomach and your vision would have fogged with burning tears.

Their bundle of joy was a lump of horror.

The future in store for this family would be one of pain and sacrifice.

And they could handle it, and George was sure there had been enough of love in their marriage to make martyrs of them both, but he had also witnessed what the torture of a child could do to a parent.

The only sensible option left was the one he had spent his entire career perfecting. Lessen the pain.

When Martha went to bed, dizzy from a half a glass of wine he had graciously allowed her to enjoy, things were already unraveling according to his premeditation. As she lay dreaming of names for their cherished offspring, he sneaked to her side and injected her with a solution to the problem. The solution he had spent most of the morning mixing up and concocting in the solace of his office.

The solution that really hadn't solved anything.

There hadn't existed a chemical compound that could have just as easily flushed the soul of that unborn baby from his wife's body. And Martha remained a mother, without ever giving birth.

He used all his influence and money to take them across the world in search for a cure for her sorrow. Pristine jungle reserves were opened for their enjoyment, elephants were ridden for their amusement, tigers were petted for their satisfaction, but no matter where their days ended, the nights were as haunted as being back in this goddamn house.

George was sure there had to exist a big enough distraction out there; it was just a matter of finding it. They could have had a second attempt at happiness if only they had searched hard enough . . .

Really?

All this horror outside, doesn't it tell you different?

A fine wet sugar started seeping inside the room through the crack under the barricaded door. A window shattered; the blankets he had used to cover it hadn't managed to muffle the sound. The snow was finding its way inside Jonathan's room.

If George were examining the symptoms of this scene profession-ally, what would be the prognosis? Knowing all that he knew, witness-ing all that he had witnessed this morning, how much would he give himself? Five minutes? Ten? Thirty, if he tried to stamp out the ad-vancing snow?

Whatever he did, the result would be the same.

An hour from now there would be no trace of him left. It would be as if he had never existed. Remember Martha's remains, remember Clark's. Remember Jonathan's.

Even your blood would dilute to nothingness.

Lessen the pain, George, any delay will only make it worse.

He wondered what he could say to it to apologize. Were there words powerful enough to describe his grief?

And there was grief. Not only in Martha.

The thing that had bothered him so much about his wife's obses-sive mourning was that it had been on par with his own. These last thirty years had been nothing but a failed quest for redemption. All the luxurious havens of this blue world were nothing but cauterizers they selfishly used to prevent the infection of their loss from spread-ing. But no beaches were sandy enough, no jungles were wild enough, no life was exciting enough.

It was all for nothing.

It was all for no one.

He'd just say he is sorry, and hope for the best.

The old man removed the barricades from the door and stood with bare feet on the snow that had gotten under the door. His toes were already being eaten, his nervous system screaming at his indifference.

He wondered how much more could it hurt (don't let it, George, own the pain like it's an itch) before finally opening the door.

A wall of snow collapsed inside the room like an avalanche. The dance that followed was clumsy and overpowering. Before he could he could say anything, the snow was already on his face, in his ears, in his eyes, in his mouth. Millions of tiny razors hungry for his flesh.

There was so much pain he could've fed a world war with it. Tiny teeth munched at his meat so eagerly he didn't have the strength to regret his decision.

Not that there was anything to regret.

Minutes ago he had been just another man fattened on his own sins. Now, here, buried under hungry oblivion, he finally found a promise of deliverance for the unrealized delivery.

Soon he would be stripped down of everything that was George Reed and left only with whiteness that could easily pass for a clean soul.

Between reading books, watching films, and writing short stories, Goran Sedlar also co-hosts a weekly podcast in which he and his friends warn listeners of upcoming bad movies. Places he's been published include *Kzine* magazine, the *Book of the Macabre* anthology, and *Futura* magazine. He was born in Zagreb, Croatia, where he still lives and shares his territory with two cats and a crazy cat lady.

Miracle Material
by
Abra Staffin-Wiebe

THE LANDFILL IS SAFE. I think. Even Tupperware frightens me now. The sight of a discarded teddy bear moves me to tears. I wonder if Meredith's teddy bear still lies abandoned on her bed, held under siege by the ever-glowing blue stars that decorate her bedroom.

I tell myself that Meredith is safe and happy. We came from the sea, the scientists said. When there were scientists. What could be more natural than for us to return to the sea? I tell myself that she is safe and happy within the bosom of the sea.

I know I lie.

Wherever Meredith may be, however she feels, she is not my little girl anymore. And it is all my fault.

Well, not all of it. Once we brought the bluflex up from the Mariana Trench, the end was inevitable. But the loss of our children . . . that was my fault.

It was a deep and lovely blue. It glowed. It sparkled and shimmered. It resisted all extremes of temperature and stress, but it could be molded into any shape when submerged in seawater with an electrical current running through it. It was even nontoxic.

When I brought the bluflex doll home to Meredith, I was happy that she loved it so much. She took it to school for her "What My

Parents Do" presentation. I was delighted when she told me that all the other third-graders were jealous of it.

I saw the marketing possibilities.

My employers, Oak Leaf Products International, already had bluflex in production for use in building material, shoes, jewelry, food containers, and electronics components. It was the miracle material, an organic compound that needed nothing more than time and seawater to reproduce under the same environmental conditions as existed in the Mariana Trench. We had a lock on the national market, but we knew that our competitors overseas were racing as frantically as we were to find new ways to exploit bluflex's amazing properties.

Because it was my suggestion, I was put in charge of the toy division. I used the extra money to buy a house by the sea. That summer I was glad I had done so.

A hundred people died in the city during the heat wave. Sales of air conditioners made with bluflex insulation soared.

I worked ten-hour days, but I was always glad to be home again. Meredith was usually heading to bed when I got home, so I didn't get to talk to her much, but she said she loved living by the sea. She seemed content. She had the entire collection of bluflex toys, and she loved them all. Everybody loved bluflex.

The demand for bluflex was so high that our R&D division focused its efforts entirely on finding a way to speed up bluflex's natural reproduction in a lab environment. It wasn't cost-effective to mount another expedition to the Mariana Trench, and the population that we had wasn't reproducing nearly fast enough to keep up with the demand.

The week they succeeded, Oak Leaf Products held a party for all employees and their families. I noticed that every child wore bluflex clothing or carried a bluflex toy. I only smiled, a drink in my hand, when parents told me that their children refused to go anywhere without their bluflex.

God help me, I only smiled.

Meredith loved her bluflex snorkeling mask and flippers. She spent more and more time in the sea. Even though it was fall, the worldwide heat wave had not abated. Everyone either stayed inside their air-conditioned homes or went swimming.

From our house, I watched Meredith swim with her friends. I had never seen so many children without parental supervision at the beach, but they all seemed to be happy and healthy. And they all wore bluflex snorkel masks and fins.

I remember when the icecaps started melting rapidly. It was December, and it was ninety degrees in the shade. Oak Leaf Products donated a hundred bluflex air-conditioners to the homeless shelters, but there were still so many deaths that the city council mandated immediate cremation.

There were rumors of plague, but sales of bluflex products remained high.

I was in the basement with the plumber when Meredith told me she would be gone overnight for a farewell party for a few of her friends. Our basement was flooded. I had noticed puddles growing in the basement a couple of months ago, but now the water was knee-high. It smelled like the sea, and I could've sworn I saw movement in the water.

I asked Meredith if her friends' parents would be chaperoning.

She was quiet for a moment, and then she said, "We won't be alone. Don't worry, I'll be fine."

In the darkness of the basement, the bluflex bracelets she wore shimmered brilliantly. Their reflection in the water made the basement alive with small gleaming lights.

After Meredith left, I gave the plumber some excuse and retreated to the sanctity of the kitchen.

Heat waves shimmered above the beach outside. They distorted the light of the setting sun until ripples of red, gold, purple, and blue ran across the sand. The children on the beach looked as though they were swimming in a teeming sea of color.

The plumber told me that there was nothing he could do. I offered him a drink, and he took me up on the offer. When he set his toolbox on the table, I noticed the bluflex logo printed on the side, and I smiled. Over a cold beer, he told me that the water table was rising.

"You should consider selling before it gets worse," he said. "A lot of other people are."

"I can't," I told him. "My daughter loves the sea too much."

He finished his beer and left without saying anything else. I stayed sitting at the kitchen table, in the dark, drinking and watching the beach. Even though all the windows were closed, I could smell the sea.

There was a bonfire on the beach. At first, I thought the small lights around it were sparks cast by the fire, but as my eyes adjusted to the darkness, I saw the truth.

They were children.

Children wreathed in glowing, sparkling bluflex. I watched them dance, watched the pulsing beat of the light. The colors seemed to respond to each other. They never did that in the laboratory tests. I told myself that I was only thinking that because I was drunk, but I kept watching until just before sunrise.

The sparkles gradually clustered together, stopping near the edge of the water. Three dancing lights kept moving out until I could barely see them. I half-thought I was imagining them, until they flashed brightly enough to leave an afterimage on my retinas. Then the mass of sparkles on the beach flared in return, and I was blinded. When I could see again, the sparks of light on the beach were dissipating.

The sea was dark.

I stayed sitting in the kitchen until I heard the front door open and close. Soft footsteps padded down the hallway. I got up and turned on the light in the kitchen. The footsteps paused.

Meredith stood in the darkened hallway.

"Meredith," I started to say and then stopped.

She didn't say anything.

"I'm selling the house."

After a moment, she continued toward her bedroom. I could see the bluflex bracelets she wore sparkling to each other long after I lost her form in the darkness of the house.

I returned to the brightly lit kitchen, threw out the empty beer bottles, and then went to bed.

The next morning, I put a for-sale sign in front of our house. Despite the flooding in the basement, I had an offer within the week.

"The heat isn't good for the wife," the man who made the offer told me. "They say it feels cooler by the sea. And Junior just loves to go to the beach."

Although the air was oppressively hot, goose bumps raised the hair on my arms. Junior stood next to the kitchen windows, watching the beach. He didn't respond to his father's assertion, but the bluflex yo-yo that spun from his fingers glinted.

Meredith was not happy.

She didn't try to change my mind, but she was subdued for several days. She fondled her bluflex bracelets constantly, as if she needed their reassurance.

I did not try to keep her from her friends on the beach, despite what I had seen. I suppose I was trying to hide the truth from myself, trying to convince myself that I'd misinterpreted what I'd seen through the haze of alcohol.

They were only children, after all. It was natural for children to enjoy the sea. And it was good for Meredith to have so many friends. The number of children who visited the beach tripled during the months it took us to prepare for our move.

Also, I didn't need to feel guilty about drinking in front of her when she wasn't there.

Our new home was twenty miles further inland. Inside, with the windows closed and the air conditioner humming, it was impossible to smell the sea. I found that a great relief. Meredith quickly made new friends. She was gone playing with them for most of the day while I was at work. She would show up for dinner, her skin glowing a healthy brown against the blue of her bracelets, armbands, and necklaces. After dinner, she would leave again.

I never met her friends, but all the children ran wild during that long, hot Indian summer. A teacher died from heatstroke in January, and the schools were closed temporarily. Most school buildings were old and could not be fully air-conditioned. It didn't seem to bother the children, but a number of teachers became ill. Once the heat wave had subsided, the government promised, schools would be reopened. Scientists were working on the problem. They thought electromagnetic radiation might be among the causes.

The heat wave is finally over, but there are no schools.

One day at work, I came across a lab technician crying at her desk. She told me that her son had run away. He hadn't come home last night, but she didn't notice until breakfast. He spent so much time at the beach, she had just assumed . . . but all his bluflex toys were gone, so she knew he wasn't coming back. She forced a smile and asked me how Meredith was doing.

I realized I didn't know.

That night at dinner, I asked Meredith if she would like to see the place where we tested and molded bluflex. I was gambling that she'd be interested. Once I had her attention, we could talk. We would spend more time together. Grow closer. I hadn't been paying enough attention to her since I'd become absorbed in developing and marketing bluflex toys. We hadn't done anything together just for fun in almost a year. I had neglected her, and she had become a stranger to me.

I took her in on the weekend. I could show her around, get a chance to talk to her, really talk to her, and at the same time, I could check on some tests that I'd left running on Friday.

I had set up a special lab room in a sealed environment, solely re-analyzing any compounds that bluflex might exude. The correlation between the toys I had suggested and the strange behavior of the children who owned them was too strong to ignore. The tests I was running were not only for the standard toxins. We had tested for those before. I was looking for mild hallucinogens, mood-altering chemicals, organics . . . anything. Anything other than the standard diatomic and carbon dioxide. Anything that would explain what was happening to our children. Anything that would give me an enemy I could fight.

The children were not the only things I should have feared for, but they were all I could see.

I showed Meredith around the building and explained what the testing and manufacturing processes were. The sparkle in her eyes and the glints in her bracelets both brightened.

I didn't explain the special lab. I didn't want my own daughter thinking I was a crackpot.

I left her in the hallway outside the lab, telling her I'd only be a moment, and went into the adjoining room to check the results of the gas chromatography tests. They were all normal. From the time the tests had been set up, there had not been one suspicious molecule in the air of that room. Not one.

I was studying the charts when I caught a movement in my peripheral vision: a door opening. I looked up, through the one-way glass that stood between the lab and the instruments I was using, and saw my daughter.

She hesitated just inside the door but then began to explore the room. I shook my head and studied the gas chromatography. Her presence would not mess up the results. There were no results.

I turned back to the stream of information presently coming in from the room. And stared.

The readings were far from normal. They were so far from normal that my first thought was that they must be wrong. There were high levels of organic chemicals I didn't recognize, a few psycho-actives that I did, and insanely high concentrations of carbon dioxide. *Meredith!* I bolted out of the chair, ready to run to the lab and drag her out. I expected to see her gasping for air.

She was leaning over one of the vats of bluflex. She reached out her hand to brace herself against the side of the vat, and a brilliant light filled the room. When my vision cleared, Meredith was standing beside the vat. The bracelets on her wrist showed only subdued sparkles. Meredith's expression shifted to normal surprise so quickly that I hardly caught a glimpse of her previous expression, but a glimpse was enough. There had been worry and suspicion there . . . and an anger as deep as the sea.

I bundled her home as quickly as I could. I tucked her into bed, careful not to touch any of her bluflex ornaments. I kissed her on the forehead and left her to her dreams.

Her hair smelled like the sea.

When I recovered the data from the gas chromatography tests on Monday, I was stunned. Everything was completely normal until Meredith entered the room. The abnormal readings lasted for only a short while. The last abnormal reading was the one I had been staring at the instant before the flare of light. After that, the readings had returned to normal levels. There was no transition period, no time for the molecules to disperse. They were simply gone. I couldn't shake the conviction that the results showed a sentient, hostile reaction. The bluflex in the lab had somehow known that it was under observation. The bluflex that Meredith wore hadn't—until it was warned.

I took my findings to the president of Oak Leaf Products. I explained that we had to recall all bluflex products from the market immediately. Ten minutes later, I carried out the contents of my desk in a cardboard box.

On the drive home, I turned on the radio to hear experts discussing the continuing heat wave and the projected disappearance of the polar ice caps.

When I got home, Meredith was out. I packed our essentials into the car, being especially careful to leave behind anything containing bluflex. That ruled out a lot. For the first time, I appreciated the endless meetings about new bluflex products that I had been forced to sit through.

I drank some courage and waited for Meredith to come home. I knew I would regret what I was about to do, but I had no other choice.

When I heard Meredith's footsteps in the hall, I got up with dread in my heart. She was surprised when I bent to give her a hug hello. Had it been that long since I hugged her simply to show my love and welcome her home?

However long it had been, this hug had no such innocent motivations.

My arms went around her and held her immobile. She didn't say anything; she just looked at me. She didn't start fighting until I removed the first bluflex bracelet. Then she fought.

It was over quickly. Once the last of her bluflex adornments hit the floor, she stopped struggling. She must have guessed what I was planning, but she didn't try to run away. She didn't reproach me. She just stared at the abandoned mound of sparkling, shimmering bluflex.

I drove as far inland as I could go. I kept the windows rolled up and the air conditioner blasting, but the smell of brine followed us, swimming through the air currents.

At the end of the second day, I rolled the windows down. The air was clean and wholesome, smelling of fresh-turned dirt.

The wind felt cold on my cheeks where it crossed the wet tracks of my tears.

Meredith had visited the place where we were going, but not in many years. When my parents were alive, we made the pilgrimage to their mountain cabin every summer. After they died, the visits stopped too. I hadn't been able to bring myself to sell the place. I was too attached to it, an attachment for which I was now grateful.

I stopped in a little town at the base of the mountain to buy supplies. Meredith was sleeping. I covered her up carefully with a car rug and entered the small grocery store. I was debating whether I should buy more than just the fixings for peanut butter and jelly sandwiches when I saw a mother and her two boys. The boys were bored, as all boys are when taken grocery shopping by their mothers. They were playing with their yo-yos.

Their bluflex yo-yos.

They must have noticed me staring at them, because they looked up. Their bland, incurious eyes summed me up and dismissed me. They returned to their discussion of the best superhero and supervillain. Through the entire encounter, their yo-yos spooled evenly from their fingers in perfect synchronicity, twin lights gleaming in chorus.

I bought enough dried and canned supplies to feed an army garrison for six months. When I went to the register to pay, I noticed a bulletin board covered with missing-child posters. There were so many that when the wind blew they danced like seaweed at high tide.

Before I carried the supplies out to the car, I turned to confront the woman whose boys I'd seen. I knew it wouldn't do any good, but I had to warn her.

"If you want to keep your children," I said, "take away their bluflex toys and stay away from the sea." I lowered my voice. "If you can."

The woman's eyes widened with fear. I felt a spark of hope until I realized that it was me she was afraid of.

"Boys," she said, keeping her tone level, "come here. We're leaving."

She headed toward the door, the boys trailing behind her. I couldn't let them leave, knowing what I did.

"You don't understand," I said.

The boys stopped and looked at me. "You can't stop us," one of them said. Their eyes were dark, as unreadable as the depths of the sea.

In desperation, I grabbed for their yo-yos. If nobody else would listen to me, if nobody else would do anything ... I would. The yo-yos spun away from my fingers, swinging away from me in perfectly symmetrical arcs. The boys turned to follow their mother. The rhythm of the yo-yos never skipped a beat.

I stepped forward.

"Hey!" the clerk shouted at me. "Get out, and leave those boys alone!"

I was defeated.

The cabin was fairly low on the mountain. I unpacked the car and woke Meredith. She was hesitant at first, as though suffering from culture shock. I kept my keys in my pocket and my eyes on her. She didn't bolt. During her tentative foray into the trees, she found the swing her granddad had put up for her.

After some false starts, she remembered how to use it. I left her with an easy heart. She was pumping her arms and legs awkwardly but with growing enthusiasm, and her face bore the closest thing to a smile that I had seen from her in more than a week. I thought we would be safe here, maybe even happy.

I should have remembered the missing-child posters.

The next month made me grateful we were safe on the mountain. Safe! I should have known better.

Low-lying cities were flooded as the massive icebergs melted. Thousands of people died in the heat. Millions more lost their homes and their livelihood to the hungry sea. And their children. I cannot forget our lost children, because it was my fault we lost them.

Refugees swarmed to the mountains, bringing their most prized possessions. They brought bluflex with them, and the sea followed at their heels. Even the smell of the pines could not mask the salty brine that the breeze carried up the mountain. Though the last of the icebergs had melted, the sea level continued to rise. Worldwide, governments admitted that they were baffled.

I was not surprised when Meredith disappeared. I had lost her to the sea, or given her away, many months ago. I thought I had found her again. I had hoped I could keep her. But hope was a fragile mist that the wind from the sea easily dissolved.

When I called to report her missing, I only got an automated service that took my information, and the line went dead before I was finished. I didn't bother trying to call back.

On my drive down the mountain, I saw two end-of-the-world signs, four refugee families huddled together under a tarp for shade, and one enterprising man building a houseboat. I wonder where he is now. I hope he's doing well.

At the grocery store, I saw the woman who had been there with her children the last time I bought supplies. She was alone, and her grocery basket held only single-serving microwave dinners. The dark circles under her eyes told me all I needed to know. I don't think she recognized me. I did not talk to her.

I did not talk to anyone. The man behind the register talked about selling the store and moving. The basement was flooding, and now his house, farther up on the mountain, was having water problems. I looked around the store, and I had a revelation.

There were bluflex toys near the register and bluflex containers scattered around the store. Bluflex was everywhere. It wasn't safe.

The sea was coming for its children. It had taken our children, but that was not enough. That was why it kept rising. It would not stop until all the bluflex was back under the sea.

I bought as much food as I could load into the car and drove back up the mountain. I didn't feel safe. I knew that the global warming would continue until the bluflex was safe beneath the sea. And there was bluflex everywhere. It was the miracle material. It would not all be returned to the sea until the whole world had drowned.

I sat in the cabin, and I didn't feel safe. I could smell the sea.

I was sitting on the porch one day, drinking, when a garbage truck rumbled past me up the road to the landfill on top of the mountain. I drank a lot. Drowning my sorrows, as they used to say.

I hate the phrase. The sea has taken everything else from me; it cannot take my sorrow.

I remembered my parents complaining about that landfill when it was built. Despoiling the beauty of nature, they said, but it was a barren mountaintop that didn't attract tourism, so the town council had voted to put the landfill there. I didn't see much beauty in nature those days, but the landfill. . . . The landfill would be my salvation.

It was at the very top of the mountain, and it should be safe. Nobody ever threw bluflex away.

I waited until the road up the mountain flooded. I listened to the radio, but all that I could pick up was old radio shows punctuated by news bulletins listing the latest flood disaster areas and designating refugee shelters. The mountain was never among them.

I heard the bulletin when the town at the foot of the mountain flooded. I waited to hear that the top of the mountain, my part of the mountain, was a designated refugee haven, but I never did.

It was forgotten. I liked it that way. I could be alone with my booze and my old-time radio shows. I had no fondness for the human race. We had done this to ourselves with our desire for more, new, better.

I had done this.

I slowly moved my belongings to the landfill. I never saw anybody. From the top of the mountain, I could see for miles. Most of what I saw was water.

Each trip, the land diminished.

Finally, all my possessions were moved. I spent most of my time sitting in a broken lawn chair, drinking and listening to *The Shadow*. The Shadow knows.

One day the radio went dead, so I just sat and drank. I watched the seagulls. They flew in great wheeling flocks across the sky. The ocean had settled. I lost no more ground to it.

A month after the radio went dead, I drank the last of the alcohol and then spent a week scavenging for half-empty liquor bottles and going through withdrawal.

Without the soothing blanket of booze, I started to think again. Meredith was gone, but was I really alone in the world?

The seagulls could not be the only survivors. They flew away from the landfill and returned days later. There must be other land nearby.

I stopped looking for alcohol and started searching for a boat, or at least an engine.

The landfill is safe, but safety is not the most important thing in life. I saw a column of smoke in the sky this morning, far off to the east.

As soon as I have finished building my boat, I will set out toward that signal. The sea cannot stop me. I would dare it to do its worst, but it already has. It took my home, my job, and my child. It took my entertainments and my addictions.

It could not take my hope, because hope cannot be drowned, not by alcohol and not by the sea.

If I survived, there will be others. I will find them. And one day, we will take back our land from the sea, and our children will play in the grass.

Abra Staffin-Wiebe loves dark science fiction, cheerful horror, and futuristic fairy tales. Dozens of her short stories have appeared in publications including *Tor.com*, *Escape Pod*, and *Odyssey Magazine*. She lives in Minneapolis, where she wrangles two small children, three large cats, and one full-sized mad scientist. When not writing or wrangling, she collects folk tales and photographs whatever stands still long enough to allow it. Discover more of her fiction at her website, aswiebe.com.

Downpour
by
Lisa Timpf

6:15 P.M., THURSDAY, SEPTEMBER 24, 2048: CFB Borden, Infrastructure Design Testing Station

"And now for the weather, with Windy William."

Patricia Griffin lowered her tablet to her lap and riveted her attention on the flat-screen TV mounted on the far wall of the monitoring center. Her husband, Jerome, strolled into the room and stood behind her, keeping his eyes focused on the newscast.

"Thanks, Arlene." On screen, Windy William grinned and extended his arms at his sides, palms outward. "Well, let's get to the news everyone's been talking about—that nasty storm that started brewing down in Texas yesterday, and is heading our way. It's spawned tornados south of the border, along with high winds and flooding, but is expected to lose some of its steam before it gets to us." His expression turned serious. "Don't be surprised to see a bit of a light show when it gets here. There may be some sleet or hail in Southern Ontario," he gestured at the map, "and unseasonable amounts of snowfall for regions north of Orillia." Snowflakes appeared on the map, dotted between Orillia and North Bay.

"In our region, the storm is expected to dump close to two hundred millimetres of rain in less than twelve hours, starting around

9 p.m. and intensifying through the evening and early morning," he said. "How are area citizens feeling about this? We went to the streets to get some comment."

The newscast cut to an image of a twenty-something man with blond hair brandishing a surfboard and declaring, "Bring it on!" A trio of college-aged girls in a canoe on the Nottawasaga River waved their paddles at the camera, and a dour homeowner looked up at his newly installed high-capacity eave troughs and shrugged to indicate his indifference.

An interview with the local Ontario Provincial Police detachment spokesperson provided a sobering viewpoint. "We'll be monitoring the roads, and we anticipate some flooding particularly in low-lying areas," the woman said. "We ask that people avoid unnecessary travel where possible."

"And now, back to the newsroom. This is Windy Willy signing off." The newsman tossed a beach ball at the camera, and the image faded out.

"I wish they wouldn't joke about it." Patricia flipped the control to turn the TV off.

"The storms we've been getting have been increasingly severe," Jerome agreed, stroking his moustache thoughtfully, "but the change has been so gradual that people have more or less adapted. A bit of flooding here and there, a few insurance claims—" he shrugged. "If Mother Nature is sending us a message, most people are tuning it out."

"From all the reports we've seen, this storm could be the worst in thirty-five years, and that's saying something." Patricia stood to look out the window, her arms crossed in front of her. "I'm glad we told the girls to head up to Jesse's place."

"It's great that your brother offered to look after them, especially since we won't be around." Jerome rubbed his hands together. "This will be a true test for our rainwater diversion infrastructure design. Are you ready?"

"We shouldn't *be* testing anymore." She whirled to glare at him. "When will people realize we need to make changes *now*?"

"In fairness, some have already bought in," Jerome, always the peacemaker, commented, spreading his hands palms-out. "But there are so many who *haven't*."

Patricia's fists were clenched. "And that adds up to property damage at best, loss of life at worst, when we get hit by a storm like this."

"People need proof," Jerome replied. "Who wants to raise taxes to pay for changes to infrastructure they aren't convinced are needed? The human animal just isn't wired to accept change lightly, especially when it means some inconvenience. The hardest kind of change is proactive change, and that's what this is all about."

"Proof," she snorted, her disgust clear in her tone. "Well, we may get some this weekend."

6:30 p.m., Thursday, September 24, 2048: Earl Rowe Provincial Park

Irma Cole, Earl Rowe Provincial Park's superintendent, was thoughtful as she turned off the TV. Was she overreacting? There weren't a lot of campers—after all, it was only Thursday, and it was the slow season. Still, those who *were* here needed to know. She had a feeling this storm was going to be a significant event. If she was wrong—she shrugged. If she was wrong, she'd look foolish, maybe shake her supervisor's confidence in her levelheadedness.

She thought awhile longer, warring with indecision. At last she came to a conclusion and rose to her feet.

Best to be on the safe side. She'd call an emergency meeting and divvy up the occupied sites, sending park staff to each location to notify the campers of the pending weather and, more importantly, urge them to come to the newly built Interpretation Centre. Equipped with a backup generator and situated partway up the hill, the centre provided a spot where campers should be able to ride out the storm in relative comfort.

Once she'd sent the staff on their way, she'd jump into the white park pickup truck and hustle to the camp store to collect provisions. This occasion justified overriding the normal protocol. If head office didn't like it, that was just too bad.

6:45 p.m., Thursday, September 24, 2048: Alliston, Ontario

Jay Baker had just placed his supper dishes in the sink when his cell phone buzzed. He paused for a moment, studying the small screen, and then rose from his chair.

"They've called all the reservists to the base," he told his wife, Alicia. "I'll have to pack. Will you guys be okay?"

Alicia nodded, noting the concern in his eyes. "We'll be fine. We're well up the hill, and we don't need to go anywhere this weekend." She paused. "Plus, we have the emergency kit. Will the storm really be that bad?"

"Maybe not," he said reassuringly. "The commander's probably being cautious." He paused, his expression becoming serious. "But we do have amphibious vehicles, and there may be a need for some search and rescue. Let's hope the storm isn't as bad as they're predicting."

7:00 p.m., Thursday, September 24, 2048: Long Point

They had flown great distances to get here, and they had much farther to go.

It was time to rest for the night.

As per custom, flocks of monarch butterflies gathered in the trees. Tonight, this particular group was roosting just north of the large lake that lay between them and their ultimate destination. They perched with their slender black feet upward, their black and orange wings closed, lining up side by side for protection.

Instinct would only protect them so far. Those on the outer edges would take the brunt of the storm, if it came, and it had the potential to decimate their numbers.

For now, all they could do is cling to the branches and wait it out.

9:15 p.m., Thursday, September 24, 2048: Airport Road, north of Highway 89

Judy Griffin stifled a yawn as she piloted the family SUV up Airport Road. She was glad the number of vehicles had dropped off after they passed Caledon. Traffic had been pretty hairy there for a while. At least she had the radio to help her keep awake. She nudged the volume higher as she checked the readout to the right of the steering wheel. Fifty kilometres of fuel left. She chided herself for not filling up at the gas station when they'd stopped just south of Orangeville. There'd been a huge line, though, and they were impatient to get to Uncle Jesse's.

A large, fat raindrop hit the windshield, and Judy groaned. Just what she needed. She'd driven here tons of times with her parents, but hadn't paid much attention to the route. She was relying on her younger sister Sharon to handle the GPS. Darkness had fallen over an hour ago, and now she had rain to contend with. Great.

"How far to our turn?" she asked Sharon, who occupied the front passenger seat.

"What'd you say?"

Judy turned down the radio and repeated her question.

"Sorry, I dozed off. Twenty kilometres. No, wait." There was a pause. "How can that be? Twenty-one and a half kilometres. We're getting *further* away."

"We must have missed the turnoff." Judy gritted her teeth, trying to conceal her annoyance. It was really pouring now and the windshield wipers, set on max, were barely keeping up.

"Sorry." Sharon's voice sounded pouty. "I guess I didn't hear the GPS over the radio."

"I'll turn around," Judy snapped. Sharon didn't comment on the less-than-elegant manoeuvre that brought them to face the opposite way, though she gripped the armrest anxiously.

"Turn left in two hundred metres," Sharon sang out at last. Judy could barely make out the dirt road, which appeared as a slash in the forest.

The vehicle crawled along as though feeling its way by touch as the narrow road twisted back on itself several times and large trees loomed on both sides. They splashed through more than one puddle, and Judy was grateful that it was the SUV they were driving and not the low-slung sedan that served as the family's other vehicle.

"If the GPS didn't say this was it, I'd be worried we were on the wrong road," Sharon said timidly.

"This is it, all right. I remember." Judy shivered. "Mom and Dad say you always have to keep a lookout for deer at night, along here."

"Maybe they're holed up for the night," Sharon replied.

"They would if they were smart."

Finally, Judy saw the word BLACK in reflective lettering on the mailbox just ahead. *Uncle Jesse's place.* "At last," Judy grunted as she made the turn. The headlights showed streams of water racing down the dirt driveway. She heaved a sigh of relief when the car rolled to a stop in front of her uncle's sprawling brick bungalow.

"We're here," she sang out, waking her youngest sister, Val, who'd been sleeping in the back seat.

9:30 p.m., Thursday, September 24, 2048: Alliston Humane Society Shelter

Glenn Chandler listened to the rain drumming on the roof. Well, the storm had arrived. So far, all was quiet—just a bit of yapping from the canine inmates. They were restless, though, he could sense it—the dogs were panting, and those cats that weren't pacing lay huddled in their blankets.

The fundraising campaign for a new building to house the animals couldn't wrap up soon enough, he reflected. They weren't exactly on high ground. Hopefully the sandbags the volunteers had put in place to address the most vulnerable areas would do the job. Otherwise, they'd all be floating.

Normally, of course, there wouldn't be anyone here overnight. He'd set the cot up for the night so he could keep an eye on things. He wasn't sure what he'd do if water started coming in, but he'd figure it out. He hoped it wouldn't come to that.

1:00 a.m., Friday, September 25, 2048: CFB Borden, Infrastructure Design Testing Station

Patricia Griffin monitored the readouts as early data started to trickle in. So far, so good. Jerome, as the other lead researcher, would relieve her at the end of her eight-hour shift while she in turn caught some sleep. Other technicians were doing on-site monitoring of their own, including driving along the "streets" to confirm the effectiveness of the water runoff measures. Of course, the computers would capture the readouts as they happened, but nothing could substitute for the human eye and mind.

Tucked away in the middle of CFB Borden's 21,000 acres, the Infrastructure Design Testing Station was a proving ground for technology. It owed its existence to funding from a variety of sources, including industry, universities, government, and a few select private foundations. Though they were situated on the Forces base, the object of their study wasn't related to the types of battles that normally came to mind when one considered the military. Instead, it was related to the war against the effects of climate change. One of the spinoffs from the earth's warming trend was increasingly intense storms, which in turn would require a different kind of thinking about infrastructure design and building codes. Here at the Testing Station, a miniature "town"—streets, houses, storm sewers, and all—had been established. The military site just happened to be an available piece of land to support a project of this scope. The key design elements were modelled after similar installations in the United States, with appropriate adjustments made for the Canadian climate.

Thus far tonight, all systems for water flow control, water retention, surge protection in the event of electrical strikes, and communications and electrical infrastructure preservation were operating as planned. This weekend's storm, if it lived up to its billing, would be the system's most rigorous test yet. She was keeping her fingers crossed. That wasn't scientific, she knew, but it made her feel better.

3 a.m., Friday September 25, 2048: Jesse Black's house

Boom! The thunder sounded like a cannon's roar, and the third blast of it brought Sharon racing into Judy's room. Val was already there, huddled at the end of Judy's bed with Latte, Uncle Jesse's red-and-white Border collie, cowering beside her.

The dog raised her head as the door leading from the garage to the mudroom opened and then closed.

"Uncle Jesse?" Judy called, hoping her voice sounded braver than she felt.

"Here," he said calmly. "Just had to fire up the generator. We lost power a few minutes ago." He padded down the hallway.

Judy noticed the wind's wild howl. "Should we go downstairs, do you think?"

"Wouldn't hurt, since everyone's awake anyway," Uncle Jesse said. "Bring some blankets. We'll sit on the couches and watch the light show."

With their uncle's help, the girls ensconced themselves comfortably enough on the lower floor, which was a walkout with large windows. Judy sat upright in the middle of the couch along the wall facing the main windows, with Val resting her head against Judy's shoulder. Sharon perched on Judy's other side, patting a frightened Latte. Jesse sat nearby in his favourite armchair.

Sharon winced as a pink flash of light lit up the sky over the woods. "What if we get hit by lightning?"

"I've got a surge protector on the main panel," Uncle Jesse said reassuringly. "That'll prevent any damage."

"Uncle Jesse, will we get flooded?" Val asked sleepily.

"The soil's extra sandy here," Uncle Jesse said. "I had to bring in topsoil for the garden and the lawn. I've never yet had a problem with flooding, touch wood. The water should just run away."

"They might get flooding in the city though, mightn't they?" Sharon asked timidly.

"Quite likely," he replied. "It's a lot of rain in a very short time."

Another bolt of lightning split the sky, followed by a ferocious grumble of thunder.

"Uncle Jesse, do you think that fawn we saw in the springtime is okay?" Val asked.

"He'll be mostly grown up by now," Uncle Jesse replied, "and the deer and the other animals will take shelter where they can."

Judy glanced over toward her uncle. *That's true enough, as far as it goes,* she thought. She knew a vicious storm like this might result in some creatures being flooded out of their homes.

Val, comforted by her sisters' presence, was the first to fall asleep despite the crashing of thunder. Her sisters followed suit.

Jesse dozed fitfully, waking now and then to check the weather conditions, and then nodding off again.

3:45 a.m. Friday, September 25, 2048: Interpretation Center, Earl Rowe Provincial Park

Irma Cole snapped awake when she heard the knock on the Interpretation Center door.

She clicked on her flashlight and hurried over. Opening the door revealed the two campers who had been holdouts when her staff had gone around encouraging everyone to come up to the Interpretation Center. The man and woman looked to be in their late fifties. Water streamed off their rain gear and dripped onto the floor. They both sported sheepish expressions.

"It's nasty out there," the grey-haired man said. "Got room for us?"

Irma smiled and gestured to a space where a pair of sleeping bags lay waiting.

"Make yourself comfortable," she replied.

Inwardly, she heaved a sigh of relief. She hadn't been able to compel anyone to come to the Interpretation Center, though most had come willingly. With the arrival of these final two, she didn't need to worry about anyone being out there in that weather. They were much safer here.

9 a.m., Friday, September 25, 2048: on the road from CFB Borden to Alliston, Ontario

Jay Baker swayed along with the motion of the troop vehicle as they headed toward town. Help where they could, offer water and supplies to those who needed it, and be on hand for further orders, that was their assignment. They were laden with several cases of bottled water and other supplies for that express purpose.

The rain had subsided to a sullen drizzle, though the air still felt heavy with humidity. Large, shallow lakes lapped almost up to the roadside in several fields that had already been harvested, while in other spots crops still waiting to be gathered lay beaten down by the storm's force. The shoulders of the road showed signs of erosion here and there, and the ditches brimmed with water. He felt a surge of gratitude that they were travelling in a large vehicle.

Behind the vehicle carrying the handful of reservists was a green Jeep hauling a trailer with an inflatable boat and an amphibious vehicle. Jay wondered whether they would need to use them.

10 a.m., Friday January 25, 2048: Alliston Humane Society Shelter

Glenn Chandler stretched and grinned as the black, mud-spattered four-wheel-drive pickup truck splashed through the gravel parking lot, coming to a halt to the right of the shelter's entrance. Mick Williams, equipped with florescent yellow rain gear and sturdy green rubber boots, jumped down from the passenger side. Mick's wife, Sarah, similarly dressed, emerged more slowly from the driver's side, taking advantage of the running boards to make her way to the ground.

"Sorry we're late," Sarah sang out. "We had to take the long way around. The bridge on the Third Concession was washed out."

"Took 'em nine months to put that new bridge in," Mick said, shaking his head. "Mother Nature just took a few hours to rip it all out."

"At least the sandbags held," Glenn said, gesturing to where the water from the pond had risen halfway up the improvised barrier.

"Well, let's get those dogs walked, shall we?" Sarah asked, walking briskly toward the door.

11 a.m. Friday September 25, 2048: Interpretation Centre, Earl Rowe Provincial Park

Time to assess the damage, Irma Cole thought as she climbed aboard the park's ATV. Several of the campers were evincing signs of restlessness and making noises about returning to their sites.

Already, it didn't look good. A large tree branch had fallen in the open area behind the Interpretation Centre, and the parking lot lay half-submerged in a broad, shallow puddle.

She trundled downhill along the paved roadway, the wheels kicking up a spray behind her. Halfway down the ridge, she stopped. The small lake had tripled in size, its waters now lapping against the walls of the camp store. The campsites below would be thoroughly soaked, with many of them underwater. Doubly glad now for the action she'd taken in herding the campers up to the Interpretation Centre, she executed a tight turn and headed back up the hill. They were going to be there awhile, from the looks of things.

Noon, Friday, September 25, 2048: Jesse Black's house

"At least the rain's stopped for now, but look at that wind!" Judy exclaimed, gesturing toward the backyard, where even the tops of the oak trees were swaying wildly. Evidence of the storm's handiwork during the night lay scattered across the yard in the form of fallen branches.

"The oaks have taken a beating lately, thanks to the oak weevil infestation," Uncle Jesse said. "It's made them weaker."

"They came over from Europe, right?" Judy asked.

"Yes. And the trees were stressed to start with, due to the drier summers we've been having."

"Drier summers?" Sharon snorted. "Doesn't look like it."

"It's fall now, smarty," Judy retorted. "And yes, there are prolonged periods of dryness, despite the storms."

"Storms are stronger, too," Uncle Jesse added quietly. "The intensity of the rainfall, the lightning, the winds."

"Hey, where's Val?" Judy asked, turning to Sharon. "Weren't you watching her?"

"She was here with Latte a minute ago," Sharon replied defensively.

"If she's gone into the woods, with that wind—" Uncle Jesse's voice was concerned. "You girls stay here. I know my way around."

"I think I know where she might have gone," Judy offered. "Check where we saw the fawn last spring."

Uncle Jesse nodded, his expression serious. His wooded property spanned thirty acres, and there were hectares of county forest behind. He hoped Val hadn't strayed far.

12:15 p.m. Friday, September 25, 2048: north of Alliston, Ontario

Jay Baker stared at the Nottawasaga River's murky, tumbling waters as the amphibious craft trundled along the riverbank. The wind lashed his face and released drops of water from the trees. Between sweat and the water that had winnowed its way through gaps between his skin and his protective gear, he might as well have stepped straight out of the shower. He ignored his discomfort, remembering the orders that had come over the commlink half an hour ago, launching him and the vehicle's driver, Jackson, into action.

Two boys, bored by the power outage and seeking adventure outdoors, had reportedly launched themselves onto the river on a small wooden raft. Their absence had been called in by their panicked parents, who hadn't seen the boys depart but had noted the raft missing from the family's dock. *They're the same age as my two guys,* Jay thought, shivering. He figured the boys thought the danger was over once the rain had stopped. They couldn't be more wrong, as water continued to flow into the river from the overloaded tributaries.

He caught movement out of the corner of his eye. "Stop," he yelled into the driver's ear. "Over there, in that clump of driftwood."

The craft eased its way toward the jumble of tree branches and dock boards where the raft had crashed. He could see two motionless forms huddled on the pile of debris. He hoped they'd arrived in time.

12:30 p.m., Friday, September 25, 2048: Jesse Black's property

"Valerie!" Jesse cupped his hands to yell, and then ducked under a wind-whipped branch as he trudged along the trail. The odds seemed stacked against his voice reaching the girl, wherever she'd disappeared to. Still, he had to try.

Jesse scowled at the tossing treetops overhead, and flinched when he heard a loud *crack* in the woods to the right. He passed a splintered branch that had fallen jagged end first into the ground, implanting itself a good six inches. It provided a chilling reminder of the hazards that Val was facing.

Suddenly a *woof* sounded from the path ahead. Seconds later, Latte appeared. She raced up to Jesse, licked his hand, danced all around him, and trotted back along the way she had come.

Slipping on the wet grass on the pathway, Jesse hustled after the dog.

2:00 p.m., Friday, September 25, 2048: Jesse Black's house

A small fire crackled in the woodstove on the lower floor of Jesse's house, providing physical and psychological warmth. Latte stretched full-length on the warm tile in front of the stove, causing Jesse some inconvenience when he needed to toss on additional fuel. Given the Border collie's role in leading him to Valerie, however, he didn't comment on her choice of resting spot.

His three nieces perched on the couch. It had taken Val half an hour to stop shivering, once she got inside the house. There had been no need to lecture her on the consequences of her unauthorized expedition. Val had been thoroughly frightened by the time he tracked her down.

A battery-powered radio sat on the oak end table to Jesse's right, and the occupants of the room had their attention fixed on the device.

". . . a state of emergency has been declared in southern Ontario, due to widespread flooding. Many roads are impassable due to downed trees or bridge damage. Power is gradually being restored, although it's expected some areas may be out until noon Monday.

"Flights in and out of all airports have been suspended due to flooded runways. Travellers are advised to check in advance for schedule alterations.

"Across southern Ontario, close to fifty people are believed to be missing, down from sixty two hours ago. Fortunately, there are have been no fatalities reported at this time, although all major cities report extensive flooding with many roadways underwater. Damage to homes and commercial establishments is already estimated to run into the billions, although it's early to pin down exact figures.

"In area news, two military reservists rescued a pair of boys who took a raft ride down the surging Nottawasaga River. The Humane Society is fielding reports of missing animals, as well as receiving calls about 'found' cats and dogs. The majority of area roads have flooded sections, and the Ontario Provincial Police strongly request that all nonessential travel be postponed."

"Uncle Jesse, will we be okay?" Sharon asked as the newscaster's voice faded out, replaced by the bouncy music accompanying a commercial.

"We're fine," he said. "We have emergency power, thanks to the generator, a secondary heat source with the wood stove and fireplace, and plenty of food. We're better off than a lot of people."

"I wonder how Mom and Dad are doing?" Judy asked.

"They're okay. I'm sure of it."

5 p.m., Saturday, September 26, 2048: CFB Borden, Infrastructure Design Testing Station

"I'd say that was an unqualified success," Jerome Griffin observed, a note of elation underlying the tiredness in his voice.

"No major issues with any of the monitored aspects, although we should make some tweaks to the storm sewer design parameters. They worked well this time, but I'd like to see more excess capacity," Patricia replied. "All other systems functioned as planned, with room to spare, and it was our most severe test yet."

"You have the ammunition you need for the next mayor's conference." Jerome rested a hand on his wife's shoulder.

"Maybe this time we'll get more traction," she replied, her voice bitter.

"It's a fine balance, isn't it?" Jerome, usually the optimistic one, frowned as he looked out the window. "As we come up with better ways to mitigate the impact of the storms, people become more blasé about the phenomenon that's driving their severity."

"It's almost as if our work, if successful, helps to blunt the message about the impact of climate change," Patricia said, nodding. "And yet, we have to do something."

"I agree," Jerome said, forcing a smile. "If for no other reason than to contribute to a safer world for the girls."

"Speaking of the girls, let's go and see how they made out, shall we?"

"After you," Jerome said, allowing himself one last glance around the command centre before he followed his wife toward the door.

Noon, Sunday, September 27, 2048: Long Point

Martin Rotheby felt his wife, Veronica, tighten her grip on his arm as they approached the tree. He grimaced, bracing himself for what they might see. *Please,* he thought, *let them be okay. Let some of them be okay.*

"Oh." That single word conveyed a depth of sadness as Veronica leaned down to examine the orange forms lying at the base of the tree. "So many," she whispered, turning to face Martin.

"But look," he replied, pointing upward. Veronica's gaze followed, and she gasped as she noted the clusters of monarch butterflies that remained in the tree. Only now, with the emergence of the sun and the abating of the howling wind, were they starting to stir.

Spellbound, heedless of the passage of time, Veronica and Martin stood and watched as the butterflies began to launch themselves off their perches, flapping bravely and soaring southward.

"There's hope then, for them, still," Martin said, raising an eyebrow as he saw Veronica's fists clenching at her sides.

"It's not their fault," she said, her voice grating. "Nothing they do in their daily lives impacts climate change, yet they, like the other insects and animals, must suffer the impact."

"And yet, they survive," Martin replied, his voice calm.

"For now."

"For now," he agreed. And as he watched the butterflies soar away, he couldn't help shivering, as though struck by a cold wind.

Lisa Timpf is a retired human resources and communications professional who resides in Simcoe, Ontario. Her writing has appeared in a variety of venues, including *Chicken Soup for the Soul: My Very Good, Very Bad Dog*, *The Martian Wave*, *Third Flatiron*, and *New Myths*. When not writing, Lisa enjoys playing with her border collie, Emma, as well as cycling, bird-watching, and reading. She has self-published a collection of creative nonfiction and poetry titled *A Trail That Twines: Reflections on Life and Nature*.

Air

Midwives

by

Tiffani Angus

MARISOL CYCLED ALONG THE EDGE of the dirt road, swerving around her Hacienda Roja co-workers as a mini-bus chugged by. *Nueva Flora* was emblazoned on its side in bright yellow and orange letters. The workers inside rode high above Marisol with no reason to look down, the buzz of their morning gossip as clear as birdsong through the bus's open windows. Marisol closed her mouth and turned her head away to avoid the debris the bus's wheels churned up. When it was dry she choked on dust. When it was wet her shoes were caked with mud and gummed up the pedals. After nearly twenty years in the greenhouses, she'd never been able to decide which was worse. She was just lucky, she knew, to have a bicycle. Even a broken-down and rusted one.

The ride to work wasn't a long one, but the change in the land from Medellin suburbs to flower farms made Marisol feel as if she were crossing the border to a different world. In her neighbourhood, householders took advantage of every windowsill and ledge to grow potted flowers and herbs and even vegetables. But here at the edge of the city, acres and acres of low buildings made of plastic stretched over wood and metal skeletons that protected the investors' livelihoods. She had once seen a photograph of the farms taken from an airplane and thought it a shame that the production of something so beautiful should be so ugly.

The final reminder of her world before she arrived at the farm was the *madreselva*—honeysuckle vine—that grew over the wall that surrounded Hacienda Roja. There was no breeze, but the vine's leaves and flowers vibrated with the industry of a hundred bees. Its scent always reminded her of the stories she had been told about *La Madremonte,* the woman who protected the forest and its animals. Not that Marisol—or her family—had been out of the city in years. A holiday in the mountains was as impossible as one in a hotel suite in the middle of the city, even though both were within viewing distance. But she had grown up hearing the tales from her mother and *abuela,* about how *La Madre* would wipe away paths and change the shape of the land to confuse those who tried to cut down trees or steal iguanas, parrots, and monkeys to sell to the northerners, who would only put them in dirty cages and tanks. Her *abuela* believed that *La Madre,* who punished wicked men especially, was kinder to women. "A mother protects her daughters," she would say as she brushed Marisol's hair. "When women destroy nature, it's because a man is behind them. *La Madre,* with her big eyes that glow in the dark, knows this."

Marisol reached out to touch the blooms as she pedaled past. Her extended arm appeared blurry, as did the ground and sky beyond it. She blinked and shook her head, sure that the chemicals had finally got to her. The usual heady scent of the *madreselva* faded and then rushed back, as solid as the wall it grew on. As the world shrunk back to clarity, Marisol found herself off the road and on her knees, the vine cascading over her shoulders. Below the drone of the bees she heard her niece's voice.

"*Tía!* What happened? Are you all right?" Gabriela, on foot, dropped her bag and pulled Marisol away from the wall. "With the vine for your hair, you looked like a *duende.*"

Marisol shrugged the girl off and picked up her bike. She had no recollection of having fallen off, just of the world shifting. "No, girl, you were the *duende,* saving me from the vine. I'm just tired, of course. Always tired," she said and pushed her bike along the road.

"You're confused. Mama used to warn me that the *duende* were going to come in the night and bite my feet if I was bad." Gabriela hoisted her aunt's bag on one shoulder and her own on the other. "They don't save people."

"Ah, *sobrina,* that all depends. The forest sprits have their own way of doing things. Some are good, some are bad." Marisol laughed through her nose. "Like people."

At the entrance to the Hacienda Roja farm, Marisol and Gabriela greeted their workmates as they filed into the long greenhouses. The scent of roses was overwhelming, underlain by the sting of antifungal solution from the vat in one corner and the always-present reek of the outhouses. To one side was a small room where the women stored their bags. Marisol kicked off her sandals and changed into a pair of heavy boots a few sizes too big that her son had outgrown. They were uncomfortable and gave her blisters even though she packed them with newspaper, but they would protect her feet. Flower work was a wet business.

The day before, she had ripped a hole in the thumb of one glove, so she rummaged through a pile of cast-offs in the corner to find a replacement. Some women had heavy-duty rubber gloves, thick enough to protect their hands against the thorns, but they were so thick that Marisol couldn't feel anything when she wore them. She believed she risked fewer punctures wearing thinner gloves that allowed her to move her fingers more freely.

As Marisol tried on a green glove from the pile, Gabriela shoved her ungloved hands beneath her aunt's chin. "Look. Look at my hands." The skin on her fingers had peeled off in patches, exposing a layer of raw new skin, red and angry. In spite of gloves and long sleeves, chemicals seeped everywhere. "Mama said to try lotion, but it just burns. And now my hands are beginning to look like hers."

Marisol took Gabriela's hands in her own calloused, rough hands and felt a tiny surge of power from the connection. She wanted to shrug and turn away. Or tell the girl about her first weeks in the greenhouses and how her hands had blistered so badly that they bled and kept her awake at night. Wanted to tell her that this was the way of things and to get used to it—to the skin rashes and sore throat if you were lucky, worse illnesses if you weren't. But Gabriela had only just had her *quinceñeara* the month before. To go from being treated like a princess one day to stooping over roses in the greenhouses almost the very next was a shock to a girl. She would learn.

"*Tía,* Mama is still angry that I have come to work here. She would rather I go to Nueva Flora and eat their free lunches than be here with her—and you."

Marisol shook her head. "She isn't angry, *sobrina.* Just worried." The girl was young and didn't know yet what it meant to take on the troubles of the world. She looked round to be sure that Hector, the *encargado,* wasn't skulking nearby. Yesterday he had docked Laura's pay for taking too many bathroom breaks. "Come to my house tonight. Bring your mama."

Gabriela's brows drew together. "You know that Mama goes to mass tonight."

"Tell her that I am going to give you the secret to my *buñuelos.* That will change her mind."

The recipe for the cheesy rolls had been the subject of more arguments than Marisol wanted to count. But she was the oldest, so her own mama had passed it down to her. Marisol kept her face still. Better for her niece to learn to lure in chickens with the best crumbs rather than chase them round the yard. And wouldn't her sister be upset to think she was the chicken in that scenario.

"Now, put on your gloves, little girl, and get to work, or Hector— that little *mierda*—will make trouble."

Gabriela's eyes widened at her aunt's language but did as she was told.

As she joined Gabriela and the others to find their spots along the line, Marisol spied Laura arriving late. She waved in greeting, but Laura, her eyes deep-set, her skin sallow, and one hand on her belly, barely acknowledged her. Six months gone this time, so maybe she would make it. It was the way of mothers and aunties to cluck over the younger ones as they grew their first babies, but in the greenhouses the workers were only supposed to be midwives for the roses. Some said it was bad luck to think of baby names or knit booties before the baby came, just in case. Inside the greenhouses that was an unspoken law.

Long hours of standing over the conveyor belt, stripping thorns and leaves, measuring stems, dipping them in the solution, wrapping the bundles in plastic, and storing them for the trip north took Marisol's mind off of her niece and sister and Laura and the others. After work she peeled off her heavy sweatshirt—necessary when working in refrigerated conditions—and boots and dropped them in her bag before unlocking her bike for the ride home. For a while she just pushed her bike along the road, too tired to pedal. Just like that morning, the Nueva Flora bus roared past, the workers inside the same, only facing the other direction. And just like that morning, she passed the honeysuckle vine and said hello again, as if it were an aunty, a force to be reckoned with. It wasn't until she was past the wall that the feeling of the vine, heavy in her hair, left her.

The women began arriving before eight o'clock. Including her sister and niece, the number at the meeting would be near thirty: only about a third of the work force at Hacienda Roja, but a good start, and a worker from Nueva Flora was there to give advice. Marisol had hoped for Lucinda and Gabriela to arrive early enough for her to talk to her sister alone, but when they arrived the front room in the small apartment was already full with four women squeezed onto the couch, four others on the kitchen chairs, four more on chairs the neighbour brought, and the rest standing against the wall or sitting on what floor space was available.

"*Buñuelo*?" Marisol offered a plate of buns to her sister.

Lucinda's lips tightened. "Marisol, why would you do this again? The owner will lock us out. He will bring in other workers."

"What workers?" Laura asked from the couch. "We are the only ones in the neighbourhood who still work at Roja. The others won't give up their bus rides and free lunches to come back."

The room filled with the women's voices, all adding their own take on the situation. "No one who lives any farther away will come to Roja." "Roja is the last farm in this area that still uses the chemicals." "The government won't listen." "The government doesn't care." "They let the farms regulate themselves." "It's us against the owner, and there's only one of him."

Marisol handed the plate to Gabriela and held out her hands for quiet.

Lucinda grabbed the plate from her daughter's hand without looking and set it on the closest flat surface. "No, Marisol. I won't be part of this again. Come, Gabi." She turned, but Gabriela didn't follow. "Gabriela, come home I said."

Marisol recognized the internal struggle behind her niece's eyes.

"No, Mama. I work there now, too."

"You are just excited by the idea of being one of the women. You're too young to remember your Uncle Oscar." Lucinda stared daggers at her sister as she said her late brother-in-law's name. "The rest of you—" She scanned the room before continuing. "You want your children on the street, digging through the garbage for food?"

"You mean this child?" Laura asked and pointed at her belly. "This child who may be healthy ... but maybe not? He might be fine. But he might have asthma, or cancer."

Lucinda opened her mouth but then shut it again with a snap.

Laura continued. "We are asking for Roja to treat us as Nuevo—and many of the other farms—treat their workers. Decent gloves, a room to change in, toilets that are clean, to start with. Sick and dying workers can't bundle flowers."

"They also cannot take care of their families if they don't have jobs. I'm leaving." With one last glance at her daughter, who avoided her gaze, Lucinda walked out the door, leaving it open behind her. Marisol wanted to call her sister back but the room shifted and the lights in the neighbourhood beyond the open door blurred and shook. Gabriela grabbed her hand and asked what was the matter. One woman stood, and hands guided her to the open chair. The heavy-sweet scent of honeysuckle filled her head and she heard the buzz of the insects.

Gabriela pushed a mug into Marisol's hand. "Drink, *Tía*." Two sips of water and the scent retreated, the sounds died away, and the lights came back into focus.

"We should go," one of the women said.

Marisol shook her head. "No. Stay. We must plan."

"But you're ill," Gabriela said as she took the mug.

Marisol shrugged. "Perhaps. But that's exactly why we must fight."

Marisol finished washing the mugs, and when Gabriela offered to dry them she shook her head and instead set them upside-down on a towel to dry. "What has your mother told you about your uncle?"

Gabriela's gaze darted to the door to her cousin's tiny bedroom. Marisol slept on the couch, insisting that Luis take the bedroom in hopes of keeping him home. But young men of nineteen didn't want to live with their mothers forever, though it would be many more years until he'd be able to take care of her.

"That Uncle Oscar fought the *policía* in the street."

"Yes, he fought in the street, threw rocks, and was beaten down. But did she tell you that the police were protecting bad men—men who own big companies and own the politicians?" Marisol leaned back against the kitchen sink. "It's a long story, very complicated. But Oscar fought for himself, for his friends, for me, and for his son. For our future."

"Mama says he was foolish, to leave you and Luis with no one to protect you."

"That's because she cannot—does not—want to imagine what life would be like without your father."

Gabriela crossed her arms. "Papa won't leave."

"That may be so, but that doesn't mean that if he did you wouldn't have anyone to protect you. Now," she said as she hung a shawl around her shoulders, "I will walk you home."

Down on the street, Marisol held her flashlight in one hand and hooked her other arm through her niece's elbow.

"I can walk home by myself," Gabriela said, her voice defiant.

"In the daytime, yes. But you know better than to be outside alone at night."

"But it's only two blocks, *Tía*."

"And you are only fifteen, niece."

"Good evening, Marisol." A man's voice came out of the dark. Marisol clicked on the flashlight, and Hector raised his hands to deflect the light.

"What are you doing here?" Marisol knew he didn't live nearby and so didn't try to lessen the accusation in her voice. Let him read of it what he would. If he had followed other workers to her apartment, she decided not to care. He didn't make much more pay than the rest of them; perhaps he could be drawn to their side.

"Visiting my cousin," he said and pointed in the opposite direction. "And you?"

"Walking Gabriela home. See you at work tomorrow." She pulled her niece around the corner.

He followed. "Wait, Marisol. Please."

Gabriela jogged to keep up. "*Tía*, slow down."

Hector drew even and stopped in front of them, only a few feet from the entrance to Gabriela's apartment building.

"What do you want?" Marisol asked. "You can't report me to the boss for being out after dark."

He put his hands up, palms out. "I was going to offer to walk with you."

"But you live that way." She pointed toward the city. "Go inside, now," she said to Gabriela.

"Goodnight, *Tía*." The girl disappeared inside, leaving Marisol and Hector alone beneath the streetlamp.

"May I walk you back home?" he asked.

Marisol didn't know how she could say no, alone and with a flashlight, even if it was a short walk. She nodded and turned around, heading back into the dark street without waiting for him.

"What did your cousin feed you?" she asked.

"Um . . ."

"Did you forget already?" She sneaked a peek at him, knowing the look of a man caught in a lie.

"No. Just a simple meal. Red beans, some pork, a bit of corn."

Marisol kept walking quickly despite her sore feet. At the corner, she said, "Nearly there. You can go now. I'll be fine."

Hector narrowed his eyes. "No. I'll walk you to the door. You can never be too careful. People may be watching."

Near the entrance to her building was a small playground. What wasn't broken was covered in graffiti and the ground glittered with smashed bottle glass. The swing set was covered in vines; they had even reached across to the slide.

"Such a shame." Hector sighed.

"The vandalism or the fact that nature is taking back what's hers?"

"Both. The children need a place to play."

"Hmmph."

"Marisol?" Hector laid his hand gently on Marisol's arm. She froze, one hand clutching her key in her pocket. "Be careful."

"We're at my door, Hector. I'm safe."

He shook his head, his lips pressed so tightly together that they all but disappeared. "Just . . . be careful," he said.

The playground behind him was dark, but Marisol was sure she saw movement. He spun around, alerted by her distraction. "What?" he asked. "Who's there?"

One of the swings moved forward and back, just a fraction.

"It's just the wind."

"Marisol, there's no wind tonight."

No matter how much she hated to admit it, he was right. The tree's leaves and the football flags on the balconies all hung slack. Nothing moved, except for the vine twining through the swings' chains.

Hector stumbled, and Marisol reached out to catch him. "Are you okay?"

"Yes, just tired is all."

Marisol sighed. "Would you like some tea before you go? To help you feel better, I mean."

"It's time I left," he said, not taking his eyes off of the swing set as he walked away.

The following weeks passed with a speed that alarmed Marisol, yet being forced to take action often defeated fear. After many messages passed from hand to hand, whispered conversations on the walk to and from the greenhouses, furtive meetings at different locations, and advice from the Nueva helper, they chose the Monday before Mother's Day in the United States. If no workers stood on the line that week, no roses would go north. And after Mother's Day came prom season, and after that the wedding season. Nueva Flora often brought in extra temporary workers that week, meaning that the most local workforce would be depleted. Hacienda Roja's owner wouldn't have a choice.

The morning of the Friday before their plan was to go into effect, the changing room at Roja was quiet.

"Did you hear?" Gabriela whispered to her aunt. "Laura . . ."

"The baby?" Marisol asked.

Gabriela shrugged. "Mama said it was early but not too early. The baby is tiny and sick."

Marisol caught her sister's eye from across the small room. "When will it be enough?"

Lucinda shook her head and turned her back.

On Monday, Marisol's nerves were as frayed as the hem of her jeans. As soon as everything was up and running, a susurrus slid along the line as the women took off their gloves and stepped away, bunching together to get to the door and out into the open before Hector or the other managers could stop them. Gabriela had taken up a spot on the line near her aunt and hurried out under her protection. Lucinda, who had avoided Marisol for weeks, was the lone woman left in the barn.

Marisol found the rest of the workers standing at the side of the road. They all still wore their sweatshirts, some with hoods pulled up against the rain. Their bags were still inside the storage room, but they had all stashed keys and wallets in their clothes. The Roja had nothing of theirs.

They waited.

After a few minutes, the management team, all men, came outside. "Back inside," the largest of them yelled at the women. "Back inside and back to work or we will call the owner. And you know what will happen."

Marisol worked to keep her voice calm. "And if we don't, no roses will go north. So go ahead, call the owner. Tell him our demands."

The man, who was said to have eaten at the owner's table, loomed over Marisol and pointed his finger in her face. "You will go back inside."

Marisol felt the women behind her, an invisible force at her back, their power strengthened by her mother, her *abuela,* their love for their children, and the stories they told. "Your hands aren't blistered," she said. She shook her head and turned her back on him while he yelled threats.

Half an hour later, Hector came outside. Lucinda stood in the doorway protected from the rain, arms crossed, watching.

"The owner says you come inside before lunch you can keep your job and you just lose half a day's pay," he called, a mobile phone in one hand. "You don't get back to work, you're fired. And the other farms won't hire you. So c'mon now, back inside."

Marisol again stood at the front of the crowd of women. She shook her head and crossed her arms, mirroring her sister. "And who are you going to get to come work here this week, when all of the roses need to go north for all of the rich mothers? Huh? We don't ask for much: decent toilets, a room where we can eat, better gloves."

Hector put the phone back to his ear and walked away into the greenhouse.

"Lucinda," Marisol called to her sister. "Come join us."

"Please, Mama." Gabriela held her hood against the rain.

They stood like that, three points of a triangle, and waited for one point to give.

Hector returned. The triangle broke down and became a line from Marisol to Hector as mother and daughter looked on. "The owner says that you're gathering illegally and trespassing on his land." The rain fell harder, drowning out the sound of the crowd of women talking.

"Then I expect the *policía* will arrive soon."

Hector shook his head. "Not *policía*. The owner's men." He frowned, and Marisol read sadness in his gaze. "If you all come back to work the owner will call them off."

The women stood firm. The rain beat down.

Marisol held up her hands to the crowd, reminding them of their own hands—of the blisters and peeling skin, yellowed nails and calluses. She imagined she could hear trucks rumbling down the road toward them. Forgetting herself, she motioned behind her for Laura, wanting to protect her. Over the weekend she had visited her friend, had seen the baby boy, so tiny, his skin ashen with an undertone of aphid green. A hand—smooth or rough, she could no longer tell—slid into hers. Gabriela, the youngest of them all, not yet sick or ruined, not yet tired and sore, not yet resigned to her fate and invisible to the world. The *madreselva*'s scent rose beneath the patter of the rain and the growling of truck engines, and beneath it all was the droning of the bees. Marisol called out, "Flowers hide death. They bloom while the women who tend them wither away and die."

The trucks were nearly upon them, but the droning of the bees had sunk into Marisol, making her teeth shake. Gabriela held her hand out to her mother in supplication and love.

"You don't know what you're doing, little girl," Lucinda said.

"If I am old enough to work, I am old enough to fight. We need you with us, Mama."

Lucinda rolled her eyes up to the sky. Three trucks slid to a halt, the men in them holding bats and clubs. The women, dozens of them but with nowhere to go, stood in empty space and waited. Hector stood in the middle of the drive and waved his arms. The rain fell harder, drumming on Marisol's head. And beneath the beat she heard—she felt—the buzz of the bees working away in the *madreselva* vines.

The men turned away from Hector, whose voice was lost in the noise of rain and men and insects, and toward the women. Marisol held her hands up again, the rain running down her palms and into the sleeves of her sweatshirt. She did not stand in surrender but in defiance.

The buzzing grew louder, deeper, and she felt it in her bones. A woman to her left screamed as one man lashed out and punched her.

Like a flock of birds, the women surged away from him, but the men followed. The sound their bats made when hitting flesh wasn't the crack she expected but a meaty thump. Beneath it all, the vibration intensified, and with it came the scent of the *madreselva*, sweet above the smell of rain and mud and blood.

The flock of women streamed away from the men, away from the greenhouses and Hector, and toward the wall at the edge of the parking lot. Marisol ran with Gabriela. A club swung down, catching Marisol's wrist and breaking their connection, and the meaty thumps were from the club on her niece's body, the man's fist on her face. Blood dripped on the mud, mesmerising Marisol, who wondered how it would look when dry. She wasn't herself anymore—she was all of them.

Lucinda screamed, distant beneath the buzz. Her sister, eyes wide and wild beneath hair that hung loose in the rain like vines in the forest, ran for the man, pushed him from behind. Lucinda was action, Marisol spirit. Gabriela now up and between them, the sisters ran. The men followed, their bats held high. The closer to the wall they got, the deeper the buzz, the more Marisol's teeth shook in her mouth. She felt the tiny bones in her fingers and toes loosening, slipping their bonds, followed by the longer bones in legs and arms, but still she ran. Her ribs became a cage of bees, her head a kettledrum, but still she ran. Another truck pulled up and blocked the exit as they reached the wall. The women, trapped, slowed down, and Gabriela cried out and stumbled, taking Lucinda down with her. A man—a different one or the same, it didn't matter because all men were keeping them from the *madreselva*—pulled his arm back for another swing and Marisol stepped between him and her family.

The vibration in Marisol's head reached such a pitch that she could hear the vines, hear the bees, hear *La Madre*. The man blinked and shook his head, disoriented long enough for Lucinda to pull her daughter up and away. Marisol linked hands with them again, leading them to the wall and behind the shrubs and into the thick vines, taking shelter in *La Madre*'s hair, foolishly hoping like children that they wouldn't be found. The rest of the women followed, spreading out along the length of the wall, desperate against the hard men and their harder fists and clubs. Marisol grabbed the hand of the woman next to her, and down the line in either direction the women were linked, each to each, the strong holding the injured, the old encouraging the young.

Hector stood in the yard behind the boss's men. Some were on their knees where they had fallen from the momentum of swinging a bat that never met its target. Hector pointed and his head whipped back and forth as he searched for what he was sure was there. The leader walked along the edge of the vines, his bat sliding over the leaves. When he motioned Hector to join him, Hector hurried over, his hands halfway up in surrender.

Marisol knew Hector was shouting, but the sound was tiny and far away. "Where are you?"

Then the leader stepped back as if leaving but really just shifted his weight from one leg to another, lifted the bat above his head, and swung it down right where Marisol stood. She shook with vibrations so fast and so tiny that she was a blur. The bat passed right through her.

Within a few minutes the men—all different yet all the same—had climbed into their trucks and left.

The rain slowed to a drizzle. The bees slowed, and their constant exchange of information became private once again, leaving the women to their own concerns.

Hector spoke into his phone, and his voice grew louder with every word. "All gone, sir . . . your men came . . . disappeared . . . No, not in the greenhouses . . . Aren't anywhere. What do you want . . . ? Yes. No, sir. The line is full of roses waiting to be shipped. Yes, sir, see you then, sir." His shoulders slumped for just a moment before he straightened up and punched the phone to end the call.

"Marisol," he said, his voice clear now. "I can see your eyes glowing at me from inside the vine. The owner says that you will get your new toilets and a new changing room. *If* you get back to work."

"What about the chemicals?" one woman asked.

"And the shuttle?" another woman shouted.

"And the lunchroom?" asked a third.

Hector put up his hands in surrender. "He's coming to see you all next week. If you get all of the roses batched and shipped in time for the mothers up north, he will meet with your leaders to work something out." He stood alone, wet from the rain, and smiled.

The women looked each to each silently, questioning the offer and only ready to accept if it was unanimous. As one, they stepped out from behind the shrubs and trees and out of the thick vines that covered the wall. Hector stood in front of Marisol. The other women moved around them like river water around a rock. Lucinda took Gabriela toward the changing room to tend her wounds.

"Oscar was a friend, and I didn't march with him that day."

Marisol flinched at her husband's name.

Hector continued. "I always regretted it. This was the best I could do for you, today."

She weighed the emphasis on his final word. "Today? What have you done until now but be the mouthpiece for the owners, the hand that writes the reports, the man that cows to them and stands over us?"

"Where did you go?" he asked, his eyes on the vines that covered the wall.

She shrugged. "Nowhere." A bee droned around Hector's head. He ducked and it landed on Marisol's arm for a second before zipping away. "We were right here," she said. "We have always been right here, taking care of the flowers, taking care of our children. You just weren't looking hard enough."

Tiffani Angus, Ph.D., is a lecturer in publishing and creative writing at Anglia Ruskin University, Cambridge, UK. A graduate of Clarion, she has published short fiction in a variety of genres (science fiction, fantasy, historical fantasy, horror and erotica) in several anthologies. Her academic research, which often results in creative writing projects, includes gardening history and gardens in fantasy fiction, women in apocalyptic fiction, and the dynamics of science fiction and fantasy writing workshops. When not languishing under fluorescent lights writing or teaching writing, she can be found geeking out in gardens that other people have planted. You can find her at tiffani-angus.com and @tiffaniangus.

A Choice in Exile
by
Stephen M. Coghlan

ONE MONTH TO GO, DUCEY "Deuce" McNellis typed into his tablet. *And it feels like an eternity. Knowing that I'm not truly isolated has been somewhat of a relief to me, but the agony of loneliness has been harsh all the same. I can't help but wonder what has gone on in the world since I was locked away. Inmates in jails have known more freedom than me.*

He paused to chew on his stylus.

I'm certain that the psychologists and psychoanalysts are going to have a field day with me. I know that all of my writings, actions and inactions have been closely monitored and will continue to be for another year as I integrate myself back into society. I have known the illusion of privacy as my sole companion for so long that I wonder if I will function at all once I return to civilization.

A piece of plastic broke off in his mouth. Deuce turned his head and spat the fragment out beside his bed. He didn't feel like writing anymore anyway. He knew that, as soon as the words were saved, they would be sent to a long list of doctors and scientists who would poor over his scribbled thoughts as if they were religious zealots looking for justification in ancient tomes. It would all be picked apart, analyzed, categorized, and graded.

Rolling out from the covers, Deuce remained nude as he performed his morning routines. It was both humor and anger that drove him to do everything naked while the cameras watched until he had nothing left to accomplish in the living quarters. Only then did he don his uniform. The coveralls were itchy but well worn.

With a final wave to his audience, with his middle finger raised in salute, Deuce left his room.

The labs were at the opposite end of the bio-dome. That way the lone occupant had to move about at least once a day. Birds sang in the air, and a small monkey chattered from a nearby tree. The air was sticky and sickly sweet with rotting vegetation, and by the time Deuce had made it to this office his undershirt was plastered to his skin. He took the shirt off and hung it over a chair to dry.

Samples lay in their containers, and a book of math questions awaited him. A computer began asking him basic questions about his mental health.

How are you this morning, Deuce? The white letters stood out against the black screen.

Just dandy, he answered, tapping away on the keyboard.

Did you sleep well?

Like a lead brick.

30 days, 11 hours. Are you excited?

Deuce chuckled as he tapped out his answer. *Does a bear poop in the woods?*

Thank you, Deuce. I will talk to you soon.

Deuce knew that soon meant noon, on the dot. Shaking his head, he was preparing to take his first readings of the day when the computer beeped again.

That was not normal.

Awaiting his response was the scientist responsible for Deuce's exile. He was a stern-faced man with dark skin and eyes that looked like burned caramel. His voice, when he spoke, was thick with his native accent.

"McNellis? Can you hear me?"

For a moment, Deuce considered ignoring the man for another month, but something about the scientist's tone worried Deuce enough to reply.

"Dr. Iyer, are you aware that your contact with me is going to ruin the experiment?"

The lead scientist coughed harshly, and only then did Deuce notice the eyes were pinker than normal. "I don't think that's going to be a problem," the doctor responded, as he wiped blood from his mouth and chin. "We anticipated that you would be shocked upon your return to civilization, but there may not be a civilization to return to."

"What are you talking about?"

The computer began downloading files.

Ever the scholar, Dr. Iyer's began his lecture. "It started halfway through the experiment, Ducey." He paused to wipe his eyes, and a crimson stain appeared where his hand passed. Beside his image, files began opening, displaying global headlines. Although many covered each other, the words were easy enough to read.

PLAGUE STRIKES PRAGUE
VIRUS IN VENEZUELA
DISEASE IN DENVER

"Is this some kind of joke?" Deuce asked, but he already knew the answer.

Dr. Iyer was dying in front of him.

"I'm afraid not." The scientist coughed and grabbed his chest in pain. "It seems to be an airborne version of the Marburg virus. It spread fast because it gave its victims no sign of illness while remaining highly communicable. The first known cases belonged to an international mining corporation. By the time we discovered that there was a problem, major cities all over the world had already become infected."

"So then . . ." Deuce tried to speak, but words failed him.

"You are safe at the moment, Mr. McNellis, but outside your dome, the nearest city is already a ghost town."

"So why call me now?"

"Because I am terminating our contract." Dr. Iyer leaned toward the camera. "Your dome is supposed to automatically release you in at the end of this phase. It won't anymore. I've ordered control of the doors to be fed directly to this console. You alone are in control of your fate. Furthermore, I have allowed you access to the Internet and various newsfeeds so that you can make an educated decision for yourself."

"Why? Why do all this for me?"

"Because I have come to admire you, Mr. McNellis. You have been entertaining, informative, and have had some surprising reactions when faced with situations. I will not be around much longer, but I wanted you to know that we appreciate what you have done for us.

"Goodbye, Ducey."

The scientist's face vanished from view.

Deuce slid into the chair and stared at the information that scrolled across the screen. The death toll was astronomical, beyond his comprehension. He scanned video feeds, watched people speak their final thoughts, and observed the creation and completion of mass graves. All throughout, he felt numb and empty although he supposed he should have been screaming and cursing.

He didn't tear himself away from the computer until the sun outside vanished, and the songs of the creatures of the night became loud in his ears.

The countdown read **29 days, 18 hours, 42 seconds.**

It took him two days to contact his sister's house. Her boyfriend answered the call. His voice was hoarse.

"Deuce?" He sounded at least somewhat happy. "How's it going, brother?"

"Doing okay, Jim, how are you and the girls?"

"They're sleeping. Government issued everyone pills a few weeks ago. When Macey got sick we knew it wasn't long. Patty was next. She got it only a few hours later. We put our little angels to bed before they suffered."

Deuce closed his eyes and fought back tears that burned as they fought their way to freedom.

Jim continued, unashamedly weeping. "Elisa decided to go with them. I wanted to join her but you know me, a fighter to the very end. I couldn't go quietly. They held each other until the end. I buried them in the backyard."

Deuce nodded, but his throat was too tight for him to speak.

"Your folks stopped calling two days ago. They were checking up on me to make sure I was all right. They blew everything on a cruise. It's supposed to be a one-way trip. Sometime during the ride, their cocktails will be spiked, and the last crewmember alive is supposed to scuttle the ship.

"Anyways, didn't think they'd let you talk to us yet. You out already?"

"Nah." Deuce tried to keep his voice casual. "They just let me talk to the outside."

"Lucky bastard." Jim paused to cough. "You're missing all the fun."

"I, I've heard, Jim."

"Look, do me a favor, okay?" Jim said quietly.

Deuce waited a moment before he answered. "Yes?"

"Don't come on by when you get out, okay? Let me have what little dignity I have left."

"I understand, buddy," Deuce whispered.

The line went dead.

152

24 days, 2 hours, 2 minutes.

The host of the talk show was in an advanced stage of infection. Her guests were not much better. The audience sat numbly, and Deuce thought he even saw one member near the back stop breathing before the third commercial break.

Maybe it was the celebrity worship for some, who took their last chance to see their idols in person. Or maybe it was a need for answers that pulled them out to a show that teased them with possible causes and solutions, but Deuce didn't understand why anyone would choose to spend their last moments sealed in with other dying people to just watch some celebrities talk to each other.

The guests were specialists in their fields. One was a viral historian, another was an environmental warrior, a third was a frontline doctor, and the last was a famous television preacher.

"We know, dear," began the historian, whose voice was smooth and gentle, "that the disease began at the mine. What we don't know is why."

"It is God's plan. He is cleansing the wicked and the unrepentant. Now, brothers and sisters, is the time to beg the Lord to let you—"

The environmentalist cut the preacher off. "Oh grow up!" she screeched. "We have ravaged our planet for far too long. Of course the disease started at a mine. That's where humanity rapes Mother Nature herself."

The doctor coughed, and all eyes turned on him.

"I won't claim to know its origin," she gurgled on the accumulating fluids in her lungs. "But I will tell you this. It is not a pathogen that is interested in survival. No one has been found yet to be a carrier. Our immune systems are useless against the disease."

"Unless you have been isolated from the world, you are doomed."

Sickened to his stomach, Deuce reached out to change to another streaming feed, but before he switched the channel he hesitated. No one objected or rose in anger over the apocalyptic view of the doctor. Most just sat there with quiet acceptance.

It was too painful to watch.

21 days, 23 hours, 10 minutes.

Deuce sat listlessly in his chair. He had unzipped the top of his coveralls and tied the arms his waist, and his undershirt was stained with drops of coffee. A requiem video played in front of him. Requiems were taking over the Net.

It was a simple concept. Stand in front of your camera, talk about yourself or a loved one, praise their accolades, leak a few dirty secrets, maybe perform a skill, and then wash down the pill.

It was tragic drama at its worst, but Deuce had become involved emotionally with so many of them that he felt like he had no feelings left to give, until the next video proved him wrong again.

Deuce watched young mothers nurse their infants for the last time. He watched a father play catch with his toddler son before sharing a beer and shaving together. He watched an old couple kiss tenderly and talk over a bottle of wine about all of their children and grandchildren, who had already left the earth.

He began to wonder if he should join them. He had control of the dome. It would be as simple as cracking the seals, letting in unaltered air, stepping forth and feeling the natural sun on his face.

Something stopped him. He didn't know if it was fear or a further calling.

He began to save every video that he watched.

He collected a young woman in China who played a multistringed instrument. He collected a five-year-old who told a memorized story of a paper-bag princess. He watched zookeepers release animals from their cages.

There was enough memory to spare.

Deuce stayed at his post, as he thought of it, for the night, and then all of the next day, and then the day after that. He filled up one memory stick after another.

He listened as airlines stopped their flights because there were no more pilots left alive. He recorded a mass wedding taking place as hundreds of doomed souls shared their last moments together. He heard a confession from a man who murdered his family in order to spare them the pain. The pill wasn't available everywhere.

He passed out at his desk, and awoke with an imprint of the keyboard in his cheek.

18 days, 3 hours, 5 minutes.

Someone was calling him. A crowd of people in white coats stood together.

"Ducey McNellis?" an woman asked. She seemed to be the oldest of them, and had a matriarchal air about her.

"That's me, who are you?" he answered.

The woman said, not unkindly, "We work for what's left of NASA. We're partly responsible for your present position."

"Glad to meet you, I guess." Deuce straightened his undershirt.

"Likewise." The woman smiled, but her bleeding gums told a story all on their own. "We want your help."

"I'm listening."

"As you are no doubt aware, humanity is dying. In less than three months we will almost all be gone. Infrastructure is breaking down. And, sadly—" She swept her arm, presenting her colleagues. "So are we."

"Sorry to hear that. What can I do for you?"

"You can help us make sure that our stories are not lost. We've programmed several satellites to broadcast messages from humanity to the stars, for as long as they hold out. We're launching five probes. We've loaded them with players and transmitters, but we have a problem."

"What's the issue?"

"No one here will survive long enough to see if all the information that we're sending will get to the probes. We want you to send information for us. We're going to connect you to the satellites, and as long as there's power, the probes will store what they can. When they are full, or haven't received anything for forty-eight hours, they will launch.

"We've sent instructions to you already, as well as a list of other people who have volunteered their time and efforts."

The computer beeped again.

"Do you have any questions?"

"No," Deuce answered as he scanned the information.

"Then on behalf of all of us at Project Goodbye, thank you," the matriarch said before the screen went blank.

Eager for a cause, Deuce busied himself on the task at hand. The countdown forgotten.

"Hello? Are you Mr. McNellis?"

"Please, call me Deuce," he replied as he hurriedly pulled his shirt over his head. The caller was a woman, and Deuce felt a need to be civil, even if she was somewhere else in the world.

Her age was impossible for Deuce to gauge. She was Asian, but Deuce couldn't place where she was from at a simple glance. She sat in a lab. The walls behind her had both English script and writing filled with straight lines and circles covering it.

"What an odd name," she said. "Why Deuce?"

"It's a holdover from my college gambling days." He laughed as he raised a bottle of water into the air in salute to times long gone. "And may I know yours?"

"Seong Sun."

"Pleasure." Deuce chuckled when she raised her own bottle of water in a return. Are you involved in Project Goodbye too?"

"Yes, and like you, I have a few days left to help."

Intrigued, Deuce waited for her to continue.

"I'm calling from a lab just outside Yeosu."

"Korea?"

"Yes."

Deuce had heard of unpleasant things happening overseas. The last report he had read stated that the North had invaded the weakened South.

"How's it going over there?"

Sun paused, and her face fell for a moment before she smiled again. "It's been better." She was obviously uncomfortable.

"So, you building a database too?" Deuce tried to change the subject.

"Yes. I was wondering how it's going for you."

He glanced at another window. "Great composers' library just finished. Architecture's next."

"I just finished the language files." She smiled, but her next words were somber. "You're the first healthy person I've talked to in over a month."

"You're one of the only people I've talked to in a year," Deuce said slowly. "And probably the last."

"Probably."

"So, is this just a social call?"

"No," Sun said. "Project Goodbye was my idea."

16 days, 0 hours, 10 minutes.

The two of them coordinated what was sent and what was collected, altered what remained, and counted their time.

He got to know her fairly well. Sun was pleasant to talk to. She had a laugh that sounded like twinkling crystal and a sense of humor to match. She was intelligent, witty, and not afraid to speak her mind. After Deuce's voluntary solitude, she was a breath of fresh air.

He wished he had known her sooner.

They were playing online poker against each other. Deuce had put his bet on an ace high, and he could only guess what Sun was playing with.

She coughed, and a speck of blood ended on her lip.

"Sun?" Deuce asked, concern ladled in his voice.

Sun wiped the blood away with the back of her hand. Her shrug was fatalistic.

"It was only a matter of time," she said.

Deuce didn't respond at first. He stared at her incredulously. "How can you be so calm?" he finally asked.

"Because no one escapes it. For some, it lay dormant in their system for weeks. I guess I got lucky. At least I got my affairs in order. Your turn?"

Deuce refused to let her change the subject. "This is your life you're talking about."

"And I've had a good one," Sun answered as if she was explaining something to a child. "And I've outlived so many. Every day is both a blessing and a curse. As long as I can complete our project, I will die well."

"You can't be serious. I didn't take you as someone who would just give up."

"Then I'm a liar," she said quietly, sadly. "I lost my husband in the first month, and my kids only a week after. I outlived almost my whole city. I started this project as a memorial to all of us, but I have been selfish, and have included all of the pictures of my family that I had, all of their videos, all of their records.

"I bluffed the rest, but thanks to you and the other volunteers, we've made this happen. Now show me your cards."

He ordered his hand revealed.

She giggled. "See, we can both play the bluffing game."

She had bet on a pair of twos.

12 days, 2 hours, 14 minutes.

"Deuce?" Sun's voice called. "Deuce?"

He lifted his head from the table. Data scrolled across the screen, but Sun's window was open. She looked concerned. Her eyes were bloodshot and her skin was flushed with heat. She had stripped down to her undershirt.

"What is it, Sun?"

"I can't breathe." She gasped, and then said something in Korean. "I hurt everywhere."

"Calm down," Deuce said, although he began to panic for her sake. "Do you know what's going on?"

"It's the infection," Sun panted. "It wants me to share it. It makes you *want* someone. Makes you want to get close to someone so that they become infected too, but there's no one around and it's driving me crazy."

"What can I do?" Deuce asked.

"Talk to me, tell me something. Are you scared?"

Deuce bit his tongue before he answered. "Yes."

"Of what?"

"Of being alone and of the outside. Before I found out about Project Goodbye, I was lost in grief for humanity. Since I've been involved with it, it's given me purpose. But I don't know what I'm going to do when we're done."

"Don't you want to live?" Sun asked, surprised.

"My primeval side does." Deuce laughed bitterly. "But I don't want to carry the grief of the world with me either. I don't want to be alone anymore."

"You're not."

"Not at the moment. But when the infection runs its course. . . ." He trailed off, swallowed nervously. "There's less and less being uploaded now. I've heard that entire cities are empty. One person transmitted their requiem from a darkened room. On batteries, I guess. Power failed along the seaboard. It's only a matter of time until the world grows dark."

"What will happen to you then?" she asked.

"The bio-dome is self-sustaining," Deuce explained. "I have rations and vitamins to spare. The trees here have more fruit than I can eat, I have vertical gardens of grains and vegetables, and I've been raising insects for protein. Do you know the reason why the dome was built?"

Sun shook her head.

"It was designed as a test facility to see if first-world people could adapt to a sustainable culture. I just didn't think it would be man's last holdout."

Deuce felt something behind his eyes. "Do you understand the irony? My isolation saved me from the worst, and damned me still. You might be lonely now, but you won't be alone much longer. If I hadn't talked to humanity I might not have missed it, either. I was okay, fine with being alone, until I realized that being alone hurts. It hurts so hard."

Sun coughed, and crimson flecked her chin.

"God, I'm sorry, Sun." Deuce felt sheepish at his own self-pity.

"It's okay." She smiled. "It's just nice to know that I'm not alone."

Deuce smiled back, and then he leaned forward and kissed the monitor.

8 days remained on the counter.

1 day, 1 hour, 1 minute.

The last of the data was sent. In celebration, Deuce raised his cup of water.

Sun smiled. Her mouth was bloody, her eyes were nearly blind, yet she hung on still.

"Care to do the honors?" Deuce asked softly.

It took all of her energy to press the single key.

The words flashed.

Launch Completed.

"To your family," Deuce whispered.

It was too difficult for her to reply.

"To humanity. To us."

Her eyes fluttered, closed, and she exhaled harshly. "To a good life."

The words were barely whispered. Then she breathed her last.

For a while, Deuce just sat in his chair and watched Sun's still form. She had died with a smile on her face. She had accomplished her mission, but at the same time Deuce felt that, with her goal completed, she had abandoned him.

Outside the dome, the sun began its descent from the zenith.

1 day, 0 hours, 0 minutes.

He left the office to wander the dome. The air felt heavy and oppressive. The songs of the birds and calls of the animals seemed to echo off the walls and bounce away into infinity. The ground underfoot gave slightly, and the grass pulled at his clothes.

In the middle of the dome was a tree that grew out of a pond. Deuce waded through the water and climbed until he was as high as he could safely go.

About him, he saw the entirety of the place he had called home. He saw the animals. He saw the vibrancy of life.

He saw how alone he was.

Tipping his head back, he roared his grief to the sky. It was a cry for all who had gone.

He slipped back down, dove into the water.

He walked through the trees and tried to lose himself.

He watched as the sun fell and the night arrived.

He watched the sun rise, and the clear sky burn bright.

1 hour, 1 minute.

Recovering his composure, he showered, changed, and recorded his own video. When he posted it, he saw that he was the first person in almost a day to add anything.

He hit the playback.

"On this day, I have made my decision. As you are no doubt aware, humanity has been ravaged by disease. We do not know where it came from, we do not know why, all we could do in the end was die.

"I have, in the last few weeks, witnessed our final moments, and have even helped launch our legacy into the heavens in the hopes that, one day, someone will find it and understand who we once were.

"I survived because I was sealed away. In less than an hour, my isolation will cease, and the place I have called home will open unless I stop it."

Standing up, Deuce began to march. The video continued to record.

"I have made my decision."

0 minutes, 0 seconds.

Spreading his arms wide, Deuce smiled as the door cracked. The air rushed by his face as it escaped into the outside world. The naked sun felt wonderful on his face.

Taking a steadying breath, he stepped out of the dome.

Stephen Coghlan writes from Ottawa, the oft-frozen capital of Canada. His novel, *GENMOS: The Genetically Modified Species* is coming soon from Thurston Howl Publications. Feel free to contact him or visit his website.

Swarms

by

James Dorr

SWARMS WERE EVERYWHERE! THE SWARMS of people in Ankara were constantly jostling and pushing, where Ryan passed through airport customs and metal detectors the old fashioned way—through carefully placed bribes. And on the airplane he sat, sweating under the long black coat that he couldn't take off, itching but not daring to scratch beneath the sixty-pound weight of the kilo bars sewn into its lining as other passengers pressed around him seeking their seats. He tried to lean back and relax by his window, to think of the chocolate-bar-sized strips of solid gold, neatly arrayed in rows within secret pockets separated by a thin white cotton shirt damp against his skin.

He tried to think of the desert he'd just left, his only human companions Collins and Lebotovski on the long Land Rover drive out of Iraq. But even deserts had swarms of their own.

Ryan thought, as he finally drifted to sleep somewhere over the Mediterranean Sea, of the twin-tailed lizard he had seen burrowing into the sand the morning they found what they had come for. He thought of pointing it out to Collins, their leader, but Collins was already gesturing elsewhere, east toward the rising sun.

"Masks on!" Collins shouted to them and Ryan nodded, pulling his gas mask out of his kit. He saw the black cloud too, low-lying, swirling and drifting toward them. Most likely it would just be the flies again, only the flies came with dawn. Tiny wasps, really, as Collins had told them, an Englishman who boasted of his degree from Cambridge; they lived on figs and dates and on the detritus that desert travelers left behind. Still, everyone knew, despite what the news reporters said, that both sides in Desert Storm had resorted to chemical weapons. So the cloud *could* be gas, filled with lethal residues left from the American missiles that blasted apart the Republican Guard on its long retreat to Baghdad. Or from the column of burned-out tanks and half-tracks itself that he and the Russian and Collins, who'd been with the British forces, had sneaked across from Kuwait to find. Some little "surprise" the Iraqis had run out of time before they could use. It paid to be cautious.

It paid to be cautious at night as well, as clouds of gray moths swarmed around the partially shielded fires where they cooked their rations. At least one man with his rifle was always at the ready. Collins had told them that the rumors of treasure he'd heard in Riyadh when the war was finished, of gold and jeweled artifacts stolen from the Al Kuwait museum by Saddam's elite guard but subsequently lost in the allied ambush, might well have been heard by other ears too. And it wouldn't pay to be caught in their own ambush after they'd found it, before they could cross the Turkish border where Lebotovski had contacts that paid for such treasures in gold of a more disposable sort.

However, the black tendrils in the sky proved to be just a new swarm of the tiny wasp-flies that had plagued desert crossers since before the conquest of Persia. Then, as Ryan exchanged his full mask for a gauze scarf that only covered his mouth and nostrils, he spied a second lizard burrowing into the sand, moving in haste to escape the rising morning heat. And then he saw something else.

A patch of gray shone where the lizard had dug. Not the khaki-tan color of military, but a blistered civilian blue-gray that proved to be that of an armored truck all but buried beneath the shifting dunes. It was exactly like the kind used by banks and museums.

High above the Atlantic, he awoke again and reflected on the almost surreal journey west to Ankara. The wasps had disappeared, as they always did just before the searing heat of noon, as he had worked alongside the others, sweat drying on his skin almost as soon it appeared, with his shirt tied around his head in a makeshift *kaf-fiyi*. Together they loaded the last of what they had dug out from the armored truck and placed them aboard the Rover, carefully hiding them under a tarp.

It was then that he saw the first foxes. He picked up his rifle, just in case, as one, curious, came near. But then others joined it, which was odd. Desert foxes, unlike jackals or wolves, always traveled alone.

Ryan shouted at it, not wasting a bullet, and saw the matted fur of its back as it turned and ran with the others, its tail thin and ratlike instead of bushy. And then for some hours on the journey west they had shared the desert trail with mounted Kurdish tribesmen—some of these half bald, half covered with tangled hair. Others had goiters, and still others had patches of skin that looked pocked and gray instead of brown and wind-burned. Their camels, too, had humps oddly swollen, although he, whose forte was navigation and knowledge of geographical features, well knew that the nearest water was days away from where they'd been riding.

But none of that counted—in any event they had been soused enough by then from celebrating with Collins's whiskey. None of them paid attention either to the curses Collins joked about some treasures possessing. All they cared about was gold, and gold alone. Lebotovski's friends had proved reliable, trading what they brought out for the yellow bars, one third of which weighed heavily now on Ryan's chest and shoulders. Enough for a lifetime.

He leaned back again, feeling its lumpiness underneath under his back and shoulders, squirming a little to try to relieve the itch that persisted. He reached the call button to bring the flight attendant.

Why not? he thought, when the woman arrived, dark-eyed and dark-haired, smiling prettily as she asked, first in Turkish and then English, for his order. He returned the smile and pulled down his seatback table. *Why not live it up some?* After all, he could well afford it now.

"Champagne," he said.

Ryan made a point of staying moderately drunk the rest of his journey. It helped quell the sweat and the itching, until their final descent into Miami. More swarms when they landed, not so much of tourists—it was, after all, May, the start of the off-season, which suited him fine—but rather of businessmen from South America, wearing their own dark coats and their suits and ties despite the humid heat outside the terminal. And then one more bribe, to get a quick taxi to Southwest Eighth Street and to an apartment over a Cuban shop where he could finally undress and shower.

Ryan turned on the TV. Dressing more touristy now in a print shirt and white poplin slacks, he poured out a whiskey over cracked ice and made several phone calls. The following evening he exchanged his gold for untraceable money and celebrated across Biscayne Bay with a high-priced hooker.

For three weeks he lived that way, drinking and whoring not just in hotel bars but more and more often sampling the cheap trade in

Motel Row. Yet the itch, and now with it a sense of growing oppression, persisted. The heat stole sleep from him, even while he lay naked beneath his apartment's bedroom air conditioner turned up to its highest. And worse were the crowds—he'd never liked crowds, even when he was growing up on the East Side of New York. But now, with the press of the swarm even on the Beach, even in the posh hotel lobbies where the Latino *comerciantes* held sway in the summer, still wearing their damn suits even outdoors where the daytime temperatures soared through the nineties, he began to feel almost a physical crawling beneath his skin.

But he needn't stay there. He bought a new car, a four-wheel-drive Cherokee. He could afford it. And he had a cabin, a fishing shack, really, but one with a dock where he could enjoy the wind from the ocean, unsullied by people, or go and come in a motor skiff he had waiting for him there.

And so, the second week in June, he loaded his car with all his possessions and took off not north, but south, stopping once for supplies, down to Key Largo and the Causeway. He drove out toward Key West but turned off before it, on Sugarloaf Key, wheeling left onto what was practically nothing more than an overgrown jungle trail. Navigating through palms and pimentas, around coral outcrops and swamp holes, he finally came out onto a sandy crescent that faced the Atlantic.

He unpacked his gear, checked the boat in its boathouse, and grabbed the extra gas he'd brought for it. He tested the motor and, as the sun retreated west giving way to a blood-colored tropical twilight, he filled the tank of the cabin generator. He left the lights off, though, turning the generator on only for the freezer and refrigerator, and took out a steak he'd brought packed in dry ice and let it thaw while he built a fire on the beach to cook it. He went for a swim just after he'd eaten—to hell with mothers' advice about waiting an hour after dinner—then checked the icebox to see if the beer was cold enough to drink.

He slept on the beach that night. The nearest human company he had were in the cars on the Causeway clear on the other side of the island. He dreamed of the moths that flew out from the jungle to swarm in spirals around what remained of his dying campfire.

Ryan woke with the dawn, its blood and coral pink splashing his face as he got to his feet, went to the ocean, and washed with salt water. He pulled on his jeans and then walked into the jungle. He didn't know why—he walked and he searched until he discovered a wild banana tree, scraggly and bug-pocked, but he didn't care. He ripped fruit from its branches, wolfing it down—he who normally didn't eat breakfast—and then went back in his cabin. A quick scan inside the freezer revealed a can of orange juice concentrate, which he mixed and drank, not even bothering to boil the cistern water that came from the kitchen tap.

He shook his head then—the itch still persisted, but not the oppression. He felt alive yet sleepy, like a lion that had hunted and eaten its fill. A picture of the desert foxes with their naked tails filled his mind. He thought about them and about hyenas. Creatures that stole kills while lions were sleeping. Stretching, scratching, he put on a loose shirt to guard against sunburn and wandered back out on the beach for a long nap.

He didn't fish, though he'd brought along tackle. He didn't swim either—he'd brought trunks, not that he'd need them alone on his stretch of beach, but after that first morning's washing he found that the salt irritated his skin.

Then one day, it must have been almost July, he saw the first tiny wasp. He'd just woken up from one of his naps and he saw it on his arm that lay outstretched in front of him on the sand. He watched as the wasp crawled, neither adding nor taking away from the itch he was used to by then—and then it disappeared. Just like the two-tailed lizard in Iraq. He got up, hungry, but rather than go to the jungle as he usually did to search for fruit, he went into the cabin.

He turned on a light and inspected his skin, noticing for perhaps the first time the network of dry, gray scales that had formed over parts of his flesh. He prodded them on his arm—felt something moving. But nothing to be seen.

Examining the scales closer, he discovered, just below the crook of his elbow, a tiny hole.

Ryan went to Key West twice, in the boat both times, the first time wearing a jacket and suit slacks over his skin as if he, too, were a *comerciante*. Both times he loaded the skiff with bananas and grapefruit and oranges, mangoes and figs and dates and dried prunes, even though he was paying Key West prices. The second time, wearing his long black coat with its lining pockets, he went to the public library as well and took out books about wasps.

He knew, somehow, he had been infested. He knew from what Collins had said on their trip across the desert that some wasps were parasites. Ichneumon wasps, for instance, laid their eggs in the entrails of fruit moth larvae, piercing their skin with their ovipositors like other wasps stung prey. But the wasp larvae in turn killed their hosts, while he, if anything, felt more alive than ever before!

His sense of smell, especially, guided him in the jungle, finding new fruit trees to augment the fruit he'd brought in on his boat. But his hearing also, as well as his vision, seemed keener and more defined, while, despite the gray, lacelike protrusions that now covered most of his body, his sense of touch was augmented equally.

Sometimes he would wake screaming from his noon naps, having dreamed of Miami and its swarms of people—knowing that he couldn't ever go back there. He couldn't even go back to Key West now, even though, as July became August, he knew the town would be nearly deserted except for the Conchs—the ones who lived there year-round. He felt, rather, that there was a perimeter somehow outside of him, around his skin, that couldn't be violated without causing what nearly amounted to physical pain.

He dreamed about violence. Like Collins, he had once been a soldier, although in peacetime. But he had trained for war. Now, in his dreams, he practiced killing. He *wanted* to kill—he didn't know what might happen in fall when the weather got cooler and he'd feel the Causeway traffic increasing, even though it was miles from his beach house.

He didn't want to know.

Rather, he read his books in the mornings while the cool breeze came in over the ocean onto his cabin porch. He read about hornets and bees and domestic wasps, wasps that made their nests out of paper. And he knew that was what was happening to him as he felt the chewing beneath his skin—not hurting, just tickling—as the tiny wasps, flying in and out openly now, converted subcutaneous fat into paper, building it out, cell by cell, on his body.

He couldn't wear clothes now. The skin-architecture, the paper palace that *was* his skin now, had become too extensive. This wasn't spherical—or sphero-conical—like the wasps' nests that hung from northern trees. In his books, he had pictures of those to look at. But, rather, his flesh was pinnacled, arched, with towers and peaked roofs and crenellations, and fantasy-castles, more like the coral reef beyond his island where wind and water had carved and shaped it. And, like the fish of the reef, his skin-castles had guardians as well. Soldiers and workers buzzed about him, flying in mini-swarms out of his body at morning and twilight, red with the blood-rose of dying sunlight, the purple-red-orange explosions of dawn.

He scarcely could walk now. He shambled to the jungle, to the beach for his naps in the hot sun, long since protected from any sunburn, to the cabin and refrigerator, the latter no longer working, where his associates—he thought of them that way, his friends and companions, more partners than parasites—still allowed him an occasional beer.

The liquor, he wouldn't touch. Once, when he'd opened a bottle of cognac, he felt a pain in his cheek—his architecture had grown higher until by now it covered his head too, allowing tunnels and transparent micalike, lenslike structures to breathe and see through. A friend disapproving. Meat, though, rotten now, he might still sample.

In fact, it was gradual, but something was changing. He started to crave meat, carrion meat, and his flying associates would sometimes lead him along jungle trails to where, days in the past, they had stung the life from a lizard or a small mammal.

And always his hatred grew—for his own past. For the swarms of the people he had left behind him.

Then one night the rains came.

It must have been August, or nearly September as he made it. Ryan had a sense for the sun's risings and settings that told him that fall wasn't far away, something he felt without needing a calendar.

He went in the cabin and battened the windows, knowing the weather would cool soon, and then it would be tourist season. Soon people would come and fill the Causeway, some even driving off, perhaps, to picnic or to fish on his island. To explore its beaches. Perhaps find his *own* beach.

He found a marker, and tore apart cardboard cartons with puffed fist-like hands. He made crudely lettered signs: NO TRESPASSING! DANGER! He even managed to chuckle with what his throat had become now, when he made one that said CAUTION! UNEXPLODED MINE FIELD. Using gore from the remains of animals he had eaten, he painted skulls and crossbones on weathered boards ripped from his cabin, and posted these and the others around the island.

And yet these would not work. Eventually people, being what people are, would ignore them. Some he might kill—he was daily famished for meat now as well as fruit—but, eventually, tourist deaths would bring police also.

He searched through the cabin to find his guns, a pistol, a shotgun, which he had brought with him, but found his fingers were too large to fit around their triggers.

Yet something *was* happening within his body. As the first storms passed, he felt a new tickling. An anticipation among his hosts—he had begun to think of them as hosts now. Joyous, not fearful.

And then he realized what it was he must do.

He used the days of sunshine that followed to inspect his boat, caulking leaks where he found them. He cut a tarp to fit snugly over its open cockpit, and oiled its engine as best he was able, taking it out on short trips from his island from time to time to test its handling in wind and surf.

And then the second wave of storms came, and he hauled the skiff back into its boathouse—this, he knew, was more than a squall. But also he knew it would hit to the north of him—he had a sense now for wind and weather—its eye perhaps striking land north of Daytona Beach. Possibly even as far north as Georgia.

And so Ryan waited, biding his time, two, three, four weeks into September, glad of a respite after what had been a fiercely hot summer. Hurricane season, still for the most part affecting cities north of Miami, had come with enough vigor to keep the tourists in check.

But the people still swarmed in the cities to the north, on the Coast, on the Gulf, on the Mississippi, on prairies and mountains west to the Pacific. God, how he hated them! How he shuddered to think what he was once—he thought of the hooker that night in Miami, his arms on her body. The others both before and after. His—

His hosts were waiting. He felt himself calming. He loaded his boat's freshwater tanks from the cabin's roof cistern, now fresh-filled itself. There were prunes and dried figs he had left from his last trip to Key West, and he loaded those as well. And he, too, waited.

Then one morning he saw the sky turn gray and scaly, much like his skin when he'd seen his first host-wasp. He felt the wind freshen and knew his time had come. He went to his cabin and brought more supplies out, sailcloth, a sharp knife, cordage, paddles, and carried them out to the dock to his boat.

He pushed off to sea, as the wind seemed to hook from the south and southeast, and headed at half speed out into the Florida Strait on a course that would take him just north of Cuba. He knew what was coming—his wasp-senses told him—a southern-track hurricane barreling down the Santaren Channel to strike Cape Sable and Florida Bay. A big one, to sweep the Keys and then veer to the Dry Tortugas, and then hook back north through the Gulf of Mexico to strike the coast near Pensacola, or even as far to the west as New Orleans. But big, big, to envelop Texas to Corpus Christi, to reach as far east as Tallahassee. And he sailed to meet it.

He heard a buzz over the hum of the engine, a buzz from within him, as he made his shipboard preparations, dogging the tarp down over the cockpit so, when the first rains came, he was able to crouch beneath it, out of the cold wind, squinting out through the spray-stained windshield into a green sky over green water. He kept himself dry as best he was able and gorged on dried figs, hearing the engine's strain.

At one point he turned on the skiff's radio, hearing the crackle of Coast Guard warnings—all small boats to come ashore, larger shipping to clear the area from the Antilles clear to Bermuda—until its battery finally failed. His boat was alone now, alone with wind and waves, still straining east and south past Andros Island.

And then his engine died, finally, as the wind whistled around him, but not as loud now as it had been before. He lifted a tarp edge and threw out the sailcloth he'd packed before, now attached to two crossed paddles to form a sea anchor.

And he waited.

He felt more than heard the wind start to die down, and felt the crawling and scurrying of those inside him. He waited, crouching, and peered out through the strong Plexiglas windshield until the sky in front suddenly lightened.

He listened, closely, until he heard nothing—even his hosts seemed to have stopped their chatter! He listened for wind, for the patter of rain, until, satisfied, he loosened the tarp and rolled it partway back, and then heaved himself up until he was standing, supporting himself on the boat's engine cover.

He stood in a dead calm—the eye of the hurricane!

Silence surrounded him.

And then, at first very faint, but gradually increasing, he heard his wasp-hosts resume their buzzing. He spread his arms wide as they climbed out from inside him onto his skin, to the paper-skin architecture that overarched his body in domes and towers, in cities and steeples, until every part of him that he could see—every part of him and every part of the boat as well—was massed with blackness.

With the first breeze from the hurricane's trailing edge, the swarm began. As one mass, the wasps took to the air, whirling around him, filling his ears with their high-pitched buzzing, taking his hatred, his revulsion for the human swarms with them. He watched as their circling rose higher and higher, darkening the sky, whirling to blend with the storm around them, to course on its winds to the Mississippi, into the heartland of the continent as the storm gathered strength out of the ocean. To rain with its rains on cities and farmlands, some to ride jet streams—he thought about Collins, in England now, but perhaps with *his* hosts even now spreading out over Western Europe, of Lebotovski somewhere east of Moscow in his Siberian wilderness dacha—he thought about what he had read about wasps and how, when they swarmed, it was for just one reason—to seek out new hive sites.

And, laughing, Ryan still stood, the remnants of his paper skin whistling as the wind freshened, this time from the north. As the new rain fell.

Ryan rigged a sail, the skiff's engine still balking at being started. He scarcely remembered *why* he had sailed out into the storm's eye, but, somehow, he had wrestled the tarp back and ridden the wind out, all night long, until the next morning. And somehow his sense of *place* had remained with him to guide him back until he stood off Sugarloaf Key.

He lowered the sail and used a paddle to ease himself the rest of the way to shore. His dock was still standing, although the boat-house's roof had been damaged and the porch of his cabin had caved in. Nothing, however, that couldn't be repaired.

When he made it to dry land, he stood there inspecting himself. His memory was fading, of *why* his skin seemed covered with wispy, dry, papery tendrils, except for their gray color much like it might have been had it peeled from prolonged sunburn. And yet he felt healthy—healthy enough, despite his thinness. A gauntness close to emaciation.

Ryan located the rest of the figs on the boat, along with bottled water and a sealed tin of emergency crackers. He ate his fill of them, and then went in the cabin and foraged more food, canned soups and stews that had lain untouched since he'd first unpacked them.

He found enough dry wood to build a cook fire.

He slept on the beach, having put on a pair of loose slacks and a shirt he'd found in the cabin to guard against sunburn the following morning. When he finally woke, shortly before noon, he packed the other clothes he could find, along with the rest of his possessions, and climbed into the Cherokee.

Threading his way out the jungle trail, he drove onto the Causeway, taking his time. The road was deserted, apparently still closed, but that was okay.

There was plenty of time. Nothing to do. A bank account waited for him when he got back to Miami, with plenty of money. He missed the people, the crowds around him—at least he did sometimes—and thought, once he'd gotten himself better cleaned up, maybe he'd check out the Beach hotels. Possibly have a few drinks. A woman. . . .

Or maybe rest first in his apartment. He'd have time enough, he thought.

He drove slowly, cautiously, avoiding felled palm trees, north and east over Big Pine Key, past Key Vaca and Grassy, Long Key and Plantation. The scent of sea air, the freshness of it, even caused him to smile, and he took pleasure in the sun shining on him through his open side window.

Until deep within him he felt a new itching.

Indiana writer James Dorr's "The Tears of Isis" was a 2014 Bram Stoker Award® nominee for Superior Achievement in a Fiction Collection. Other books include *Strange Mistresses: Tales of Wonder and Romance*, *Darker Loves: Tales of Mystery and Regret*, and his all-poetry *Vamps (A Retrospective)*. Also be on the watch for *Tombs: A Chronicle of Latter-Day Times of Earth*, a novel-in-stories due for release from Elder Signs Press in June 2017.

An Active Member of HWA and SFWA with more than 500 in-dividual appearances from Alfred Hitchcock's Mystery Magazine to Xenophillia, for the latest information Dorr invites readers to visit his blog at http://jamesdorrwriter.wordpress.com.

Earth Mother

by

Paul Du Jat

All that was—would never be.
All that would be—never was.

I'D BEEN IN THE OLDUVAI Gorge in Tanzania for two weeks. The searing heat of day and the bite of night couldn't deter me. I had learned that modern human remains had been unearthed in an ancient layer of African rock. Carbon 14 dating revealed the fossilized bones were found in a layer dating back millions of years before any human had ever walked the earth.

My degree in paleoanthropology didn't prepare me for what I discovered. My political connections from my days working at the United Nations allowed me access to dig at the secret site. The human remains were long gone now, claimed by the local government. They weren't going to let another national treasure be stolen like so many other artifacts. What I found at the site perplexed me to my core.

I unearthed a stainless steel attaché case. It was dirty and dented, its once-shiny metal skin covered in a film of prehistoric dirt. I poured a bottle of water over the case to clean it. Etched into its side was a human name. My name, Oscar Crevaliz.

There was no combination lock or key access to the case. A small notch, which appeared to be a fingerprint scanner, located on the top of the case was smashed. I wondered how any of this was possible.

I immediately called Professor Thurgood, my old mentor from grad school, and told him what I had found. "How can an attaché case be buried in rock millions of years old?"

"The earth is alive and is a sentient being," Thurgood said.

I didn't believe him. I should have.

He continued. "Planets live and die, like every creature in this universe."

"Doc, how does this pertain to the question I just asked you?"

"It does, lad. Just be patient for a change. Planets can communicate with each other. Some even have a sense of humor. Mars once told Earth a joke about Jupiter being filled with custard. Jupiter remained pissed off for eons." Thurgood paused for a moment. "Ozzy, you are in grave danger." His words ceased.

"Doc? Doc?" The phone call had dropped as the satellite moved out of range. My heart fell too. He had never answered my question, although he must have sensed the urgency in my voice. The object I found couldn't be explained within a rational discussion. I needed to get home to New York. It took a week of bribes and anguish to smuggle the attaché case out of Africa.

Under dark gray skies, I arrived home. I would seek the guidance of my best friend, Milo, as well as that of Professor Thurgood. I handcuffed the cryptic case to my left wrist and placed a revolver in my coat pocket. One can never be too careful.

The cold Manhattan wind stiffened my muscles and caused my bones to ache. Wind-driven snow froze in my entire face. Fresh snow disguised the dirty concrete of the city with a lush carpet of white. The police sirens echoed as they bounced around the towering buildings. I could barely hear myself think in the cacophony. It felt like home.

I pondered the inconceivable discovery I had made in Tanzania as I walked along Fifth Avenue. If anyone would know how to solve this dilemma, the professor could. My thoughts were interrupted by a commotion across the street. I looked up to see an enormous hairy humanoid beast holding an old woman by the throat. Her scrawny legs flailed about as she was lifted from the ground. Frightened people scurried away; some remained to watch the spectacle.

"Stop! Put her down," I shouted. The attacker turned and glared at me. His blood-red eyes fixated on the attaché case. He tossed the elderly woman onto the busy street and darted toward me. My fear rose as I inhaled his putrid smell. Suddenly, he stopped. The snow melted as it landed on his hairy head and broad shoulders. I sensed the cold, depraved anger that consumed him.

"Who the hell are you?" I said.

The beast lunged forward. I swung the heavy metal case at him and knocked away his long outstretched arms. I unleashed a series of hard kicks and punches, hitting the evil creature about his thick body. A feeling of alarm filled me to see him unaffected. The beast struck me in the gut, knocking me backward. My skull smacked hard against the pavement.

Searing pain in my arm and left wrist brought me back to consciousness. The beast straddled me with his hideous face inches from mine. I couldn't get free and became angry. Then he spoke to me. "Your language is the same as the Luxorgs, but you are weak." He tore at the flesh of my left wrist, lacerating my skin as he cut the titanium handcuffs with his razor-sharp fingers. In seconds, he'd pulled the attaché case from my wrist and ripped the case open, separating the top from the bottom. The broken case unleashed a bright yellow flame that sent violent blue and orange sparks swirling into the air above me. The beast discarded the pieces of the ruined case into the street. The onlookers who stayed to watch were long gone now. A bus tried to escape the melee by changing lanes and ran over the remains of the attaché case, crushing them to useless bits.

The red-eyed beast howled in delight and beat his chest in triumph. I drew my revolver and fired three times. The thing fell to his knees and then bounced up from the cold concrete, screaming. Streams of yellow blood spewed out of his body. He leaped on top of another passing bus. Helplessly, I looked at those evil eyes disappearing into the thickness of the storm. I lay there in the freezing puddles of bloodied snow and slush, as yet unable to rise. Strange thoughts of confusion and anger crept into my head. I was cold, wet, and alone.

My head hurt, but the blood seeping from my wounded wrist concerned me most. I wrapped my scarf around it to stop the blood. I managed to hail a cab and headed uptown to the professor's townhouse. Upon my arrival, I saw Milo's bright green hair through the hazy glass of the mighty front door. He possessed Ph.D.s in atomic molecular physics and engineering. He unlocked the door's many deadbolts and opened it. His familiar smile quickly disappeared when he noticed the bloodstained scarf around my wrist. He flicked his Marlboro away and helped me inside.

"Ozzy, what the hell happened to you?"

"A hairy beastlike man attacked me. He destroyed the attaché case that I emailed you about last week. If I hadn't shot him, I'd be dead!"

"Since when do you carry a gun?"

"That reminds me." I retrieved the gun from my coat pocket and handed to Milo. "Here, put this in your bag. You know the professor abhors guns and I don't want him to find it on me."

"Yeah, thanks."

Milo placed the revolver in his backpack and escorted me to a small bathroom on the ground floor. We cleaned and bandaged my wounds. He gave me a set of brand-new clothes that possessed the fruity scent of spring. Milo's white T-shirt, black leather vest, and blue jeans reeked of cigarettes.

"You're as good as new!" he announced with a wry smile.

He then led me into what he once referred to as "the tree elevator." Its rounded walls were covered in living tree bark. We slowly descended while Milo lit another Marlboro. "The Doc's been worried about you," he said. "He's acting stranger than usual. He keeps referring to me as *Guardian* and seems like he's expecting something."

"Or someone," I said.

The tree elevator doors slid open and revealed Professor Thurgood. The professor's stringy white hair waved as he moved. His stern and wrinkled face reminded me of those old Uncle Sam posters. Those piercing opal colored eyes fixated on me. His irises lighted up with iridescent red and blue flashes.

Thurgood stood underneath a colossal globe of the earth. It was exquisitely detailed and at least a hundred feet in diameter. Every detail of the earth's surface seemed to be represented.

I felt overjoyed at such beauty. "Wow, look at Mount Everest jutting through the clouds." I took notice how half the globe was in darkness to simulate night and day.

"Look at the devastation of the rain forest in South America," Milo added.

"It sickens me, Mr. Moss," the wealthy old man said. "Let us return to the matter at hand. I was concerned for your safety, Ozzy. It is good to see you."

"It's good to see you, Professor."

"Where is this attaché case?"

"A manlike beast attacked me on the way here and destroyed it."

"So, the time has come," he muttered, his eyes widening. "This is very grave, Ozzy, very grave indeed."

"What's going on, Professor?"

"The creature that attacked you is named Zarr. He is a Luxorg."

"That thing? How do you know this? And how can my name be on an attaché case that was buried in prehistoric Africa?"

"The same reason why Mars is now dead, lad. It's because of the Luxorgs." The professor explained how the Luxorgs came and destroyed every living thing on its surface. They drained the planet of all her natural resources and reduced the red rock to a wasteland.

Thurgood's eyes teared and his face winced in pain as he spoke of the Luxorgs. "They are vile creatures from beyond our galaxy," he said. "The Luxorgs claim a planet only to decimate all life on it for sport. Now they want the lives on earth, and Zarr is their leader."

"This is the same thing that attacked Ozzy?" said Milo.

"He is a cruel and single-minded creature, unyielding in his mission to destroy the human race. Once he is dead, all other Luxorgs will retreat from our solar system."

"How do you know all this?" I said, grimacing from the pain in my wrist.

"Let me see your wound," he said, ignoring my question. The professor gently took my hand into both of his and cradled it. I felt a weird tingling sensation that seemed to pass from his tender grip to my skin, the muscles in my hands, and then my very bones. Power surged through my entire body. I stared at my hand, disbelieving. The bandages had fallen away and the painful and bleeding gashes they once covered were reduced to tender pink scars.

"Thanks," I said, dumbfounded. That sounded flat to my ears, but I couldn't conjure the words to express my amazement and gratitude at what he'd just done.

"Don't thank me," he said. "I am the being who will crush your most cherished beliefs into dust."

I heard Milo cough as he extinguished his cigarette.

"Prepare yourselves, for what I am to tell you is the brutal truth," the professor said. He placed his old hands on my shoulders. "I tried to tell you during your trip to Africa, but you weren't ready to hear it. The earth is alive, like you and me. She is our mother and created all life on our world. I'm sad to say our mother is slowly dying at Zarr's hands. Bless her soul."

"Earth has a soul?" It was a concept I'd never considered.

"Indeed, a worn and tattered one."

"These Luxorgs don't seem so likeable, Doc," Milo said.

"They are wicked parasites."

"So, what did Zarr do to the earth?" I wasn't sure I was ready for the answer, but I couldn't help but ask.

"Lads, this may be hard for you to accept." The professor sighed as if the weight of worlds rested on his shoulders. "Two million years ago, Zarr invaded the mother. Our earth burned and shook that day and much life was lost. However, many species survived, including the hominids, which could be a threat to him and the other Luxorgs."

"How did this Zarr respond to the hominid threat?" Milo said.

"Zarr savagely raped thousands of the young hominid females just for fun. He injected your distant ancestors with his perverse genes. Zarr altered their DNA, eventually polluting the entire gene pool." Thurgood paused. I could see by his scowl, he was disappointed in the look of disbelief projecting from Milo's face.

I tried to be more receptive to the news, although the tale seemed like something right out of a B-grade sci-fi flick.

"So what happened to them?" I asked.

"The Earth Mother molded and evolved them into vicious and intelligent creatures."

"What kind of creatures?"

"Human beings."

"Get the hell out of here, Doc," Milo said. It was clear he didn't buy the story.

"I'm afraid Zarr is the father of all humanity."

I somehow knew he spoke the truth.

Milo lit another Marlboro and looked up at the giant globe. "Ozzy, do you believe him?" He turned and gazed at Thurgood. "Doc, I think you need to either take some really good drugs or quit the shit you're on!" He took a deep drag on his cigarette. Its fiery head burned as bright as Thurgood's flickering opal eyes.

"You doubt me, Mr. Moss? I am a son of Mother Earth. I assumed this form ages ago—I am eternal. I am immortal!"

"Yeah, right," replied Milo.

Thurgood pulled out a sharp, shiny knife from underneath his coat in freakish slow motion.

"Wait a minute, Doc, there's no need for violence," warned Ozzy.

The professor brought the blade up to his face. He smiled as he sliced a gaping hole across his throat. We stood there, spellbound. A jet of hot blood spurted outward toward us. Milo shrieked and his blood-speckled Marlboro fell from his mouth. It hit the white marble floor the same instant Thurgood did. And our reality seemed to close in around us, drawing our world tight.

I will never forget the sight of the deep, rich blood exploring the bright white marble floor. But suddenly the expanding puddle stopped and then retracted into Thurgood's pale, immobile body. The great wound closed up and disappeared. Thurgood's eyelids blinked, and then he opened them wide. He looked at Milo as I cautiously helped him to his feet. It took the old man a moment to speak.

"I'm disappointed in you, Mr. Moss."

"He's as good as new!" Milo proclaimed.

"We believe you," I said, hoping to reassure him.

"All humanity is doomed if Zarr isn't destroyed, Mr. Crevaliz." Thurgood closed his worn eyes. "The Earth Mother has felt Zarr in Central Park. Find him. You must be careful whenever you're outside. He sends the storms of rain and snow. They are his eyes, his ears. Do not speak of him. Keep your teeth together!"

The specter of uncertainty haunted my mind. Confusion filled my thoughts. I felt like one of those characters in a Stephen King novel, suddenly caught up in something you can't understand and waiting for the monster to come after you.

Central Park at night can be a deadly place. By eleven thirty, the air had turned much colder than earlier in the day. The snow had gotten deeper as fear spread inside me. Milo followed tentatively a step be-hind. We had been searching for an hour when we came upon a hill near the pond just north of the zoo.

Milo stopped. "There's something down there," he said.

I pointed my flashlight onto a dense group of bushes and trees. As I panned my flashlight slowly, the small red reflection of Zarr's eyes stared back at us.

"That's him!" Milo gasped. He took a drag from his cigarette and threw it into the snow.

We slowly walked down the hill into the darkness of the dense thicket. Soon the path came to a fork. I took the left path. Milo treaded along the other. Quietly, I searched alone. The frozen bushes and trees stood tall in the cold night, collecting snow. They seemed to surround me. I became more anxious with each deep footprint in the deep snow. I heard a crackle of electricity and saw bright blue flash of light through the thicket of branches. Moments later, I heard Milo yell for me. I could hear his footsteps crunching the fresh snow and I ran toward him.

"Milo, where are you?" I yelled.

I saw him running toward me. Somehow, he had an undamaged, pristine attaché case in his hands.

"Run, Ozzy, he's coming!"

I didn't see Zarr, but I ran anyway.

Milo was a step behind me. "Take it," he wheezed as he handed me the attaché case. "I can't run anymore. Head toward Fifth Avenue. I'll meet up with you later." His eyes told me otherwise.

"I won't leave you," I said. I slung him over my shoulder in a fire-man's carry. "Take my gun!" I tried to run for my life, though in truth I couldn't manage more than a clumsy lumbering. Milo started shoot-ing. The shots rang in my head. I stumbled toward the orange glow of the street, not stopping until we reached a subway station.

Milo climbed off of me and together we scurried down the icy steps. I fell once, my buttocks bumping down part of the way. There'd be bruising there tomorrow, I had no doubt. If I had a tomorrow.

We caught the uptown 4 train, dashing off into the labyrinth of tunnels cut out of old bedrock and Manhattan schist. Milo looked different. His hair had changed to a chestnut brown and it was shorter, his body language now displayed purpose not fear, and he looked older.

"Thanks for not leaving back there," he said.

"Hey, I wouldn't leave you to die. Friendship is forever." I glanced at our booty. This inconspicuous attaché case in a crowded train in the middle of the night had caused us so much trouble. "I saw Zarr destroy this case. How can this be?"

"Dude, we've been enlightened to the age-old questions of the creation and the purpose of humanity. Let's get back to Doc's house. He'll know the answer."

I looked at him and smiled. He was a weird one, my friend. "You always seem to clear the fog from my thoughts."

When we departed the train at the 86th Street station, we could hear the angry howl of the wind. We proceeded through the freezing subway station with caution, and then climbed a multitude of urine-stained steps until Milo suddenly cried out, "Oh shit, it's a blizzard!"

I saw the thick waves of anger-driven snow sticking to all it touched. Zarr still searched for us. We turned around and hurried back down the steps.

"Go find something to cover the case," I said.

Milo searched the littered station. He returned with a black plastic trash bag.

"Perfect," I said, hoping it really was. We covered it the best we could and ascended the stairs once again. "Cover up and remember, teeth together!" I wondered what dilemma would happen next.

Shivering and silent, we slogged against the relentless storm. Every step we pushed forward tested our wills. My face felt frozen, and there was ice in my eyelashes.

We arrived at Professor Thurgood's house. He met us in the foyer, and before we could say anything he spoke with urgency. "I was worried, lads. Zarr searches for the attaché case as we breathe. Our time here is fleeting." Quietly, we followed him down to the giant globe room.

"Professor," I said, "how can this attaché case be undamaged, and why is it important to Zarr?"

"Your attaché case is a time device. It will allow you to cut through the fabric of spacetime."

"How does it work?" I ran my hand over it, the memory of seeing it ripped apart and crushed still fresh in my head.

Milo answered me in a firm and friendly tone. "It works by bending spacetime. Given a certain configuration of matter, the actual spacetime fabric of the universe can be altered and a time bubble is created."

"You will be able to travel anywhere, to any time," Thurgood said.

I was beyond disbelief and had no more energy for doubt. I accepted them both at their word, yet I paused to think for a moment, considering an idea.

"Professor, I could go back and stop Zarr."

"You could do much more, lad."

"Wait a second. This creates a time paradox. If we destroy Zarr, won't we erase our own existence?"

Professor Thurgood raised his voice. "You have been betrayed by your ignorance, Mr. Crevaliz. Such ends are not yet written."

I began to understand and raised the attaché case. "I want to open it. Does the finger print scanner unlock the case?"

"Good powers of deduction," Thurgood responded.

I placed the source of my determination onto a small table carved from solid granite, feeling like I was opening gifts on Christmas morning. I placed the middle finger of my right hand on the scanner. The magnetic lock disengaged and the case sprang open.

"Wow! Look at all of that sweet technology!" Milo laughed with glee. "Whoever created this is a genius." He gazed at the friendly green and blue buttons beside a hand-shaped sensor. The display screen remained dark and silent. Milo fiddled with some buttons and a small panel opened. Thin curved metal rods popped out and unfolded into a working gyroscope. The entire case began to hum.

Anxiously, I joined him at the control panel and placed my left hand in the aptly shaped sensor. Red and green lights flickered to life. The display screen came alive with an array of split prism colors. Today's date lit up on a panel. To my delight, a friendly female voice spoke to me.

"Hello, Mr. Crevaliz. What destination, please?"

I knew it was silly, but I liked the fact that the phrase rhymed. Suddenly, we heard a loud crash from high above. Professor Thurgood jumped up and sniffed the air. He grabbed us both.

"Zarr is here, lads. We must leave."

A long, painful, angry howl echoed throughout the vastness of the domed room.

"Where are we going?" I said. Were we really going to travel through time?

Thurgood glanced at me with urgency. "We must go to where this all started."

I understood what he meant, but had no idea how this was going to happen.

"Hello, Mr. Crevaliz. What destination, please?"

"Northern Tanzania," Milo said. "Two million years ago!" He flashed a confident smile.

"Destination confirmed," the device replied. Zarr's incessant howl grew louder.

"Wait," the professor said. "I cannot leave Zarr to run amok in my home. We must find him."

Each of us scanned different areas of the room, looking for Zarr.

"Do you see where he is?" Milo asked.

"There!" Thurgood said, pointing aloft. "He's placing some type of device onto the main cables that hold up the globe. I fear it may be some type of explosive device."

Zarr leapt from atop the enormous globe and crushed a chunk of the marble floor where he landed. He stood underneath the enormous globe urging us for a fight.

"Milo, hand me my gun." I asked. He reached into his bag and complied. Thurgood flashed me a look of stern derision. "I have an idea," I added.

I dashed into the tree elevator and ascended to the top floor of the domed room. When the doors slid open, I rushed down a catwalk to the edge of a platform overlooking the room. My eyes found what I was looking for. I aimed my revolver at the bolts that anchored a thick, compressed cable attached to the faux world. I emptied the gun of its deadly fruit, but amid the sparks and smoke, I soon realized this to be a fruitless effort.

I strained my eyes and saw the bomb. To my horror it had a timer. "Holy shit!" I ran back to the tree elevator and joined my friends in the standoff below.

"Zarr knew the human would lead me here, old fool," the beast said.

"Foolish wretch," Thurgood replied loudly. "It is I who has led you here!" From his hands, Thurgood shot beams of amber light at Zarr. Again and again he shot the beams into his nemesis. Zarr became smothered in a sticky sap, which held him at bay, trapping him underneath the giant hanging globe.

"Zarr shall cut you open and bathe in your blood."

"Professor, we have thirty seconds left. We need to kill Zarr and leave."

"No, we must destroy the Zarr from two million years ago," Thurgood said. "Come with me. The time device is set." He locked eyes with me. "Leave the gun here."

I complied with his wish and took position in front of the time device, placing my hand in the hand sensor. The warm voice echoed in the vast room.

"Destination confirmed."

I became scared—the bomb would explode any second. "How I do I make it work?"

"Ozzy, I think you just need to tell it to proceed," Milo replied.

"Do it," I said.

The spinning gyroscope created a growing field of energy. A crackle of blue and red lightning surrounded us. We were soon enveloped in a whirling ball of colored light within a time bubble.

We heard the bomb explode and saw a flash of light. The bomb destroyed everything Thurgood had built. We were unaffected, however, and I now sensed the lonely silence of the universe as we rode the lightning into the past. When the lightning dissipated, I felt a chill from the clean, crisp wind of Tanzania. The three of us stood in a boggy marsh. I gave the time device to Thurgood to hold and clambered onto dry land.

I felt safe for now. I shouldn't have.

"We must find him," Thurgood said as he joined me.

My eyes scanned the grassy landscape and a nearby lake. A stand of trees blocked the horizon to our right. We searched the area, using the tall grass to keep ourselves out of sight.

"This is definitely the place and time. Look there," Thurgood said, pointing to the other side of the lake.

My attention quickly focused on three screaming hominid males of the type that scientists would later call Australopithecus. I was both terrified and fascinated at making this discovery. We made our way around the lake to get a closer look.

Each hominid was covered in a layer of bristly hair and had an apelike face. Underneath the large, extended brow sat two forward-facing, very human-looking eyes. The hominids were running toward the lake and carrying wooden spears. Suddenly they stopped and raised their spears in defense. Zarr stood at the shoreline. They let out a series of grunts and intimidation calls to deter their foe. They threw their spears, but the beast easily swatted the primitive projectiles away. The hominids retreated, yelling in fear. Zarr bolted from the water's edge and grabbed one of them.

Without effort, Zarr ripped off the creature's head and tossed it away like one of Milo's finished Marlboros. The other terrified hominids scattered and Zarr chased them into the trees and out of our sight.

"This way. Follow me," I said.

"We must kill him before he finds the females," Thurgood yelled.

We trudged through the thick muddy landscape toward the trees. Puddles of blood lay on the ground. I knew we were getting closer and soon heard terrible screams.

"What's that?" I said and ran to a clearing. I saw him. His eyes were on fire as he beat and kicked a small female. "Give me that knife of yours, Professor." He handed it over without trepidation. "Milo," I added, "let's finish this."

"Aye, Captain," he replied, giving me a firm salute and his wry smile. I still couldn't understand why his hair was brown instead of green.

We ran toward the violent rape in progress. The female's cries of agony made me sick.

Zarr turned his huge body. I could see those red eyes peering from underneath his large brow. He stood up and the terrified female scurried away.

"Who are you?" asked Zarr.

"The man resolved to kill you."

Zarr lunged at me and flung his strong, bloodstained, powerful hands outward. Just then, Milo grabbed my shoulder and jumped in front of me. The impact of Zarr's attack knocked him to the ground. Milo's feet and hands violently flailed about as Zarr lifted him off the ground. Zarr stared at him intently as he dug his razor-sharp fingers into my friend's slender frame. Milo screamed as he writhed against Zarr's claws, his steaming blood spewing out onto the ground.

"Does it burn, boy?" asked Zarr.

Anger filled every cell within me. An adrenalin-fueled rage over-took me.

I screamed some angry words that even I couldn't decipher. I bolted toward Zarr, swinging the sharp knife with broad vicious strokes. I slashed him and he took a step backwards. I stabbed him good and deep in the gut. Zarr's hot slimy yellow blood spilled onto the ground. He shrieked and swung his arms, throwing Milo to the ground.

"You cannot defeat Zarr."

"I can destroy you, pig!" declared Thurgood. "Step aside, lad, I will finish him. I have tirelessly waited for this moment for two million years!"

He shot an amber lightning bolt into Zarr. This wasn't the same beam of light as in New York. This was deadly lightning that burned the beast from within. Zarr screamed in torment. Smoke rose from his body as he convulsed in agony. He collapsed face first into the water and died.

The earth shook. Thunder rumbled beneath clear skies. I fell to my knees and wondered if the earth was dying. But when the earthquake had subsided, I collected my bearings and looked for my friends. The professor cradled Milo's broken body in his wrinkled hands.

"Professor, how is he?"

Thurgood looked at me sadly. "I'm afraid he is gone, lad."

"Can't you revive him?"

"I cannot bring back the dead."

"No. It can't be true!" I cried out and sank to ground in anguish. "He gave his life for mine!"

"For everyone, lad."

Utter sadness overcame me. I sat there while Thurgood created a grave by using sacred hand motions of the sort I dare not mention. The soil moved at his will. It piled up next to the solemn hole. .

"Just before Milo died," the professor said as he worked, "he want-ed me to impart a few words of wisdom: *Friendship is forever.*"

Thurgood's words didn't ease my pain. My salty tears fell hard and fast.

"You need to activate the time device, but don't give the command to engage just yet," he said.

I opened the case.

"Hello, Mr. Crevaliz," it said. "What destination, please?"

Thurgood closed the lid and placed the attaché case at the bottom of the deep grave and covered it with mud. I could still hear the voice of the time device in my head. We now shared a telepathic link. Thurgood then rolled Milo's body into the grave. We covered him with mud and dirt and I said a quick prayer to honor our fallen comrade.

"Why did you bury my attaché case with Milo?"

"He will guard the time device until you unearth it two million years from now. We knew it was vital to hide it from Zarr and any other Luxorg who wished to destroy it."

"Who are 'we'?" I asked.

"Myself and Mr. Moss, of course."

"Milo—Milo was aware of all this beforehand?"

"No, no, lad."

"What do mean?"

"Milo will develop the time device in 2029. He will travel back to 2017, when you two separated in Central Park, and inform his younger self about our plan. He will then replace his younger counterpart and give you the time device."

"I'm very confused, Professor."

"The fog will clear soon after we reach home."

"Hello, Mr. Crevaliz. What destination, please?"

"Thurgood's home," I said. "January 8, 2017."

"Destination confirmed," it replied.

"Do it!"

The blue light of eternity surrounded us once again. A moment later we were back in 2017. The blizzard had vanished. The skies were clear. The Earth Mother beamed with happiness again.

The mighty globe hovered above us once more. It seemed to be alive. Its rainbow of brilliant colors was beautiful. Every mountain peak glistened with majesty. Every ocean, lake, and river exuded joy. Every speck of foliage seemed to sing.

"It's as good as new," a familiar voice said. The younger version of Milo smiled at me.

I looked at him with sublime joy and hugged him. His bright green hair reeked of cigarettes.

"You're alive!"

"Of course. My older self made sure of it."

"I thought I'd never see you again."

"Friendship is forever," he said, and his grin was like a beacon of light.

Paul grew up on Staten Island, New York, and currently resides in sunny Tampa, Florida, with his wife and two daughters. His work has appeared in *The Dark Side of the Moon: A Song Stories Anthology*, *These Vampires Still Don't Sparkle*, and *Happy Little Horrors: Alienated*. He can be reached at facebook.com/pmdujat/

She Had a Lot of Problems

by

Christopher Fox

THE POSTCARDS FROM AFRICA WERE supposed to be exotic. Lions, meerkats, ostriches. Look at all the fun she was missing. Leopold made sure to deface the pictures with hurtful sentiments—laughing hyenas taking down a wildebeest, *You* scrawled at the top with an arrow pointing to the dying animal. *Thanks for nothing, dumbass*, said an aardvark.

Leopold, the geologist obsessed with sand.

Last winter, he accepted a job in Botswana and Mona was expected to tag along, no questions asked. Of course she would, right? Not much of an adventuress, she wanted to stay in Asheville where there was no sand. Africa was too hot, too dry, too strange. Leopold's dismay was almost comical in its spluttering shock, as if he'd just realized that Mona was constructed out of tightly bound batches of stones rather than the soft, fertile loess he'd previously supposed.

An elephant with *your ass here* scrawled across its backside. Brown stink lines squirmed above the letters.

When the bugs showed up, Mona was drunk. She staggered over to the window to gaze out at the gray clouds and feel poignant but what she saw through the panes brought relief instead. She smiled for the first time in weeks. Butterflies! Thousands upon millions of them following their invisible, willy-nilly pathways like tossed confetti. Large ones, too. They were the size of sparrows and richly mottled with orange and rusty-purple splotches. Bruised butterflies. Mona identified with them on a fundamental level. Leopold had beaten up her heart.

Life had been hard since they'd split the sheets. Mona quit going into work, lost her job. Now her only income came from placing want ads in the newspaper and selling off her furniture piece by piece. She had diseased feet. A virulent fungal infection spread under the arches and between the toes like moss. Not to mention wrecking the car, bouncing checks, gaining weight.

But suddenly, here was her consolation prize, a reason to stop sluffing around the house in tears, festooned with martyrdom and unsightly folds of blubber. She stared at the butterflies in delighted disbelief. Never had she seen so many at one time. Where had they come from? It was a once-in-a-lifetime event, magical and wondrous as if creatures from the land of faerie had emerged from beneath the depths of the hallow. Everyone liked butterflies. They signified rebirth, were metaphors for the soul.

Mona ran downstairs and all but kicked the door to get it open. Months of being cooped up with stir-crazy delusions and relentless charley horses had made her desperate, irritable. She needed a break. She needed potassium.

The fluttering of so many large wings sounded like a sustained sigh of contentment. Butterflies probably made whooshy noises all the time, only Mona had been too preoccupied living her life, dwelling on past hurts, being an ordinary person, to notice. Not in on the secret. Yet another nameless drone who didn't bother to pay attention to the big, beautiful world. The butterflies' destination was unimportant. Far more interesting was how they flaunted their determination to get there. Each individual flapped and flew and had a reason to exist, a motive for being here and going there. Otherwise, they wouldn't be here. They'd be somewhere else. Or dead.

I used to be like that, Mona thought. *Places to go, people to see, things to do.*

Gusts of displaced air teased her greasy hair, waggling it like the snakelets on Medusa's hideous skull. Ten revolting toes stung with a fungal itch. Dried ham glaze, eaten straight from the jar with an unwashed tablespoon, encrusted her muumuu. She hadn't felt this alive in ages. To celebrate, she sang a ditty, danced a jig. Painful burdens lifted from her shoulders, which were dappled with moles.

Across the street, a gang of children ran around catching butterflies in old mayonnaise jars. To kill them. The brats embodied everything that was wrong with America. They oinked at Mona and made fun of her for being a frump.

"She's got no makeup on," said Cammy Franklin, who was only six. "She'll never find a husband."

Mona didn't want a husband. Not since Leopold exited her life like a sudden soda pop belch. When had little girls become so cynical? And how galling to be judged by a child who picked her nose and gobbled up the boogers she found.

Mona kept a terra-cotta planter next to the front door. The fern in it was dead from neglect. She hurled the planter at the children. It hit the ground and exploded several feet short of the target. Exposed roots poked out of the dry soil like shriveled penises.

"Ha ha, you missed!"

The children laughed even harder when Mona rushed back into the house like a lumbering rhinoceros from one of Leopold's vindictive postcards. She slammed the door hard enough to rattle the walls and make the house say *Screw you!* She trundled upstairs and dove headfirst into bed.

The children were right. Mona was too fat. The bed collapsed from the strain and landed on the floor with a crash. The headboard tipped over, knocked her stupid.

Mona went on a crying jag, moistening the pillows with meepy tears. She chugged cheap vodka from the bottle on the nightstand. Then she blacked out.

Only to awaken in a puddle of vomit.

Mona groaned. Puke was caked across her lips like bad cheese. She'd hit a new low, wallowing in filth. One thing was certain. She couldn't go on like this much longer. Friends and family members had quit feeling sorry for her months ago, because nobody likes a whiner. The day was fast approaching when she'd be too emotionally exhausted to feel sorry for herself either. Then she'd have nothing. Time to wake up and smell the coffee. If the butterflies had a reason for being alive, then by God so did Mona. She refused to be a victim for another moment.

Getting out of bed was a struggle—she had the twirlies—but down in the basement it was cool and damp. Musty dimness soothed her bloodshot eyes. The shotgun and ammo were stored in an old wheelie cooler. Mona was going to shoot the children. Not kill them, just hurt them real bad.

Step one: Wreck up the place; use eyeliner to write spooky poems on the wall; take a dump on the rug; scratch her face with toothpicks.

Step two: Mow the kids down.

Step three (for when the police arrived): Sway to a mysterious, inner groove and keen like the madwoman she was, completely out of it, an emotional catastrophe. Everyone knew she had inner demons and battled depression. A battle she had sadly lost. Not guilty by reason of insanity.

Postscript: As the children recovered from their injuries, grew up, got married and raised families of their own, taunt them with anonymous poison pen letters. Her life hadn't panned out. Why should theirs?

She clambered back upstairs and peeked out the window sniper-style.

Too late. The children were already dead. Four ravaged skeletons sprawled across the sidewalk like the remains of a fried-chicken dinner. Butterflies feasted upon the scraps. Their pulsing wings bulged with fresh infusions of protein.

Mona screamed and dropped the gun. It shot a hole in the wall.

Dammit!

Not only were the butterflies going around eating people, but Mona had lost her chance to revenge herself upon the children. It was so unfair. Nothing ever worked out for her. Now what was she going to do?

Calling the police was a bust because the phone lines were down. Her cell phone was useless—disconnected due to nonpayment of funds. Television and going online weren't options either, because she no longer owned any electronics. Sold them for a song. And the car sat in a weed-choked lot next to Billy's Garage, waiting for her to scrape together enough money to have it fixed.

Radio was her only link to the outside world. The one frequency still broadcasting was the college station where the deejay went by the name Dick Whiplash. He raved about dead coeds, dead professors, general pandemonium, nothing Mona hadn't figured out already. In between hysterical outbursts, he lectured about how vinyl records sounded better than any form of digital media, and played punk rock and harsh industrial bands. Mona hated the music, but what could she do about it? She had to stay tuned in case Dick had something important to say, what to do, where to go. Why didn't he put on a few decent tunes by someone like Hank Williams or Patsy Cline? Poor Patsy! She'd flown into a mountain. Mona could relate, only instead of getting it all over in one fell swoop, her plane crashed in stages, losing a wing here and a landing gear there, and then the cabin depressurized. At least Patsy got to be famous and sing beautiful songs before she cashed out.

Every few minutes, Mona peeked out the window and watched the flood of killer butterflies flow down the street. She wondered if any animals in Botswana were running amok. It was a real gas to think of Leopold being terrorized by swarms of furious termites or being gored by a water buffalo. *Tee hee, ha ha.*

Dick was playing a song by some freaks named the Snot Hurlers when he suddenly cut in screaming, "They're getting inside! We're all gonna die! Black Flag rules!"

After that, dead airwaves.

Mona wigged out. If the butterflies could breach a radio station with soundproof walls, what was going to prevent them from invading a forty-year-old tract home? It used to be kind of nice but was now more than a little run down. Just because she had nothing to live for didn't mean she wanted to die.

She raided her hope chest. *Although in my case it's more of a no-hope chest.* Mona gagged on tears. Why did she get such a perverse thrill from hurting her own feelings? Proof she was messed up.

She forced linens with a high thread count down the bathtub drain. She crawled underneath the sinks to cram hand towels into the U-bend and then wrenched the pipes back together. Her bad knees cracked with every move, making her wince in agony. She shut the drapes and tacked antique tablecloths across the windows. At least they hid the dead flies in the sills. She sealed the mail slot with duct tape and stuffed Beanie Babies into the cracks under the doors. At no time did she utilize any of the linens she used on a regular basis. They were filthy dirty and she worried that this might attract the butterflies. By the time she finished, she was drenched with sweat. Her muumuu clung to her like cellophane. The swish it made when she moved sounded like butterfly wings, so she took it off. Also, there was barf on it.

She wondered about her family. Even though she loved them, they were probably dead. Dad, probably from running outside with a handgun, blasting butterflies from the sky. Mom likely from codependency, following fast behind him with rollers in her hair, wagging a finger at him, nag, nag, nag. And Rhett, the lazy mooch, thirty-two and still living at home rent-free. Mom cooked his meals, did his laundry and cleaned his room while Dad paid the bill whenever the Firebird broke down. True, Rhett did have a job, tending bar at Smiley's, but that was so he could pick up cheap floozies with names like Starla and Dee Dee. Nothing the spoiled, golden wonder boy ever did was wrong. But Mona was labeled the *difficult* one. The problem child.

A door slammed. Mona peeked out the window and saw her elderly neighbors making a break for it, John and Gwen Mortensen. Unlike with the children, Mona didn't want anything bad to happen to them. Gwen had knitted snoods out of brown yarn for Mona, nice ones that caught flyaways on days when she didn't feel like doing her hair, and John always had a kind word, was confident that it would be easy for someone as "smart and lovely" as Mona to find another man. Out of gratitude, Mona baked batches of fresh snickerdoodles for them. There was no way to tell if they ate any or not. They were wonderful people.

John bolted for the car while Gwen fumbled with the house keys, wanting to lock the door so no burglars could get in while they were away. Both flitzed pepper spray at the butterflies. They doused their bodies as if applying perfume. While not stopping the attack, it did keep the butterflies away for short stretches of time. Individuals taking a heavy dose dropped to the earth and flopped around.

The Mortensens would take her with them, Mona was sure of it. They were her friends, perhaps the only two left who felt bad about how things had worked out for her and weren't of the opinion that she was somehow to blame. Mona doubted that she could make it to the car without being savaged but she had to try. If only she weren't in such bad shape. There was no point in blaming Leopold, depression, or a glandular problem. She was fat because she had chosen to gorge with wild abandon. No one forced her to overeat.

Mona flung the door open and ran. Being a large woman, she couldn't go very fast. More of a lumbering canter. Stained bra, ripped panties, unshaven legs and armpits, hair on her head a positive fright—she looked like the Yeti.

"Wait for me! I'm coming with you!" There was no shame in admitting that she needed help and couldn't survive on her own. Not today. Maybe tomorrow when everything returned to normal. Then she would be okay. She would get her life together and emerge triumphant. Leopold could go shit in a hat.

Butterflies honed in on her with the narrow-minded deliberation of raptor birds. Mona noticed with disgusted dismay how they had changed, as if their grisly diet of human flesh and offal triggered some kind of rapid evolutionary jump. On the wings, the dark, violet hues throbbed against the duller orange sections, refusing to touch as if miscegenation was repellent to both. Their mouths lacked a proboscis. Specialized palps curved into wicked, mandible-like pincers gouged chunks out of Mona's flab. She swatted at them furiously, squealing in pain.

Their bodies were segmented into a bulbous sequence of rounded sectors reminiscent of the head, abdomen, and thorax of typical insects, but not quite the same—they appeared to be more closely related to annelids or slugs, an unholy hybrid. Surviving them was going to be quite a challenge. But wasn't everything about life a challenge? When Mona thought about it, today was no different than any other day. It's just that the danger was more apparent than normal. Hopefully, this realization hadn't come too late. All she wanted out of life was to be happy.

There was a sudden stabbing and burning at her belly. Mona looked down. The butterflies were carving into her abdomen in an organized group! She crushed two handfuls of them against her rolls of fat, their greenish-yellow blood squishing between her thick fingers. Their blood smelled sweet and feculent like honey-suckle on top of feces. She licked her thumb, and shuddered. The goo tasted like three-month-old rotten chicken and was horribly bitter. Eating them would not be a survival strategy.

John must not have seen Mona or known she was on the way. He gunned the motor to encourage Gwen to hurry up, stop dawdling, but in his alarm he must have placed the gearshift in reverse. The car peeled out and ran Gwen down. Mona cringed. It sounded like a card table collapsing at a bridge party. Now John was parked on top of her. The old fool. There was no reason for an elderly man with ague and cataracts to still be driving.

Mona couldn't help but burst into tears. If only she had gently broached the subject months ago, offered to give him rides around town so he could run errands safely. But she hadn't wanted to upset him, knowing from past experience with elderly members of her own family that giving up the car was a traumatic decision. Aunt Milly claimed that the only thing worse that had ever happened to her was being widowed. Mona shook her fist at John and called him a moron. Sometimes old people drove her nuts.

John floored it and finished running over his wife. He was probably in a flustered tizzy, not thinking clearly, and very much like any older driver whose keys should have been taken away long ago, he left her there and sped down the street backwards. The car vanished around a curve. Then the sound of a loud crash. All that was missing was a lone hubcap making a return appearance as it rolled down the street.

"Help me," Gwen croaked before several butterflies slithered between her lips and into her mouth to devour her from the inside out. She was a pile of tattered rags.

Mona spun in indecisive circles. She wanted to save her friends but didn't think it was going to do any good. John was too far away. She'd be half eaten by the time she got there. And Gwen was fatally banged up and swarming with bugs. She looked like that guy at the state fair who wowed the crowds by wearing a twenty-pound beard of honeybees. Mona didn't think she could carry her to safety.

Butterflies continued to dine upon her own nourishing fat deposits. The pain was unbearable. She was covered all over with their squashed bodies but new ones just kept coming. Blood loss sapped her strength. A terrible realization seared her to the core. Backed into a corner, did she have the ability to make bold, difficult, necessary choices? Absolutely she did. She'd done it before *(No, Leopold. I will not go to Africa with you; I shall get revenge on the children)* and was going to do it again *(If I help my friends, I will die too; I'm going to get my life back on track; nothing will intimidate me again).*

Mona told Gwen, "Sorry. I love you," and then ran for her life. Her kneecaps popped and her lungs sizzled from the unaccustomed strain. She had a gym membership but never went. Letting herself go like this was inexcusable.

Once back at her house, she tottled inside and slammed the door. Butterflies clung to her body, chewing holes in it. They flew around her head looking for a place to land, like pesky mosquitoes. Mona stopped, dropped, and rolled. That killed twenty-one of the damn things outright. They popped like squeezed grapes, gooey splats of bug juice that stank of corruption. She chased the rest around the house with a fly swatter. Killing them was hard work but enjoyable. She gave them names—Leopold (*whap!*), Heidi (*bam!*), Sutton (*pow!*), Florence (*whammo!*)—people who'd hurt Mona's feelings at some point in the past.

Pfffft went Joel, who'd laughed at Mona when she fell down playing kickball at vacation Bible school in 1982. And as for Chris, whose butt crack showed whenever he sat down but had the audacity to tell Mona that she looked bad in shorts, she yelled the loud *WONK!* used on game shows to let the contestant know they'd given the wrong answer and lost any chance of winning a new car.

The final butterfly glared at Mona from the dining room chandelier. She knew exactly who it was. That boy in the dune buggy. She'd been staring at him, admiring his chest, when he flipped her off, the arrogant jackass. To fool the creature, Mona lay down on the floor and pretended to fall asleep. *Zzzzzzz.* Moments ticked past. Woozy from blood loss, she worried about losing consciousness for real. She yawned.

Fuzzy legs tickled her stomach. It felt like a wooly-booly caterpillar crawling across her bare skin, leaving a trail of livid rashes. Mona repressed the instinct to bat it away, an atavistic memory from the prehistoric past when insects were apex predators and devoured human invertebrate ancestors with chittering relish. The plan was to pounce when the creature was distracted, its guard down. There wasn't long to wait. The butterfly bit into a chunk of belly flesh.

"A-ha!" she roared, eyes snapping open. She snatched at the butterfly with piano-key fingers. "Gotcha!"

Mona stomped into the kitchen. The creature was desperate to escape, wings flapping like tentacles.

"I am so sick and tired of you," she hissed. "I'll fix your wagon."

She placed the monstrosity in between her infected toes so she could root around in the junk drawer for some twine. It made no attempt to bite her foot. Mona felt bad about herself. Toes so diseased even long-leggity beasties refused to touch them.

There was more than enough string to tie its legs together. Once the knot was secure, she let it go, swinging it around and around in the air like a whirlybird as she hurried down the hallway to the bathroom, where she doused it with hairspray. Back in the kitchen, she turned on the gas and lowered her enemy to the tips of the bluish flames until it smoldered, pulling it back up only at the last moment. She tortured the butterfly like this for twelve minutes. Then it burst into flames.

"Well, that was fun," she said, brushing the ashes onto the floor.

She went back to her peeking vigil. Where was everybody? The police, a SWAT team, some jerk in a Pinto. Anyone? She doubted that she was the only survivor. They were butterflies for God's sake, not an alien invasion or Godzilla. Just kill the stupid things! Mona felt dumb about being victimized by something as silly as butterflies and found herself sympathizing with characters in killer-doll movies. Up until now, Mona would have hollered at the screen, "Kick it, you moron! Kick the damn thing across the room! It's a freaking toy!" But when something like that happened to you. . . . It seemed that she was as helpless as any scream queen. And her toes! Dead skin flaked off them like peeling paint. Lead-based. If children chewed it, they'd get brain damage. Still, if some dumb-ass kid was stupid enough to go around eating paint, they deserved to wind up a retard.

As Mona's thoughts raced, she lost control of her appetite. Hunger struck her down like a speeding ice cream truck playing a crazed ditty. The refrigerator and pantry were thoroughly grazed. *Old Mother Hubbard with a serious alcohol problem and clinical depression.* All she found was a can of cream of mushroom soup, a forgotten bag of jellybeans, a canister of Italian-style breadcrumbs, and some sour cream, which she mixed together in a dirty bowl. When she spooned it to her mouth, it was kind of like munching on an uncooked casserole while having dessert at the same time. She sipped water from a butter dish because all the glasses were filthy.

Mona suddenly burst into tears. What a hypocrite to look down on brain-damaged kids gorging on paint chips. Look at what she was eating! No wonder she was a heifer. Closing her eyes and not having to look at the food lessened the impact. That was when she choked.

She felt like a complete loser. *Look at the fat chick gagging on a meal.* Of course, labeling herself as a loser indicated that she had something worthwhile to lose in the first place. The only thing Mona had to lose was weight. She recalled one of Leopold's most hurtful postcards: a rock python swallowing an entire gazelle. *Babe, take smaller bites.*

Spiraling blue flickers spun in officious circles—sirens with the sound turned off. *Here we are,* they announced. *There's nothing to worry about. Help has arrived.*

Mona stumbled over to the window. People in biohazard suits with rifles slung over their shoulders surrounded a slow-moving procession of anonymous government trucks. Jets flying overhead released clouds of poison. Butterflies dropped from the sky like daredevils with tangled parachutes. Finally, the Army! They were going to have to give Mona the Heimlich maneuver.

She lobbed open the door and hurried towards the soldiers with outstretched arms, unable to form the words that expressed her gratitude for being saved and the swelling love she felt for her rescuers. The only sound that came out was a garbled retch. *Hheeccchhhh! Hhheeeeccccchhhhh!* She knew she was turning blue.

Four soldiers broke away from the main regiment. Hidden behind hoods and breathing masks, it was impossible for Mona to tell if any of the soldiers were handsome. She made the universal gesture for *I'm choking.*

They aimed their guns at her. They made comments she couldn't quite hear. Mona just knew that they were judging her chubby body covered with dozens of squished butterfly carcasses and their bite marks marring her skin. Maybe even gauging the droop of her boobs. If they didn't help soon, she was going to pass out.

A decision was reached.

"Ready! Aim!"

Mona shook her head furiously. *Millions of people starve to death each year. There's rampant child abuse, global climate change, terrorist attacks, and the government decides to tamper with Mother Nature and develop a mutant strain of superbug? What a bunch of imbeciles.* She'd never been so angry. *I haven't been parasitized! My brain isn't infected with mind-controlling larvae. I'm fucking choking on jellybeans!*

"Fire!"

They shot Mona dead.

"You have five minutes to rejoin the regiment," the leader said before jogging off down the street.

They made fun of Mona's weight as they cut her head off. They wrapped it in tinfoil and placed it into a large metal box with several others, including John Mortensen's. There was going to be a lot of lab work to do, checking for disease and contagion. Then they'd blame it all on foreigners so the fat cats in Washington would have another flimsy reason to invade more non-Christian, non-white countries to rape, pillage, and plunder. For no good reason. For fun.

"Get a load of those feet," the tall soldier said.

The one with the clipboard agreed. "Man, those are fierce."

She was one of the ugliest women they'd ever seen. An absolute pig.

Christopher Fox lives in a small town in the southern Appalachians where he sells vinyl records. Previous work of his has appeared in a variety of markets.

Fire

b.E.L.F.r.y.

by

Dan J. Fiore

WHEN, EXACTLY, THE TOWNSFOLK OF Babel started acting strange, Reed Groom couldn't tell for sure. Ornery just runs in the mountain springs, some say. But, in hindsight, it was probably safe to assume the Confusion hit its stride when his mother's neighbor, frail, shaky Amelia Sever, after fifty-two years of marriage, decided to stab her husband seventeen times with a knitting needle.

Old Marvin Sever bled out on his front patio—the same spot where passing locals always knew they'd find him toking a cigar in his handmade rocking chair. Curious what all the commotion was about, Reed shuffled over to the Sever house and saw the blood-spattered cement. He approached the open kitchen window by way of the side lawn, keeping his metal crutches quiet so he could hear the words spoken inside.

When the sheriff asked Amelia why she did what she'd done to her husband, she said Marvin had once cheated on her with Silvia Stanwick. But, on account of a car crash out along Clay Pike, Ms. Stanwick was dead going on two decades by that point.

He then asked Amelia if perhaps her husband suddenly confessed to this long-past affair, spurring her moment of enraged violence. She pondered the question and then shook her head. "No," she said. "But I know I'm right."

After getting one more good look at the patio, Reed hobbled back to his mother's house and figured the event for just *one of those fucked up things* that sometimes happen in hick towns like Babel.

Reed never did talk much. Townsfolk would see him around quite a bit and, while they all knew him—Reed could tell by their snickering—they knew very little *about* him. Before disappearing forever into the mountains, he lived all his thirty-three years in this tiny Appalachian town. And yet only a handful of locals knew more than the basics. He went to Mount Kindling High, used to drive a beat-up yellow Datsun, grew up out past the cemetery, and he was a roofer—or, rather, he'd *been* a roofer until one false step sent him flailing.

He fell four stories. Landed headfirst on a thick slab of sidewalk. It was a fall that robbed him of his depth perception, clarity of thought, and use of his legs. He would never, the doctor assured him upon waking, walk again. Thirteen bones in all—bruised, broken, or shattered. They even drilled a titanium plate where the back of his skull used to be.

When he finally could, Reed asked the doctor, "Was I out fo' vewy long?" and the slow realization of what he'd said—*how* he'd said it—thickened in his chest like mill smog. "Weed," he said. "Weed … Gwoom. Weed Gwoom! Weed *Gwoom!*" He repeated his name, ignoring Dr. Peters. Echoes of cruel laughter reached from the recesses of his mind. The doctor had to send nurses in to sedate him.

Because, for nearly three decades around Babel, nobody ever called Reed *Reed*—besides maybe his mother. You see, there was a reason for his quiet demeanor, a childhood catalyst to even his adulthood shyness:

Growing up, he couldn't even pronounce his own name.

No matter how hard he tried. No matter how intensely he focused on each syllable, each letter, each careful maneuver of his lips and tongue. Every time until well into his teens, *Weed,* he'd say instead. *Weed Gwoom.*

And so that was the name that stuck with him. Even as an adult, long after his rhotacism had faded.

Until, of course, that fall of his robbed him of his R's again.

And, lying in that hospital bed, as his speech sputtered back to silence, his thoughts wavering and his vision dimming, he first heard it—the whispering. Long before the Confusion, it popped in his head like a thought, but not a thought of his own. Its voice—a woman's voice—was distant, distorted. But calming, too. The muffled words crackled as if played through a buried, broken tube radio.

Dr. Carl Peters is a liar, it said.

And as Reed drifted into the calm pond of narcotic sleep, he distantly realized that the doctor had yet to mention his first name.

But just three months after Reed first heard the whisper, he proved the doctor wrong. Proved him, just as the whisper promised, a liar. Sure, his legs were far from agile. But he managed to work himself free of the wheelchair. Got upgraded, as it were, to the relative mobility of forearm crutches.

Though that affliction of his tongue did persist.

Once he'd gotten his first unsteady steps behind him, the hospital let him return home; home *not* to the two-story he'd been renting along Babel's outskirts, but home to his mother's house in the hills just past the cemetery.

Throughout that long trip back, his mother refused to let nary a silent second pass between them. As she talked, Reed watched out his window, focusing on rolling, rambling hills. Gas drills spiked up across them, like religious relics awaiting worship.

The new wave, Reed thought. Same as all the old—the poultry conglomerates, the crop tinkerers, the coal mine companies, even the government folks a decade back doing their weather studies up in those same mineshafts. In the boom days, Reed's grandfather worked in those mines, as did most Babel men of that time. And ever since, the town saw a long line of outsiders coming in, promising they'd be the ones who would return the struggling backwoods town to prosperity and importance.

Importance, Reed repeated in his head with a single huff of laughter. *How could these small-minded animals believe such . . .*

But his thought trailed off.

In its place, beyond the drone of his mother's gossip and the rattle of her minivan's engine, Reed heard something . . . *unusual.*

A growing murmur.

The nagging, knocking pressure at the back of Reed's head built, mile by mile, to a pounding. A sea of voices spoke at the same time some far ways off, both inside and all around him. They grew stronger the closer he got to his little hometown at the foot of those mountains.

"Here we are," Reed barely heard his mother say. Pulling into the driveway, the strength of the colliding whispers now crowded his brain. "Home sweet home."

Throbs of sharp pain clattered inside his reconstructed skull. He had to hold his head with both hands. Drool dripped from his lips. He shut his eyes and moaned while his mother clawed at his shoulders and asked what was wrong.

"Should I drive back to the hospital?"

She had the van backing down the driveway already when Reed noticed the whispers beginning to converge. Words were forming.

"No, Mom," he said. The pain let up. "Just need out of the caw."

With a worried frown, she slowed the van to a stop. Reed got out. And as he opened his watering eyes to those mountains towering over him again, the whispers overlapped to finally speak as one in that woman's confident yet comforting voice:

Welcome home, Reed.

Not long after Amelia Sever, there was Jacob Nilinski. Nilinski was a respected man in the community. Dependable. Likeable. He was even-tempered and a successful business owner. Known as Big Jake to most everyone, Nilinski lumbered into the First Pennsylvanian Bank on a Tuesday morning with two pistols in his meaty fists, a tactical shotgun slung over his shoulder, and a bag of homemade explosives on his back.

He wasn't there to steal money, he told the four employees at the counter that morning. He'd come so he could move in with his earnings.

"Them damned Koreans," he said, would soon hack the American banking system, wiping out all the coin he'd worked so hard for. All he wanted was to live in the vault with what he'd saved throughout his life. Like a bunker. He wanted to keep an eye on his cash until all of the Korean hackers were wiped out.

Terrence Dolman, the bank's manager, tried to reason with Big Jake. So Big Jake took the butt of his shotgun to Dolman's face until it caved in.

Three days into the ordeal, Big Jake's chapter in the mounting Confusion was brought to an abrupt end by a SWAT sniper's bullet. His last and, according to the bank employees who survived, often-uttered words: "I know I'm right."

Soon enough, the whisper spoke to Reed daily. So often, in fact, he barely paid it much attention. He never told anybody about it—he feared what they might think and say behind his back—but figured at least a few folks spotted him from time to time mumbling angrily to himself.

In the wake of his accident, he made a point to get around town as much as possible. Any chance he had of proving his worth he gladly took. Groceries. Mail. Gas for the lawnmower—which his mother's neighbor opposite the Severs had to run for him.

With the frustrating help of his crutches—left-*clack*-balance, right-*clack*-balance, left-*clack*-balance, right—he could go just about anywhere.

And the whisper always followed.

There were others, he was sure. More than just the one, the woman's lulling, throaty voice that addressed him and him only. A layer of maybe hundreds. A babbling brook, always just over the next hill. They never clarified and came together quite like they had the day he returned home, but as he'd travel eastward toward the mountain side of town the whispers would grow louder, like a brook building to a raging river.

People—many of the same who made his childhood miserable—would see Reed walking, cocking his head with his eyes shut as he tried to listen for words drifting out of that rambling din, and they'd smile. Sometimes they'd even coyly wave. But their mutterings and snuffed giggles as he passed always gave them away.

They're laughing at you, the whisper would tell him.

Children yelled from school buses and bicycles. They heckled and threw things. They'd even mimic Reed's walk.

Doesn't it make you angry, Reed?

It wasn't until a drunken confession from an old employer that Reed found out what the townsfolk now called him:

Wobbly Weed.

A few weeks after Nilinski's death, Reed was out on an errand and decided to stop at the baseball fields behind the junior high school. The

Hawks were playing their cross-town rivals, the Indians. He stood at the fence in left field, reminiscing over the few years he played for the Hawks himself. Back when he was young and healthy.

In the sixth inning, Kenny Kane—cleanup hitter for the Hawks and a beast among his twiggy teammates—cracked a low, humming shot along the third-base line. Reed watched it land in the grass and roll toward him to the fence.

The umpire, a young man likely working for next to nothing if anything at all, called it fair. The stands exploded in argument. Before Kane even rounded second, the parents were filing off the bleachers and approaching home plate. Reed made his way along the fence as the left fielder threw the ball in. At the rain-faded line Reed stopped, squinted.

"That was foul," he muttered.

And the whisper agreed, *You're right, Reed. It was foul.*

But while the Indians' parents yelled at the umpire and the Hawks' parents yelled at the Indians' parents, Reed noticed something off about the infield. Due to a dark, deep mud puddle from yesterday's rain, third base had been shifted a few feet to the right from where it usually was.

The ball *was* fair, Reed realized. The umpire had made the right call. Reed opened his mouth but then shut it again. Nobody would listen to him.

And he would've been too late anyway.

The crowd around home plate had the umpire on the ground. They were pulling off his equipment, pummeling him with their fists and feet. A few of the Hawks came out of the dugout with aluminum bats and sent dull dings across the field with blows to the young man's bones.

Turning to hobble home, afraid the mob might come after him next, Reed heard, just below the young umpire's inhuman squeals, the pops of his joints as the parents pulled his body apart.

Talk of the umpire incident spread fast. Panic seeped into Babel. Doors and windows across town were boarded up from the inside. Gun and ammunition sales at Big Jake's Hunt & Fish Depot—now run by Big Jake's brother—skyrocketed. The schools closed indefinitely.

Within days, the township supervisor called a town hall meeting, and no one realized how bad an idea that was until *after* the municipal building burned to the ground. Across the mountainside, savage fights broke out over the smallest issues, from property line infractions to interpretations of traffic right-of-ways. One night, the electricity—lights, sockets, batteries, *everything* technological—failed and never turned back on.

A small group calling themselves the Babel Peace Unit banded together and patrolled the darkened streets for weeks. On a brisk autumn morning, they pulled Thomas Hampstead from his secluded woodland home and hanged him with an extension cord in his own front yard. Why they blamed Thomas—a kind, unmarried, middle-aged man who never bothered anyone—for all the insanity, nobody knew.

But the insanity continued, well after all but one member of the Babel Peace Unit murdered each other along Main Street.

A few days after winter's first snowfall, the governor sent in the National Guard. They came as close to town as their technology allowed, then barricaded the base of the mountains. They blocked everyone from coming in. No one could leave, either. There was no word from the outside world as to how long this might last, or what was being done to help the people of Babel.

Nobody knew anything.

Nobody, that is, except Reed Groom.

Boards now covered the entrance to the southernmost mineshaft, which Reed's grandfather had always called Emmylou. It'd taken Reed two hours to reach the mines. His legs ached. His back roiled with painful spasms. His overworked muscles were taught and twisted from the long frost-slick trek through the woods. Cold sweat soaked his clothes.

This is it, he thought. This is how he'd prove his worth. Show the tiny, ignorant people down there that they were wrong to doubt and ridicule Reed Groom. He imagined the shame they'd all feel when they found out who discovered what was going on and saved them all. It filled him with a euphoric wave of pride.

He'd tried to talk his mother into waiting out the escalating violence inside the cemetery's mausoleum—an old favorite hiding spot of Reed's from when he was a boy—but she refused. "This is my home," she'd said, unfazed by the clatter of gunfire drifting across the cemetery. "The home your father built for us. There ain't a place safer, Reed."

While she calmly chopped carrots, he told her about the big, solid doors. The concrete walls. The deeper level, underground. "Twust me—it's not safe heeah," he said and grabbed her arm. "It's only a matta of time."

"We're safer here than anywhere, Reed." She tugged her arm free of his hand and raised the knife above her head with wild heat in her eyes. "I know I'm *right!*"

But now, standing at the blocked threshold of those endless tunnels, manmade veins and arteries winding through the mountains, Reed knew *he* was right—despite, or maybe because of, the whisper telling him over and over, *There is nothing in there, Reed.*

Signs were plastered sloppily across the boards. Over the years, kids had covered most of them erratically with spray paint, but Reed could still make out what was underneath. Graphics of skulls and gas masks and a logo for a company called Tlaloc Technologies. Words: NO TRESSPASSING . . . FEDERAL LAW . . . PROJECT: b.E.L.F.r.y.

And it sounded to Reed like that cascade of distant whispers was now just past the boards—a looming tsunami about to break.

Turn around, Reed, the whisper urged. *Go back home.*

Reed used his crutches to pry free the planks. One crutch snapped in the process.

The cruelty will be over soon.

Inside, the cold, damp air stuck to his skin like swamp slime. He took careful breaths at first. Eyes closed, focusing. But it smelled as most caves would—must, mold, dirt. Nothing he'd figure for toxic or flammable. Still, it took a few moments before he could work up the nerve to flick the butane lighter he'd brought along.

What exactly do you think you're doing, Reed?

The ground was soft and unsteady under him. His lone crutch would stick or sometimes sink into the muck, throwing off his already poor rhythm and balance. He stumbled to his knees repeatedly.

His flame's yellow light glimmered off the wet walls as he went deeper. The tunnels forked at times and Reed simply followed the escalating assault of murmurs in his head. With each trudged step, the whispers clarified and amplified and the pressure around that plate in his skull swelled. Sweat and tears fell in streams from his face as he hobbled on. His arm operating the crutch ached and quivered. Again and again he'd stumble, and more heavy muck clung to his weakening limbs.

The tunnels narrowed. The mud thickened. While the other voices built in volume, that booming whisper continued. *Why would you help these cancerous things?* The cluster of other voices grew so loud it was hard for Reed to stay focused on his surroundings. *We have been here for centuries.* Almost all of his attention was monopolized by the sounds and the pain pulsing through his brain. *This isn't just our world, Reed.* He tripped, his balance completely lost. *We are the world.*

His face hit the ground and sank into the mud. His arms were swallowed by the muck. He'd managed to tighten his fist around the hot lighter but his crutch had flung out from under him and disappeared into the dark.

That plate may help you hear through our deception, but can you accept the truth when you hear it?

Each syllable thrummed his skull.

You've seen what your people are capable of—their cruelty.

Reed tried his best to ignore the voice, but he couldn't fight those memories from returning. The mocking. The bullying. The laughter, the grins, and the pitying glances.

We have willed the end of man for countless seasons. Yet, each spring you find a new way to oppress us, poison us, and bend us to your will.

He struggled to his knees, feeling through the mud for his crutch.

The men who made what gave us voice thought they could control the weather. They left this place when they thought they had failed. They left behind all their equipment. Their litter. They moved on to new ventures, new ways of oppression and ruin.

Reed's fingers hit something metallic and he noticed its unfamiliar girth as he began lifting it. The weight of the thing nearly pulled him back down.

Kill them all. He wiped off the lighter and flicked it on. *Kill your loved ones.* In his other hand, a leg-thick cable rose from the muck. *Kill yourself.* Its wire-mesh coating hummed in his grip and he realized the words he heard weren't the woman's, but those of a cluttered mess of strange voices. They whispered at a blasting volume that made Reed worry his brain might burst—words, names, secrets, and urgings all overlapping and intersecting between his temples. An ocean of voices convincing a sea of simple minds.

. . . you're right you're right you're right you're right you're right . . .

He dropped the cable. His familiar whisper returned. Again it assured him. *The cruelty will be over soon, Reed.*

Man's ignorance will swallow itself.

Reed found his crutch and followed the cable deeper into the mountain. After hours of ignoring the whisper while working his way through the murky sludge lining the mines, he came to a large cavern.

Do you believe they'll raise you to their shoulders?

The width and height of the space he'd found, he couldn't gauge—his tiny flame couldn't reach that far. But the clacking of his crutch as the ground rose and hardened echoed back seconds at a time.

Do you believe they'll cheer your name?

The cable snaked out of the mud. It thickened as Reed lurched deeper into the cavern. Then more cables crept into the bubble of yellow light around him and converged with the first. He followed them all, that growing braid of humming metal, until he came to the foot of a knotted tower of steel, cable, wire, and what looked like roots and vines.

Do you believe they'll finally hear you beyond your pathetic speech impediment?

Reed couldn't tell in the weak light where the technology ended and the nature that'd taken it over began. He reached up and ran a hand along a length of root. The rough bark rippled, the tendril recoiling as the entire knot convulsed.

Imagine how wonderful this world could be again.

A moan jumped from Reed's mouth as he backed away, the shadows cast by his lighter shifting and gyrating with the massive jumble's movement.

Imagine a world without cruelty . . .

He turned, ready to escape as fast as his tired, ruined legs could carry him.

. . . without ignorance . . .

Huge wooden fingers reached out and grasped him from behind.

. . . without hubris.

His crutch dropped and the lighter fell from his hand as the cavern went dark.

Or do you enjoy being shy, pathetic Wobbly Weed?

The vines tightened around him. They lifted him, pulling him into that great thrumming knot. Twig and wire intertwined, fed into his ears and nose, breaking through his canals and soft tissue in brilliant flashes of pain to worm between brain and bone. The plate at the back of his skull blew out from his scalp in an explosive clap and the sharp ends of that biotech webbing stabbed into his cortex and lobes. His mind sparked alive, surging with sensations Reed barely grasped during his time spent on rooftops, standing high above the tiny people of Babel.

It was an odd and awesome feeling—the potent thrill of power.

Then the whispers receded, as if waiting. He heard instead the thoughts and dreams and emotions of every man, woman, and child in Babel.

They are listening, Reed, the familiar whisper then said, clearer and closer than ever. *They are all listening.*

And they had no choice. He held each of them in the palm of his mind.

Have anything you would like to say?

Dan J. Fiore is a freelance writer from Pittsburgh with fiction previously published by *Writer's Digest*, *Dark Fuse*, and *Thuglit*, among others. His work won the 82nd Annual Writer's Digest Writing Competition, LitReactor's Arrest Us! Crime Writing Challenge, and Pittsburgh Filmmakers' First Works Grant. He is currently writing his second novel while finishing up the MFA in Writing Popular Fiction program at Seton Hill University. In his spare time, he also tinkers in music and photography. You can find out more about him at danjfiore.com.

Mean Green
by
James Pyne

VANDERBOLT ENTERPRISES WAS INDIRECTLY THE cause of the apocalypse, but their latest deforestation scheme wasn't the culprit. One of their employees beat them to it by kicking apart an anthill out of boredom. The ants had done nothing to him. Not one painful bite, which they were more than capable of doing. It was unprovoked and Mother Nature had enough. She had been keeping tabs on humanity's offenses every day since she created the Original Two, and that last act of bullying was it. There's only so much of your skin being shaved off and being tunneled into and jabbed and things exploded off it and poisons injected into you before enough is enough.

It didn't start quickly—the payback, that is. Sure, there were worldwide earthquakes and volcanoes, and some buildings collapsed with a few casualties, but that's as far as it went for natural disasters. Basically, the earth shook and cracked open just enough to spray red dust into the air, while the volcanoes did the same. The storm winds gladly carried the dust worldwide. Experts concluded the crimson dust was harmless since no one was dropping dead from it and it wasn't up there long anyway, not more than a day before sudden storms would soak the lands with the blood rain, or as the religious called it: "holy rain."

Kayla set up her tripod and canvas along the riverfront where waves slapped the boardwalk. People strolled, roller-skated, ran, or jogged by her. A hippie floral band didn't do much as the wind scattered her hair all over her polar-bear-covered smock dress. She proceeded to oil paint what was in front and above her, soaking in the beauty of the bloodshot sky. The dust was spreading its squiggly arms over the city; making this, according to the news, the last place in the entire world to be graced with this divine gift. There were reports all over the globe of vegetation growing faster in areas where the blood rain had fallen, with people complaining about having mown their lawn the evening before only to awake to ankle-high grass. It sounded exaggerated, but whatever.

Kayla overheard conversations passing her by:

"Great, here it comes. I hear this stuff stains everything once it rains."

"Stop being so negative," a woman said through her gasps for air. "Our lawn could use a burst of *blood rain*."

"Everything's a joke to you. You just wait and—"

Their voices trailed off into the intermittent sound of splashing waves.

Kayla looked up. The red dust was almost over her. She brushed in clouds to look like an iris to give the sky a true bloodshot look, as if it were angrily looking down at the city. A city she lived on the outskirts of and only visited for food or when she had a part-time job. She didn't hold jobs for long. The place was too loud with silence, even with arrogant car horns, random gunshots, and arguing lovers. Everything was horribly dead in it and death to her muse.

"I guess it makes people's allergies worse," another person said, as paired-up joggers panted heavily past.

She shaded the city in, giving it an abandoned look. This was the first time in awhile she included the city in one of her paintings. She despised it. Not because of the evil in it—that was everywhere—she loathed it because of its unoriginality. It had no pulse. It was a place where old artists with nothing left to give went to die in obscurity. The buskers themselves had lost their artistic edge and went through the motions. People still tossed change their way, because everything had become routine.

"Doomsday's upon us," a man said behind her. It was her boyfriend, Matt. He had dropped her off and then gone to get some errands done, which translated into him sneaking into work and checking up on the weekend crew under his supervision. "Anything that beautiful must be a harbinger of doom."

"Oh stop it," Kayla said, not turning around, touching up the skyline. Above, the red dust stretched across the sky like wiggly lines fattening into scarves.

"There's a spicy chicken sandwich and some fries waiting for you."

She was basically done, with minute details left that she might or might not include. She joined him at the bench. Even though it was Saturday and his day off, he dressed formal.

"How many of my fries did you eat?" Kayla knew the answer but couldn't help but needle him some.

"A few. Look at me like that all you want. We both know you won't eat all yours."

"Is that so?" She gnashed on the sandwich, talking with her mouth full most times, which drove Matt up the wall. She dipped into the fries. "Beautiful, isn't it." She was referring to the sky darkening with natural clouds, but none looked menacing, or would bring rain, so there was no need to pack up just yet. There was just enough color to give the heavens some oomph. Now that she got thinking about it, the firmament looked a lot like her painting right now; even the city seemed darker. "It's just amazing."

"Your painting? It sure is. You're going to make money off it. You just need to start networking."

"I meant the sky, and you know it." She playfully bumped him. "It's not all about money, you know."

"Dreamer."

"Excuse me?"

"Look, I support your art. I totally dig it, but you hardly sell any, and when you do, you have enough for coffee and donuts. That's about it. You need to get yourself out there. There are tons of art galleries in the city. It's time for the world to know of Kayla Strasberg."

"I make a living."

"You could have so much more. Look at that." He motioned at the canvas. "It's so lifelike. I feel like I could pull out a building and eat it like celery or splash up a tidal wave and flood the city." He crossed his legs and put an arm along the backrest. She smiled, remembering their first date when did the same thing in Macintyre Theater before he kissed her. "No one paints like that. You put your heart into this day and night. Don't you think you should be getting more than you're getting back? The world needs to see your brilliance, you're—"

"Okay, okay."

Kayla didn't like being pushed. She only resisted more. Maybe it was the Capricorn in her, planting firmly her feet, resisting any force of encouragement when it came to her art. It was a complex she had. When people pressured her to do something it was usually out of their own selfish needs, making her less trusting of people.

"You're a perfectionist to a fault, that's your problem in a nutshell. You got confidence, someone of low self-esteem doesn't paint like that. Stop overthinking. Just do it."

"Do you make deals with clients without doing extensive research on them?"

"That's different, a lot of money could be lost—"

"Just like my reputation could be."

The thought of putting subpar art out there gave her anxiety. She didn't want to be one of those people who looked back at their old stuff and wished they had incinerated it. Sure, this painting was worthy of the world stage but no way in hell was it being introduced in that city. Anywhere but there.

"I appreciate your encouragement, hon," she said, "but it's my life."

"Now, you don't have to snotty about it." He turned for an eye-to-eye argument.

"Want a fry?"

He shook his head, laughing, and pinched a fry from the cardboard holder. "Like I said, you always end up giving me the leftovers."

"Shit." She jumped up at the first warm raindrop on her arm. It ran down her skin like blood. Drops splattered on the concrete like an invisible person's nosebleed, leaving splotches everywhere. Scarlet raindrops blotched the painting. Some of them wormed down the canvas.

Matt helped her gather everything up and they rushed to the car. There wasn't much traffic on this side of the river. Most of the buildings were residential. The painting was upright against the backseat. Kayla examined it, and was initially perturbed at Mother Nature graffiti-ing her painting. But then she realized it didn't look so bad.

"It kind of adds to it, you know," she said.

Matt shut the driver's door as he wiggled himself into comfort.

"What are you going on about, everything is going to be stained with this red stuff. Look at our clothes, ruined."

"I'm talking about the painting. Look at it. It's like Mother Nature added the final touches. I know that's crazy sounding, but every drop and streak is perfectly placed." The sudden downpour pounded the roof. "It's like I'm looking out at the world through my painting."

"Well turn around and look out at this."

The holy rain ran in rivulets down the windshield. The city gloomy, abandoned looking. Just like her painting. She saw the YouTube videos of other places experiencing the blood rain and the things it stained but there was nothing like witnessing it firsthand. The runners kept up with the roller-skaters and the joggers were keeping up with both, looking for shelter, as the blood rain ran down their faces and bare arms.

The world's bleeding on humanity, she thought.

Matt turned up the radio and turned the knob back and forth. Only static.

"The music was just on and it cut out. I can't find a station anywhere."

She checked her phone settings. "No Internet either."

"Holy shit. Look!" He pointed at the city.

Five passenger planes, a few helicopters, and a crop duster darted toward the city from different directions. One by one they exploded into the buildings.

"Oh my God, what's happening?" Kayla didn't know if she'd said the words out loud or not. Her brain was reeling.

"Terrorists, that's what."

He revved the car up.

"Matt." She couldn't believe what she was seeing.

From within the fire and thick, black smoke, buildings toppled over, including ones that hadn't been impacted. Skyscrapers fell into each other. Dust flew up and rolled out like an angry grey monster. The sky was clearing quickly, with the exception of one storm cloud round like an iris. It gave the sky an angry look until it blew away in threads of grey and faded into nothingness, like the sun was burning it all away.

"What the hell is happening, Matt?" She clasped her head with both hands, as dust fell over the river like a fog.

Matt reached for the radio again and tried every channel. Still only static.

She tried calling her mom. No signal.

"Kayla, Jesus, look at that."

"Shut up for a second." She was trying to text her mom but nothing would send. He tugged at her. "I said, wait —"

The fallen buildings lifted from the billowing dust. Chunks of brick and concrete fell. Sparkles of glass fairy-dusted the area.

"They're—joining together?" She dropped the phone.

A gigantic skyscraper-arm rose with a headless body of crammed-together buildings, its hand made of mangled cars. It tugged at a battered skyscraper and attached it as its second arm with twisted iron beams for a fist. It bent over and reached into the water and lifted, with both hands, another building that it placed as its head, horizontally. Water dripped like saliva from its concrete and broken-window face. The car shook and rattled while the city monster went ape crazy, pulverizing everything into rubble and dust.

Matt turned the car around. Cars sped by on the main road leading out of the city. He joined them, almost colliding with one.

"This can't be freaking happening. How's this happening, Matt?" She looked back to see the city monster rise on one bent leg and push itself slowly upright. Then she looked past the monster. "There's a second one." Miles away, another city monster moved in their direction fast. The nearest one took one step, causing the car to shake and rattle, and almost skid out of control.

"Watch out." She motioned at a car whizzing by them.

"You want to drive?" He kept his stare straight. "I didn't think so. Now shut up and let me concentrate."

On the driver's side, another city awakened into the blue sky and looked like it was moving their way, or so it appeared due to the immense size of it. She glanced back to see their city yank the suspension bridge from its tower foundations. Cars dropped into the water as it attached the bridge as its tail. Was this happening all over the world?

"Jesus!" Matt shouted.

The car swerved as creatures made from stone advanced on vehicles. One was made of tombstones and coffins with corpses and skeletons dangling here and there like macabre jewellery. Matt avoided the last one as she looked back to see the cars behind them being crushed, or picked up and slammed.

"They're crashing into each other," Matt said. "They've gone mad."

She turned around to see cars farther down spin around and ram into each other, some of them overturning and rolling over still others. It was a crash derby on a grand scale.

Matt squealed to a stop.

"What are you doing?"

"It stopped on its own." He pushed his door open. "Get out."

"What do you mean it stopped on its own? I'm not going out there."

"Will you listen to me, it won't start. Come on." He darted around the car.

Had he lost his mind? Stone creatures behind them and people gone insane in front of them, and city monsters walking toward them seemingly in all directions, and he wanted her to step out of the car?

He flew her door open and pulled at her. "Let's go, hon."

A truck and two cars raced side by side in their direction. She really had no choice.

They bailed out of the car and rushed to the steep bank and climbed up it, sometimes slipping, reaching the tree line just as the three vehicles converged on their car. In one of them, a woman pounded on the driver's window, silently screaming through her tears while holding a baby. The car was driving itself, much to Kayla's disbelief.

"Oh my God." She turned away and hugged Matt. The sound of metal and glass collided, throwing up pieces into the woods.

"We got to go." The ground rumbled and shook, lifting them from their feet. The sound of metal screeching across the pavement became deafening. She turned to see vehicles pulled along by an invisible force, lifting and spinning into the air. One car grazed the side of the woods, knocking small trees down, enough for her to see cars gravitate toward the city monster, becoming its armor.

Matt pulled at her as the ground trembled. They kept running away from where their city once was, from everything, deeper into the woods, into the thick spruce and sugar maple trees, with no idea how far the forest reached. Animals ramped in every direction, wolves, bears, deer, none concerned with the others or the fleeing humans. The forest canopy hid much of the outside, but she saw glimpses of the monster city. A few more steps and it would pass them. Suddenly, humanity was insignificant on its own turf by its own creations. It was a long time coming, but why couldn't it have waited another seventy years when she was long dead?

"It can't see us in here," she said, gasping for breath. "I got to stop."

"It doesn't need to see us to accidentally squash us." He stopped. "The thing's huge. Those smaller ones are out there, too, and I saw three more big ones from a distance. We got to keep running."

A loud deafening roar, and then another, and two more, as if the city monsters were communicating. The ground quaked and trees rattled. Matt stumbled and she fell on top of him. They scrambled back up, fighting their way through a forest where they stopped and stared at the people in the trees. Branches around their necks and mouths as they struggled to get loose.

"The trees are alive too." Kayla felt like vomiting from the anxiety hitting her. There was nowhere to run. Every leaf had crimson raindrops, every branch, every tree trunk was streaked in red. "It's brought everything to life," she said of the holy rain. "We're not safe anywhere."

The ground moved again, knocking them over. She could see through a break in the treetops that the city monster had stopped before stepping into the forest as birds of every feather peppered the sky. It was looking down their way, as if it knew they were alive in here but couldn't advance for some reason. Of course, she was imagining it. It couldn't see them. They weren't even ants compared to the size of it.

"We got to keep running."

"But the trees, look at everyone, Matt." People reached out to them, the branches tight around their mouths and chests and legs. "We can't just leave—"

"Don't look at them." He grabbed her hand. "Look straight down and I'll lead us through this."

She kept looking down, letting him lead, and everything was okay until there was a collective snap. Bodies started dropping all around them. Children or adult, there was no discrimination. They looked up at her, their eyes condemning her for being alive, for not helping them. She was too frightened to cry for them; too confused to make any sense of it. She covered up from the sudden sunlight as she was pulled into a clearing. They stopped.

Matt said nothing. When her eyes adjusted, she almost collapsed from the dizzying vision of the city monsters standing over them. The forest wasn't that big at all. There was enough space between the city monsters to give the illusion of an escape, but one step from either of them would squash that attempt easy enough. Even if Kayla and Matt got through, they'd be snatched up by the smaller monstrosities that were made from wrecked houses and apartment buildings, who were flinging the dead into one big pile. They had nowhere to go. Everything was a wasteland except for the forests which remained standing.

One of the city monsters lowered itself into a kneeling position, and the breeze from its movement almost blew her over.

"The last of humanity," a female voice boomed from a mouth of brick and twisted metal. "Humanity's seed in the balance. Convince me to let you live."

Matt went speechless, his eyes wide, as if he had gone silently mad. He let go of her and staggered backwards, mumbling incoherently.

Kayla didn't have to think about what to say. Only one thing came to mind.

"Let us start over again," she shouted, as Matt fell back into a seated position and rocked back and forth with arms folded, humming, as if trying to drown out reality. Not her; she stood steadfast, hoping it couldn't sense her fear, hoping it would be impressed that such a tiny thing could have such spunk. "Let us start over, like Adam and Eve."

A silence filled the world as the city monster considered her words. The last of the dead were piled up and a fire lit. The house and apartment monsters held hands and clumsily danced around the blazing bonfire, then one by one they entered the flames.

The city monster's mouth turned up at one corner. Its eye suddenly glowed like the sun.

"Made that mistake once before."

Its enormous fist came down on them.

James Pyne was born in New Glasgow, Nova Scotia. His writing has recently appeared in *Grey Matter Monsters, Clockwork Wonderland, Only the Light We Make, Death and Decorations, Jack O'Lanterns,* and is forthcoming in *Renegades of Prose, Missing, Buried,* and a few other anthologies. He's also working on the completion of his latest novels, *Woe* and *Big Cranky.* If you dig his work, or want to troll him, feel free to add him on Facebook: facebook.com/jjamespyne.

A New Kind of Eden

by

J.T. Seate

WERE THEY MERELY LUCKY, OR had they been chosen? It was like a hole in the fabric of time had opened and they had slipped into prehistory. As far as Evelin knew, she and Aaron were the only two people left on earth.

Huge branches of large trees hummed in the wind, making empty music while providing shelter. Evelin looked across a land that bore no house, no lean-to, not even a chicken coop, and felt fortunate the disaster had fallen during a warm summer. The early morning mist hanging over the landscape created a scene mirroring the dawn of time. They might actually be the second Adam and Eve, even though they had clothes to wear when choosing to and more than just an apple to be tempted by. Although it wasn't a time for childish notions, Evelin didn't attempt to chase them away because notions were the only indulgence left to them.

She and Aaron fled to the remote countryside not long after the catastrophe. Populated areas were dangerous and the electricity had failed almost immediately. Truth be told, she enjoyed the pastoral scenes devoid of manmade objects such as power lines that carried no power and phone lines that carried no communication.

Aaron lay asleep next to her inside their double sleeping bag. They couldn't just waltz into a supermarket and pick out what they needed,

237

because buildings were off-limits. The two of them had been camping out for a couple of days when it happened. Evelin had reached the time when she wanted to get pregnant, and conceiving with the stars as their canopy seemed the perfect way to begin a family.

When they hiked back to the road the following morning, they saw a vehicle parked next to theirs with its driver's door open. Half in and half out of the truck was a set of clothes. It was as if the truck's driver had dematerialized. They examined another vehicle. Behind the wheel was another set of clothes settled in the car seat.

They set down their gear and hustled toward an outpost less than a mile away. Along the road were other vehicles. They all contained the same scene—clothes without their owners inside them.

Reaching the convenience store, Aaron made tracks for the building, but Evelin grabbed his arm and held him back. Just inside the glass door were more empty clothes.

"What happened?" he asked.

Before she could answer, a figure appeared from a nearby stand of trees. He looked like a modern-day mountain man—scraggly beard, weathered features, a hunting knife in his belt. He and approached them in a rush. "You kids know what the hell's going on with folks around here? Heard anything on the radio?"

"We've been camping. We don't know anything except people seem to have disappeared right out of their clothes."

"Been inside the store?"

"No," Evelin said. "But there are empty clothes in there, too. Look." She pointed.

"This is some kind of crazy-ass joke. It's got to be," the man said and headed for the door.

Evelin and Aaron watched as the man opened the door. One fatal step. The man dematerialized as he entered. His fatigues fell in a heap on top of the other garments. The couple gasped. The shock couldn't have been more jolting if they had bitten into a plugged-in electric cord while wearing braces. Too frightened for expletives, they backed away from the store and the sight their unbelieving eyes just witnessed.

Evelin was shaking. "I know this will sound crazy, Aaron, but maybe this is that Rapture thing."

Aaron held her. "Where everyone but us is taken? I can buy alien abductors before I can swallow some religious hocus-pocus. Or, *more* likely, Mother Nature has finally had enough of us."

They hurried toward another storefront and, without getting too close, peered into the window. Inside, more clothes without their occupants.

"Holy Christ, Aaron. Maybe we should go hide somewhere. We could walk back to the truck and get the cell phone."

"I don't think I want to climb into anything right now. Being out in the open seems the best idea."

A frantic notion popped into Evelin's head. "Maybe it's the cameras in the stores. There are cameras everywhere now. Maybe it's when people are on camera that something happens?"

"It doesn't explain all of those people disappearing in their cars," Aaron said. "Somehow, the environment in enclosed places, manmade places, has turned toxic and is disintegrating living cells, something like that."

"What are we going to do? What about our families? How can we survive being outside indefinitely?"

"As long as we can find food. But for now, let's walk toward home. Maybe everything is okay away from here."

"It has to be," Evelin said, starting to cry. "It just has to."

Two years earlier, Aaron sat in a corner booth of the Mountain Man Café and slowly, sadly, all by his lonesome, ground a slab of beef into submission. Happy couples wined and dined. He was a pathetic image—a testament to liaisons gone wrong. Getting over another breakup in a series of breakups left him wondering what exactly the hell he was looking for.

The day after his tough steak with sautéed mushrooms, he contemplated his fizzled summer while browsing at Barb's Book Bin. Looking through the Mystery/Suspense section, he hoped to find a handful of used books to get him through a solitary autumn, expecting no more thrills than what storybook fantasies might provide.

She was standing at the sales counter with a pile of textbooks, offering them to Barb for some aspiring student. He stood next to the book-bearing woman and tried to act nonchalant with his paltry haul of two beat-up paperbacks.

Aaron listened as the woman talked to Barb. Her melodious voice was soft and kind. She was an attractive creature in her mid-twenties. A heart-shaped face surrounded her blond curls. Her wide eyes were the color of a deep ocean. Her smile revealed perfect teeth.

Her loose, gypsy-like summer dress ended at her curvaceous knees. Her tanned legs ended at sandaled feet. He always noticed women's feet. Hers sported silver-pink polish on each toe, long and slender like her tapered fingers. They could have been pearls dredged from the ocean's floor created merely to accentuate each piggy.

His mind searched for something semi-intelligent to say—something that wouldn't sound like a come-on. Barb took the final book from the woman, a Russian textbook. But before this tantalizing female could get away, he said, "I read *War and Peace*. Do you think I'm ready for one of your books?"

A broad smile re-carved her features, making her even more fetching. "Into Russian literature, are you?"

In spite of himself, he couldn't help thinking about the soft, yielding tissue between her legs. "I'm into whatever it takes to buy you a cup of coffee while we discuss famous revolutions, or other things."

She hadn't the time just then, but she told him he could Google her, Evelin Benedict, in case his interest lasted beyond the present afternoon. His interest certainly did, but it took him a month to pin down this very busy lady. He finally managed a rendezvous at a Mexican restaurant where he took a table in the establishment's courtyard. He brought her a long-stemmed rose, which he planted in the dining table's centerpiece.

They talked for a very long time. She was extraordinarily open, an animal-rights and Greenpeace supporter. They shared an encapsulated version of their life stories—tales of successes and failures. Evelin was too attractive for Aaron to keep his mind totally on social issues. An image of those tree-hugging, animal-loving legs wrapped around his waist was enough to make him squirm with renewed verve in the contemplation of a new and sweet relationship.

After a second lime-wedged Corona, Aaron wanted to be her professor emeritus of love, but he knew if he were to conquer this beauty, it would have to be accomplished in some shared activity that would appeal to her kind, animal-loving nature.

Aaron called Evelin the next week. "How about letting me take you to the zoo this weekend?" he asked her.

She accepted. On a Saturday afternoon, they walked their legs off for most of the day, moving from the sleeping big cats, to the monkeys doing nasty things, to the noisy birds, and finally to the playful pachyderms. While taking a break on a park bench, they observed a woman on another bench catching her breath from pushing a stroller through the park. The little boy parked next to her was busily scraping a lollipop on the asphalt. Then he decided to stick it in his ear for safekeeping.

"Oh, Jimmy," the mother tiredly exclaimed, and removed the sticky earplug.

Deprived of his toy, Jimmy started to bawl. Evelin exhibited an unpleasant expression.

"Don't like kids?" Aaron asked.

"Of course I do, but I would rather teach them than make my own. I'm not sure I want to bring any into this world, with all the pollution. For now, I'll settle for baby elephants."

"At least one of *them* would have more sense than to stick a sweet treat in its ear."

She laughed and gave Aaron a look every man wishes for. It was one of not only pleasure but of admiration—the look that said he had been accepted as a good guy. He flattered her back with his lingering eyes and marveled at her down-to-earth humor, and the prospect of a more involved relationship. She seemed to have it all, and in the mind of the beholder, nothing else was necessary.

The next year, Aaron and Evelin were married, just six months before the fateful camping trip. Six months after that they were vagabonds, leaving their hometown because staying would have been unbearable. The event turned out to be more than a local phenomenon. The whole world had gone tilt. In the beginning, the couple camped outdoors in town parks and open places. Everywhere they ventured, including their parents' homes, they found the same thing. Bodies were not piled up. People had simply vanished inside structures, their clothes and ornaments left behind as if to prove they'd once been here.

Aaron and Evelin spent time speculating on what nature, or God, or aliens had wrought. Disease and viruses and poisoning were ruled out because *they* were alive. Were they the only two people with some kind of immunity?

"When the end came, it almost seems appropriate to have happened in a way that defies explanation," Evelin told Aaron during their flight from what had been civilization. "Mankind has abused nature for so long, it must have become too much."

Those statements were followed by a nostalgic period in which they discussed the things they would never be able to do again. Parents, friends, parties, pecking order, getting ahead—all those things were just vapors, all replaced with the dawning of a pristine world with its centuries of history wiped clean except for the memories of them.

Evelin never thought she'd miss food shopping, but she did. Doing a mundane, numbingly normal task would have been therapeutic.

Evelin's heart was heavy with pondering about the kids she would never have the opportunity to teach. She tried to dwell on more frivolous things. "No more movies," Evelin said one evening. "Unless we run across a surviving drive-in somewhere."

"Sorry. You'd have to go into the projection room, and even then, no electricity."

As they checked off things enjoyed and accepted the present, they soon left the towns behind. They both abhorred the burned-out yards and unchecked weeds coming through the pavement. Home gardens were few and far between and they couldn't risk going indoors. Aaron even speculated the event might have had something to do with being below metal, but such musings soon lost their meaning.

They preferred the countryside. The animals they most often spotted were horses. Those grazing in open fields could manage indefinitely, they supposed. But most pets had met the same fate as people. Those left outdoors, however, had either starved or had had the cunning to head for the hills themselves, which fostered a fear of stray, carnivorous packs. Evelin had considered returning to the zoo and trying to free the animals but, in the end, couldn't bear the thought of finding all those beautiful creatures lifeless or mad with hunger. Those that survived would be hungry. She and Aaron would be fresh meat. Bad idea.

They passed abandoned vehicles and empty buildings. Wherever people had been, it was the same shit, different day. The multi-colored machines that once prowled the streets were now stilled sentinels of a civilization past. The empty clothes seemed more haunting than if they had contained decaying bodies.

"How could there not have been others camping out somewhere and figuring it wasn't safe to go inside?" was Evelin's standard mantra.

"It's a big world," Aaron offered. "There might be millions somewhere. In India, for instance, half the population lives on the streets.

In Africa maybe, but around here everyone must have been indoors or mistakenly run for shelter."

After abandoning the familiarity of their area, they made their way southward in search of milder climates. They would have used bicycles if it hadn't been for Aaron's metal phobia. An eventual beach sounded inviting even though the foraging might not be as good. Besides, what was the hurry, and there was a whacky liberation in having nothing left to lose and no timeframe to adhere to.

In the year that followed, Aaron and Evelin never ran across another living soul. The disappearance of mankind would remain a mystery, but their survival skills soon kicked in. There was no processed food in the great outdoors, but fields had been planted. After living on what crops provided, they learned to set traps because they couldn't go into a store and pick up a gun and rounds of ammo. "We'll have to live mostly on love," Aaron told Evelin at the outset.

They found their shelter from the elements in forests under tree limbs, but never built a structure that would have provided more protection. Nor did they enter a manmade structure of any sort, even those of earth or wood. By the end of the summer, they had truly become a sequel to the Adam and Eve story, but without a pesky snake to complicate things. They hunted together with spears made from scavenged hunting knives and tree branches, and became quite skilled at bringing down small game.

In addition to living on love, they also lived on their cunning, once being attacked by a group of hungry wolves. As terrifying as the experience was, the skills they'd mastered at hunting served them well. And after they'd killed one of the wolves, the rest of the pack sought other prey.

On another occasion, they came upon the remnants of a crashed, mid-sized passenger plane. This was inevitable. With all the air traffic at any given time, thousands of planes must have fallen from the sky. What remained of this one's burned-out skeletal wingspan reminded them of a pterodactyl. They had no desire to approach the wreckage.

Aaron and Evelin stayed mobile, never entertaining the possibility of farming or even staying in one place. "When you're on the move, you don't think so much about your past or your dreams," Aaron told Evelin. "The key to serenity is to have a goal." And theirs was to reach the coast.

They fancied the idea of following in the footsteps of the first nomadic Americans, free to go where food led them. There was plenty of fresh fish and water, seasonal nuts, berries, and protein from their acquisitions. And they never took each other for granted, knowing the world could be much lonelier than it presently was.

Clothes worn twenty-four seven didn't last long. As the weather cooled, they found outdoor fabrics to fashion into warmer protection. But until then, and in the following spring, they wore nothing but boots or tennis shoes picked up where vacated—in doorways where feet had once been.

Outdoor living revealed certain drawbacks, but Evelin came to think of herself as Sheena, queen of the jungle, more than Eve in the Garden of Eden. She was Aaron's equal in all they did, which included their lovemaking. Both of them let their hair grow long, and their bodies bronzed under the sun. They had grown stronger and healthier through necessity. Their muscles were toned. They'd returned to an athletic form and moved almost catlike on their feet. Their minds were sharp and bright with no smog or pollution to mix with their gray matter. No traffic or loud noises except for those produced by nature. And, in time, most of their regrets fell at their feet like sprinkling summer rain.

Although humans had disappeared in the blink of an eye, it took a year for their absence to become obvious. Electricity had gone quickly, but the inattention to property and roads now showed in definite signs of nature eradicating man's intrusion. Aaron and Evelin had long since quit looking into windows. It only made them want to risk going inside for canned goods or supplies that would make their lives easier.

Instead, they beheld the mysteries of nature with new awe and wonder. When leaden storm clouds rolled across the sky with thunder rumbling behind them, the couple would hold each other and watch the rain from beneath a tarp carried in their pack. If it was a summer shower, they might bathe each other or make love in it, allowing the rain to temporarily wash away their fear of an uncertain future.

They marveled at the spectacle of the star-filled heavens, which glittered from one horizon to the other. Orion, Little Bear, Draco, all vast and beautiful. It gave Evelin a feeling of timelessness, and maybe even immortality—one with the universe. Their distant ancestors had set out in small boats with only the stars to guide them. They too were crossing a new kind of wilderness to an unknown destination.

"Beauty is in the mind of the beholder," Aaron told Evelin whenever running across some unpleasant reminder of man's sudden exit that threatened to sweep away their resolve. Oftentimes near towns, pieces of paper and tattered garments would flutter in the wind, having freed themselves from doorways or open cars. "All of this is returning to nature," he philosophized. "The sky and the water will be clean again."

"You've become as much a nature-lover as I am," Evelin teased. She was glad for Aaron's strength. At least one of them saw their glass as half full. He constantly reminded her they had each other. In a land that could be both beautiful and terrifying, they took time to dance among wildflowers, to lie down in grassy meadows, and to hold each other and have sex early and often.

They liked the freedom of nudity. There was an innocent delight in not having to disrobe. For Aaron, it was a hint of wildness in Evelin's ever present, sleek hips, toned body, and the promise of luxuriant sex. For Evelin, it was the shedding of a lifetime of social mores. Like Aaron, she tried to find positives in a world that seemed to be theirs alone. And, truth be known, their body parts' swinging freely while walking was a turn-on. They mused over the image they would present if they ever came across anyone else—two naked humans with spears, one with dark hair, the other with fair hair, carrying a rucksack full of dried berries, nuts, and fruit, tethered by a strap between Evelin's breasts.

Their lovemaking was often frenzied, swimming in kisses with no definable dimension, attacking each other as if their survival had been a mistake. Sometimes when they kissed, Aaron felt Evelin's warm tears on his face. All his dreams focused on the miracle of their heavy breathing and making the world new. With sex they could suspend the knowledge that everything was lost save their passion and dedication to each other.

Making love any time and any place, as long as it was outdoors, was their gift in this scary, brave new world. They didn't worry about access to pills or condoms. Their world began and ended with a beautiful encounter, and it might be up to them to repopulate the planet, after all. At night, Evelin nestled into the space between Aaron's arm and chest.

"When I first realized we were surrounded by death, I cursed the world," he told her. "Then I learned to rejoice when we accomplished some little task."

She turned her head and kissed his neck. "It doesn't really matter whether we ever find anyone else, does it? Not really?"

"We always want what we can't obtain. If suddenly there's a village, I'll be the first to run toward it. But I can tell you that for the first time in my life I'm content with who I am and what I have."

"Me too," Evelin replied as twinkling stars gathered overhead, their pinpoints of light beaming from suns burned out millions of years before.

Aaron looked into the heavens. "Even when we can't see the stars, I know they're there. I think about other surviving humans we haven't found, feeling their way along, looking for meaning in their forever-altered lives." He kissed Evelin tenderly and then said, "Here we are on this blue bauble in a sea of night. It still turns as it always has and the universe doesn't care if its creatures have eyes or wings or dreams. Everything just is."

It wasn't often that Aaron waxed poetic, but his attempt seemed apropos. "We can't lose each other," Evelin said and wrapped her legs around Aaron.

"We won't, baby," he answered before they fell asleep with their separate dreams of the new world order.

Lost in thought while walking, Aaron and Evelin heard something unusual—the clanging of a bell. Following the sound, they approached quietly, knowing if they encountered other survivors it wasn't a given they would be friendly. The noise came from a large tree near a farmhouse. Cautious inspection revealed a bell hung from a piece of lumber. A tree branch brushed against it every time a strong gust of wind came along.

"A tree house," Evelin exclaimed. "Let's check it out."

Aaron watched as Evelin scampered toward the huge oak and placed her foot on the first two-by-four nailed to its trunk. She started up as nimbly as any kid who ever climbed up to his or her special place.

"God, Evelin. Stop!" Aaron suddenly screamed. He ran to the base of the tree and grabbed her nearest booted ankle, almost causing her to come crashing down.

"Aaron!"

"It's a structure, honey. I almost forgot."

Evelin glanced up. The tree house had a tin roof. A piece of material, a checkered wool sleeve, fluttered over the edge of the platform in the breeze. Her emotions once again climbed aboard a roller coaster. The day had begun with birds singing in the trees, only to end in a meteoric descent into the void.

"Oh God, Aaron. I wasn't thinking."

With Aaron's frightened upturned face below her tanned legs and bare bottom, she backed down and fell into his waiting arms.

"I'm such a ditz sometimes," she said, fighting back tears. Hopelessness swept over her as she looked into her husband's eyes.

Their naked bodies pressed together for reassurance. Sudden reminders of what had changed the world—like the crashed plane or the armless sleeve—were a nasty shock. Evelin rested her head against Aaron's chest and let the tears come. They trickled down his chest. Without platitudes or attempts at wit, he held the back of her head until it was all out and her tears began to dry, until the catharsis gave both of them the strength to move on.

"I'm all right now," she finally said, and wondered why there were never better words to soothe fear and regret. Only God, if there was one, could know how many times they had averted disaster since the world went quiet.

"All I know is a few years with you will be more rewarding than a world filled with other people," Aaron said. He kissed Evelin's lips to try and make her forget what could have happened.

Would they ever know if it was safe to enter anything? Aaron often thought of catching a rabbit and tossing it inside something, but Evelin wouldn't allow it. It was better not to know than take a life of any kind unnecessarily, she believed. To the north, the direction they had come, thunderclouds were gathering. South was where their destiny waited. They'd learned to survive in the elements, and as long as they avoided injury and kept moving south…

By mid-summer, a year after their nomadic life began, they reached the ocean. They momentarily pondered the possibility of ships or sailboats. Seeing none, they reasoned that controls were in cabins and probably led sailors to a fate similar to everyone else. And if not, why would anyone be on the water after a year?

They played like this was a vacation to some exotic destination. They dropped their packs and weapons, pulled off their footwear, and ran happily into the surf. They frolicked in the waves, rising and dipping like fishing bobbers. Aaron kissed Evelin's lips with greedy abandon, mashed his wet chest against hers, and enveloped her in his arms.

"What happens on the beach stays on the beach," he joked as they ran their fingers through one another's wet hair and stroked each others' toughened, sun-baked skin. Their goal was realized. They let the waves carry them toward shore and then back toward the abyss, not much caring where they were taken as long as they were together.

Upon returning to shore, Aaron asked Evelin if she would care to dance. A smile crept across her face, an honest good-natured smile he hadn't seen for a while. He started to hum "Unforgettable."

"A tummy tickler," she laughed and melted against Aaron the way every man hungers for, clinging like a vine long familiar with the stone it intertwines. With her head against his shoulder, she hummed along with him.

When they were hummed out, she asked him to sing a fast one. He sang a bastardized rendition of Michael Jackson's "Billy Jean." Evelin began her own variation of booty shaking. With her arms raised above her head, she resembled something between a Spanish *contessa* clicking castanets and Botticelli's painting of *The Birth of Venus*, enjoying the freedom of her own space.

"You move beautifully," he told her.

She didn't answer. She was caught up in the rhythm of the song. It had been so long. She hated to stop, but finally did. "Thank you, honey." She reached out and touched Aaron's arm to show her appreciation for bringing just a speck of their former lives back to them.

He felt very close to the treasure that spoke to him, the schoolteacher who'd traipsed across half the country with him. He believed they had never loved each other any more than now. They lay next to each other and sunbathed, the long stretch of beach hauntingly reserved just for them. After a while, they reluctantly picked up their supplies. It didn't seem to matter in which direction they went, but they chose to go south.

After beachcombing for a couple of miles, Evelin suddenly stopped and clutched Aaron's arm. He looked at her and then down the stretch of coastline. He froze. Something was lying on the beach. Either mannequins or—?

One of the forms moved. A man. *Holy Christ!* And a woman. A couple lounging in the sand, as brown and as naked as Aaron and Evelin. The pair sat up. Aaron and Evelin approached cautiously, wanting to rub their eyes to make sure the sun hadn't gotten to them.

Not a mirage. The couple stood.

"Well, I'll be damned," the man said. He walked toward Aaron and Evelin and offered his hand. "Tarzan and Jane, I presume?"

Aaron and Evelin thought they might be embarrassed by their nakedness if encountering other people, but they weren't. They'd been naturists too long. Neither had any idea what to say to the couple, who looked to be in their thirties.

"There are eight of us," the man said, anticipating the questions sure to come. "We left our camp and went for a hike. When we got back, everyone else was gone."

For a year, Aaron and Evelin had only heard each other's voices, so this new audio sounded almost alien. "Just their clothes, huh?" Aaron asked.

"Oh no. No clothes. We belonged to a nudist colony."

"A nudist camp," Evelin said with a look of surprise. "Those most likely to be outdoors."

"We think it was some new organism with the sudden power to eradicate living cells within all enclosures," the man said matter-of-factly. "Something completely illogical."

"Kind of like *The Andromeda Strain*?" Aaron hypothesized.

"We'll probably never know. There *were* nine of us. We watched Jack disappear at the door of a men's restroom. It was a good month after the event. Whatever it is may have mutated to something safe by now, but we don't plan on testing it again. Not until one of us is at death's doorstep and is willing to volunteer."

The woman now stood by the man. She said, "We're all independent types, but we do have a bit of a civilization going, if you care to join us."

Aaron hesitated. "You'll have to forgive us for staring," he told the couple. "We haven't seen anyone for a year. I think we're both in shock."

"Quite understandable," the man said.

"Where do you sleep?" Evelin asked.

"Under open-air configurations with palm frond roofs. Protection produced by nature is no problem," the man answered. "Come along with us and let us at least feed you. Our digs have a nonconventional ambience if nothing else. We have a nice garden and a few head of livestock, so you won't need your spears unless you like to throw them at trees."

"Convention is in the mind of the beholder," Evelin said. "Do you ride bicycles?"

The couple looked at Evelin and laughed. "All the time," the man said. "They're good to scout for useful items. We even rollerblade and skateboard just for fun."

"If you want to stay with us, you're welcome," the woman added. "If not, we can appreciate your new life is just meant for the two of you. You might find our company tedious or irritating."

"Have any beer?" Aaron asked.

"Golden nectar from the land of sky blue waters," the man said with a smile. "Found cases and cases in bottles at the site of an outdoor soiree. Keep them cold in a swimming pool."

Evelin and Aaron looked at each other and passed a silent message. The four humans stood naked in the sea breeze, concerns gradually easing.

"I might add one thing," the woman said. "One in our party is a nurse. It looks to me like she might be a handy person to be around in a few more months." She glanced at Evelin's bare tummy. "Life is a miracle and we're all very lucky."

"You might be right," Evelin answered. To Aaron, she said, "Let's go have a look-see, hon. See if we can remember what after-dinner conversation in mixed company is like."

Evelin and Aaron did go to dinner and stayed for many more. Five months after their sojourn ended at the coastline, Evelin had a baby boy. They named him Adam. The small band of survivors was elated over the baby and neither Aaron nor Evelin minded that Adam inherited a handful of godfathers and godmothers. An extended family made it possible for the young couple to sneak off occasionally to try and make a brother or sister for Adam, but they were never gone long. Not with their new arrival waiting at camp and a new reason to stay in one place—a reason for starting fresh.

Not long after Adam's birth, something else happened. On one of the men's reconnaissance bike rides, they came across a huge sign. It revealed the existence of another group of sixty people. Coordinates left behind placed their destination about sixty miles north from the Naked Ten Plus One. The NTPO, that's what Aaron and Evelin's little band called themselves now.

One member of the group to the north was a chemist who knew something about natural science. He left a lengthy note protected in plastic with the large sign. The gist of his theory was that the hole in the ozone layer had grown to critical mass, allowing deadly rays to permeate the atmosphere. Although the rays were everywhere, they were somehow drawn to artificial creations, which absorbed catastrophic levels.

The note rambled on a bit concerning conspiracy theories about how scientists probably knew the danger, but couldn't have predicted exactly when such an event might occur. As with the nuclear tests that devastated the Bikini Islands with radiation, it might be decades or longer until structures were safe. Or, more likely, until the ozone layer was able to repair itself. The truth was, Aaron and Evelin's group cared little about the cause. They were doing fine without the use of buildings and machines and the trappings of rules and regulations, thank you very much. They had their lives and each other to care about.

The northern group must have included a philosopher as well, because the missive about the apocalypse's cause ended with another note that read: *Every beginning is only a continuation and the book of fate is always open in the middle.*

The NTPO were delighted to discover the existence of another pocket of humans, but were reluctant to seek them out, not at all sure they wanted to join a larger group. Large communes had a history of not being all they were cracked up to be. And the group was none too keen about putting clothes back on.

But one thought resigned Evelin and Aaron to move north. There might be children who could use a teacher or other infants in the larger group. Survival of the species would require several new babies.

And in the end, the other eight followed, because they had grown to love their new family and would cast their lot to whatever situation might confront their very own Tarzan, Jane, and boy.

After J. T. Seate read a few of his stories to his parents, they booted him out of the house. Undaunted, he continues to write everything from humor to the erotic to the macabre, and is especially keen on transcending genre pigeonholing. His tales span the gulf from *Horror Novel Review*'s Best Short Fiction Award to *Chicken Soup for the Soul*. They may be told with hardcore realism or fantasy, bringing to life the most quirky of characters. Novels include *Valley of Tears, Tears for*

the Departed, And the Heavens Wept, and *Paranormal Liaisons.* His story collections are *Carnival of Nightmares, Midway of Fear, Sex in Bloom,* and *A Baker's Dozen,* available at melange-books.com and bookswelove.net/authors/seate-troy.

Earth

Don't Fool with an Earth Witch

by

J. D. Blackrose

My fingers burrowed into the ground and I cast a healing spell for the Earth. She hurt today and I could feel her pain as my own. Recently, she was always hurting, but this spot of land was my responsibility.

Rumor was that a careless driver had thrown a lit cigarette out the window and started the fire that left all this ash. The area was already dry; one spark had been enough to set the area ablaze. But dryness or no, there was an undercurrent to this particular fire that felt like dark magic.

"Sadie, bring me that watering can, will you?" Sadie, a Golden Rottie, a combination of a golden retriever and a Rottweiler, grasped the handle with her teeth and carried the full can to me without spilling a drop.

"Thanks, girl." I gave her a pat. She sniffed as if to say, *of course.*

I dug a hole in the ground and poured the water into it, chanting an incantation of seeing. The water formed a smooth surface and my reflection peered back at me. I repeated the chant two more times. Vapor rose from the water's surface in the shape of a human being, masculine in form, who leaned over a hole in the ground, as I was, but this man was not healing anything. He was pouring a thick liquid into the ground and the Earth was unhappy about it, which is why She showed me this image.

Fire is part of the Earth's cleansing cycle, and actually brings new life to the forest, but this was a violation.

I walked home, Sadie in tow, thinking about what I'd seen. My other dog, Gimli, a bulldog, waited on the steps.

The air became heavier, and I caught a peculiar scent on the breeze. It made my arm hair stand on end and a shiver run down my spine. I spun, looking for the intruder. Both dogs were growling at something to my left so I focused my attention there.

"You're already looking for me," said a voice. "That was fast." A shimmer in front of me coalesced into the man I'd seen in my vision.

With a gesture and a whisper of my will, a nearby oak branch bent down, snagged him by his robe, and lifted him high into the air even as he solidified. "Never surprise an earth witch," I said.

The warlock, swinging in the wind, nodded. "It's not nice to fool with Mother Nature. I get it. May I come down?"

"I'm not Mother Nature, but I do know Her. You're correct. You really, really don't want to mess with Her. Why did you poison the Earth?"

"I wasn't trying to poison the Earth, per se. I was trying to ascertain how much silver is buried here. I used a seeking spell and then the magic got excited by the fire and accelerated."

"You ravaged this mountain because you were *careless*? Nice. You're working for DB Miners?"

"Yes."

"We have nothing to talk about."

"Holly, you need to be reasonable. Since the Fae came out of the shadows, the price of silver has skyrocketed. The miners have a right to access the silver."

"No, they don't. This mountain and the neighboring forty-five acres belong to my family, as they have for generations, and I say no. And it's Ms. Springfield to you. Don't presume to use my first name, *Mr. Walker.*"

"You can call me Gareth. My feet are falling asleep. Can you please let me down?"

I flicked my wrist, and the branch flung him a far distance. I had no idea where he set down, but I considered the warlock sufficiently skilled enough to land without breaking a leg. I didn't feel any reverberating pain, so he was unharmed. Unfortunately.

Sadie and Gimli were fine after the warlock left, as dogs live in the moment. I didn't have that luxury. If the miners were desperate enough to send a warlock then I'd have to get ready to fight.

The squirrels on the roof of my cabin chittered at the catapult move. Squirrels have funny senses of humor. My closest squirrel friend, Chuck, jumped on my shoulder, came into the house with me, and perched on the back of a wooden chair. He chittered again.

"I'm glad you approve, Chuck, but I might have gotten myself into trouble." The squirrel flung himself from the chair to the table in an elegant backwards arc and landed with a splat, imitating what he hoped happened to the warlock. I couldn't help but smile. "I doubt he fell like that, but that would have been fun to watch."

A chuff from the floor made me look down. Gimli sat next to his food bowl, forlorn.

"It's not yet time for dinner," I said to him. He sighed and lay down next to the food bowl, waiting.

I needed to talk to my other witch friends, so I did what any self-respecting witch would do. I picked up my cell phone.

"Why is a warlock working for the miners?" asked my best friend, Flo, a water witch.

"He needs the money, Flo. You know how warlocks are. They go to the highest bidder. They're guns for hire."

"Still," said Flo, clucking her tongue, "disgraced wizards they may be, but being so careless with magic that he pushed the fire as far as it went? That seems more than careless. I'm calling the Council. Maybe I can learn why this particular wizard went warlock and if the Council is looking for him."

"Thanks, Flo. I appreciate it."

"Holly?"

"Yes?"

"How close was the fire to your cabin?"

"Less than three miles."

"Get some protection spells up."

"Flo—"

"What if he's a patsy meant to take the fall when they mean to harm you? Not the land, but *you*."

I hung up, mad at myself for not thinking of that. I should have flung him harder.

I hiked down to the nearest town, a middle-sized place called Mathersville. Mather was the last name of the founding family. Miners, all of them.

Gimli and Sadie accompanied me to the diner. It was an old place with worn red stools, wooden booths, and a perpetual air of grease. The food was delicious.

I slipped into a booth, and Sadie and Gimli snuggled under the table at my feet. Most people wouldn't let two dogs into the restaurant, but Minnie didn't mind.

"Hey, Holly! Good to see you." Minnie rested a pad of paper on her swollen stomach. "After you eat, would you be willing to check the baby?"

"Of course, but you know everything is fine. I checked him out last week."

"I know, but it would make me feel better," she said with a shrug. "The usual?"

"Perfect," I said. "But hold the ketchup for Gimli. It gives him gas."

In record time, Minnie was sliding a plate on my table holding a grilled portobello mushroom with onions on a homemade roll. She slid another plate with two beef hamburgers under the table for the dogs. Sadie took a single, delicate bite but Gimli snarfed his down. Then the poor guy was stuck watching Sadie eat the rest of hers.

"He never learns," remarked Minnie.

"Nope. Bulldog through and through."

"I'll be back for that baby check when you're done eating."

The scent of the mushroom and onions was heavenly. I took a bite, eyes closed to savor that first wonderful taste. I opened my eyes when the dogs growled, and was met with a most unpleasant sight—Gareth Walker.

"What the hell?"

"Holly. Ms. Springfield. I need to talk to you."

"No mining."

"Humans are scared. The Fae are powerful and the only thing that hurts them is silver. There is a huge demand for it now and we owe it to the general public…"

"*I* don't owe them anything. What they fail to realize is that that humans have *always* existed side by side with the Fae. The only thing that's changed is they now know about it."

"Ms. Springfield, I have great respect for witches, but I am here to warn you. At the risk of sounding cliché, D.B. isn't going to take no for an answer. Your land is full of silver. He wants it, and will do anything to get it."

"Including burning down my woods and cabin?"

"That was an accident. OUCH!"

I craned my neck to look under the table. I eyeballed Gimli but he gave me an innocent stare. Sadie hid her eyes behind her paw, laughing.

"Just so you know, he bites liars."

"That's it. I've tried to play nice, but you refuse to see reason. They're going to get you, and your little dogs too!"

"Seriously? That is *really* a cliché."

He stormed out, leg bleeding from Gimli's bite. I worried he'd get an infection. Gimli, not Gareth. A little bit of blood had dropped on the floor. I swiped at it with a napkin and put it in my pocket. Not sure what I'd do with it, but blood was always handy.

"Come over here, Minnie. Let me see how that beautiful baby is doing."

I placed my hands on Minnie's stomach and closed my eyes, linking to the fetus. He was strong and peaceful. All the parts were in the right place. Midwifery was one of my favorite things about being an earth witch.

"He's great, Minnie. Strong and healthy. Two more months."

"Thanks, Holly. Pack something to take with you? On the house."

"Thanks, Minnie. That'd be real nice."

I exited with two dogs and two doggie bags. I hadn't walked but four paces when a new set of feet stepped in time beside me on the right, Gimli between us.

"Ms. Springfield?" said the man, doffing his cowboy hat.

I turned to gaze at him. Levis, a black T-shirt, and a blazer. Big belt buckle to match the hat. Mousey brown hair with sideburns. Texas corporate chic. But it all looked a little forced, like he was trying to be something he wasn't.

"Yes," I said finally.

Sadie slipped around and got on the right side of the man. Now he was surrounded by dogs. He noticed for sure, because he cleared his throat with a little warble.

"Douglas Brant, ma'am. I've wanted to meet you."

"Douglas Brant, as in DB Miners Douglas Brant?"

He gave a small bow and a tight laugh. "The very one."

"I've wanted to meet you too."

"Really? Well, that's great. I'm here to make you a serious financial offer for your land."

"Forget it. Stay away from me. You're getting me angry."

"Well, I'm getting mighty upset too, ma'am. You haven't heard my offer yet."

"It doesn't matter. The answer is no."

I reached out to the Earth and asked for a little help as I stalked away. D.B. tried to follow, but was shocked to find his feet were glued to the ground.

As I hiked back up the mountain, I noticed someone in the shadows. An extremely tall man with a long leather duster and a staff. I sensed him looking at me. I wanted nothing to do with him, because if he was who I thought he was, he was Council, and those conceited, arrogant morons could bite me. I did like his gigantic dog, though, and Sadie gave the dog a sidelong glance of interest.

"No, Sadie. We'd best let those two pass on through," I said.

I hiked up the mountain, which was easier for me than for others because the Earth guided my steps and gave me strength. As I got closer to my cabin, there was a sense of urgency. I stopped for a moment and listened. The forest was quiet. Truly quiet. No insects. No owls. No bats. Even the pink petunias in the window box were still, as if the Earth had stopped breathing. Maybe She had.

Gimli and Sadie sensed it too, and stayed silent, with only a baritone rumble in Gimli's chest so deep it was almost out of hearing range. I dropped my bags and felt out with my magic to find out who was there. The Earth showed me four men, all carrying rifles, hidden at various spots around my home.

A raccoon scurried up to me, eyes frantic. I knelt down and petted him. "Yes, I know, little one. I see them. Don't worry." The raccoon gave me a little nudge with his nose and scampered off to hide. I felt my anger rise. Now they were scaring my animals and bringing guns to kill me. I was done.

Mother Earth helped to muffle my steps as I crept forward. I didn't want to kill these guys, but they had guns. There might not be a choice. I noticed one man hiding under the limbs of my friend Grand Daddy Oak. I chuckled. *This will be fun.*

The old oak slithered a thin branch down and touched the man on the shoulder. He jumped and looked around, eyes wild and white with fear. Another branch tapped him on his other shoulder, and the man shouted, "Who's there?"

"Howard!" hissed one of his comrades. "Shut the hell up!"

"There's something hunting us, Jim. I told you this place was creepy. This woman is a witch, remember? We shouldn't be waiting for her *here.*"

"Howard, stop being such a pansy."

At that moment the oak leaned down, wrapped a branch around the terrified man, and flung him over the trees and out of sight. He howled as he catapulted through the air, and I hoped the man didn't get seriously hurt, but seeing as he was there to kill me, I didn't waste time thinking about it. I didn't feel any sympathetic pain, so he was most likely fine.

His cry spooked the others. They ran from their hiding spaces, and as soon as they were in the clearing, the ground shifted. Rocks rose from the Earth and gathered into a landslide. All three men lost their footing, dropped their guns, and tumbled ass over teakettle down the mountain. I could tell from my body's reaction that they had some bumps, bruises, and a few scratches, but no one died.

The forest erupted with happy twitters, amused growls, and scurrying sounds as the woodland creatures collectively exhaled. The raccoon emerged and offered me his paw in formal handshake, bowing from the waist as he did so. Chuck dropped onto my shoulder and groomed my hair, chittering the whole time. Birds swooped in circles, crickets chirped, owls hooted, and the forest came alive. The dogs ran, not sure where they were going but back and forth, back and forth.

Gimli, not a natural sprinter, tried to keep up with Sadie, and the sight was simply too funny.

And then it suddenly stopped again.

Gareth Walker emerged from the shadows.

"I advised them not to send men with guns to your sanctuary," he said. "But *they* wouldn't listen."

"*They* were idiots. Why are you here?"

"Because now it's my job to kill you."

"That's not going to work out for me. I have a dentist appointment next week."

The warlock drew back his hand and, with a word of power, threw a ball of fire at my head. The fireball missed but blasted the trees behind me. As they started to burn, I could *feel* their pain.

Scuttling to my right in a crouch, I aimed a round rock, the size of my palm, straight for Gareth's head.

"Let my aim fly true, Mother," I whispered. The rock struck him hard and he fell to his knees, bleeding from a large gash on his temple. But he didn't stop. Fire was his game and he was going to use it. He struggled back to his feet, and another ball of flame flew from his hands and exploded onto my house. My heart sank. All I owned was being consumed by the fire. The forest was screaming.

My dogs circled around Gareth, and the warlock grinned as he pointed a long crooked finger at Gimli. A needle of flame flew straight at my dog's face. Gimli turned to escape but the fire lanced his side and he fell to the ground, yelping in pain. I shrieked.

In a rage, Sadie dove for Gareth's legs and bowled him over. She leaped on top of him and held him down, baring her teeth, staring straight into his eyes. I ran to them, but before I got there, he'd grabbed Sadie by the collar and shoved her off. Gareth staggered to his feet and he glared at me, eyes black, mouth set tight.

Sadie recovered in a flash and dashed to Gimli's side, but he was standing on all fours by the time she got there. He didn't appear badly wounded, just mad as hell. Sadie gave him a reassuring bump and licked his nose.

A surge of water bubbled up from the ground and rose at least fifteen feet in the air, dousing the burning trees and building. *Thank you, Mother.* The cavalry, finally.

I turned and focused on heaving the ground beneath Gareth to the side, creating a pit. He fell straight down into the hole until he stopped at his neck. He was trapped and he knew it. I pulled the Earth close against him and he gasped for air. I struggled to breathe just as Gareth did. Earth witches couldn't escape physical law. An action always has an equal and opposite reaction.

Flo hurried up. "I'm glad I got here in time," she said, watching me fighting for a breath. "I checked with the Council."

"And?" I wheezed.

"He was labeled a warlock because he started a fire that killed several humans, an air witch, and a couple of lesser Fae."

"Don't certain members of the Council regularly start fires?"

"Yes, but this was malicious. Intent to murder."

The warlock in front of me was turning blue and I felt his panic. I studied him for a moment and made a decision, knowing the cost.

I pulled the bloody napkin out of my pocket and whispered a single word, *maak*, Hebrew for to squeeze or to press. I opened the pit wider and deeper and, with the push of blood magic, he fell in all the way. I closed the pit and compressed the Earth.

My arms pressed into my sides, my legs pressed together.
My feet—my feet. The Earth pressed me from my feet up. Searing pain roiled inside my body as my toes, then ankles, were crushed.
No more . . . no more . . . let this end. Let this end!
Unspeakable pain shook me as first my legs broke, and then my pelvis.
I screamed as my blood watered the Earth.
My manhood, ripped from my groin.
My stomach. My innards.

Finally, my heart, pressed flat, weighed down by the weight of the world. Then a millimeter-by-millimeter compression, until, finally, my heart burst.

Relief. No pain. Floating. Wait.

Something was ahead. Fire? What was this . . . ? Oh my God . . .

Flo held my head in her lap as I came too.

My price was to feel it as he did, to experience the death I caused. I dragged myself to my knees, crawled away, and vomited into the dirt.

I managed to whisper, "That's for my dog. And my trees. And my house. And for the people you murdered."

That's right. Don't fool with an earth witch when death was on the line.

Spent and bruised from the inside out, I fretted about would happen next. I knew it wouldn't be good. If their gunmen failed, and their warlock failed, DB Miners was going to send something worse.

Flo sat cross-legged next to me and poured healing magic into my body like mountain water streaming into a cool lake. Most of my physical injuries mended quickly, but my spirit still suffered a wound that might never heal.

I gave thanks to the Earth and to the animals and trees surrounding me, and apologized for the fire and noxious smoke. Grand Daddy Oak got a special pat. I double-checked that Gimli was okay and then we all piled into Flo's truck, dogs in the open back, tongues out, and drove to her home, which was, naturally, by a lake.

We entered the house and immediately the phone rang. Then my cell phone rang. Then Flo's cell phone rang. Then mine again. We rushed to pick up anything that was ringing. I answered my cell.

"Holly, it's Marc, Minnie's husband," said a breathless voice.

"Marc, I know who you are, silly. What's going on?"

"He's got Minnie!"

"Who has Minnie?"

"Douglas Brant. He is holding her at gunpoint in the diner. He wants you. You have to come!"

Flo's cell phone was up to one ear and her landline to the other, obviously getting the same news from both. She gave me a grave nod.

"Marc, I am fifteen minutes away. I'm coming. Tell him not to touch a hair on her head or so help me, I won't just kill him, I'll kill him painfully. Make sure he knows that."

We piled into the truck and drove into town at top speed. The dogs flattened themselves against the floor and hung on. They knew something was very wrong. We were all exhausted but the new kick of adrenaline was doing its job. So far, we'd fought four bad guys with guns, and a crazed warlock. Now we had to go face a different danger. A thug with a gun held my friend hostage. This was a long day.

I let my anger grow. It fueled me. Beneath us, the road trembled.

Flo said, "Holly, calm down. You can't go in there this hot. And I can't drive if the road keeps shifting, so lock it down. Now."

I did. Barely.

We pulled up to a cross street and parked. Flo said, "You should be calm when talking to this guy—restrained. Remember your top priority is Minnie and her baby. Anything else can be fixed later."

I had no interest in experiencing another death, but the lives of my friend and her unborn child were on the line. "Am I an earth witch or not?" I muttered.

I stalked to the very center of the abandoned street. I could practically hear the spaghetti western theme song. Flo stood behind me. The dogs stood on my sides, Sadie on my left, Gimli on my right, heads down, ears back. You would have thought they were pointers with the way they were focused on the diner's front door.

"Let my friend go and I might, just might, let you live," I bellowed. The road trembled and the trees along the side streets swayed. An entire flock of birds took flight.

Out of the corner of my eye, I saw residents coming out onto the street to stand behind me. Marc's neck muscles bulged with his fury, and two large men had to hold him back. I was afraid he'd do something stupid, so I gestured to Gimli to go calm him down. Gimli trotted off, stood in front of Marc and looked up at him. Marc bent down and the two stared into each other's eyes. Marc gave a curt nod and Gimli came back to me.

I called again.

"My name is Holly Springfield, earth witch of the seventh order! By my name and my power I call you to come forward and explain yourself!" I put a little more mojo in those words and the storefront shuddered with the movement of the earth.

Douglas Brant pushed a terrified Minnie through the door first, his feet fighting for purchase as the ground rolled. He had a gun to her head, and, in the other hand, a piece of paper. I pulled the mojo back, worried the gun would go off.

"I tried to do this nicely. I tried to offer you money. I tried sending a warlock to warn you. My guys were sent to scare you . . . "

"Your guys were sent to kill me."

He waved the paper back and forth. "Scare . . . kill . . . you say potato, I say potahto. Like I really believed they could kill you."

"Well, with the guns and all, I think maybe you thought they could."

"And look how wrong I was! Gareth didn't come back either."

"He's not going to. He had a pressing problem."

D.B. shook his head in confusion, but let that last comment slide. "So, we are going to do this the hard way."

Minnie sobbed. That sound broke me. I made up my mind. I took a deep breath, and then another. I closed my eyes and focused on an image of the baby growing inside my friend. Flo was right. The priority was Minnie and the baby. Everything else could be fixed later.

"I assume that paper is for me to sign over my rights to the mountain and surrounding acreage to you?"

"Well, aren't you the smart one? Sign it and I don't kill her. Don't sign it and I do kill her—and, of course, the baby."

"I'll sign it. Sadie, go get the paper from the evil man." She gave me the eye. "No, you can't bite him yet."

Shaking her head as if to say *Why the hell not*, Sadie walked over to D.B. He leaned back a little and held the paper out by one corner, trying to stay away from the dog's teeth. She took the other edge of the paper and trotted back to me. D.B. grabbed Minnie by the neck with his now free hand.

"Someone give me a pen." Someone did. I didn't notice who, just signed the paper and handed it back to Sadie, who trotted back to D.B. and placed it at his feet. She gave him a quick fake lunge and he almost fell backward in fear. Unfortunately, that caused him to pull on Minnie's neck and Minnie gave a cry of pain. Sadie gave Minnie an apologetic glance and came back. I shook my finger at my dog. She looked at me, and I swear, she shrugged. I didn't even know dogs could shrug.

"There. You have it. Now let Minnie go," I said.

"As part of this contract, you have to abandon your house and leave the land."

"No problem. Your warlock burned my house. Nothing to go back to."

"Burned it?" He smiled. "Delightful. Now, I'm going to let Minnie here go slowly, and you are going to stay still or I'll shoot her in the back. Got it?"

"Yes."

Minnie pulled away from D.B. and staggered across the street, hurrying as she got closer, wrapping her arms around her tummy. Marc enveloped her with both arms and they held each other, gripping tight.

"Now, Ms. Springfield. I'm getting into my truck right there and you are going to let me go."

"Why on Earth should I do that?"

"Because I planted a bomb in this diner and I'll blow everyone to hell if you don't."

D.B. held up the detonator, which had been clipped to his belt. I hadn't even noticed it. He backpedaled all the way to his truck, got in, and drove away with the detonator and his thumb where we could all see it.

When his taillights faded out of sight, whispers about the bomb flittered through the crowd. Flo nudged me with her elbow. "We need to remove that explosive."

"I know. Let's go look. Everybody else stay back."

We tiptoed into the diner and peeked in. D.B. wasn't lying. There was a small device sitting on the counter.

We walked in close to the bomb, my heart fluttering in my chest. Flo turned the water on in a nearby commercial sink, letting it gush full blast, and gathered her power. The water flowed in a beautiful wave over to the explosive and completely encased it inside a dense water bubble. She floated the water-enclosed bomb toward the door. I shut off the flowing sink and opened the door for her and the bomb. Flo was drenched with sweat from the effort of using both air and water magic. She jerked her head toward a patch of dry scrub.

Suddenly understanding, I ran ahead and opened a hole in the ground several hundred feet deep. Flo dropped the water-encased bomb in and I moved dirt to fill in the empty space. There was an eerie moment of silence and then a concussive blast rose and rippled across the surface. Storefront windows shook. Car alarms shrieked. I'm pretty sure a tree house fell down and a swing set collapsed in the neighborhood park, but no one was injured. Flo and I sank to the ground, exhausted.

Minnie waddled over. "Oh, Holly, thank you! I was so scared for my baby."

Marc joined her and so did about three dozen other town citizens, all thanking us for saving Minnie and the buildings.

"But Holly," said Minnie. "You gave up the mountain rights. You've lost your land."

"Don't worry about that. All that matters is that you're safe."

Both dogs grunted their assent. Gimli gave Minnie's hand a lick.

"You want food, don't you, big guy? Well, a hamburger for you seems fair. Sadie?"

Sadie's tongue lolled out.

"I guess so. Anyone else hungry?"

The entire town crowded into the diner. My dogs enjoyed some treats. I finally moved to a corner chair and dozed. Tomorrow, I was getting my land back.

The earthmovers and men in hard hats started at sunrise, roaming *my* land with impunity, poking here and prodding there as if the Earth had no feelings. I hid in plain sight with the Earth's arms wrapped around me. True camouflage. The workers could have bumped into me, of course, but that didn't happen.

Before leaving Flo's, I had checked the town's bylaws to make sure I remembered an obscure town statute correctly. That was my ace.

Several men had gathered a few yards yonder. Douglas Brant was with them, his back to me. Looking at him made my heart pound in my ears, and my hands itched to reach out with my magic and drop him into a hole too. But I didn't. No matter how vile he was, I didn't want to risk harming the men that worked for him. They had done nothing except their jobs.

The men were planning where to dig and were trying to understand the density of the soil and rock beneath them. That gave me an idea.

I touched the ground and asked the stones, boulders, and even the pebbles to rise to the surface, and asked the Earth to harden Her shell. Some rocks spoke back, explaining that if they moved, the mountain would become unstable. Those stayed where they were, but others travelled up and lay down in a several-foot layer right under the surface. At my request, the Earth moved the silver veins deeper toward the center of the mountain.

The Earth's movements caused the mountain to shake and roll. Several of the men lost their balance, even though we were nowhere near the steepest part of the mountain's incline. The tremors continued for several minutes as the entire internal configuration of the mountain changed. Men struggled to hold machines in place, but despite their efforts at least two earthmovers rolled backward down the mountain slope, then tipped over the sides, enormous booms announcing their inevitable acquiesce to gravity. One man, charging after a machine, almost followed it into a crevasse, but a co-worker grabbed his shirt in time.

Shouts reverberated across the mountain and valley below. When the tremors stopped, men struggled to their feet and got their wits about them.

"What the fuck was that?"

"We don't get earthquakes here!"

"The *hell* with this!"

The foreman said, "Mr. Brant, we can't stay up here with active tremors. We have to evacuate and get some engineers out here to double check the stability of the mountain." Then he turned and said, "Collect only necessary gear and move out!"

The men jumped into their vehicles and skedaddled down the mountain, taking the switchbacks a little too fast. When a few of them glanced behind, I gave the mountain a little shake to convince them to keep going.

Douglas Brant was soon the only one standing there. He looked around him in fury.

"I know you are here, witch," he shouted.

I released the camouflage and stepped forward where he could see me. He was above me, about twenty-five feet up the mountain.

"You stole my mountain. And my land."

"Stole? Naw, I used extreme measures to procure it, but you signed. You gave it to me."

"You threatened lives. Minnie's and then the whole town's with that bomb."

"In the end, it doesn't matter, Ms. Springfield. I have the signed document and it is filed with the county clerk, nice and proper. You can't prove anything."

"I have dozens of eyewitnesses."

"Who will tell their stories to Judge Glenn, the most rampant anti-witch, wizard, and Fae man I've ever had the pleasure to meet."

"Who gets the land if you die?" I said through gritted teeth.

"What?"

"Did you already deed the land to next of kin?"

His eyes narrowed.

"The law says that the land reverts to the previous owner if the death comes within forty-eight hours of sale without a designated heir. I, of course, would be expected to return the money that you paid me to your business or family, but since you paid me nothing, that isn't a problem."

Dougie-boy's eyebrows shot up as he realized that he was in trouble. There was no one else around, no backup.

I sank his feet into the dirt about six inches. Eyes wide, he pulled his feet free and jigged to the side. As he did so, he fell to his knees. The sharp jolt to the knees was minor, but it reminded me of the price I would pay for causing a death. The warlock's death still lived in my mind.

"Okay," he said, voice quavering. "You win. I see your point. There's nothing to keep you from killing me. I'll give you back the land. We'll go down the mountain together. We'll go to the county clerk's office and I'll re-deed it back to you. No need to get crazy."

I didn't trust him but I was hoping not to kill him. "Exactly my thought, Douglas. Glad you can see reason."

I took careful steps toward the one remaining Jeep. Douglas mimicked my actions and did the same. We both got in at the same time, with him in the driver's seat. I didn't like that he was in control of the vehicle but he had the keys. I would rather have walked, using magic to make good time, but I wasn't letting D.B. out of my sight.

We drove the switchbacks at a steady but safe pace. As repugnant as he was, it seemed like D.B. was going to play ball on this one. We could get out of this with no more deaths.

I was mulling this over when we accelerated. D.B. shoved me out as we hit a hairpin turn smack in the middle of the mountain. The momentum threw me out of the vehicle before I could grab hold of the Earth and I flew downward, hitting the ground with a thunk, rolling and rolling until I stopped. My right side hurt like hell, particularly my right wrist and elbow that took the brunt of the fall. It all happened so fast I hadn't tried to even grab Air.

I saw the Jeep on the escarpments above me, taking an alternate road to leave me as far behind as possible.

That was it. The last straw.

Asking the Earth for help, I staggered forward. I called Air to push me and bounded across the mountain like a man on the moon. I stopped right in front of him, only a few yards away, and then reached down and rippled the Earth like I was shaking out a long carpet. The ripples jostled the Jeep, toppling it over, and destabilized several larger rocks from above, which came raining down on our position. One of them hit D.B. a glancing blow on the head. That hurt us both. He was bleeding now and his left leg was pinned under the car.

Ignoring the throbbing in my head and the pressure in my leg, I said, "Douglas Brant! I find you guilty of sins against the Earth, humans, and witches. For that, the punishment is death." I gestured toward rocks higher up the mountain and they pelted down. D.B. looked up one time, hid his head with his right arm, and was swallowed by a hell storm of igneous badness.

I fell to my knees with the pain.
Sharp, pounding hits on the head.
Crushing weight.
Heart hammering, agony and shock.
Gasping, begging for breath.
One final hit.
Then, finally, blackness.

I was shaking hard and barely conscious when I heard a huge crack. I scrambled back in time to see a pine tree fall on top of the rocks with a resounding crash. The Earth yawned and swallowed Jeep, rocks, and man. The tree lay on top like a grave marker.

I touched the Earth. She seemed settled. Creaking and groaning, but satisfied. I whispered a word of thanks and limped back down the mountain, aching from injuries no one could see.

I took it easy and didn't ask any more help of the Earth. While I had sent the rocks to plummet down on D.B.'s head, I hadn't made the tree fall or caused the Earth to gulp him down. She did that on Her own.

It's not nice to mess with an earth witch, but Mother Nature is a true bitch.

J.D. Blackrose loves all things storytelling and celebrates great writing by posting about it on her website, slipperywords.com.

When not writing, Blackrose lives with three children, an enormous orange cat, her husband and a full-time job in corporate communications. She's fearful that so-called normal people will discover exactly how often she thinks about wicked fairies, nasty wizards, homicidal elevators, treacherous forests, and the odd murder, even when she is supposed to be having coffee with a friend or cheering her daughter on during a soccer game. As a survival tactic, she has mastered the art of looking interested.

J.D. Blackrose is the fantasy and dark fiction pen name for Joelle M. Reizes

sliperywords.com

@JReizes

Joelle M. Reizes on Facebook.

A Mother's Fury

by

C.W. Blackwell

CORA WAS SCREAMING.

Jeanie was the first to react. She threw off the wool blanket and curled her left arm around the girl with her bowie knife raised in the other hand like some Abrahamic parable. She shushed the girl and patted her forehead and kissed her behind the ear.

"It's all right," she breathed, searching Cora's small form in the pre-dawn light. "Tell Mommy what's wrong."

Joe was on his knees with the Beretta cupped in both hands, blinking away the numbness of sleep. He sat that way until Cora settled into sort of a weeping pant and then he rose stiffly to his left leg. His prosthetic struggled for a grip on the leaf-littered aluminum roof.

A cluster of pine needles was in the folds of Cora's sleeping bag and she was pointing at it with her finger trembling.

"Get it off, Mommy," she managed with halting breath. Jeanie scooped it with the knife and flung it aside.

"Those pine needles aren't gonna hurt you," she said. "We're safe up here."

"Cross your heart?"

"Cross my heart."

They had camped atop the canopy of an eight-pump ARCO station and built a small fire that was more for reassurance than for warmth. The fire had sunk to a mound of ash and the sun was still just a foggy rumor in the eastern hills. Joe walked the perimeter of the pump canopy, peering onto the road at the minivan below. The windows of the minivan were intact. The ladder they had set across the chasm between the minimart and the pump canopy was still stored safely where they'd hauled it up for security. He watched a fat raccoon growl and chitter across the road with two juveniles close behind and then disappear into the bushes.

Cora was still breathing hard.

"Everything's okay," said Joe. He tucked the Beretta in his pants. "Not more than fifteen minutes till sunrise."

"How long till the desert?" asked Cora, wiping her tears.

"Tomorrow," said Jeanie.

"So one more night?"

"Yes."

They ate a bag of stale tortilla chips and waited until the sun cleared the trees before they crawled over the ladder to the roof of the minimart. When they got across, Joe pulled the ladder and winked at Cora and kissed her on the head. But he turned to Jeanie with a worried look and tapped on the side of the ladder. There was a spiral mark around the ladder's frame as if a vine had probed it while they slept. Jeanie rubbed at it with her fingertips and then shook her head.

"It's growing higher," she said grimly.

Joe nodded and then lowered the ladder to the ground.

They sat in the minivan for a moment with Joe turning the stereo knob, but there was only static. Jeanie and Cora were buckled in the bench seat with a blanket tucked around them waiting for the heater to warm up.

Joe thumbed the knob and killed the static.

"I'm gonna take a look around the gas station before we leave."

Jeanie's eyes were like stones. "We have enough," she said. "Just drive."

"We have enough to get there. Who knows what kind of setup Vernon has, or how many folks he's taken in already."

Jeanie looked out the window and pressed her hand against the glass. There were wavy marks that ran up the dusty surface from the outside. Cora was lying in her lap, her curly hair blooming from the folds of the blanket.

"Fine," she said. "Be quick though."

"I'll leave the van running," said Joe.

The door to the minimart was propped open with a garbage can. When he entered, he found the shelves toppled over and the floor littered with crushed bags of junk food and lottery tickets. The coolers had been emptied of beer and wine, but he found a few unbroken bottles of tea and diet soda and he stuffed those in a pillowcase. There was a package of juice boxes, and he threw those in too. He found a quart of milk, twisted off the top and gave it a sniff. He winced, turned it over and a glugged a gooey stream onto the linoleum.

Beyond the cash register was a door that led to an auto repair bay. There were a few cars lined up with their wheels lying flat on the shop floor. Joe rummaged through the toolboxes that were lined against the wall and slid a crowbar and a ten-inch flathead screwdriver into the pillowcase. He found a case of cigarette lighters and threw that in too.

There was a noise behind him and he spun around. There was a form hunched in the driver seat of a late-'90s pickup, dark and motionless. He raised the Beretta and edged closer. A rat leaped from the shattered driver window and scurried under the truck. He tried the latch and it clicked open. Inside was a human body, its skin a thick pelt of green moss, dappled with dark nodules. Mushrooms grew from the eyes and mouth in strange bouquets, like something left in a compost bin. The corpse wore a polyester jumpsuit with the name "Buddy" embroidered on the breast.

Joe fished a pack of cigarettes from Buddy's front pocket and lit it one with a lighter from the case. A sense of well-being filled him as he inhaled. He blew the smoke out into the repair bay and leaned against the bed of the pickup, just staring at the corpse.

"Ain't no way to die, Buddy," he said, and took another drag. "But I thank you for the smoke all the same."

Outside there was a scream.

Joe dropped the cigarette and ran back through the minimart with the pillowcase in one hand and the pistol in the other. Another scream. The minivan jostled in its frame. He could see Jeanie inside, shielding Cora with her body. A large stag swiped at the van repeatedly with a heavy rack of antlers. It reared and attacked the side window as if trying to break the glass and then bounded stiffly into the air, landing with its eyes dark and mad. Joe dropped the pillowcase and raised the Beretta. The animal took notice. It pranced around the front of the van and lowered its antlers to the ground, steam piping from its heaving snout. Joe inched closer and curled his finger around the trigger.

He never had a chance to fire. The engine roared and the minivan leaped forward, knocking the animal onto its ribcage. The stag kicked its feet, trying to right itself but the tires spun and smoked and the beast couldn't get clear of the front bumper. Joe ran to the van, slid the door open and jumped inside. Jeanie was in the driver seat, her teeth clenched and her hands gripping the wheel as if she were wringing the life from it.

Joe wrapped his arms around Cora.

"Let's go," he said.

Jeanie threw the transmission into reverse with her foot all the way into the pedal. The stag slumped and then began to right itself, but she already had the vehicle in drive and swerved out onto the main road with the animal lost in a cloud of tan dust.

Jeanie gunned the minivan down a straightaway, her knuckles white on the wheel. "Find anything good in there?" Her voice was cool, and she said it without taking her eyes off the road.

Joe peered at the rear window. He thought he could make out the pillowcase still lying in the dirt. He sighed, and then slid a roll of lottery tickets into the cup holder of the center console.

"Maybe we'll get lucky," he said softly.

Jeanie whipped her head around with a piercing look, and then turned back to the road without saying a word. She glanced at the stack of lottery tickets a few times. After a moment she started to laugh. Her laugh grew sort of wild and then Joe started laughing too.

"Why are you laughing?" asked Cora.

"We could win the lottery," said Jeanie, still laughing.

"That's good, right?"

Joe reached over the driver seat, squeezed Jeanie's shoulder and hugged Cora with the other arm.

"Yeah," he said. "That would be great."

They drove along a cinder-colored highway through a forest of tall pines. The ridge on the other side of the valley was charred and barren from a recent wildfire. Near the town of Hume they passed a wood-paneled station wagon headed the other direction, crowded with old and young alike. The car slowed as it passed, their faces sharp and wide-eyed and pressed against the glass. A dog glowered in the rear window like a gargoyle.

"Where are they going, Daddy?" Cora said.

"The other way. Back where we came," said Joe.

"Back home?"

"No. Somewhere else." He handed her a canteen and twisted off the top. "Home isn't safe."

Cora drank a few sips and then wiped her mouth.

"Because Mother Nature wants us all to die now," she said, staring into the passing trees.

"Nature doesn't want us all to die," said Jeanie. "It just wants balance."

"Because we unbalanced it?"

No one replied at first, as if her words had landed somewhere and needed time to disembark.

"Yes," said Jeanie. "We did. Not you or me or your father, but all of us. It'll take some time, that's all."

"How much time?"

"I don't know."

By evening, the pine forest had given way to old and tired oak trees that splayed from the hillsides like the hands of the dead. They pulled off the highway at a crossroads where some pioneer-era general store rotted alone in the dark. Joe untied the ladder from the roof rack and tilted it against the weathered eves of the old building.

"Can't build a fire up here," he said. The piston in his prosthesis groaned as he climbed the ladder. "But we got plenty of room and it's far enough from the tree line."

A coyote yipped somewhere in the distance and Cora clambered up the first few rungs with her eyes wide.

"Can we use the lantern, Daddy?"

"Yes, but only for a bit. I'll let you sleep with the flashlight though."

"Okay. Promise we'll be safe?"

"Cross my heart."

The girl fell asleep not long after dark. She lay nestled in the blankets with her breath deep and steady while Jeanie and Joe watched the sky blacken and the galactic core pierce the horizon like some strange frond unfolding in the void. They lay silent for a long while.

"Do you believe it?" Joe whispered. "That nature's just trying to make some correction?"

"Maybe. I don't know," she said. "It's the simplest answer. Doesn't nature always find balance?"

They were silent again. Joe watched a satellite sweep across the dome of the sky.

"I wish I believed in balance," he said. "It would make this all worth it somehow. I just think chaos is more regular. You know, maybe a system forms here and there like a bubble, and everyone thinks it's perfect. Maybe it is for a while. But then it pops and there's nothing left but the chaos that was waiting the whole time."

"Like what you saw overseas?"

"Yeah, like that. The bubble just popped and everything filled with . . ." His voice trailed off and he shook his head.

"With what?"

"Chaos. Mayhem."

She found his hand in the dark and held it as they fell asleep.

"Mommy," Cora said, shaking Jeanie awake. "Daddy's choking."

Jeanie launched to her knees and grabbed Joe by the shoulders. The moon was now overhead and she could see a bright froth trailing from the corner of his mouth. His eyes were white and upturned. He was gasping for breath.

"Find the flashlight," she told Cora.

"I don't know where is," she cried, scooping the blankets in a pile. She lifted them and shook, and a small Maglite clattered on the wooden roof. Jeanie grabbed it, flipped on the light and shined it at Joe.

Around his wrist was a tight loop of vines that grew from the rotten gutters of the old building. They had bored into his radial artery and anchored to his wrist with a pulsing green sac like some kind of kelp pod. Jeanie screamed and tore at the vines and sliced them off with the bowie knife. She stabbed at the sac but it kept pulsing like some angry heart. Joe arched his back and kicked out his legs.

"Joe! Just hold on, honey," Jeanie pleaded.

"Don't die, don't die," Cora sobbed.

Jeanie groped for the propane lantern and twisted the filaments from the canister. She stabbed at the canister valve with the bowie knife until it began to hiss.

"Stand back, Cora," she said.

She flicked a cigarette lighter and a blinding stream of fire poured from the valve, jolting the shadows all around them. Cora tumbled to her side as Jeanie leveled the stream of fire over the pulsing node on Joe's wrist. The thing quivered and shrank from the heat and then detached, tumbling away as it sizzled against the old dark wood.

Joe gasped and choked. His eyes rolled back to center and he reached out to Jeanie with his hand shaking. She threw the canister down to the road and held him there while he tried to breathe. Cora grabbed his hand and wept, her tears falling in the webs of his fingers. The glow from the road faltered and darkened, and Joe's breath stopped.

"No baby, no, don't you dare," said Jeanie.

Joe's head fell to the side. A single vine emerged from his mouth and searched the contours of his jaw line before lying still against his cheek.

They sat there for a while, listening to the sound of rustling all around them. The building was creaking as if it were shifting off the foundation.

"We have to go," said Jeanie.

"We can't leave him," said Cora, still holding Joe's hand.

"It's not safe, honey."

"We can't," sobbed the girl. Her tears glistened on her cheeks.

"He'd want us to go. Let's go now."

When the sun rose they had travelled two hundred miles in the dark, stopping only once at a weigh station to empty the last gas can into the tank. By now the hills had flattened to a wide sandy pan dotted with endless sagebrush.

"Maybe he thinks we're dead," said Cora. She was sitting in the passenger seat with her feet on the dash and a pair of purple sunglasses on. It was the first thing she said since they started driving.

"Who thinks that?"

"Uncle Vernon."

"Well, we're not, are we?" said Jeanie.

"Daddy is. Maybe he is too."

"I think Uncle Vernon is alive."

"How do you know?"

"Because he lives in the desert, just like Daddy said. Things don't grow well in the desert."

Cora looked out at the desert scrub toward the bald hills on the horizon as if she were waiting for everything to dry up and die.

"Remember back home when you had me spray the weeds when they grew out of the cracks in the porch?" Cora said.

"Yes, I remember."

"Maybe we should look for more of that stuff."

"Weed killer?"

"Yeah, weed killer."

"That's a good idea," said Jeanie.

They came across the town of Randsburg, a choked-out mess of pitted stucco shacks and crooked trailers. Many of the buildings were charcoal shells, burned to the ground as if sparked by nothing more than the noonday heat. The entire town looked like an extreme comment on spontaneous combustion.

There was a billboard ad for an Indian casino on the side of the road, and beyond it Jeanie noticed what looked like a junkyard. Two Winnebagos were parked out front. She slowed the van and parked it in the shade of the billboard.

"Why are we stopping?" Cora asked.

"We need gas."

"I don't see any gas stations."

"Those RVs have big tanks. We can siphon the gas out like—"

"Like Daddy showed us?"

"Yeah, like that."

Jeanie unhooked the gas can from the back of the van and slung the garden hose over her shoulder. She was wearing one of Joe's sleeveless T-shirts, and she could almost feel her skin turning red in the baking sun. She had only taken a few steps toward the junkyard when Cora rolled the window down and called to her.

"I want to come," she said.

"No," said Jeanie.

"Please can I come?"

Jeanie looked at the girl over the top her sunglasses. She seemed so small in the van window.

"Fine. Just stay close."

They walked together up the dirt path to the junkyard, past a broken-down modular home that squatted in the shadow of a desert willow. There was a garden of pinwheels and dead grass around the front door of the modular, and a faded American flag that billowed from a bracket by the door.

"Think someone lives there?" Cora said.

"No, nobody lives there."

"How do you know?"

"All that dead grass blocking the door. Plus, no footprints anywhere."

When they reached the Winnebagos, Jeanie set down the gas can and garden hose and pulled Joe's Beretta from the waist of her jeans. She circled both vehicles, looking in the dirt for tracks. She leaned underneath the chassis.

"Still safe?" Cora said.

"Yes. Nobody's been here for a while."

Jeanie plumbed the filler housing with one end of the garden hose and started the siphon with the other end. There wasn't a lot in the tank, but there was enough to fill half the gas can. She moved on to the other RV, but that one had a lock on the gas cap. It took some time to bust it with the bowie knife. By the time she got the siphon going she had lost sight of Cora.

"Cora?" Jeanie called. Gas was flowing into the can.

Cora didn't respond.

"Cora?" She shouted this time.

There was a loud boom like a shotgun blast, and Cora screamed.

Jeanie ran around the side of the RV with her pistol drawn. The door to the RV was open and Cora was crouching beside it, still screaming. Jeanie scooped up the girl and drew her away from the door, the Beretta pointed at the opening.

"Are you hurt?"

"I don't know," said Cora, sobbing.

"Any blood?" Jeanie was patting her down while keeping the gun in the air.

Cora held out her palms and there were red scrapes where she had fallen in the dirt. "A little," she said.

"Tell me what happened."

"I just opened the door and it exploded."

Jeanie crept slowly to the door of the RV and peered in from the side. A string was looped around the door handle and led into the darkness of the vehicle. She squinted into the shadows and saw a shotgun leveled at the door, anchored onto the opposing counter with silver duct tape.

"What was it, Mommy?"

"A trap. A gun tied to the door."

"Was I shot? I felt wind on my head."

"No. You got lucky. It was set for someone taller."

Jeanie cleared the trap and untaped the shotgun from the counter. Inside the RV she found a mummified corpse covered in a crust of orange lichen. It was lying on a Formica table, its mouth agape, with green polyps crowding its lips and eyes. In the bunk above the corpse were six gallons of distilled water, a box of shotgun shells and three cans of chili con carne.

They loaded what they had found into the van and emptied the scavenged gas into the tank. The sun was now cooking the ghost town in a wave of hot, undulate air that blurred the road. It only took a minute or two before they passed the last shanty and were headed into the open desert.

"Did that man die the same way as Daddy?" Cora asked. She was looking in the side mirror as the town faded behind her. "Did nature kill him when he was sleeping?"

"I don't know how," said Jeanie. She reached across the cab for her hand. "It's possible."

"I thought it didn't happen in the desert."

"We're not all the way there yet. When we get there, we'll sleep in the dunes where there's nothing but sand."

"And during the day we'll stay with Uncle Vernon?"

"Yes, he runs the visitor center. He's a ranger, remember?"

"I remember. There were big palm trees and a rose garden out front. He baked us a loaf of raisin bread."

"Yes, that's right."

Cora was scratching at her scalp and pulled something from the curls. She was rolling it around between her fingers. He noticed the blood.

"What is it, Cora?"

The girl shrugged.

Jeanie opened her hand and Cora dropped a shiny round ball into her palm.

"It's buckshot, from the shotgun," said Jeanie. She checked her head for more, then after not finding any, squeezed her hand. "You got lucky."

By mid-afternoon, the scrub had become sparse and only a few gray shrubs sat upon the land like piles of cigar ash. They turned off the highway onto a two-lane road that had been paved within the past few years.

"Will we ever go back for Daddy?" asked Cora. She was playing with a Lego mini-figure dressed as a pirate. "You know, after Mother Nature stops being mad at us."

Jeanie's eyes welled with tears, as if Joe's death was something she could no longer bury.

"Yes," she said. "We'll go back for him."

"Badger," said Cora.

"What?"

"Badger. That's the town he died in. I saw it on a sign."

"Okay. We'll go back to Badger when this is all over."

"And we'll cremate him? That's what he wanted."

"I know, honey," said Jeanie. "I know."

The road turned sharply south along a bend where a few Joshua trees angled to the sky like dark scarecrows and a sage-stubbled hill lobed at the sky. Jeanie suddenly pressed the brake with both feet and the tires smoked and skidded to a halt. A barricade of fence posts and barbed wire stretched across the road and into the desert on both sides.

"What is it, Mommy?"

"I don't know. Just stay calm, and stay inside the van."

"Okay."

Jeanie reached behind the seat for the shotgun and checked both chambers. She handed the Beretta to Cora.

"The safety's off," said Jeanie. "You just point it and pull the trigger, okay?"

Cora held the gun like it was a piece of wood.

"I need you to say okay."

"Okay," said Cora.

Jeanie stepped out slowly, leveling the shotgun over the barricade. The sun was a white blot in the sky that bored into her skin as if through a magnifying glass. She stepped toward the jumble of wood in the road, and as she did so a man rose from behind the barricade with a pistol in his hand. Another man appeared on the other side of the woodpile. The long blade clutched in his fist glinted in the bright sun.

"Hey there," said the man with the gun. He brushed his dirty blond hair over his scalp and spat on the ground. "Where you headed?"

Jeanie didn't answer. She kept the shotgun pointed square at his chest.

"We don't mean no harm," said the blond man. "Just wonderin' if you got any food or water to share."

The other man turned to the van. He was older than the blond man, with a bushy black beard.

Cora curled into a ball in the passenger seat, peeking from beneath her hands.

"Don't look at her," said Jeanie.

"Earl don't mean nothin' by it," said the blond man. "He just ain't seen no young'uns in a month er so."

"Earl," said Jeanie. Her eyes shifted back and forth between the two men. "If you look at my daughter one more time I'm going to kill you."

Earl's eyes were large and wild. He flicked at the stubble on his throat with the blade and then patted it against his palm and spat.

The blond man took a step toward Jeanie.

"I can't be responsible for what Earl does, ma'am," he said. "Since the world ended he's been high every day. Not much else to do."

"You tell him to stop looking," said Jeanie. "I don't care what he's on."

The blond man laughed, and Earl laughed too.

"You can't blame us. I'm sure you've seen 'em too. All them bodies wrapped in vines and growin' mushrooms out their eyes. It's every man for himself."

"Just let us through," said Jeanie. "We've got family down the road."

"You talkin' about Kelso Station?" said the blond man. "We've been tryin' to get to Kelso for weeks. They ain't lettin' nobody through."

Earl took another tentative step toward the van.

"Don't fucking look at her, Earl!" yelled Jeanie.

"Or what?" The blond man grinned. "There's two of us. I've got a gun too."

"I've got a bigger one," said Jeanie.

"Don't listen to her, Earl. I got this."

Earl was fidgety. He looked at the blond man and then at Jeanie. He licked at the patch of hair below his mouth, took a long, hard look at Cora and then took another step toward the van.

Jeanie swung the shotgun in his direction and pulled the trigger. The shot sent him tumbling into the sage. She brought the barrel back toward the blond man but he fired twice and she fell to the road.

"Mommy!" Cora screamed.

The blond man stood over Jeanie and squeezed the trigger again. The gun clicked on an empty chamber and he looked at it and thumbed the hammer and it clicked again. He cussed and kicked Jeanie where she lay, ran to Earl and yanked the blade from the sagebrush beside him. He stomped across the road with the blade in his hand and kneeled over Jeanie, but there was another blast and he fell backward in a mist of blood.

Jeanie appeared in the driver window and pounded on the glass. Cora reached across and pulled the handle and Jeanie hauled herself onto the seat and locked the door. She groaned and choked, and a dark stain bloomed from the belly of her shirt.

"The gun," said Jeanie. Her voice was nothing more than a raspy whisper. "Give it to me."

Cora handed her the Beretta, but it dropped from her weak hands and clattered on the floorboards.

The blond man was righting himself against the barricade, his leg a mess of exposed flesh and bone. He had the long blade in his hand and turned to the van, his eyes like a feral dog. He teetered on his good leg and then wheeled at the van with the blade in the air.

"Pick up … the gun," said Jeanie, barely.

Cora was already fishing for the pistol before Jeanie finished speaking. She found it underneath the brake pedal and pulled it up with the barrel pointing the wrong way.

"No," said Jeanie, and pawed at the gun. "Careful."

The blond man was now banging at the window with the hilt of the blade.

"Let's get this over with, ladies," he shouted through the glass. He spat when he talked, and the blood on his hands smeared wide, red streaks on the window. "See this knife? It ain't just fer killin'. I'm gonna carve you into steaks and fuckin' cat you." He banged on the window again and a crack forked out in a star pattern.

Jeanie's head slumped against the headrest and her eyes rolled back for a second. Blood was gathering in the corners of her mouth. She snapped her eyes open as if awakening from a dream.

"Shoot," said Jeanie. "Now!"

Cora raised the Beretta at the man in the window, her hand shaking. She closed her eyes and cried.

"Both hands," said Jeanie. "Do it."

Cora put her other hand on the grip and looped her finger over the trigger.

Something dark filled the windshield.

"Mommy, look!"

A turkey vulture had landed on the hood. Its talons clacked on the metal as it bent its bald head over the windshield and peered in. There was a sound on the roof as though another had landed. Then another.

The blond man had stopped pounding and was now waving his knife at the birds.

"Mommy, over there!"

There were more vultures perched along the barricade, maybe a dozen. Some waddled across the road and pecked at Earl's corpse, but most seemed interested in the blond man.

"Go away," he yelled. He swiped at one that was eyeing him from the roof.

A few more gathered behind him, and one took a brave nip at the blond man's wound. He screamed and stabbed at the bird, but it only launched into the air as another one landed beside him and gobbled at a hanging piece of flesh. The man swiped again, and this time he lost his balance and fell hard onto the road. This was the signal the others had been waiting for. The birds from the barricade hopped to the ground and hustled over to the man, hissing and growling at each other for a spot on the kill. The man tried to crawl underneath the van, screaming and weeping, but was quickly enveloped by a writhing dome of black feathers.

"Oh god, my eyes!" he screamed.

Cora dropped the gun in Jeanie's lap and lay against her chest. Jeanie rested her hand weakly on the girl's shoulder.

"Cora," said Jeanie. Her voice was low and wet.

"Mommy, no," she cried. "You can't die too."

There was another thud on the roof as more vultures arrived. The man was now shrieking hysterically.

"Listen," said Jeanie. "After they're g-gone," she choked the last word. "Clear the road."

"I'm not doing it without you. No!"

"Listen. Shhh. Twenty m-miles."

"No!" Cora screamed into Jeanie's chest.

"Twenty m-miles to Uncle Vernon."

"I can't drive, Mommy, I'll crash! I can't do it!"

"Yes you c-can. I love y—"

Jeanie made a choking sound, and her eyes fell to the window as if she were staring thoughtfully across the plains toward the dark and faraway hills.

Cora lay on her mother's hard and silent chest until sweat began to stream from her forehead. The temperature was rising inside the van, and Cora was feeling faint. She drank the rest of the water from her canteen and refilled it with the water they had scavenged. She fiddled with the air conditioning knob, but realized she would need to turn the engine on for it to work. She searched Jeanie's blood-soaked pockets for the keys, and found one that matched the emblem on the back of the van. She placed it in the ignition, turned it and the engine started. Cool air began to blow through the vents.

"I did it, Mommy," she said.

After an hour the turkey vultures began to lose interest in Earl and the blond man. One by one they launched into the sky, their bald heads matted with gore. Cora picked up the Beretta and opened the van door, pointing the gun all around her with her arms fully outstretched like in a TV cop drama. She saw what was left of the blond man and quickly squeezed her eyes shut.

She tucked the gun into her pants like her mother had done and began to tug at the fence posts blocking the road. She managed to drag one out into the desert, but when she let go, it left a painful splinter in her palm. She pulled the next one and her hand slipped. Another splinter. Cora shook her hand painfully and narrowed her eyes at the barricade.

"Stupid woodpile," she said.

She untied the gas can from the back of the van and shook out what remained on top of the bone-dry wood. She found the cigarette lighter in her mother's pocket and lit a spot where the gas had soaked in. Cora stumbled back as the fire roared to life, and soon she was standing in front of the biggest bonfire she had ever seen.

The wood burned hot and fast, and it wasn't long before most of it was reduced to a chalky ash, stirring in the desert wind. She folded a blanket over Jeanie's bloody lap so she could sit there and see over the dashboard. She knew she had to pull the shifter, but she wasn't sure where to land it and what the letters stood for. She pulled it down one stop and the van began to roll backward. She shrieked and shifted it back into park and the van jolted to a halt.

"Mommy, how do I get it to go?" she said, pointing down the road.

She saw the "D" three stops down and tugged it all the way. The van rolled forward, and she gripped the steering wheel with both hands like a racecar driver and steered the van over the smoldering ashes.

"I did it, Mommy. Just like you said." She held her mother's hand, but the van began to veer off the road so she let go and righted the wheel again. She couldn't reach the pedals though, and the van simply rolled by the power of its own torque.

The sun was now low in the sky, and Cora passed along an interminable straightaway so scoured and pitted by the desert sand that the tires whined and shook beneath her. The wind began to shift the van in the lane, and she sometimes drove down the broken yellow line to keep herself straight. She wondered if she had run the car too long back at the barricade and would run out of gas soon. She also wondered if there was anyone at the end of the road, or if they had just given up waiting.

She curled her mother's arms around her lap, and the weight reassured her, as if she might wake up any moment and praise her for driving so far.

"Should I honk the horn, Mommy?"

She pressed the steering wheel and a short bleat rolled out into the desert. Cora smiled, but it faded quickly. She held her mother's hand again, as if suddenly realizing she was alone and there was nobody around to hear the horn if she pressed it. There was a curve in the road, and when she made the turn it opened up into another straightaway, this one longer, flatter and sandier than the last.

The girl drove on. The sun shrank and faltered over the dried-out basin and a light blinked on the dash next to a symbol of a gas pump, but there were no gas pumps as far as she could see. She didn't really know what twenty miles felt like, but she thought maybe with each sandy washout or brambling Joshua tree or crumbling rock formation that maybe a new mile had been reached.

Soon she began to cry. But as she did so, an object appeared in the distance: two white silos standing together like factory exhausts, piercing the desert monotony. There was a dark patch on the road and as she drew nearer, she saw it was another barricade like the one from before.

She could see at least four people scouting the line in the road, hurrying from their positions. She heard a shot, and then another, as if they were warning her to stop the van. Cora kept the wheel steady, but as the barricade drew closer she panicked and chucked the wheel toward the open desert and the van bounced into the sand and scrub and halted quickly in a shallow wash not more than a few feet from the road. She grabbed the Beretta and stood in the back of the van, watching as the people ran up the road with their weapons drawn. A young man's face appeared in the driver's window and then fell back. He looked confused at the corpse behind the wheel. He looked through the side window and disappeared once more.

"She's got a gun," he shouted.

Other faces popped into the side windows. A woman with braided red hair took a long look and then called out to the others.

"It's a girl," she said. "A young girl. Stand down."

They backed off for a moment, and Cora sat in the back seat, petting the sides of the Beretta like a security blanket. The red-haired woman appeared again and called through the window.

"Honey, you need to put the gun down."

Cora looked at the Beretta and shook her head.

"Are you like the people from before?" she said.

The woman turned and waved at the others.

"I don't know what people you're talking about. Are you alone?"

Cora's face drew tight.

"No, my mommy is there, in the seat."

The woman sidestepped to the driver window and stood there for a moment, looking in. Then she returned.

"Did your mommy bring you here?"

"Yes," said Cora. "My daddy too, but he died in Badger. We're looking for Uncle Vernon."

The woman's eyes widened.

"You said Vernon?"

"Yeah," said Cora, "He's a ranger. He's my uncle."

The woman backed away, and for a few minutes Cora was alone in the van. She kneeled by the console and held Jeanie's limp hand, watching out at the people circling the barricade. After a while, a golf cart zipped down the road and over the sandy wash. A man stepped off the cart and ran to the van, unarmed except for a bottle of water. He peered inside with his hand cupped over his brow.

"Cora?" said the man.

He had a gray beard and large bushy eyebrows. He eyed the driver seat and his face washed of expression. Cora squinted at him, and then dropped the pistol. He looked like an older version of her father, but still hard to make out in the dim gloom of evening.

"Uncle Vernon?"

The man didn't answer. He pulled the van door open and kneeled in the sand. He reached out and Cora stared, and seeing his face she tumbled toward him and wrapped her arms around his neck as if he were her own father.

"You made it," he said softly. "You did great, Cora. You made it."

Cora wept and held Vernon tight.

"Is it safe here?" She asked.

"Yes, you're safe."

"No vines or animals?"

Vernon lifted the girl and handed her the bottle of water.

"You're safe here," he repeated.

"Cross your heart?"

"Yes. Cross my heart."

Vernon set the girl in the golf cart and drove around the barricade toward a wide two-story villa painted the same color as the dunes. The palm trees were cut down to stumps and the rose garden had been plowed under the dry and sterile sand. A man in a yellow coat was swiping at the ground with a drip torch, and in the air was the smell of burnt grass and freshly baked bread.

C.W. Blackwell was born and raised in Santa Cruz, California, where he still lives today with his wife and two children. His passion is to blend poetic narratives with pulp dialogue to create strange and rhythmic genre fiction. He writes mostly dark fiction and weird westerns.

Nature's Promise

by

Daniel Conyers

MAN IS NOT SEPARATE FROM nature. An entitled species will rot on a web of privilege.

The doe's body was a speed bump in the desolate road. Eve begged Lawrence to stop the car, but the college polo champ responded with a chuckle and took another swig of cheap beer. The rest of the college kids in the car laughed as Eve protested. "Please, Lawrence. We might be able to help it."

"We're almost there. It'll die and become food for something else," Lawrence said.

Eve looked out the rear of the car. The sight of the doe's limp body tightened her stomach. She could faintly make out its stomach rising and falling.

"I think it's still alive," she said.

"Lawrence, please stop," Kathy said from the back seat.

Lawrence glanced at his roommate, Sam, sitting next to him. Sam shrugged his shoulders.

"Wouldn't hurt," Sam said.

Lawrence slammed his foot on the brake and put the car in reverse. The vehicle swayed on the dirt road, tumbling through mud and over mountains of dead leaves.

Tearful, Eve stumbled out of the car and knelt by the doe. Kathy and Sam appeared more eager to see the body than Lawrence was. Kathy squeezed Sam's hand as they approached. Lawrence rolled his eyes and followed, dragging his feet through the mud.

The doe's stomach had caved in where Lawrence's tires had hit it. The animal stared into Eve's eyes as she stroked its head. Its raspy breathing pierced her ears and echoed through the silent forest.

"Can we go now?" Lawrence asked.

"We can't just leave it," Eve said.

"Look at it this way: We did a predator a favor. Saved it a step." Lawrence slipped back into the car and honked the horn.

Kathy put her hand on Eve's shoulder. "There's nothing we can do."

The doe's dying eyes followed Eve to the car. She watched the doe fade into the forest as Lawrence sped along the road as if late for a game.

Eve tried getting the image of the dying doe out of her head by flipping through her journal. She read through passages about the camping trip she was on, college, and her hopes for what she'd do after graduating.

"Anything interesting in there?" Kathy asked.

Sam took a sip of beer as he turned around from the front seat. "Probably just thinking about Professor Holton," he said with a smile.

Eve smiled back and shut the journal. "How long till we get to the campground?"

"About that," Lawrence said, "I thought we'd find our own."

"Off road!" Sam cheered and tossed his empty beer can out the window.

"Are you sure that's okay? Won't the park rangers be looking?" Eve asked.

"Relax. I don't think the park rangers care." Lawrence glanced over his shoulder and gave her a rebellious smile.

"Besides, didn't you want to live outside the box?" Sam asked with a grin.

Eve sank into her seat. She gripped her seatbelt tight but then relaxed. The forest looked thicker and more expansive than her research led her to believe. What harm could there be in finding their own private camping spot?

It's not like we're going to tear anything down or build something. What harm is there? Eve thought of Robert Frost's poem, and liked the idea of going somewhere less traveled. Just then, she spied the ideal place to go.

"Turn here," Eve said.

Lawrence gave her a thumbs-up and turned off the dirt road. The vehicle bounced like a hydraulic roller coaster as it barreled through the forest. Lawrence and Sam cheered and laughed, but Eve couldn't stand to look out the window. The rapid passing of trees upset her stomach. She ran her thumbs over her broken rosary. They passed over each decade, not out of faith but out of habit. Eve imagined her mother coming back with disappointment, knowing her daughter broke her rosary and wore it as an accessory rather than a conduit to God. And yet, it was an accessory that bound her to the memory of her mother. It was the only thing she had left of her.

Lawrence parked the car at the edge of a small clearing, having left a long trail of bent grass and broken branches behind them. Large, looming trees with thick branches and leaves surrounded the clearing, allowing little sunlight in. The four college friends got out of the car and looked around.

A small cypress stood in the center of the clearing with a large hole at the base of its trunk. Lawrence and Sam circled the small tree.

"This place looks great, but this is kind of standing in our way," Lawrence said.

Something felt off about this place, and though Eva loved the idea of camping off the beaten path perhaps this spot was best left alone. "Maybe that's why we shouldn't camp here," she suggested. "We could find another spot."

"Don't worry. I brought something that'll solve our little problem."

Lawrence smiled as he opened the trunk. He threw out tents, sleeping bags, and coolers. He reached farther in and pulled out a two-handed saw, giggling as if he'd just won a new toy.

"Give me a hand," he said, holding up the saw.

"I don't think so," Eve shook her head and took an unsteady step away from the weapon.

"It'll be fine." Lawrence took Eve by the hand and led her to the other side of the tree. Eve grabbed the handle and watched Lawrence grip the other end.

"We are just going to rock back and forth, okay?" he said.

Eve gave a reluctant nod and pulled the saw toward herself. Lawrence pulled it back. She heard the blade tear through the bark of the tree as they sawed their way through its trunk. The bark creaked and groaned as if the trunk were crying. Pleading. Eve smiled as she watched their progress.

"All right, stand back," said Lawrence as their weapon neared the opposite side of the trunk. He and Sam gave the tree a few swift kicks. It screamed as it crashed to the ground. The ground shook and bugs scattered. The surrounding trees waved as Lawrence lifted Eve's arm in the air.

"See, that wasn't so bad."

Eve had thought she could barely operate a hammer let alone saw down a tree. She couldn't help but feel as if she'd accomplished something grand. She bundled herself up and smiled. Sam handed her a beer from the cooler, and she toasted the start to a wonderful camping trip.

Lawrence and Sam wasted no time chopping apart the tree to clear room for their camp, gathering stones, rummaging for dry wood, and igniting a fire. Lawrence watched the flames with a cruel grin. He reached for a section of the chopped tree that had blocked their path and threw it on the pile, just to watch it burn.

Kathy helped Eve set up the tents and organize the site.

"I'm glad you decided to come along," Kathy said. "Lawrence is glad too."

"My mother said camping was where she discovered herself. I figure I'd give it a try."

"Did you fit that into the eulogy?"

"I didn't give it. Felt odd giving a eulogy to an empty casket." Eve nailed a metal spike into the ground. Crimson liquid spewed from the dirt as if the spike had struck bloody oil. "Oh my God! Is there an animal under there?"

Kathy dipped her hand into the wet soil surrounding the buried spike, but she only found water. "Must be the light."

Eve took a swig of bottled water and finished setting up the tent.

The doe's dead eyes plagued Eve's thoughts throughout the evening. Lawrence's self-absorbed stories about polo victories were drowned by the rasping sound of the doe's breathing. Sam and Kathy laughed at a joke Eve missed. Lawrence's eyes gazed over Eve's legs as she recalled the joyous sensation she felt sawing down the tree that gave its life.

The evening persisted with beer, food, and recollections of their junior year in college. The group laughed and shared their hopes for what they'd wish to accomplish after finishing one more year. Lawrence attempted a few advances toward Eve, which she quietly ignored. It was difficult to consider being with him when she thought of the deer and his indifference to its suffering. He escorted Eve to her tent later but she chose to sleep alone that night.

Eve wrapped herself tight in her sleeping bag. She fell into such a deep sleep that she hardly noticed the long, jagged legs of an oversized creature dragging across the top of her tent.

A shriek from within the woods snapped Eve from her slumber. She catapulted out of the tent as best she could without getting tangled.

The scattered morning rays glittered through the ceiling of branches and leaves, and thin trails of smoke rose from the deceased campfire. Kathy and Sam sprinted back and forth screaming Lawrence's name.

"What's going on?" Eve felt her heartbeat quicken.

"Lawrence's tent is empty," Sam said.

"Maybe he got lost going to the bathroom."

"Lawrence!" Sam yelled, "We need to look for him." Lawrence's car was just as they'd left it, and nothing was missing from his tent. Sam grew more frantic as the sun passed over them at an unusual pace. He honked the horn over and over again. The sway of trees and an eerie breeze was the only response.

"Where would he have gone? Eve asked.

"I'm sure he'll be back. He's probably recovering from all the beer last night," said Kathy as she pulled her jacket from her tent.

Sam, Kathy, and Eve waited. Eve glanced at her watch periodically. The second hand slowed down. She tapped the crystal. The second hand stopped.

"I'm going to look for him." Sam examined the grass surrounding Lawrence's tent. He paced, growing more upset with every step.

Kathy stopped him and rubbed his shoulders. "Calm down. We'll find him."

"I don't get it."

"Get what?"

"There are no tracks." Sam knelt. His fingers surveyed the untouched grass and dirt. "There should be something: footprints, bent grass, something."

A scream erupted through the trees. Sam sprinted into the woods. Kathy and Eve followed with reluctance.

The three friends passed tree after tree as they ran, crying Lawrence's name. The scenery blended together and direction became lost. Sam led Kathy and Eve through the woods, slowing down only to carve an X into the trunks of trees.

"How far could he have gone?" Sam asked, struggling to get the words out in a coherent breath.

"Do you know where we are?" Eve asked, trying hard to make herself believe her own words.

The light dimmed as the sun sank in the west. Eve checked her watch again. Time remained frozen on her wrist.

Sam reached into his pocket for a compass. A look of fear and puzzlement plagued his face. "That can't be right."

He showed Kathy and Eve the compass needle spinning in a rapid circle. Sam surveyed his surroundings and proceeded to follow the trail of X's left on tree trunks.

Eve's fingers rubbed against the beads of the rosary as if out of faith not habit.

The chill in the air stiffened Eve's legs, making it tough for her to keep up with Sam's pace. Her knees buckled and she toppled to the ground. Thick webbing decorated Eve's entire hand. She pulled her fingers off the ground, discovering the web's extreme length and thickness. Her eyes followed the web across the landscape.

"Sam, stop."

"We're almost there."

"Stop!" Eve's throat, dry as sandpaper, made it difficult for her voice to reach a reasonable distance.

Kathy came to a halt and lifted her foot. Thick, elastic silk stuck to the bottom of her boot. She raised the other and found more of the same.

Sam looked as if he had to use extra effort to lift his foot. The webbing grabbed the bottom of his boot as if it didn't want him to move.

"It's a spider web, so what?"

"It's all over the ground," Eve said with a vibrato of fear.

The webbing beneath them slowed their pace through the woods. Each step felt like trudging through a dense lake of quicksand made of silk webbing.

Sam collapsed against a tree. He dragged himself around the trunk and slammed his fist against it. "It should be here." He circled the tree again. Tangles of webbing stuck to his back.

Kathy fell to his side. "Sam, what's going on?"

"I don't know where we are. This tree should have an X on it. The camp should be here."

"Don't move," Kathy said. "We'll get the car, drive out of here, and we'll tell the rangers to look for Lawrence."

Eve and Kathy walked away from Sam. They didn't make it a few feet before a strong influx of wind pushed through them. A faint yelp followed the sudden gust.

"Where's Sam?" Eve turned to the tree that had supported Sam's exhausted body. The lonely tree made her spine chill. Eve looked up. The crowded skies revealed nothing but bloated leaves attached to gargantuan branches. Light bounced off a cloud of hanging webs above them.

"Where the hell did Sam go?" Kathy's eyes were wide.

"I don't like this." Eve walked slowly backwards. "We should leave."

The temperature suddenly dropped, and no coat in the world could have warmed Eve's slender physique. Steamy breath escaped her chilled lips. The trees swayed in the wind. She grabbed Kathy by the arm and dragged her away from the trees. The trunks and branches screamed against the wind. Eve recognized the agonizing moaning of the forest. The screams erupting from the branches sounded like Sam and Lawrence.

"Sam!" Kathy called.

"It can't be them."

Eve dragged Kathy through the forest. Kathy struggled to keep up with Eve's frantic pace. The trees pounded against each other. A large shadow passed over them with lightning speed. Webs grew thicker on the trunks of the trees. Eve looked up at the sky and felt as if she were running in a large circle. A loud thumping erupted behind them. Kathy and Eve ducked. Dense, prickly hairs grazed their heads. The two women kept their eyes closed, but they smelled rotting skin in the air. A massive surge of wind blew them to their knees. They got to their feet again and staggered forward.

An aged wooden house emerged in the distance. Eve and Kathy ran to the building and barged through the front door.

Exhausted, Kathy slid down the wall to a sitting position. She curled into a ball and sobbed.

Eve held her close. A subtle creak from a floorboard grabbed Eve's attention.

"I'll be right back," Eve said, with a sense of dread growing in her stomach. She journeyed through the single-level house, growing more and more astonished as she found each room absent of furniture, pictures, or people.

"What the hell just happened?" Kathy asked.

"Your guess is as good as mine," Eve yelled from the other room. She rubbed her fingers across the broken rosary her mother had given her. Her fingers slipped against one of the beads. She looked down, and her hand trembled. The beads were smeared with blood. She examined her body for any open wounds but found only more dense layers of webbing.

"Have you seen spiders anywhere?" Eve asked.

"What? No."

"Where did this webbing come from?"

Darkness jetted through the house as if something colossal had stepped between them and the sun. A piercing screech dug across the house. Whatever stalked Eve and Kathy circled the building, increasing in speed. Rapid thumping climbed up the walls and landed on the roof. Glass shattered at the other end of the house.

"It's gonna get inside," Eve said, stepping backwards toward Kathy.

Kathy reached for the doorknob, which was also wrapped in webbing. She tried to yank the door open, but thick coats of gooey webbing kept the door shut. Strips of her skin ripped off her palms as she yanked her hands away from the knob.

Kathy screamed and the thumping persisted. The creature crawled along the house in a frantic pattern. Eve tore up a loose floorboard. The shadow passed over the house again. Eve ran through the halls with the floorboard held close.

Kathy cradled her bleeding hand and backed up against the wall.

What have I gotten myself into? Eve thought. Nothing in her studies could've hinted at something like this happening. Sam and Lawrence disappeared, and suddenly the laws of nature had gone haywire.

The passing shadow and thumping stopped. The wind calmed and an eerie silence engulfed the forest. Eve hurried over to Kathy, her footsteps echoing against the old floorboards. Eve froze and dropped her wooden weapon in terror. Strings of webbing stretched across Kathy's mouth, silencing her screams.

A powerful force reached through the window and snatched Kathy. Eve leaped for her, managing only to grab her boots. Kathy's body jettisoned out of her footwear and through the window. Whatever force took the young college student was too quick for Eve to get a solid look at it.

Eve ran out of the house and found herself staring into a gigantic tunnel of webbing. The screams of her friends echoed deep inside it.

Eve hesitated. The surrounding forest looked nothing like it did when she arrived. Thick webbing painted the trees and the sky. She climbed into the tunnel. The webbing made her feel as if she were climbing across rope ladders strung together. The sun's light faded the farther she ventured into the web. She could hear Lawrence and Sam crying for help. The walls of the tunnel vibrated with their agony.

The light vanished. The grunts she made as she pulled herself through the tunnel bounced in odd directions, and the scent of rotting flesh burned her nostrils. The floor of the tunnel broke, and she fell into an abyss of darkness.

Instead of hitting the ground, she landed lightly and discovered she was standing upright. She stretched out her hands, and discovered spidery cocoons surrounded her. The darkness made it difficult for her to discern who inhabited the cocoons. She squeezed between the hanging coffins.

"Sam! Lawrence! Kathy!"

"They cannot hear you," said a feminine voice in one of the silky cocoons.

"Where are they?"

"They are suffering," said a male in a cocoon to her left.

"Soon," every soul around her spoke in unison, "you will join them."

"Why?" Eve screamed as her eyes fervently searched the darkness.

"Nature's children don't belong to you. A single tree houses life beyond your sight," said a sea of voices.

Eve recalled the tree Lawrence and she had cut down. She remembered the pleasure and sense of accomplishment she took from seeing it fall.

"One tree?" she asked.

"ONE TREE!" all of the voices replied.

Eve fell to the ground at the power of everybody speaking at once. Slowly, light filled the space, but she couldn't see where it came from. She scanned the area. The monochromatic eyes of the figures in the cocoons glowed. Eve found herself kneeling before Kathy, Lawrence, and Sam. Their eyes were black and hollow, as if something had sucked the life out of them.

"Men walk as if they are entitled to the ground beneath them. They take nature's gifts like spoiled children," said a feminine voice.

Eve turned to run, but the body of an old woman wrapped in webbing knocked her to the ground. Her eyes glowed bright orange. She wore a dress aged in decay. Her skin matched the gray of the webbing holding her up. The silken coffin squeezed her body; the cracking of her frail bones echoed through the farm of hanging bodies. The light in her eyes shone brighter. Eve looked at the woman's familiar features, and it took everything in her power not to scream.

"Mom?"

"My sweet child." Her voice cracking, like the sound of old parchment crumpling.

"What happened to you?"

"I found myself; I found truth."

"What truth?"

"We are all one, and punishment is swift for those who overstep their bounds."

"I'm so sorry. It wasn't my idea."

"There is a price you must still pay."

Eight monstrous legs, attached to an epically sized spider, loomed over Eve. Its fangs dripped with the flesh of ancient victims. The creature fell on her.

Months passed. The forest cleared and returned to what it once was, and the season for camping returned again. A car filled with a boisterous family journeyed through the woods and parked in a clearing. The father got out and stretched his legs. He leaned against a small cypress in the center of the clearing. His eyes wandered to the tree's trunk.

"Hey kids, look at this," he said.

Two kids and a beautiful woman emerged from the car and joined the father by the tree. The man ran his fingers across the tree's bark. Its design looked like an old broken rosary had been wrapped around its trunk.

"Kind of a neat design, huh kids?"

The kids agreed.

"Who wants to help the old man chop this down?"

The children cheered as their father pulled an ax from the back of the car. The tree screamed with every swing.

Daniel Conyers was born on an Air Force base in New Mexico. Coming from a military family, he moved around a lot, but he found his home in Colorado. Daniel fell in love with storytelling after reading Greek mythology and comic books. He received his bachelors in general philosophy from Colorado State University, and he received his MFA from Full Sail University. Daniel has written in a wide range of media: film, fiction, web series, and comic books. His debut novel, *Owen of Anthea: The Warlock's Curse*, will be released on eBook this year. When Daniel is not writing, he is reading, exercising, and playing video games.

The Path

by

Jeff Dosser

DUST SWIRLED AROUND THE JEEP in a gray tornado as Tanner's Cherokee bounded into the gravel parking lot at the end of the long, dirt track. He dropped it into park and waited for the dust to settle before swinging open the door and stepping into the dry mountain air. Finally, their vacation had started. He turned in a slow arc, taking in the wonder of towering pines and cloudless blue sky. He breathed deeply of the earthy scents of evergreen and rich forest floor, and let the tension of the workweek flow out in a slow, relaxing exhalation.

His daughter, Stacy, wriggled free of her safety belt and stared out of the window with a gap-toothed grin. Tanner clicked open the door and she sprang out in excitement.

"Let's go daddy! Let's go daddy! Let's goooo!" she shouted, jumping up and down.

Hands on hips, Tanner shared a knowing grin with his wife before looking down on his daughter in mock disapproval. Stacy was his and Mary's only child, and at six years old she was the joy of Tanner's life. Her thick, red hair bounced on her shoulders as she danced about, her delicate white complexion kissed by just the right number of freckles.

"Hold on, kiddo," Tanner scolded. "You and Mom have to put on lotion so you don't get burned. We're going to be walking for a long time."

Mary rounded the rear of the Jeep and unzipped her pack. She foraged inside and withdrew an industrial-sized tube of sunscreen. They shared a smile when Stacy spotted the tube and assumed the standard "sunscreen application stance." Arms held wide, legs apart, and chin raised, she waited patiently for Mary to slather her with lotion. Mary spread a thin white film across arms and legs and ended with a dot on her nose.

"Hey! Cut it out." Stacy laughed and swiped away the glop of cream.

As Mary applied the lotion to her own arms, neck, and face, Tanner stood a moment admiring his wife. "You know, next time we come out here," he said as he moved closer and wrapped an arm seductively around her waist, "maybe it could be just you and me. I'll bring a blanket and some wine. But you'll need a lot more sunscreen. What with all the skin that will be exposed."

"In your dreams," she laughed and hip-bumped him away.

Tanner dragged his backpack from the rear seat and slung it over his shoulders. Then he hit the button on the key fob and locked the doors. The Jeep chirped noisily, and for the first time he noticed the oppressive quiet. There were no sounds of birds or breeze, just the scrunch of gravel beneath their feet.

Mary glanced at a dirt-covered pickup parked in the corner of the parking lot. "Are there other hikers on the trail?" she asked.

"Could be," Tanner replied. He marched over to the truck and ran a finger across the dirty hood. It exposed a streak of dark blue paint beneath a thin layer of silt. "Based on the amount of dust, it looks like this one's been here for days. It probably broke down."

Tanner checked his water bottles and then shrugged on the pack and followed his wife to the trailhead.

"So will it be extra hot because of the drought?" Mary asked.

"No, it hasn't been much hotter than usual," Tanner said, "just no rain. The drought's been bad the last couple of years, but this summer has been the worst on record."

He'd hiked this trail many times but never seen the undergrowth look so scraggly … and dry. "We'll need to watch out for fires, but otherwise everything will be fine. A wildfire in these conditions could be dangerous. But we'll stay close to the car. Besides, Stacy can't walk too far."

"You think we'll see animals?" Stacy asked.

Tanner squinted into the woods, troubled by the preternatural silence. "I'm sure we will, honey. There are birds, and chipmunks, and elk all around."

"But where were they?" Mary asked. "Do you think they're having trouble finding food and water because of the drought?"

"What's a drought?" Stacy asked. She looked at him questioningly with her deep green eyes.

"A drought is when it doesn't rain enough," Tanner explained. "And the mountains have been very hot and dry for a long time."

"It's caused by climate change, honey," Mary added. "Too much pollution can make the air stay hot too long."

Stacy's brows beetled in confusion but she nodded her assent.

"Okay, then. Enough talk," Tanner said. "Let's get started." He looped his thumbs beneath the straps and led them onto the trail.

Stacy rushed past, giggling, as Mary stepped up beside him. They followed the path as it twisted away into the coniferous woods, but it soon lost itself behind a large boulder far ahead. To either side, the underbrush was cut back four or five feet, but, beyond that, the tangled plants grew thick and wild. The normally lush leaves were brown-edged and brittle.

Tanner guessed they'd hiked almost three miles when Stacy suddenly dashed ahead.

"When do you think we should stop for lunch?" Mary asked.

Tanner watched his daughter round a tangled deadfall and disappear from sight. He was uncomfortable losing sight of her. Although you heard nightmare stories of cougars grabbing children, he knew it was statistically almost impossible. Yet, there were bears out here. And that abandoned truck.

When Stacy's frightened squeal echoed thorough the silent trunks, Tanner's heart leapt into his throat. He had taken two running steps along the trail when she darted into view and raced back toward them. She skidded to a halt and gripped Tanner's leg. Breathlessly, she pointed a tiny finger up the trail.

"Daddy! There's ... something ... dead ... in ... the bushes."

Stacy took several gulps of air as Mary ran a calming hand over her daughter's head. "Slow down baby, slow down," Mary cooed.

"And it smells really *bad*!"

Tanner took a deep breath and whistled it out. "Boy, you had me goin'," he smiled. "I'm sure it's nothing. Not uncommon to find a dead deer or opossum along the trail, especially given the heat conditions."

Tanner busied his daughter with a water bottle and squinted up the trail. "You two stay here," he said. Mary regarded him with concern but she nodded in agreement.

Just a deer or opossum, he reassured himself. He strode up the trail into the sickly sweet stench of summer-rotted flesh. Where the path rounded the deadfall, he spotted the ravaged body of a large dog. The air was alive with the buzz of black flies that crawled and flitted across the carcass. The animal still wore its bright red collar, and a nylon leash dangled in the skeletal branches.

It was clear something had fed on the body, as its innards and muscles were scavenged to the bone. Now the maggots feasted on the hanging remains decomposing in the arid, August heat.

Poor creature must have escaped its owners. Gotten lost in the woods, Tanner mused. *When its leash got snagged in the deadfall, it was all over. In this heat it wouldn't last two days.*

Tanner turned and scanned the woods. A few steps beyond the body, a bright-blue tennis shoe lay in the tall grass. Although it was eerily quiet, nothing else seemed out of place.

"Come on down," he called to the girls. "But hurry past. It's a dead dog and it's pretty stinky."

Mary and Stacy rushed past. Stacy held her nose dramatically and shot frightened glances toward the spot that Tanner tried to block with his body. When they were well past he jogged up to join them. Yet something tugged at his mind. He was missing a detail about the scene. He turned and stared back toward the carcass.

"You two go on ahead," he called with a wave. "I'll be right there."

"You sure?" Mary asked.

"Yeah, I'll be fine. I just want to check that dog."

Stacy was already skipping up the path, singing, as Mary turned to follow.

Tanner stepped up to the body and circled the scene slowly. The brush near the carcass was broken and trampled but that could be explained by the scavengers coming to eat. Glops of dried, dark fluid dotted the ground among the fallen needles and tree trunks. Kneeling, he picked up the shoe and examined the dried red speckles on the toe. Then Stacy's scream broke him from his reverie. The shoe dropped from his fingers and he looked up in surprise. A second panicked cry sent him running along the trail. Ahead, Mary called his name in a gale of anguish.

Rounding a large boulder, he found Mary at the edge of the trail, staring into the brush. "What happened? Where's Stacy?" he yelled.

Mary turned, her eyes dark pools of fear. She pointed a shaky finger toward the woods. "An animal! An animal took her! It came from the woods and it took her."

Tanner dropped his pack and ran into the brush. He followed the sound of Stacy's high-pitched cries and thrashing bushes.

"I'm coming, Stacy!" The thorny branches and dry bramble snapped and whipped across his face as he tore through the scrub. "Fight it, girl! Fight!"

Tanner chased his daughter's frantic cries into a clearing. "Stacy!" She was nowhere to be seen. Her screams had ended. He scrambled atop a boulder for a better view. *Where was she?* He turned this way and that, the slow fingers of panic wending their way around his heart.

"Daddy." The call was gasping and weak. He glanced to his right and caught a glimpse of creamy white legs before they were dragged behind a tree.

Roaring in rage, Tanner leapt down, crashed into the bushes where he'd seen her disappear. He shoved his way into another clearing and found one of her shoes. He picked it up. It was warm from her foot. His eyes flicked across the trees and rocks. *Which way! Where is she!*

In frustration, he tore through the thick bramble, shouting her name until he halted in horror. There, on the ground, lying in a splatter of thick black blood, was a tiny white finger.

Tanner gaped in uncomprehending horror. He bent to pick it up and his hand froze. *If I pick this up I make it real. This cannot be real, none of this is real.* "This can't be … real!" he shouted. Anguish and impotent fury exploded in his breast, "Stacy! Where are you!"

Tanner crawled along the ground searching for any signs of where she could have gone. He found nothing. No trail. No trace. Around him, he could hear movement in the bushes, but when he followed, the sounds fled before him into the thicket.

Then, faint and far away, he heard Mary's cry. He cocked his head toward the sound. He hesitated before pushing farther into the brush. He was not ready to surrender his daughter, not ever. Around him, the tall pines gave way to tangled junipers and thorny wild roses. His progress slowed as the branches tugged and snagged.

Again, Mary's cry echoed through the woods; this time louder. He could make out the words.

"Oh, my God! Tanner! Tanner!"

Maybe Stacy's back. She must be back. She ran back to her mother. But she's hurt. There was so much blood. She must be hurt. He turned and ran toward the sounds of panic. Shoving through the woods, he became unsure of his way. Then he heard Mary again. She was no longer calling his name. She was screaming, shrieks of gut-wrenching pain that left no question of direction.

Tanner turned and ran. Heedless of the branches and thorns that snapped and bit, he broke free of the woods and onto the trail. The screams stopped.

"Mary! Where are you?" His eyes flitted up and down the dry path, unsure of the way. Above, the bright sun beat down from the cloudless blue sky. From his left, he heard a sharp growl and a barking snap.

"I'm coming!" he roared, and flew toward the sound. As he ran, he noted for the first time that shadowy forms ran in the bramble beside him. They seemed to be paralleling his flight along the trail.

When he rounded the turn, he came upon a scene that shook him to his knees. There, on the ground, was Mary. Or it had to be her. He recognized the pale legs kicking weakly from beneath a pack of coyotes.

There were twenty or thirty of the carnivores roaming about. Most were gathered around Mary's head and torso, gnawing on chunks of savaged flesh. The gaunt creatures were two feet tall with long brownish fur and the protruding ribs of starvation. Dozens of smaller coyotes slunk here and there around the larger animals, whose heads were bent to feed. As he stared in paralyzed shock, they lifted their bloody muzzles in ones and twos and glared at him with hungry malice. One held a dangling strand of red meat, which Tanner mistook for sausage. Then horror widened his eyes as the truth sank in. It was intestines the creature ate, his wife's intestines.

A wave of madness overtook Tanner. He bellowed in pain. Then he rushed them. Those who didn't flee he kicked and smashed away. One larger animal stood his ground but Tanner yanked it from its feet and slammed it into the trunk of a pine. The creature yelped in pain and crumpled to the ground. The others fled into the woods.

He tumbled to his knees beside his wife's torn body. He stared in confusion, his breath coming in short panicked gasps. Mary's chest was ripped open, her innards roller-coastered onto the dusty ground. Thick gore pooled in the dirt and seeped into the knees of his jeans.

Mary turned her head, green eyes fluttering open, considering him with a faraway expression. Then she lifted her hand and placed it on his forearm. He flinched away when he saw her grip held him with mangled stubs.

"Stacy," she gurgled through bloody lips.

"I couldn't find her," Tanner sobbed. He met her fading gaze. "I couldn't find her."

Tanner held her damaged hand and stared into her eyes. It was several heartbeats before he realized she was gone.

Around him, the hungry pack began to close. Several crept out of the shadows of trees and onto the trail. Heads down, their eyes glared as they circled. Tanner spotted dozens of dark forms moving here and there through the thicker woods.

A howl rent the air. It was joined by others. They were all around. A primal dread deeper than any he had known seized him as their yapping cries built to a crescendo. That fear catapulted him to his feet and sent him sprinting down the trail. The one rational spark that he grasped onto was the car. The only hope was to get to the car. To get help.

Ahead, the coyotes on the trail scattered into the woods while the ones behind him followed at a lope.

Panting in exhaustion, Tanner risked a look over his shoulder. He did not see the coyote rush in from the side and between his churning legs. With a grunt, he cartwheeled to the ground. He rolled from the trail and slid to a stop in the tall grass.

They descended upon him. Jaws flashed and pain exploded in his shoulder, his bicep, his calf as vicious fangs sank into his flesh. He threw the clinging animals aside and struggled to his feet, but was driven down again as a larger beast dove in and snapped its teeth across his Achilles tendon. Hot agony shot up his leg and tumbled him to the ground.

Again the starved predators attacked. With a howl of adrenaline-fueled rage, Tanner flung them aside. Kicking and punching, his blows landing with thudding, deadly effect. Bodies flew. Some hit the ground, immobile; others yelped and fled into the woods. But for every animal he felled, two more took its place.

Mad with fear, Tanner kicked a hole in the savage circle. He sprang through the opening and limped off as fast as he could. But there was no escape. This time, they did not falter. This time, they closed ranks. Ears laid back, the snarling circle tightened.

"Help! Help!" Tanner yelled in breathless desperation. His voice fell flat among the dusty pines.

When the attack came, Tanner kicked away the first assault. More followed. Ripping fangs slashed at joint and tendon and brought him to his knees. Tanner punched and raged. He raised himself up but fangs sank deep into his neck and he heard, more than felt, the crackling snap of his spine.

The animal pulled him over, pines tumbling across his vision. He lay on his back, the majestic trees rising above him like huge, green arrows. Around him, the shaggy brown forms surged and yammered. He heard the ripping and tearing of clothing and flesh but felt no pain.

He tried to move, but the attempt was futile. Eyes wide in disbelief, he watched as the horde snapped and fought over his dark organs. The thick, iron smell of blood mixed with the scent of pine and dust and filled his panting lungs.

One animal raised his head from the feast and met Tanner's eyes. It licked the blood from its snout. Then it lunged, ending Tanner's silent scream.

Jeff spent several years as an IT developer before making the next logical step in his career and joining the Tulsa, Oklahoma, police department. For the next eighteen years, he relished working the night shift in the worst parts of that southern town. Jeff has returned to the software field and spends his free time writing, hanging out with his fantastic wife and kids, and contemplating the horrors prowling the woods behind his rural home.

Jeff's stories can be found in several magazines, including *Shotgun Honey, Bewildering Stories, Down in the Dirt* and *Yellow Mama*.

Stones are Breathing Tonight

by

Russell Hemmell

I MET ELLEN AND SHAUN in Canongate, in an Edinburgh devastated by the Iron Plague. When I first saw them, coming out of the South Grey's Close like ghouls from another age, I almost pulled the trigger. My hesitation saved us both—Ellen and me. She was on the point of shooting back.

Shaun laughed and walked in between us, extending his hand. "Peace and love, mate. It's not us you have to fear. Lower your gun. You too, sis."

"I guess you're right," I conceded.

We shook hands, while Ellen acknowledged me with a nod.

I looked around, trying not to flinch at the view of the melted buildings among stumps of black stones half-eroded by inorganic decay, and ignoring the stench coming from the ruins.

"Yes, here it's not any better," Shaun said with a smirk. "If you had expected the Old Town standing like it was in the old good days, you were having a fanciful dream."

Yes, and that was the awakening.

I sighed. *It's going to be a long day.*

Days were indeed unbearable long in the Scottish summer—along with nights too short and troubled. I woke up sweating, my hand ready on the gun near my pillow. The silvery titanium surface was cold between my fingers. And precious. Nothing else could be used any longer, for whatever artefact—civilian or military—because not just iron, as the moniker would have suggested, but most of the metals were vulnerable to the Iron Plague. Like humans or animals, and even some plants. A few creatures remained alive, sure, but that proved a mixed blessing, since they were rabid and famished. Damn dangerous for all the others. I considered myself no exception.

I gave a sidelong look at the two figures wrapped in blankets sleeping on the other side of the fire. After travelling alone for so long, I was glad to find survivors—healthy ones—even without actively searching for them, many or few though they could be. I had only tried to escape as far away as possible.

Images of doom that I had tried to push away without success crept back into my mind. We would have never forgotten that moment, 2,325 days ago, when apocalypse came to us into the form of tiny stuff out of nowhere—nanoparticles of a technology turned badly wrong and, worse, alive on its own. The worst thing? Nobody knew the extent of that catastrophe, nor its scientific explanation. What remained was under the eyes of the ones who got away, looking like nightmares too persistent for sanity.

I went back to sleep. Nothing to gain by indulging in them.

"Raven? What the heck of a name is this?" Shaun said, while, the morning after, we were sharing a breakfast in one of Canongate's derelict houses.

"Mine, you Shaun of the Dead. Anything to say?"

He laughed, and threw me a bottle. "Drink. Water in Edinburgh is not safe everywhere. This one is."

I grabbed it on the fly and drank. It had no taste, indication good enough there were no metal particles. I revelled in that simple pleasure, like a man lost in the desert sipping drops of oasis water he had searched for too long. Not a casual metaphor either.

"What have you found out about it?" Shaun said after a moment.

"The Plague, you mean?"

"Yes. You're from the South. You should have seen more of that in London than we had here."

"I guess so," I replied, trying hard to forget the accuracy of those details. "But we haven't discovered much either."

Ellen made a sign with her hands that Shaun translated for me. "We?"

"Yes. The people I worked with. I am a biologist—or I should say, I *was*."

Shaun had not asked until that moment why somebody from a place several hundred miles away was strolling around in his city, when no form of transportation existed any longer. He asked no questions, and I had not explained. What for? Stories from the Plague were appallingly similar, and nobody had any tears left. Not even me. I couldn't cry any longer, apart out of hunger pangs.

"Has it happened in the same way?"

"I wouldn't know. I wasn't here," I said. "But from what I could see, pretty much."

"Which metals are affected the most?"

"As far as I know, all metals except the platinum group and titanium—don't ask me why. Some of them more than others, of course. Only old stones and wood remain unmelted, even though structures made up with high concentration of the most vulnerable minerals in their bricks have collapsed too. This explains the ruins here, and the fact they are not uniform."

Shaun nodded, looking around. "What about contagion?"

"That depends on the minerals of the water people drank. They might be lucky or not. In London, we weren't." I thought again at the delay we had discovered that and how long it took us to find a remedy. Looking at the statistics too long. Half of the population was infected by then, and the images of the sick created a new category of clinical horror. Ebola was a mild cold in comparison, even though it bore some resemblance in terms of symptoms.

"After a while it didn't make any difference."

"No. Not for us. And not for any other living beings on planet Earth."

Iron. Iron is the key of the problem, I mused in silence. *There are four stable isotopes in iron. It has taken an awful lot of time before realising only one of them, the rarest of all, was somehow more resistant to the degenerative particles. Having known it in advance, maybe some preventive measures could have been taken, infrastructures maintained, lives saved . . .* "Plants—many plants adapted to survive without, or used the more resistant isotope: we didn't know until the end, and now I wonder . . ." I said, cutting short a long line of reasoning.

"About what?"

"If this was a punishment for what we have done to this planet. The hubris of the ancient Greeks, you know, that attracts nemesis. If plants have started to recover, maybe one day the whole planet will. Except us, the real virus, eliminated forever for the better good."

"Whatever you say, mate. Personally I don't know anything about your Greeks, past or present." Shaun shrugged. "But if I were you, I wouldn't be overly concerned about any future day."

"Why?"

"We might not live to see one. Come on, let's go exploring Meadows."

"Have you given up the search for survivors?" I already knew the answer.

"No. This is how we found you, wasn't it?"

We suited up and walked toward a gaping hole that once was a prime residential area of the city, something I could still remember from my high school travel days. I braced for the cringing sight I knew awaited me there.

I was not deluded.

As if Meadows had not been enough, a couple of weeks later I was in for a treat: the core of the Old Town, the Castle itself.

"Clear," Shaun said, his wooden torch casting a cone of light into the half-collapsed corridor. Flames and shadows made the old castle frightening even to my jaded eyes.

We had waited a few days preparing as much as we could for the exploration of the dungeons and the rest of the subterraneans. It was the last thing we had left to do before moving out of the city and going to the countryside. It was not accidental. I dreaded what we would find, and yet I decided to accompany them, fighting my resistance.

While we were sure nobody and nothing could possibly live in what remained of the upper floors, the basement and below were most likely standing, even if in a badly damaged fashion. *If there's anything still alive in Edinburgh, it is here it's going to be. And it won't be pretty.* I repeated the words to myself, trying to keep my head cold and my senses sharp.

Ellen moved forward, silent and attentive.

"Careful," I said to her. "We don't know what awaits us there."

"Sis can't hear you, Raven," Shaun reminded me gently.

I kept forgetting Ellen could only read my lips. She showed nothing of the typical hesitation of disabled people when put into unfamiliar environments. I guess because in that hell she was more at ease than us.

"Don't worry for her." He smiled with pride. "What she can't hear, she can smell."

And it was true. A few metres later, she gestured for us to stop and got onto her knees, examining the lurid path, mired with rain filtered from the upper levels and debris. Then she turned, looking at her brother and signing.

"Stones were breathing here," he said.

"What?" I wasn't sure I'd understood him.

"This place *was* inhabited. Ellen detects an animal presence," he said. "But she can't tell if there's anything still around, dead or alive. The stench is strong but not unbearable."

"There might be something alive. Maybe even humans."

"Or what they have turned into," Shaun said.

"You don't believe they've become zombies, do you?" That was one of the rumours, at the beginning. And for a simple reason. It would have actually been reassuring, considering that a few governments did have a zombie contingency plan, as fanciful as that sounded.

He shook his head. "No such luck. Sick and demented, yes. Nowhere less dangerous, maybe more."

"Certainly more. Before London went still, there were a few massacres." I looked around, trying to guess what was lurking beyond the entrance of the vaulted chambers of the dungeons.

Ellen stopped, extending her arm to keep us from proceeding. She signalled something to Shaun and leapt alone inside the chamber.

"What is she doing?" I wasn't happy she'd disappeared.

"She has sensed something."

"One more reason to join her."

"No. If there's anybody there, it's in the obscurity. She can perceive it quicker than we can hear it, let alone react. Trust her, mate." He stared into my eyes. "Without Ellen, I won't be alive."

I waited, impatiently, for something to happen, amazed by Shaun's attitude. My fingers kept fidgeting nervously on the stock of my gun.

The wait wasn't long. After ten minutes or so, her slim silhouette emerged out of the dark pool in front of us. I searched for her expression in the shadow, or to understand what she was communicating to her brother, but I relaxed.

"What did she say?"

"That whatever was breathing here before has already left. Not since long. Everything on the ground is dead. Only animals, for what she could see."

This sounds as a good moment for us to leave as well. There was nothing to be gained by hanging around a graveyard, regardless of its historical merit.

"Do you know the most terrifying thing about having hordes of sick people chasing us?"

Shaun asked the question, pensive.

"I am sure you're going to tell me." I knew he couldn't help himself.

"That there's no one else normal," he said. "What if there's simply nobody else in this city or on the whole goddamn planet who hasn't been infected?

That was a thought I was not ready to entertain. "Let's go," I said, turning on my heels.

"Wait. I still want to explore," Shaun said. "I'll see you at the World's End, mate."

"You mean the place, right?"

"Where else? " Shaun snickered. "For the rest, the world ended long ago."

I walked out of the dungeons, creeping up from the half-collapsed stairs and helping my ascent with ropes. There was an uncomfortable feeling of failure niggling inside me. Somehow, I was sure the twins were feeling the same way.

We can't admit it, even with ourselves, but we hoped for those marauders. We were alert and ready for battle. Yes, even willing. Nothing is worse than being alone, not even death. But alone we are. We have explored the whole Midlothian County, and haven't been able to find a single, breathing creature. The truth? There's nobody else here.

The world did end long ago, Shaun was right. Or at least the Scottish portion of the world. We had the confirmation a few days later the

Castle's episode, on a sunny afternoon when Ellen came to search for us.

"There's a trail," Shaun interpreted for me.

"Which kind of trail?'

"She's not sure. But there were traces of something alive, and they lead to a place outside the city."

Ellen led us across Leith Walk to what, before the Plague, used to be one of Edinburgh's seaside suburbs. And it was there that, just a dozen of metres away from the shore, we had an amazing view. The sand was littered with corpses—animals of all forms, species and dimensions. There were hundreds of thousands of them, covering the beach past where our stare could follow, and probably further. It looked to me like if, in a sort of hive-mind instinct, they had tried to escape en masse from the ravaging disease to a safer place and had been stopped by the sea. Some of them where bloated with water. An evident sign they all died in the attempt of swimming.

Shaun and I did not say a word. Ellen knelt on the ground, and cried.

That same night, when we were sitting outside looking at the sky—a pastime we seemed not being able to get rid of, Iron Plague or not—Shaun caught me following Ellen with my regard.

"What are you waiting for, Raven?"

"Excuse me?"

"That day in the dungeons . . . I have seen you."

"So?"

"You were worried, mate." He continued. "You fancy her."

"Correct."

"Bummer! And I thought you had a crush on me." Shaun laughed.

"I could, if I had not met her."

"Well, sincere condolences. Ellen was not dating anybody even before the Plague, when she had quite a choice." He smiled. "I guess the shortage of breathing preys has not changed a thing for her."

I was not surprised. I shrugged.

"But she likes you, I feel it. I know my sister." He continued with a smile. "You should ask her out. She can't talk, but she would make herself understood nonetheless."

I nodded slowly. "I will."

But I didn't. Not that day, not any time after. I preferred living side by side with the woman I loved, adoring her in silence rather than risking her refusal or worse, being sent away. That was something I could not bear. I could not live alone any longer.

We kept doing what we did since we had met, searching for survivors, of whatever kind. Not trying to find not a solution—there was probably none—for a cause that had lost any relevance to us. What we wanted was just a reason to remain alive.

Days became weeks and then months.

We travelled looking at our stars, in a sky often clouded.

"Do you need assistance, Fidra? Have you fed the dogs?"

"No, Raven. Ellen will help me."

After one year or so of roaming a desolate, silent Scotland, we eventually found a place in which stones were still breathing—the remote island of Fidra in the East Lothian, where a derelict church was preserved almost intact. A young girl with two dogs lived there. She couldn't have been older than seven. God only knows how she had survived. She didn't remember a great deal, apart from her parents taking her to that place and then dying of the same disease that claimed the rest of the world.

She is with us now. She has no memory of her name either, so we called her Fidra, from the place where we found her. She's especially attached to Ellen, and the two are inseparable. But we all love her, and not only because she's adorable and she's the only other survivor we have found so far. She has given us hope.

Now we know the Iron Plague is not the end.

Maybe it was in Scotland, in Europe, in the advanced world. But not the entire Earth. Somewhere on this planet, people like us, with strange genetic disorders that metabolise iron in their blood in a different way, are still alive. And if they are, they will be living with nature. Not in metal structures but in wood huts and underground caves. It is from them that civilisation will be built again, one more in harmony with life.

Us? After our long tour across Scotland, we returned to Edinburgh, settling in this Canongate, melted and stinking, but where millenary dark stones stand stubborn. I guess history made them in the first place and keeps them alive. And they're going to live on, longer than us. But we offer our contribution—we make them breathing.

It's only 3:45 am, but at this latitude dawn is already breaking.

I look around at our room made of plastic and synthetic scraps. We sleep on a pallet of straws and rags. Sometimes there's only enough for Fidra to eat while we rely on berries and weird-looking but edible sprouts.

Later in the morning we will go fishing in a loch. Ellen thinks life is returning in the countryside. She has seen flies near the water, and possibly there's something brewing there. We are all excited at that perspective.

I take Shaun's hand while he's still asleep, and I put it on my breast. He squeezes it a little, and without waking up he starts making love to me. I have no illusion he feels real attraction, but, as he said once, only Ellen has not been affected by the lack of available mates. To me, it makes no difference. It's an animal instinct that needs to be satisfied, a species that has to survive and if thanks to our lust we can generate one precious life for a depopulated land, that's something good for everybody.

I allow him to pleasure me and I close my eyes. This day's going to be as long as the others, but it's a promising one.

Russell Hemmell is a statistician and social scientist from the U.K., passionate about astrophysics and speculative fiction. Recent stories in *Gone Lawn, Not One of Us, Strangelet,* and elsewhere. Blog: Earthianhivemind.net. Twitter: @SPBianchini.

A Cautionary Tale

by

Tom Larson

PORT BELLA WAS JUST A whistle stop in those days. A tree-lined street running to the river, the business strip whittled down to a general store and the saloon next to it. Half that since the bar went bust. Then Juanita showed up in a rental truck with a pair of bruisers and a liquor license. She parked in the shade while the boys pried the boards from the windows and doors, ten years easy since they'd seen the light of day. The rest was just lifting and lugging, and by late afternoon she was all moved in. For a week or so it was nonstop contractors, local boys to spread the word. Nobody knows when she started serving. Someone pulled on the door and it just opened.

She worked the bar and served up chili, trading barbs and barking insults. To belly up was to be fair game. She was hell on the regulars, singled out bad points, picked and poked until they couldn't get enough. Started ducking in two or three nights a week, brought their pals and girlfriends to sample a dose. More than a few took to the challenge and most nights the banter was blistering.

"Well, if it ain't Malloy, the ventriloquist. The only man who can suck on a bottle and talk out his ass at the same damn time."

"Speaking of ass, Juanita, rumor has it you have my likeness tattooed on yours. Any truth to that?"

"Yeah, and *it* talks too, with an Irish accent."

"Damn shame to cover it up, girl."

"If I had your face I'd wear pants on my head."

Trash talk, maybe, but just the thing for the day's unwinding. Juanita had a mouth, all right, sassy as a Nob Hill madam, which she'd been until returns diminished. Her number scribbled in little black books from City Hall to Sausalito. It wasn't the whoring that brought her down, more the courtroom tirades and media mugging, Bordello Queen Slaps Suit on the City. In the end they rode her out on a rail.

On to Port Bella and a brand-new leaf, no girls this time, just chili and chatter. But don't let the town council boys snow you. They read the papers. They knew the score.

The décor was trademark Juanita, moose heads and suits of armor, funhouse mirrors and penny arcades. She had mannequins poised to take your order and dressmaker dummies in leather and lace. A pair of coffins stood on end, one for the condoms, one for the cancer sticks, mismatched tables ringed in sofas, beaded lampshades, and brass spittoons.

At first it was barflies, a fair number given the town's size. The kooky setting and sheer joy of boozing kept the old girl in the black. Things picked up on weekends, trendsetters checking the buzz, the old crowd coming up from the city. The place got loud but no one complained, just laughter rolling down the street.

The saloon had a wide concourse, so Juanita leased space to help pay the bills. The weirder the wares, the less rent she charged. Shoppers ran the goofball gamut, a thirsty crowd with money to burn.

That spring an antique dealer leased the telegraph office. There was token opposition, but strings got pulled, zoning got finagled, and the rebirth of Main Street was underway. Marge Rawlins opened a teashop where the plumbing supply used to be and Phil Nash turned his place into a B&B. Crews came up from Oakland to rehab the fire-house and by fall the old town was back in business.

Not everyone was happy with the renaissance. The clergy considered Juanita's a scandal and worked the pulpits to muffled yawns. Letters to the editor warned of social discord and moral decline; the price of doing business, Juanita would say. Mostly the locals took a hands-off approach. What was good for the town was good for the townsfolk, providing things didn't get out of hand. They repaved the street and put in a stoplight and watched as their town went from hayseed to hip.

Problems started when she got the black rooster. Part of it was the bird itself, mean and spiteful, his turf marked in a wide swath of shit. Strutting out to challenge motorists. Mad at the world and everything in it, Juanita as sole exception. They held court under the willows, Juanita in muumuu and Spanish combs, the rooster charging anything that moved. People tried to overlook it, but a few times sent scuttling or stonewalled in traffic and nerves tend to fray. Rumor spread that the bird was dangerous, that he'd pecked a baby or killed a kitten, that the shit smear was rife with parasites. Not to mention the commotion at sunrise. A touch of barnyard was rustic for a time, but not every freaking morning! Still, the differences might have worked themselves out had it not been for . . . the children, their collective fixation, especially the girls. The big black cock as hottest topic, the way they said it curled papa's toes. It was crude. It was salacious. It was impossible to object to without sounding ridiculous.

Juanita knew how to handle a scandal and had a lock on the bottom line. Like her or not, the old girl kept the coffers clinking. Her Half Price Nights shored up the week, while Fridays through Sundays the place was rocking. And being the savvy sort, she courted the competition, threw in with Chez Bella and the newly opened bistro to host a weekend festival, live bands, arts and crafts, street vendors, and beer by the boatload. Revelers started arriving on Thursday and by show time traffic was backed up for miles. The told-you-so set saw their victory at hand, but the crowd was good-natured, and a fine time was had by all.

It didn't take long for the new prosperity to trickle down. Word spread that Fred Davis sold his house for three times what he paid for it. Fred refused to confirm or deny, but the seed was sown and response was immediate. House after house scheduled renovations, and contractors scrambled to keep pace, adding new decks and tasteful additions, pricey restorations inside and out. It only stood to reason that, if your house was due to triple in value it was worth even more all gussied up. The effect was to transform the town into a showplace. Who knew how handsome these old homes could be? And with the houses looking so fine a little landscaping was in order. Trucks and mowers, trimmers and blowers, crews of Mexicans putting things right. Before you knew it the town was sitting pretty.

Of course, not everyone reaped the benefits. Faced with soaring taxes, some old-timers were forced to sell. And with their situation being obvious, offers came in the lowball range. A few of the newcomers felt guilty, but most would agree it was what the place needed, weeding out the pensioners and welfare cases, ridding their world of the wrong element. The old-timers behaved just as badly, pissed and moaned to anyone who'd listen. They refused to acknowledge the town's transformation and went on ad nauseam about how it once was. Back when everything was falling apart, always the case in places like Port Bella. The ones who could afford to paid no notice. Those kinds of problems would solve themselves as the losers were priced out of the equation.

Then the bikers showed up. How did they not see *that* coming? As a Sunday destination Port Bella was ideal. It was in the country, had two cops, one cantankerous saloonkeeper, and you could get there in an hour from just about anywhere. So there they came. Not just the gangs, though they were in evidence, but dweebs and dykes and geezers galore. Before long it was hogs curb to curb and noise enough to wake the dead. You might think this would be an issue everyone could get behind, a quality-of-life, common-cause sort of thing. But the bad blood ran deep, and watching yuppies work themselves up was worth the ruckus to the born and raised.

Biker Ban One lost by a whisker, but time for the townies was running out. Winter took a toll on the old folks, and the up-and-comers smelled the edge. In May the campaign was re-launched, the board, revamped, and Biker Ban Two slipped right through. *Democracy in action*, the yuppies hailed, but the ACLU took a dimmer view. The ban was challenged, the lawyers swarmed, and the years just seemed to sail on by.

Meanwhile, Juanita raked it in. With the concourse booked solid and the merchants thriving, the joint had the look of a gypsy bazaar. The sort of place you might find an Iron Maiden or the Last Supper painted on the head of a pin. Items so one–of-a-kind folks came from far and wide. No real pattern to it. Monday could be a circus while Wednesday might be strictly regulars. Only weekends were the same year-round, wide open and jammed to the rafters.

With the ban in limbo, the bikers descended. Some of the more unsavory types even took up residence. When their prep school daughters started sporting colors, the yuppies went around the bend. They blamed Juanita's for the riff-raff invasion and vowed no child would go down that road. They'd worked too hard and spent too much to see it all go belly up. Hoo boy, no sir, not in this tax bracket, uh-uh.

Art Forrester, father to Becky "Hoover" Forrester, last seen on the arm of Sal "the Barber Pole" Magglione, was first to go on record. Braced by a bracer of boilermakers, he commandeered the podium for a town council rant. Juanita's was a sin pit, a cesspool, a blight and bane, also a den of evil, a temple of doom, and a quagmire of iniquity.

And yeah, Art's metaphors were all over the place, but his point was well taken. The ungodly noise and the bad actors, the townies and the goddamn ACLU, it just wasn't right. No sir, they hadn't worked this hard and spent this much to see it all blow up in their faces. No way, José, not when there's a narcotics squad and a vice squad and the Board of Licenses and the goddamn Republican Party. Not when there's sound ordinances and health inspectors and Mothers Against Drunk Driving and . . .

Juanita shrugged it off at first. She'd been dealing with breast beaters all of her life; some say she even thrived on it. But the raids made a dent and the fines piled up and the legal fees, *¡Ay, caramba!* More telling, the groundswell of support she'd counted on never really came around. The oddballs proved impossible to rally and the trendsetters left to set the next trend. Also the train derailment didn't help much, taking out the back deck like it did, and the black cock getting flattened by a Japanese tourist, and a barmaid walking off with a week's receipts, etc.

Besides, the old girl wasn't getting any younger. She'd been as shrewd as she was shady, and with a pile like hers who needed the grief? So she brought in bruisers and the rental truck and blew town the way she'd blown in. Nobody knows exactly when it happened. Someone pulled on the door and it was locked.

And that's how Port Bella got rid of Juanita.

Things simmered down after that. The losers took their lifestyles elsewhere and the winners hoped they'd seen the last of them. The saloon went to a Santa Cruz developer, and for a while there it was business as usual. But the oddballs didn't seem as odd, more like misfits and malcontents. The mood was different, not that the town was hurting. Weekends were still money in the bank, even if the rents were going through the roof. They kept the old girl's picture over the bar and folks came to see what used to be. Changed the name to the Silver Palace but everyone called it Juanita's.

Being a developer, the new owner couldn't leave well enough alone; started making "improvements" and introducing things, a salad bar and an ATM, lottery tickets, televisions. Tore out the condom machine and put in central air. Then came the micro brews and that whole crowd, bigger spenders, that's the ticket. And with a kitchen that big it made sense to expand the menu, fix that back deck, maybe put in a beer garden.

Then, without a word of warning, he sold off the cigarette machine, shit-canned the ashtrays, and plastered the place with NO SMOKING signs. And, okay, he saw the writing on the wall, but things at Juanita's changed overnight.

"And remember how she used to come over and just sit down at your table?"

"And insult you, right?"

"Talk about hilarious! First she'd yell over from the bar, some wise crack about what you're wearing or the size of your butt. Anything, really."

"And it sounded like she'd known you for years."

"Right, like some cranky old pal. And then she'd come over. I mean I'd heard about it, but the first time? I nearly peed my pants!"

"With the rooster?"

"Oh my God, the big, black cock! My ex gets a tic when I bring it up."

"You know Carl Helliman, Nora's husband? He heard his daughter talking about it on the phone and ended up in the hospital with chest pains."

"My Michael is that way with the bikers. Rants and raves all weekend but never a word to their faces."

"Tell me about it. We married a bunch of weenies."

"Honestly, there's a part of me that could go for one of those types, you know? Big and hairy?"

"Just drag one home for the night. . . . Maybe two nights."

"Hey, remember the Bloody Buck? Basically a Bloody Mary in the mason jar with the Old Bay?"

"And the string bean? Jesus, two and you were shit-faced."

"I kinda miss Juanita. I mean there was never a dull moment."

"Don't forget the chili to die for."

"Please. Whenever my Herbie indulged I had to sleep in the guest room."

The trouble with prosperity, it comes at a price. For the first time anyone could recall crime became a problem, which led to more cops, a fleet of cruisers, and a state-of-the-art justice center. The old sewer system couldn't keep up so they put in a new one, screwing up business for most of the summer. And putting it in meant cutting down some of the old trees, but hey, all in the name of progress. Since it was dug up anyway, the street was widened to the horror of curbside homeowners. They could like it or lump it, the merchants snickered, and the town council seemed to agree. Then came the railroad parking lot turnstile, then the speed bumps. And with curbs and sidewalks finally in place, could parking meters be far behind?

Over at the Silver Palace the smoking ban was holding firm. The micro-brew crowd didn't smoke anyway and the bikers just ignored it, leading to yet another ordinance that came with a summons and a healthy fine. The bikers ignored those too, ending in a series of high profile raids, mass arrests, lawsuits and countersuits.

And that's how the town rid itself of the bikers.

Funny thing about those bikers and oddballs, they were pretty free with their money. And as marginal characters they were more likely to patronize the offbeat merchants than, say, the micro-brew crowd. Not to a degree you'd notice right away, but turning up in the monthly tally. And, as any developer will tell you, the numbers never lie. After two months in the red Silver Palace Limited was sold to an Asian consortium. They did the bar over in Hard Rock glitz with the big screens and the pricey memorabilia.

The thing about consortiums, they have no concept of shabby chic. The way they saw it, if you could make the rent selling tchotchkes and curios the rents were probably too low. And they *were* too low, considering what the galleries and antique stores were shelling out. When you factored in renovation expenses and the inherent greediness of consortiums, in general, and Asian consortiums, in particular, a little restructuring was probably in order.

And since this was business, not some grubby small-town squabble, the restructuring was handled in a businesslike way. Rents were doubled, the chains moved in, and that's how the town rid itself of the oddballs.

But times were still good. Not for the restaurants so much, what with the limited parking, the glut of competition, and the gourmet renaissance going on in Vallejo, of all places. Those old warehouses were so easy to convert and that bridge backdrop was picture perfect, not to mention the parking. Vallejo was a Chamber of Commerce concern, all right. Port Bella's antiques were doing okay—not as well as expected, but hanging in anyway. Again, parking was the problem, as anyone could tell you. The railroad leased just so many spaces, and with one main street, well . . . something had to be done. Spend half a Sunday trying to track down a spot and you won't be back again soon, especially with Vallejo being closer with that damned bridge.

Parking. They proposed putting meters on the three side streets but the locals turned it down. They proposed a paved lot at the far end of town but the locals turned it down. They offered Josh Sheppard a small fortune for a corner of his pasture, but old Josh died and his daughters nixed the deal. They ran shuttle buses to the city, but nobody takes shuttle buses.

What happened to the Asian consortium remains a mystery. Word went around that paychecks were bouncing and a balloon payment was well past due. Two days in a row the bar didn't open. Then the doors got padlocked and big red For Sale signs were plastered in both front windows. The concourse kept at it for a while, but try doing business when the place is screaming bankruptcy. Rumor had it the Asians were smugglers and the bar just a front for money laundering. Someone said the Japanese government froze all their assets; someone else said it was the Vietnamese. Whatever happened, the effects were wide ranging. Creditors got stiffed, tax revenues dwindled, and the local banks took a big hit. Add to that a title search turned up liens going back to pre-Juanita days sending the whole ball of wax back to court. Through it all, the place stood empty, paint peeling, For Sale signs fading to pink.

Port Bella was adrift, a ship without a captain. With leases in limbo the chains pulled out, some to the burbs, most to Vallejo. The swank shops that swept in on Juanita's coattails were left with no coattails and no clientele. Even the yuppies were in trouble. Their gussied-up houses failed to appraise or sat on the market to nary a nibble. Which played hell with their equity, but did nothing to lessen their tax burden. After all, the new toys had to be paid for, even if they weren't needed so much anymore. With belts tightened and deficits looming, panic wasn't long in coming. One by one the restaurants folded, then the boutiques and the B&Bs. New shops opened but quickly floundered, until no one was left to risk a venture. A few refused to cut and run, but even die-hards die in the end. It got so bad that Dixon's Hardware closed shop after five generations. Only two years since Juanita pulled out and the main drag was as dead as a doornail.

And that's how the town rid itself of the parking problem.

But it didn't end there. Faced with financial ruin and a house full of bastard grandkids, Art Forrester drove his car into a bridge abutment. Claiming temporary insanity, a real estate agent gunned down a suddenly remorseful buyer. Neighborhoods were polarized and families were in turmoil. Wives couldn't break the credit card habit, husbands couldn't stay off the booze, and kids who should have been in college were flipping burgers for minimum wage.

Back in town the empty buildings attracted vandals, mostly high school kids blowing off steam. That drove real estate values down even further, but gave the police force something to do. The New Year's Eve fire could have been worse, but with the insurance companies balking and the lawsuits languishing, the row of charred buildings worked on the nerves.

Bad as things got, folks might have pulled through, some of them anyway. With a single break, an amusement park, say, or casino gambling, they could have weathered the storm. It was still pretty country and you couldn't beat the location, even if most of the charm had been lost to progress. All it would take is one fat investor to get the ball rolling again, one Arab sheik or non-Asian consortium. If they could reinvent Vallejo why couldn't they do it here? Just one break and they could turn the corner. One small piece of luck, for fucking Christ sake!

What they got instead was the oil spill, the river being part of the Carquinez Straits and deep enough to float the tankers. Not so many, one or two a day, slipping past like great floating cities, giving the illusion that it was Port Bella moving, the whole town adrift, not just fiscally but physically. The tankers were a thrill for the tourists back when they had tourists. Their kids running along the bank, calling out to the hands on deck, the biggest thing they'd ever seen, passing so close you could hit it with a rock. One so wide it took out the retaining wall by the railroad loading dock. A real mess what with the spill spreading halfway up Main Street before the salvage boys got a handle on things. The oil fouled up the new sewage system, seeped into groundwater, coated everything in crude and stank to high heaven. What with dead birds and dead fish, the whole bouquet settled into carpeting and clothing, washing out with the tide and then back in again. Every day for months until the yuppies buckled, packed it in by the carload, taking their kids, their incomes, and their tax base with them. Cut their losses, turned and ran, leaving the old-timers holding the bag.

Some say they brought it on themselves. It's how folks go about things that does them in. Others scoffed at the notion. Folks were the same everywhere, their strengths tempered by their weaknesses, the bad balanced by the good. Why it went south is anyone's guess. Newcomers muscle in, the old guard tries to stem the tide, and this old world keeps wobbling along. Maybe they just moved too fast or maybe it was an unnatural progression. And maybe, just maybe, they got what they deserved.

I'm thinking it was the lack of a thing, the air of something special, loud talk, laughter, and more fun than you've had in a long time. Some places have that going for them. Not so much pretty as pretty damned interesting. A place like, say, Monte Villa, way down on the Baja. Coming out of nowhere for who knows what reason? Strictly one-horse, with the post office, the bodega, the old cantina with the windows boarded up. Just a whistle stop really, until . . .

Tom Larsen has been writing fiction for thirty years and his work has appeared in any number of obscure literary reviews. His two novels are available on Amazon.

Annals of the Allred Clan

by

Mark Mellon

I. A RAID BY SAVAGES

RULON WALKED OUTSIDE TO THE yard. Moroni had already fetched the hoes. He handed one to Rulon and headed toward the fields, not bothering to see if he followed. Rulon quickly caught up. Long hoe balanced on a narrow shoulder, he followed Moroni and ate the breakfast his mother Nauvoo made, cornbread and an apple.

The fields lay some distance from the house. Hyrum, Rulon's father, farmed twenty acres of bottomland, his allotment. Despite baking heat and drought, he raised crops by irrigating soil from the Bear Stream's gentle flow.

The sun, just past the horizon, silhouetted the scarecrow amid neat rows of knee-high corn stalks that cast long shadows. Beans, potatoes, and melons grew in other fields while some were left fallow in keeping with Allred tradition. The air was clamorous with birdcalls. Barren land flanked the fields, cracked into yellow-brown clods by decades without rain.

Moroni vigorously weeded. Rulon followed his example. They worked quietly. The boy knew this was necessary, but was still bored. His quick mind craved distraction.

"Grandfather Moroni."

"What, boy?"

"When do you expect the men back?"

"The Sabbath for sure."

"Maybe they'll have cowhides. Do you think we might go to the Salt to sell hides?"

Moroni laughed. "So you can see some girls? See what the Lord provides, boy."

They worked steadily after that.

"Last Sabbath, Grandfather Abinidi said a road used to run by here and people traveled in wagons on it like the ones in books."

"Abinidi makes such a mystery. You can see what's left of Highway 91 on the trail to the Salt. A big jumble of broken rock, thanks to the Lord's wrath."

"Did you ever see the wagons, Grandfather Moroni?"

"They stopped making 'em after I was born, but I saw 'em, like Abinidi. Just machinery that quit."

They finished weeding. Moroni removed his black elder's hat and mopped his bald, sweating dome with a homespun kerchief. Despite the early hour, it was hot.

"Let me get my breath."

"Did they quit because they ran out of gasoline?"

"I'm glad your father teaches you something. They just ran out. That's why your sisters walk the treadmill for light and power while we work here."

Rulon looked back at the house, high on a bluff that marked where the Bear River once flowed broad and wide. Hyrum had built the solid, two-story home with locally made brick and lime. White solar panels on the roof gleamed in the sunlight. Beyond rose barren mountains whose peaks had gone snowless for generations.

"That's also why it's hot and dry?"

"Some so-called educated man might spout some fool theory like that, but Allreds know better. The drought and the famine are the Lord's wrath because the Church abandoned polygamy. Rain comes again if we stick to Joseph Smith's revealed truth. Every last tenet.

We'll have a new century in ten years, maybe a new age, but only if we're holy. I won't see it, but you will. You have to sanctify yourself. Understand me, boy?"

"Yes, Grandfather Moroni."

"Good. Get back to work."

In a nearby thick canebrake, Sangrito crouched and spied, reins held lightly in one hand. Insects bit him viciously. He ignored them. Sangrito slowly crept away, his ride trailing behind him. Out of eyesight and earshot, he mounted his horse and trotted northward. Dressed in deerskin leggings, he rode bareback with only a hackamore to control his mount. He'd stolen the swift, tireless brown and white paint near the Albikerk from a Tohona O'Odham he'd murdered. Armed with a Bowie knife and a bow, he wore a quiver that was filled with arrows painstakingly made by hand. His long, lank black hair was tied back with bright ribbons. Three scalps hung from his belt.

The camp was hidden in a dusty draw where a small tributary stream once flowed. Sangrito rode in to find the crew chewing cold deer jerky. Fearful of detection, Kid Crip allowed no fire. Sangrito dismounted, led his horse into the corral, removed the hackamore, and joined the crew. His brother Manolo handed him jerky and a corn tortilla.

Kid Crip ran his fingers through thick, greasy blond hair. He wore a padded black vest, antique armor from the Fat Times, bought with five horses at the Albikerk's market. At his waist was a Colt .45. Reluctant to fire, having limited ammo, the Kid used the pistol to whip errant followers or other offenders into line. Two shriveled brown ears strung on a copper wire hung from his neck, previously attached to Kid Blood, the crew's former leader, defeated by Kid Crip through a treacherous ambush. The sidearm, armored vest, and his murdered predecessor's ears were tokens of his status as crew chief.

"Dog, what did you find?"

"Like you said, *jefe*, the next place is a long ride away. I sneaked up last night while they were eating. The men are hunting. There's just an old man and a *chico*."

"What about horses, cattle?" Muerte Frio demanded. He wiped his rifle's barrel with an old rag.

Sangrito grinned. "*Mucho*. New mounts for all. And cattle, fat enough to last to the Albikerk so we can sell them at the market."

"Didn't I say crew chief can smell a juicy steak from across the Big Desert?" OG crowed.

"There's more. Women."

The men exchanged knowing looks, leering smiles, and sudden wild, raucous whoops of lustful laughter.

"The crew's getting wives today," Mo Ali crowed.

"Shut up," Kid Crip hissed, "You want to give us away?"

Abashed, the men bowed their heads. "Yes, crew chief. Sorry, crew chief."

"That's better. Sangrito, where's the old man and boy?"

"Out in the fields."

"Okay, we'll go now."

The crew's faces lit up.

"Remember, this is the biggest job we ever done. Do it right and we're rich, a real crew with good horses, fat cattle to sell, and wives."

"No more cooking or chopping wood," OG said.

"So pop the old man and *chico* first. Everything's easy then. Ride in slow. Smile. I say we want to water the horses, trade for beef and salt. When I signal, OG and Manolo spear them. Make sure they don't shout. Understand?"

"Yes, chief."

"Good. Mount up, then."

He put on his war bonnet, an Oakland Raiders ball cap, torn and faded with age, worn backward for strength and courage. The crew stroked ritual amulets and prayed to small, stone *bultos*. OG and Mo

Ali saddled Kid Crip's horse. Muerte Frio saddled his own. They were the only ones with firearms and saddles. The others slipped on hackamores and draped blankets over their mounts. Armed with handmade but effective lances, bows, and daggers, heads shielded from the sun by broad-brimmed straw sombreros, they had faces that were lined by constant exposure to sun and wind. Forgotten in the Big Desert, ignorant of civilization or humanity, the crew had banded together like feral dogs to hunt prey. Despite the long, nearly fatal journey to the far reaches of the upper Ute, they were eager, chins up and grinning, rapine and plunder ahead. They rode from the draw toward the Allreds.

The sun had neared its peak when Moroni stopped for dinner. Bevenee, Rulon's little sister, fetched bacon and cheese sandwiches and a pitcher of milk and then left, complaining about the heat. Moroni also cut up a small melon, which Rulon found refreshing. Full from their meal, the old man and the boy resumed work.

A horse's sneeze, a loud snort from the canebrake, was the first sign something was wrong. Moroni stared uncertainly into the thicket.

"Is that you, Grandnephew Brigham, playing another practical joke?"

A man on horseback pushed through the cane and onto open ground. Others followed. Rulon stared openmouthed. Horses he'd seen before, although these were poor nags compared to his father's. The men startled him. He'd never seen anyone other than Allreds before.

The riders moved slowly, well spread out, open grins marred by gaps in their teeth. The six men were a mixed bunch. The one in the lead had blond hair like an Allred. Despite the heat, he wore a curious, bulky black vest. Two brown lumps hung from a wire around his neck. Another was pale, closer to a scarecrow than human, bone-thin in a long coat. Two had black skin, something Rulon had previously seen only in books.

"Wassup," the blond said. A strange flat bill hung from behind his faded hat. "Want to trade beef and salt."

Moroni's hard, horny hand caught Rulon full in the chest. The boy staggered backwards.

"Run, Rulon. Warn the women. Get Great Uncle Enos's gun."

Moroni's tone brooked no argument. Rulon took to his heels.

"The *chico*'s getting away," one man cried.

"Manolo. Get him, dog."

A rider galloped after Rulon. He rode by his legs alone, an arrow already nocked to his bow, dark eyes alive with excitement and pleasure.

"Gentile scum."

The edge of Moroni's hoe caught the rider full in the face, swung with all the strength the eighty-four-year-old farmer could muster. The rider fell from his horse with the awful scream of a hog under the butcher knife, features split wide.

"Manolo."

Moroni faced the riders. Hoe raised high, breath heavy and labored, it was increasingly harder for him to move.

"Evil Lamanite dogs."

The scarecrow rode close to Moroni. He unlimbered his long rifle and fired into his belly.

Rulon heard the shot. He turned to see Moroni slowly sink to his knees.

"No."

Another man rode up to Moroni and shot an arrow into his chest.

"That's for my brother."

"Dog, you slipping," the blond shouted. "Get the *chico*."

Rulon ran faster than ever before in his life, but he was a boy against mounted men. There was only enough time to rush into the yard where his mother and sisters were gathered, anxious about the gunfire.

"Rulon, what's wrong?" Nauvoo cried. "Where's Father Moroni?"

"Run. Strangers, bad men. They killed Grandfather Moroni."

Bevenee began to cry. Nauvoo slapped her hard across the face.

"Stop that. Girls, run as fast as you can to the hiding place. I'll be right behind. Godlove, look after Bevenee. Go."

The girls fled, long blond pigtails streaming behind.

"You come along," Nauvoo said, "We'll hide until the men return."

"Once I get Great-Great-Granduncle Enos's rifle."

"There's no time."

"Grandfather Moroni said."

Rulon ran up the stairs.

"I'll wait."

Over seventy years ago, Enos Allred returned after fighting overseas in the Babylon War. Afflicted by a severe concussion and a severed leg, he brought back an AK-47 assault rifle. Like other Fat Times artifacts, the rifle was treasured as a family heirloom and hung from a place of honor in the parlor. Rulon put a chair next to the wall, stood on it, and took the rifle from its hooks. He took out a magazine from the glass case where it was stored. The banana clip was loaded with special-caliber bullets made to his father's order by gunsmiths in the Salt. He slipped in the magazine and pulled back the charging handle.

"Let me go," his mother screamed.

"Pretty strong for an old woman."

"Yeah, but where's the rest?"

Rulon burst through the door out onto the porch. Two men held his mother, a black and the blond. The other three were still mounted.

"It's the *chico*. Shoot him, Muerte Frio."

The scarecrow raised his rifle, but his intended victim was armed this time. Before Muerte Frio could fire, Rulon put the AK-47 to his shoulder and shot a controlled burst into the center of mass. The bullets' impact knocked the raider off his horse into the dirt, where he lay motionless. Muerte Frio was now dead himself.

An arrow whizzed past Rulon's head at a hairsbreadth distance. The man who shot Moroni screamed abuse.

"Stinking Mormon."

He pulled another arrow from his quiver. Rulon shot him in turn.

"Ain't any you any good?" the man in the cap said. He shoved Nauvoo aside and shouted. "Hold her, OG, while I take care of business."

He pulled a heavy pistol from his belt and fired in one motion. The shot went wild. Rulon was raised not to waste precious ammunition. He aimed slowly, deliberately, again for the center of mass. The raider pointed his pistol straight at the boy, a confident sneer on his face.

"Last day, dog."

His tanned face turned dead white, leached of color by the bullet's force. He hit the ground like the others. Rulon turned the assault rifle on the man with his mother.

"Let her go."

The two surviving raiders had knives and lances. Rulon's voice cracked high with strain and fear, but the bodies scattered about the yard were mute testimony he was just as dangerous as any full-grown man.

"Here, *chico*, take her."

The man shoved Nauvoo toward Rulon so hard she fell to the ground. He jumped onto his pony and rode off with the other man. Glad to see them go, Rulon ran to his mother and helped her to her feet. Her long, graying hair had come undone and she was badly shaken, but otherwise unharmed. He held her tight, fighting hard not to cry.

Nauvoo stroked his hair, gently lifted his chin, and said, "You were right, son. If we left without Enos's rifle, they'd have caught us in the open. I guess we can fetch the girls."

Rulon basked in his mother's esteem. "First I better look these fellows over. I should at least get that rifle and pistol."

Nauvoo smiled. "Very well."

She left. Rulon walked over to the scarecrow's body and picked up his rifle. In death, his face kept the same expression, but was even more shriveled and pale. Rulon wondered if he should go through his pockets, but rejected the idea as mean and low. He went to the blond and bent over him.

BLLLAAAMMM

The .45 slug whizzed past Rulon's left ear, ruptured his eardrum, and left him half-deaf.

"I'll kill you," the blond said. He pulled the trigger again, but the clip was empty.

Head spinning, in horrible pain, Rulon still had enough presence of mind to slap the dead scarecrow's rifle butt flat into the blond's face. Rulon raised the rifle high by the barrel.

"No. Wait. We can talk."

Rulon brought the butt down with all his strength.

The blond said no more. Rulon took his kerchief and put it to his ear to staunch the streaming blood. Dead men sprawled around him. They had to be buried before they rotted and drew flies. Poor Moroni and the other raider also lay in the fields. Unannounced and unbidden, manhood forced itself on Rulon that day, years before he should have played that role. In the aftermath, what remained was grief, injury, and the awareness that life in the Lean Times was indeed so much harder than Rulon could have ever known.

II. A RAID ON THE GENTILES

It was late when the cart pulled into the barnyard. Hyrum handed the reins to Obadiah.

"Untack the horse. Put him in his stall. Brush him down and see he's fed. Then go to bed."

Hyrum went into the house.

Rulon heard his mother's voice raised high in greeting. A wet puff of breath invaded his left ear. He whirled around, hand cupped protectively over it.

"Obadiah, leave my bad ear alone."

"Or what? You going to help me untack the horse like Pa said?"

About to speak further, Rulon thought better of it and went over to the horse. He slipped the bit off while Obadiah undid the harness.

"You didn't seem eager at the convocation."

"You made up for that, Obadiah."

"Guess you don't like the bad wilderness, far from Ma and home."

"Don't see the point, that's all. Besides Manolo, I got the other fellows."

"You mean Splitface?"

"That's not what a good Mormon says. His name's Manolo. I'm just saying, why look for trouble?"

"You're afraid. That's it. It's just dumb luck you got those fellows."

Rulon put a halter on the horse and led him to the barn. Obadiah followed. Both boys brushed the horse.

"Not my fault I was here that day and not you. I wish you got the praise and attention. I hate it."

"No, you're the hero, Rulon."

They finished brushing the horse and spread fresh hay.

"Come on into the house. We got a long ride tomorrow."

"After I check the stock."

"Ain't you the good farmer too. Please yourself."

Obadiah left the barn. Rulon went out back to the pigsties and stock corrals. He climbed a corral fence and whistled.

"Hey, Manolo. You awake?"

"Yeah. That you, kid?"

"Yes, it's Rulon."

There was a clink of chains. A shadowy figure got to his feet and shuffled over, hands and feet shackled. Darkness mercifully shielded his disfigured features, the curled, blackened ruins of a shattered nose and the open, smashed-teeth grimace of a caved-in upper jaw, torn open by Grandfather Moroni's hoe.

"You know, only you say my name. Got tobacco, kid?" His mangled, breathy voice was unintelligible except after long listening. "Homebrew a Jack Mormon cousin made?"

"Allreds don't do that. I got some rock candy from the Salt you can have."

"Sure, kid."

Rulon fished rock candy from a vest pocket and handed it to Splitface. The slave loudly sucked on the candy.

"Thanks, dog. Your *padre* don't feed me much, specially nothing sweet."

"Pa said tonight at convocation he's going to lead an expedition with you scouting. Parley and Nephi are coming here first thing sunrise."

"No surprise. All he says when he ain't beating me."

"Pa said you claimed there's a ranch your crew had near the Albikerk full of stolen cattle. That true?"

"Sure, kid. Sweet hideout in a box canyon. Got spring water and rustled stock."

"I hope so, Manolo. I don't want to shoot you like I did your brother."

Splitface chuckled, a death rattle rasp.

"No fear. I ain't go tell you wrong. Nobody mess with Kid Allred."

Rulon scowled. "We got to get up early. You need a blanket?"

"No. Used to the dirt by now. See you, kid."

Nephi and Parley rode into the barnyard before sunup, each man on his best mount with two spares trailing behind as instructed. Older than Hyrum at forty, worn and wrinkled by hard toil outdoors, Nephi was small, fox-faced, with brown teeth. Parley was another big Allred with flaming hair and a freckle-jammed face, the clan's blacksmith and farrier. He brought a hand-forged, single-barreled shotgun. Nephi carried a century-old Ruger MK III hunting rifle he'd bought at the Salt for an impoverishing sum. Hyrum waited in his shirtsleeves, thumbs in his galluses.

"Howdy. Nauvoo's got tea with strawberry jam."

"Now, that is thoughtful," Parley said. He hopped off his horse.

Nauvoo came out of the house with three steaming clay mugs of Mormon tea. The men drank deep of the sharp, sweet, hot tea.

"I'm glad to see you, Cousin Parley. Cousin Nephi," Nauvoo said.

Rulon and Obadiah emerged. Obadiah already dressed with his hair combed. Rulon stretching and yawning, still half asleep.

"Glad you boys decided to join the men. Ob, get the string lined up and see to our mounts. Rulon, get the cobwebs out of your head. You and Splitface get the pack mules loaded and ready."

Hectored by Hyrum, they left soon after. Rulon rode a dirty white gelding, a strong mount with an unfortunate tendency to booger. He carried Enos Allred's AK-47, the same weapon he killed five Gentiles with, tacitly understood to be his alone now. Obadiah rode a sorrel mare and was armed with the Springfield rifle that belonged to one of the men Rulon killed. Hyrum rode the big roan stallion only he could handle, armed with his hunting shotgun and a Colt .45, another trophy from his son's killing spree.

They headed down a dirt path and came to the marker for the trail to the Salt, a huge, crumbling concrete pillar. The expedition rode for two days down the path that paralleled old Highway 15, well outlined by hoof prints and cart tracks. Rulon had never been this far and was fascinated by the highway's jumbled remains. Long, weed-choked stretches of asphalt were churned and cracked into an impassable shambles. The arid landscape was dotted with burnt, giant hilltop mansions and frequent ancient, wrecked cars, tires long ago stripped off, glass senselessly smashed.

"Kinda spooky, ain't it," Obadiah said, "Sure you don't want to stay home with Ma?"

"Ob, hush up and tend the mules. Rulon, pay him no mind." The edge in Hyrum's voice made it clear he wasn't in the mood to listen to heckling or verbal sparring.

They traveled the sixty-some miles to the Salt in two days. The only sizable settlement for hundreds of miles in any direction, the once large and prosperous city was reduced to three hundred souls. Salters literally scraped a living from the heap of coarse brown salt that marked the spot where legend said a lake once stood, using it to cure hides and jerk meat.

Shacks and rusted mobile homes clustered near the salt heap, outside the ruined city, dominated by the enormous temple's gutted hulk, the giant, discolored husk of a once-splendid edifice, like the corpse of the Fat Times itself. The Salt was the place to buy manufactured arms and ammunition, to recharge batteries, to get canned goods, and (quietly and secretly) alcohol and other vices through Jack Mormons. Hyrum sprang for a night at the one hotel, a ramshackle affair of several Winnebagos in a row, with solar-powered lights, clean sheets, and running water, the lap of luxury to Rulon.

They emerged from their motor home suite in the predawn morning, ready for a day's hard riding, but Obadiah found Splitface unconscious in a horse stall in the livery stables where Hyrum had shackled him for the night, plainly sodden from alcohol. He snored loudly through the black, crinkled gap that was his ruined nose and mouth.

"Oh my freaking heck," Hyrum said.

"Mind your language, cousin," Nephi said.

"Don't lecture me. Help me get him on his horse."

Nephi and Hyrum slung Splitface onto his horse and tied his hands to the saddle horn. He spent the day in a daze, nodding in and out of sleep, but somehow stayed on. They rode south along Highway 15, the mules heavily loaded with provisions and bulging water skins.

"Who gave Splitface liquor?" Hyrum said.

"Probably a Jack Mormon, Pa," Obadiah said.

"Yes, but why? Splitface got nothing."

"He's good at talking, Pa. He talks folks into doing things by acting nice."

"Keep quiet, Rulon. See to the mules."

Perpetual drought had stripped already austere terrain down to bare rock and parched earth. The Allreds rode through a near-lifeless landscape, red plains bare of trees or grass, topsoil stripped away long ago by a punishing wind. Occasionally they passed battered relics of the Fat Times, roofless U-Totems, looted, razed strip malls, and fly-speck towns whose residents had picked up stakes and fled generations before. Hyrum passed without a glance.

"Any stores got took a long time ago. Only good for rats."

In the late afternoon, when the heat peaked, they made camp in an old Arctic Circle restaurant. They penned the stock in the gutted building and slept outside on bedrolls. Rulon shot a brace of rats with Nephi's hunting rifle. Parley carefully skinned and gutted them. Splitface built a fire and Parley roasted the rats on spits.

"These old buildings are still good for firewood," Parley said.

"That was tasty, Cousin Parley." Hyrum licked grease from his fingers.

"Hyrum, I want to know," Nephi said. "You want more out of this than stock?"

"What do you mean, cousin?"

Nephi licked his lips and grinned. "Women. Splitface claims the crew had squaws waiting. Ain't that right, Splitface?"

"Sure, *jefe*." Splitface took a sliver of rat meat Rulon had given him and carefully put it into his ruined mouth. "Three, maybe four young *chicas*."

"So besides new stock, you want new blood for the Allred clan."

Rulon grimaced at the open lust on Nephi's face. He was notorious. The only unmarried adult male Allred, his first and only wife having died years before. The Elders refused to let him remarry for some mysterious reason, whispered about among adults when they thought children weren't around.

"That's no fit way to talk, Nephi. Everybody sleep except Obadiah. You keep the first watch and then Parley."

Several weeks passed of wearying travel. They rode early in the morning and late into the evening with a long afternoon siesta to avoid the worst of the heat, down narrow, winding canyons and up sharp, ridge-backed mountains, through an eternal, unchanging stone landscape devoid of humanity. Rations were quickly eaten. Men and stock grew lean from much toil and little food. Mules and especially horses consumed hay and oats at an alarming rate.

"We got enough to last, Pa?"

"You fret like Nauvoo, Rulon. We'll be fine when we reach the Colorado."

Hyrum proved right. After another long, punishing day, they descended another seemingly endless series of switchbacks to another narrow draw. Long shadows hinted twilight would soon come. They could look forward to another cold camp without water or fire.

"I see something," Obadiah cried.

There was a glint at the valley's bottom, the gleam that only came when sunlight reflects off water. The men lashed their mounts forward, eager to slake their thirst.

"Easy," Hyrum said. "Don't want a man thrown or a horse with a broken leg."

At the valley bottom lay a winding creek, what remained of the once mighty Colorado, freed of mankind's trammels, but shrunken by drought to a fragile, frequently interrupted rivulet. Steep cliffs were striped by great, discolored stone bands that marked former waterlines. The thin stream was nonetheless a godsend to the weary travelers and their stock. They loose-hobbled their mounts and made a rope corral for the mules. Hyrum got on his knees to give thanks. The others followed his example.

"Heavenly Father. Thank you for this day, and for the water you led us to, and the grass for the stock, and our many other blessings. Please bless me that I will have all the things I'm searching for on this expedition. Bless my wife and children and Parley and Nephi. We ask these things in the name of Thy son, Jesus Christ. Amen."

"Amen," everyone else said, even Splitface.

They passed two days by the creek. Hyrum allowed them to sleep and rest, but insisted they also hunt game and gather forage for the stock. Obadiah cut long tobosa grass with a sickle while Rulon bundled and packed it. Parley smoked squirrels and doves by a fire. Rulon was sad to leave the rare verdant spot, but Hyrum insisted.

After six more days, they reached the Four Corners Monument. The parking lot was cracked asphalt, the museum and Navajo craft shacks carried away by wind long ago. The only remnant besides the parking lot was a bronze disc set in a concrete platform that marked the sharp, arbitrarily drawn corners of four extinct states.

Hyrum pointed to the direction marker for New Mexico.

"We're in your territory now, Splitface, Lead us to that ranch. Take us straight or you'll die in a gully."

"Sure, *jefe*." Splitface's open grin made his gaping orifice even more hideous. "We get there soon."

Yet they traveled on for days without sight of even a jackrabbit or a desert rat, much less a well-watered, well-stocked ranch. Often they walked to spare the mounts, down narrow canyons and past jutting mesas with nothing to see but an occasional horned toad. Even avoiding the worst of it, midday heat still crushed them like a vise while dust choked their mouths. Bone weary after each long day's trek, the arduous journey took its toll on men and stock. Once again, they grew rib-sticking lean and supplies steadily dwindled.

Splitface's cheery optimism never ceased. Always ready to help with any chore, he was first to rise and the last to seek rest at camp after tending the stock. He continually pointed to the crest of the next ridge.

"Not far now, *jefe*. Just one big hill and we real close."

Never known for patience, Hyrum grew angry. Things came to a head one night after a mule broke a leg on the trail and had to be shot. Parley sawed off a haunch to roast later on. The rest was left for carrion. They made camp in a motel courtyard. Hyrum told Splitface to get wood and make a fire. The slave broke some boards off the side of a ruined cottage with an ax. He was about to bust them into kindling when Hyrum hit him on the side of the head with a two-by-four. Splitface slumped bonelessly to the dirt. Hyrum stood over him, brandishing the plank.

"Don't like a wild goose chase, Splitface. Just a taste of what you'll get if you don't lead us to that ranch. Tomorrow. Understand?"

"Sure, *jefe*." Splitface put a hand to his head. "We get there tomorrow, you bet."

"That's it, Hyrum," Nephi said. "Show him who's boss."

They fed the stock what little grass remained and ate jerky and hardtack themselves. One cottage was still relatively intact and Rulon had the rare privilege of a roof over his head for the night. Obadiah woke him before dawn.

"You hiding? Didn't like Pa showing your pal Splitface who's in charge?"

"I don't like any of this, Obadiah. I told you at the start."

They drank coffee and ate johnnycakes and the rest of the mule meat, saddled their mounts, and rode southeast. Splitface led them along the shoulder of an old highway. The horses had trouble making their way along the soft gravel shoulder, much eroded by the wind. Nephi's mount stumbled and almost fell.

"I ought to shoot your Gentile slave, Hyrum."

"Be quiet. Everyone stop. I smell smoke."

They reined in their mounts. Countrymen with keen senses of smell, they inhaled the faint tang of wood smoke, a sign of nearby human habitation.

"Just like you say, *jefe*," Splitface said. "Today we find the ranch."

"Count your chickens when they hatch. I'll go look with you. Rulon, you got sharp eyes, so come along. Nephi, Parley, Obadiah, stay here. Keep the stock back and quiet."

Hyrum made them dismount. He had Splitface walk ahead and kept his shotgun on the slave's back. After a short distance, when the smoke grew strong. Hyrum murmured, "Tether your horses."

Crouched low, they crept to the edge of a wide arroyo from which twin streams of white smoke spiraled upward. In the gray, predawn light, two small shacks made from adobe and plywood huddled close to a muddy creek. There was a flicker of firelight from a solitary window in one shack and the sound of a woman's voice raised in song from the other one.

"Stay low."

They lay flat behind rocks. Hyrum handed a folding telescope to Rulon. He put the telescope to one eye. The sun had just crested the horizon. Down below, two men emerged from the shacks, dark as Splitface, but whole featured. They took hoes and worked on gardens irrigated with creek water. They tilled tomatoes, corn, and beans. A woman stepped out of one shack. Young and slender. She squatted to grind corn on a flat stone.

"It's a farm."

"Give me that scope."

Hyrum studied the laboring men. He handed the telescope to Splitface.

"Tell us if that's it."

"Sure, *jefe*. That's Paco and Antonio. The *chica*, she Manuela."

"Let's go back."

Slowly so as to make no noise, they walked back. Parley had broken open his shotgun and was oiling the barrel. Nephi leaned against a rock, rifle at port arms.

"Pa, what'd you find?"

"Hush, Obadiah. Come here, all of you."

They gathered round, heads bent conspiratorially low.

"It's the place all right. Near the Albikerk by water, like Splitface said."

"This ain't the place, Pa."

Hyrum glared sharply at Rulon, blue eyes full of the baleful rage that terrified the boy.

"Did you sass me, boy?"

Rulon had blurted out the truth. Now there was no retreat.

"I ain't trying to sass you, Pa, but this can't be it. He said there was a ranch in a box canyon with a spring and this is a farm in a gully with a creek. And where's all the stock? He's telling a story, Pa."

"Rulon, hush. I 'preciate what you done for the family, but you forget your place. I'm still head of this family and I make the decisions."

"You obey your father, boy," Nephi said. "Shame on you. Sticking up for Lamanite trash against your own."

"But—"

"Hush up, Rulon." Obadiah punched Rulon in the stomach, a blow that doubled him over.

"Stop that, Obadiah. Rulon, if you're scared, you watch Splitface, Me and the rest will ride down and ask some questions."

Hyrum and the others rode out at a loud, clattering trot, without pretence of stealth, firearms ready. Splitface helped Rulon sit down in the shadow cast by a rock and gave him water.

"You *hermano*, he mean as you *padre*."

"They're Allreds and that's it."

"Sure, kid, sure."

In the full light of dawn, the day's heat steadily grew. The sky was a light blue dome scarred by fuzzy patches of clouds in her upper reaches. They rested in the shade. Rulon was startled and delighted by a dove's coo, drawn by scarce water.

"Is pretty, huh, kid?

BDAM BANG BLAM

Startled by the gunfire, Rulon stood up and ran a few steps toward the gully.

"What did they do?"

Hooves clattered behind him. Rulon turned to see Splitface astride a horse, riding away at a gallop.

"Manolo, stop."

But Splitface kept riding. Rulon shouldered his AK-47, sighted down the barrel, and shot him in the back. Splitface pitched off the horse to the ground. Thoroughly spooked, the horse kept running. Rulon hurried over to him. Splitface lay on his back. A pool of black blood steadily spread in the dust around him. He laughed, an awful gurgle, and a blood bubble popped from the gaping hole in his face.

"Kid. You shot me like my brother."

"I'm sorry, Manolo, but why'd you run away?"

"Chance to go to the Albikerk, get tortillas."

"So it was just a story?"

"Had to do it, kid, get away from them beatings."

"You'll go to the spirit prison, Manolo."

Splitface laughed again. "Sure, kid, su—"

He lay dead, blood spilt on the barren red earth. Rulon fetched a pick and shovel to bury him. He'd just started to dig a hole in the hard earth when the others returned. Two women were with them, one older, the other not much more than a child. They walked on either side of Nephi's horse, hands tied to the saddle horn. Both wept continuously.

"Did Splitface run?"

"Yes. He gave me no choice."

"You did right. Good burying him too. We'll camp here a few days, water and graze the stock, rest up. Obadiah, help your brother."

Obadiah grabbed the pick and went to work. He took a breather while Rulon shoveled out the dirt.

"What happened?"

Obadiah was unusually quiet and subdued. He looked around to see if anyone else was listening.

"We rode down. Pa tried talking, but they just jabbered foreign, like Splitface did. Then they got real mad because Nephi was looking at the women."

"Is that when you shot them?"

"Pretty much. I don't know just what happened. Maybe one raised his hoe first. I know Nephi fired straight into one from the hip and Pa finished the other."

"And now they're just out there?"

"Pa said bury them later. He said get the women out first."

When the hole was several feet deep, they grabbed Splitface's body, dragged him over, and lowered him into it. After the earth was tamped, Rulon prayed for him. The rest of the day passed quickly. The men ate a pot of cooked beans with chunks of rabbit meat from one of the shacks. Hyrum fed the women too. He made Parley and Nephi bury the dead men. Rulon was set to hunting game.

Grateful to get away, Rulon wandered for several hours, as far from the shacks as he could. The water drew what little life remained, small game like quail and rabbit. Unaccustomed to humans, they were pitifully easy to shoot. Bag full, Rulon lingered and didn't return to the campsite until after dark.

"Where were you? Never mind, least you got a lot. You want supper?"

"No thanks, Pa. I'm not hungry."

"Please yourself. Go to bed."

"Yes, sir."

"Parley, take the first watch. Keep a sharp lookout by the gully. Someone might be out there. Take a three-hour stretch. Take my watch to keep time."

He handed Parley a digital wristwatch with a luminous dial, one of his most treasured possessions. Parley left for his post, studying the shining gadget as he went.

"Everyone else sleep. Got another long day."

Rulon laid out his bedroll next to Obadiah's and crawled into it.

"Why'd Pa give Parley his watch? He never lets anyone touch it."

"I don't know. Go to sleep."

Rulon rolled over onto his side and closed his eyes. He eventually lapsed into an unhappy, uncertain slumber, haunted by gray shadows and without real rest.

"AAAAAAUUUUGGGHHH."

An awful scream tore through the night, the roar of a wounded bull in mortal pain. Rulon and Obadiah both leaped up, bolt awake.

"What was that?"

"I don't know. Get your rifle and I'll get a light."

Obadiah pulled a flashlight from a pack.

"It came from the corral."

They found Hyrum just outside the corral, naked and covered from throat to chest with deep stab wounds, his clothes in a heap nearby. Ashamed and aghast, his sons stared at his blood-smeared corpse.

"What happened?" Obadiah finally choked out.

"I'll tell you," Nephi said.

He strode into the light, rifle slung over his shoulder, flashlight in one hand. With his other hand he dragged the young woman along, pinned by the wrist.

"Your father was a fornicator, ready to lie with a harlot in the dirt."

"You be quiet, Nephi," Obadiah said.

"How do you think he died?" Nephi said. "The whore took his knife when he wasn't looking. See her around, boy? No, you don't. She ran away. Well, I made sure this one didn't get away. She's mine now."

He yanked her close and shoved his grizzled face next to hers. She shrieked and tried to push him away. Rulon strode over and shoved Nephi full in the chest. Nephi reeled away. The girl broke free and ran behind Rulon.

Nephi bared brown teeth in a snarl. "What do you think you're doing, boy? Offering violence to your own elder kin? What kind of Allred are you?"

"One that's had enough. I knew this was wrong from the start, but I couldn't tell Pa. Now he's dead. This has gone far enough."

"Give me back my woman, boy."

Rulon pointed his rifle at Nephi.

"No."

"Pull on your own kin, will you? I'll kill you first."

He snatched for his rifle,

"Stop that, Cousin Nephi."

Parley walked up, shotgun leveled at Nephi.

"Rulon's right. We've done enough. We'll bury Hyrum and leave tomorrow. Nephi, sit by the fire with me until you've calmed down."

"She's mine, Parley."

"No, she's not and that's the end of it. Now get to the fire."

They left.

Obadiah said, "Let's get something to cover Pa."

"Yes."

Rulon faced the young girl. Even by torchlight, he could see her large, luminous pupils were black, totally unlike an Allred. He held his hand out.

"Come on, I'll take care of you now."

Mark Mellon is a novelist who supports his family by working as an attorney. Short fiction by Mark has recently appeared in *Deadman's*

Tome, Yellow Mama, and *Thuglit.* Four novels and over fifty short stories have been published in the USA, U.K., and Ireland. A novella, *Escape from Byzantium,* won the 2010 Independent Publisher silver medal for fantasy/science fiction. A website featuring his writing is at mellon-writesagain.com.

Ursus Horribilis

by

Nick Manzolillo

IT USED TO BE A special occasion when I would stay up to hear the echo of coyotes howling throughout the forest, as if they were declaring over and over that man can't own everything. Now that I am alone, I hear them nightly. Sometimes, barefoot, holding a can full of back-washed beer, I meet them at the edge of the woods. I howl back but receive only silence.

My dad told me how to hunt, but he didn't teach me. On the rarest of occasions, he would disappear in the woods with his friends for one or two nights and then he'd come back with stories of polishing off thirty racks of beer and shenanigans that ended with the drunkest fellow being dunked into a lake. He took me shooting at targets out in the woods, sometimes but not often. He's long dead, and now that I am alone in a house meant for four, I've been in need of a hobby. I've been teaching myself how to hunt, although I don't want to kill anything.

I want to aim down the iron sights, take a deep breath, lower the rifle and watch something roam free. I still have Dad's gun from when I ransacked his garage after the funeral, before my sister sold everything. It's got all sorts of gizmos and attachments I never played with and in the outside compartment of the gun's case I found a "Fisherman's Guidebook," although the times Dad went fishing were even fewer than the times he went hunting.

Still, all the people I've ever met who take their guns or bows out into the woods to kill things and maybe eat them or wear them do it because their fathers taught them, because their family's been doing it for generations. It's a strange sensation, picking up a loose thread and trying to spin it into something real. I don't have any traditions I follow, not anymore. Just meaningless habits, motions you can go through without thinking, like the morning piss. That's what I've been; one long morning piss, even as the stars poke through the sky.

The woods here are older than most, with sturdy-as-rock oak trees silently screaming their century-long domination. The animals come from generations of their kind—the land has always been their home. Summer and then winter, which runs longer here below the mountains than it does in other places, they have witnessed the extinction of the vast majority of this country's native inhabitants. Their children survive an endless wave of hunters with guns that evolve faster than they can.

It's a walk through the woods with a metal stick that can make a loud noise and a stink that burns your nose. I've got my wallet in the pockets of my sweats and I almost didn't bring the gleaming little knife I bought at Walmart until I realized the shirt I had slept in had a front pocket. There's something about hunters waking up at four-thirty or something. It's eleven a.m. when my running shoes crunch across a toppled pinecone. I didn't bring a beer. There is no beer in my hand, so fuck it. I have the same intentions as any professional stalker of the forest. I am okay.

Sober or not, I slip into a ditch about ten minutes into my walk and my ass gets soaked from damp mud. A cluster of thorns snares my wrist and I lie there in that sudden trench on the forest floor I thought was so clear. Tears run down my cheeks. I tell myself they're only from the sudden pain. I've lived in the woods my whole life, but when was the last time I went for a walk in them? She was with me then, that last time, I'm sure of it, although I can't remember it.

You hear about people from the city who venture out here below the mountain's shadow. To them, they may as well be in Puerto Rico or something, for how different, for how special, this all seems to them. It just goes to show that when I thought I was leaving, for that same city in the valley, when Jill had that job offer she worked so hard for, balancing an internship on top of her career for the magazine, I thought I was really going to miss this place. I thought I needed the forest around me, blanket that it is. I thought I needed to know that the animals were close. I was afraid of breathing toxic air. Then we never left. Then she got pregnant.

I have nothing to teach anybody. I have nothing to pass on, besides a few acres of land and a house in need of renovations from fixing the plumbing to clearing out the termites chewing through the floors that hold my bed up. I shouldn't have to worry about any of this anymore. I live alone now. Jill is in the city. The baby never arrived.

I am a hunter. I pull myself up from the random ditch, like the half-dug grave that it is, and I swing up my rifle. I am also the hunted. There are enemies in the forest. They have hidden something from me. I get down and crawl, gently parting the twig fingers and bush-top canopies around me as I creep forward, imagining strangers up ahead surveying my approach. I am a hunter, and this is my forest.

At one point, in the distance, I see a family of turkeys running two by two behind a large mound of glacier-dumped rocks. I run after them, swinging the rifle in my arms, feeling like a soldier. Roots grab my foot but I pull it free. By the time my untested lungs are running hoarse in their attempt to feed me air, I've scaled the top of the mound of rocks. Crouching on one knee like a wild hunter from the eighteen hundreds, I peer through the scope for a sign of the walking thanksgiving dinners. Nothing. I wonder what's harder to chase, a turkey or a chicken. I'm delivered a sudden flash of a small boy or girl, running around a screaming chick in a backyard that is now strewn with weeds and the old rusted door of a pickup truck. I'm playing

Rambo instead of learning how to garden, to farm ... hah. I'm still taking the easy route.

If I did cap a deer, that'd mean something, I bet. Somewhere, in a place where dreams exist, there would be a complete circle and my father would nod down from whatever eternal blackness he now resides in. I remain perched on the rock with a scope for eyes. I can't go blasting at tree trunks or snipe off pinecones; that's the difference between this and playing in the woods like a kid. I have to stalk the inhabitants of this forest. I need to have one of them in my sights and then, like a six-year-old with a light-up gun, I'll say "pow" and lower the rifle. As if I've already fired, a scattering of palm-sized birds rises in the distance. I don't know their names. If it's not a thing of prey or a blue jay or a crimson cardinal or a hummingbird then it's a nameless thing with wings. Glancing across the tallest branches of the treetops, I wonder whether there are bats hiding somewhere in plain sight. They've got to go somewhere. I feel like I know them better than the birds, when I'm sitting on the porch at night. They come right close, chasing insects that in turn chase the beams of light from just above my plastic chair. The only caves around here are no more than burrow holes, unless those leathery little things fly all the way to the mountains to rest.

In the distance, what I've mistaken for the crumpled remains of a bark stripped tree with branches rising up from the ground like the arms of the living dead becomes something else, as I inspect it with my scope a second time. Bones. A collection of them, forming the physical memory of something, likely a moose. I haven't seen a live moose since I was a kid, from the back of my father's pickup as my mom cried out and he hit the brakes. That massive, horned thing stood there, unimpressed by the greasy roar of the pickup. My father switched the engine off and we sat in a silence so alive with the creature before us that my ears hurt from the strange beauty of it all.

I slide down the boulder. My stubborn brain's reminded I'm not in my twenties anymore when I try to spring to my feet and end up rolling through the underbrush. My rifle bellows out a great, fiery yell and as the tumble ceases I'm lying on my back, staring at the black mouth of my rifle. The pain fades and I'm left thinking, staring down that little precisely round abyss. From the ringing in my ears, the round had been close.

I've looked down the barrel before. Half serious, I've pressed it against my forehead. Click, click, click. More serious, I've even loaded it before turning that little mouth to myself, to give me a kiss. From the porch I've enjoyed pulling the gun away, firing it single-handed into the forest. I've slept with it, pressed skinny and cold against me in my bed, the scent of its barrel beneath my nose like freshly roasted cigarette fog in Jill's hair, back when she used to come home, to our home, and smoke her Virginia Slims after every shift.

Any living beast around me for a mile or so is running, hauling ass, hiding. I can't even pretend to hunt. Most I can do is pick through the bones of something great, and dead.

The pebbles of deer shit I find on my way to the bones nearly revives the hunting fantasy, but I have no way of telling how fresh the poop pellets are as I prod them with my shoe, other than that they squish instead of crack. Some ancient Sioux tracker from a dead age could follow dozens of animals through this forest based off broken bits of foliage, and I can't read a pile of a shit. Game over.

I have some vague idea about collecting the moose's antlers and I wonder just how old the bones are. There's a junk pile accumulating on my kitchen table; a pair of horns would make a nice bowtie for it, until they too become buried. Maybe I could collect the whole skeleton, put it back together with wire. Maybe being an artist is a cure. I've driven by isolated lunatics with strange displays in their front yards. Collections of strange, welded things or woodcarvings of animals similar to totem poles. I need to do something. I need what I don't have. I need what I had.

I'm carrying the rifle backwards, so that its mouth points off behind me. It's no more than a sentimental toy I can't leave out here. I'm at least an hour past my property lines, wherever they're officially drawn. The adrenaline went, scattering with the rifle shot, which I never should have loaded until I got back to the house and set up beer cans as targets. It's going to be a long, boring walk home, where I will find the restlessness tenfold until I do something about it. Until I drink.

The bones seemed whiter through the scope and in my head. Up close they are as yellow as my teeth. Faded clumps of skin still cling to them. There's no smell as I peer over the thing. I've gotten used to the dampness of the woods. Once you start thinking something a certain way, it's hard to change that train of thought. I'm standing over these massive bones in the middle of the woods, looking for the antlers I plan on taking for a prize, when I realize I'm not looking at the remains of a moose. Another moment of applying imaginary skin, claws, and a black-lipped snarl to the thing, and then I realize it's a bear, its jaw lined with thick pointed teeth as if the thing died screaming.

You hear stories of bears venturing in these parts, a stray that's gone for a stroll. This is a big one. Bigger than any oversized raccoon of a black bear I've ever seen a picture of that was trespassing through a backyard in some nearby town. What do bears die of? Old age? Indigestion? Tumors, probably, like everything else. Old men, young women with life in their womb.

I prod the skeletal face with the end of my rifle. The desire to take something is stronger than the urge to knock a shot glass into my sweatshirt pocket the only time I ever shoplifted. Like some voodoo priest, I'm plotting over what to take back to the house with me. The skull? How long before bones rot, disintegrate, whatever they do … Do they stink? As soon as I move the skull from where it's partially sunken into the wet earth there's a flash of yellow larvae, maggots squirming through the mud around it. Maybe they live in the bones, as if the thing's foundation is corrupt. Even in death, the memories of life are feasted upon.

My attention is drawn to a sprawled arm or leg, whatever it could be called, and with a poke of my rifle I unfurl a clenched paw, revealing a collection of black, crescent moons. An image of fabled natives and gritty hunters wearing bear claws along their body, their costume, comes to mind. As I scoop the claws up, mindful of grabbing a fistful of maggots that may be hiding beneath them, I'm suddenly wary of the great skeleton springing up and over me like a fabled bear trap. Bones, if properly assembled, could be a cage more than anything else. A box that death built.

I squeeze the claws tight in my palm. A child would absolutely love these. There are three of them. Enough for a small family to make necklaces out of. I pull away from the memory of a predator. Ten paces away, I come across a paw print.

A track, in fresh mud from the two previous days of hysterical rain. Unless that skeleton was walking ... I peer over the track mark. I'm not close enough. I squat, dip my head forward, and nearly stick my face into that massive, perfect track. The sloshing, churned wet earth around me suddenly becomes a map as the other, less impressive paw prints begin to pop to my attention. Bears, oh my.

Am I afraid of being eaten? I don't think they eat you; no, they maul you, drag you along the dirt and then prance upon you like an overweight cat combined with an ape. It's a black bear, surely, despite its size. Grizzlies are farther northwest. They have got to be farther northwest. Am I afraid of being killed by a bear, or am I afraid of lying abandoned and torn up in the dirt as I bleed out? I think I may be fearless, with aberrance to pain.

I don't want to let the claws go, but as I absentmindedly brush them across the pocket of my mud-stained sweats, I realize my wallet's missing. Relief or not, I'll never be cured of idiocy. Why the fuck did I bring a wallet into the middle of the woods? *So they could identify you,* the voice of a shrouded thing whispers from the outer reaches of my mind. As much as I want to spit at the thought, in the cheer of daylight at least, I could almost mutter a "maybe" to myself.

Swinging the rifle in my arms, perked up at the idea of there being worse things than coyotes in these woods, I head to retrieve the wallet, cautious now that the shadows between things could hold something. The little leather money holder is right where I left it, beside the pile of boulders, between a cluster of trees with fresh green claw marks dug into their moisture-thick trunks. Am I oblivious? Am I losing my mind? I walk up to the closest trunk. I don't need to hold the claws up to the scratches to know they fit. Instead, I run my fingers over the scratches and wonder just how silent a big lumbering beast can be. There's something in these woods, and it's been right in front of me this whole time. Has it been watching me from my porch as I moan and drink my nights to waste?

When I was little, I wondered if the world and everything and everyone I knew was fake, and if I was in a mental asylum somewhere. I think it's a common thought experiment, or maybe I'm just nuts. Maybe I could have been a scientist somewhere. I used to wonder if I was actually alone in the woods, talking to a bunch of trees that I thought were the people in my life. At this point...

I stick my wallet in my pocket and start running. My feet find the confidence they were missing earlier. I don't trip, I high-step through the ever-tripping bite of roots, and my lungs—those untrained, unpracticed bastards—are my real enemy as I heave and cough and taste the cold in the air worse than anything else. The cold claws into my stomach, forming cramps. I pass by the hunched-over beast like it's a stopped car along the side of the road. Only when it twitches do I realize it's not a part of the forest.

Thing's an underhand toss away, as I veer, letting out a yell that wastes half my lung capacity, and then I'm squeezing through a trio of trees that have formed close together, thinking it won't be able to follow me. It's not black, but muddy, its brown fur stained with grime, like it's a sewer bear. Idiotic curiosity causes me turn around to look at the thing and it's chasing me, just as I expected it to, just as I pretty much willed it to. Something wrong with its face. The fur is missing in scattered patches, like it was burned. A shine emits from its eyes, like the pale glow of the moon. Each cascading extension of those four limbs hauls it ever closer. The bear is silent.

I don't make a beeline for home. It's faster than me, it has to be with how almost mechanical its ability to run is. Will it tackle me or will it swipe at my ankles? Was it alligators or bears that I read about being capable of running down a sprinting man? What I do know about bears is that they will do anything to fill their great, empty belly.

Running, even with all the desperation and what must be adrenaline—that woozy, thought-clogging feeling of action, of instinct—it can't be an infinite thing, no matter my reason. I can't run forever. My lungs are going to explode and my chest is pierced by pins. I collapse, dive forward onto my knees when I've had enough of running because I can't go on anymore and my rifle's fallen by my side and survival instinct with no training doesn't give you the magic know-how to use a gun as a reflexive killing tool. I'm hunched over, ready to be violated, but it doesn't come. The bear is gone. I am alone on the forest floor, sweating, wheezing, choking on myself, because of myself.

I've lost my wallet again along with my knife. Maybe the bear has them. To the victor go the spoils. I can't even try to run; the cramps are invasive anchors, stripping away logic. As I pick myself up, I realize the bear claws have been in my hand the whole time, dug tight into the flesh, drawing blood. I push on with the little I have left, sparing a look over my shoulder every few steps.

The clouds are invading, choking out the sun when my home returns in my sight. It's been nearly an hour since I gave in to the idea of a mauling and the crushing of my skull. This is real, I'm not crazy, I didn't imagine the thing chasing me.

I'm thinking about a cold beer, because a hot shower is out of the question. I haven't paid my oil bill in a while. I'm slinging Dad's rifle over my shoulder and I'm almost feeling something nice. I have a story to tell, even though I have nobody to tell it to. Nobody that I can—nobody that I want to tell it to.

My front door is wide open and the interior of my oil-less home is black. An angry, hungry monster inhabits this place.

Somehow it's the bear, with the same scorched face and lunar eyes as it slowly thumbs down the steps of my porch. I raise my rifle, clutching those blood-slick claws against the side of the barrel. I fire, having aimed right for the head, right between the two silver-dollar moons. I swear, I swear it hits. I don't know why I hear the crack of my porch being struck by a bullet, not when the bear's face remains untouched, unmarked. Whole. No burst of blood.

I forget even pain as the bear hauls itself toward me. My home is gone, along with the world of men. There is only the bear and me. It is beyond hungry. It has been sent to mop me up, an emissary of the forest sent forth to reclaim its kingdom. I squeeze off my rifle's last two rounds and then toss the useless sentimental thing away as I flee into the forest.

The bear comes from every angle. It is not a living thing but a ghost, a spirit, a mirage of the sun. One moment I can feel its hot breath on my heels and then it's leaping out of a bush to my right. Nick by nick, it slashes the backs of my legs. Somehow it gets ahead of me, pops out of the ground like the forest has a trap door and it dives toward my chest, vanishing just as I close my eyes. Is this what happens to you when you lose your mind?

I close my eyes once more and a jagged vice grips my ankle and begins dragging me along the forest floor as I howl and beg, my face alive with thorns and bludgeoned by rocks. No matter how many times I blink it never releases me. It's quiet, without snarl or roar or whatever it is bears do. I'm not even sure if I can hear it ripping through the woods. That's just my back as I crash through the underbrush.

I tilt my head up, craning my neck, stuck in a half sit-up, trying to avoid bashing my skull in. The bear is near sprinting, pulling me with such frenzy that its energy can only come from pure emotion. The woods are chewing me up. The bear, the memory of a bear, is just a reflexive digestive pull, a swallow that sends me deep through the throat to the stomach.

The forest doesn't let me sleep as my body grows numb and the silence of the bear scrambles my dimming mind. I think of myself as flowing on my back down a savage river of thorns. If I were religious, I would pray, but I only believe in the finite black. The bear can shrug off all the bullets it wants, and be a thing made of shadows to its very core, but I will not accept faith, only suffering.

I'm not sure how long I have been free of the bear's grip. Eventually I roll over onto my stomach and a moan escapes from my mouth as the air meets the ragged wounds pulsing along my back. If my ankle hurts at all where the thing's teeth had met, the pain is lost in the whirlpool of every other sting and sore.

There is logic, still, like the impulse to breathe and, some mornings, to remove myself from the floor. To switch the stove off or slip on a pair of shoes. This same logic forces me to sit up and, after a cautious bundle of minutes spent waiting for the bear's re-emergence, to stand. Above me I see a hill. Pecked into that hill is a black mouth no different from the barrel of my gun. A cave, open and hungry.

There is a thing about logic, and then there are a great many things to know about pain; and below what can be understood and felt, there is something else. A hunger of my own. A craving, an insane desire for something I cannot have, because death is the final barrier and its emissaries can only drag you so far. I don't know why I limp toward that mouth in the hill. I know what I want, but I don't know why. I don't need answers. I don't need the world to make sense. I don't need sense with death, or what comes when your life veers too close to it, or all the anger, all the empty lust that follows. I stumble and have to finish climbing on bleeding hands and aching knees so I can meet the mouth, so I can give it a kiss.

The cavern is a shallow thing, no more than shelter from wind and rain. A resting place for wretched beasts. I could just lie down and sleep, heal and live. I don't have to go too far in before I see the scattered sticks of white along the ground. Bones, of course. Not human, after all. Sifting through the dirt, minding maggots and worms and other fellow burrowers, I come across the skulls of two cubs. Both bashed in, cracked and near ruined beyond comprehension. Hope doesn't exist when you realize that children are not exempt. When you realize they die just like the rest of us, hope becomes a prayer that you don't live to see just how fast the rot can spread.

I try to deny the tears streaking down my filthy face, but they're an element, they are impervious to manipulation. I brush a hand over one of the innocent skulls. I then turn, limping home, sure the bear is following me through the trees. I no longer run.

The sun is falling away by the time I get home. I am not dying, I don't think, not any faster than anybody else. I pick up my father's rifle and eye the four blast holes scattered around my porch. I'll need to go to the store tomorrow. Maybe I'll even drive all the way to Home Depot. There's work to be done around here.

Beside the rifle, in the dirt where I left them, are the three bear claws. I don't have anybody to give them to, so I bring them to the backyard, where there may have once been a garden and may yet be again. Crouching, half keeling over to the point that I just may spend the night out here, I set about digging a little hole. I feel the presence of something mighty, scorned and sorrowful behind me. I place the claws into the earth, and as I bury them the image of the necks they might have once adorned turns to ash.

Nick Manzolillo is a Rhode Island native who finds himself living in Manhattan. His writing has appeared both online and in anthologies such as *Thuglit*, *Wicked Witches*, and *World Unknown Review Vol. III*. He is earning an MFA in creative and professional writing from Western Connecticut State University.

Mud Babies

by

Soumya Sundar Mukherjee

WHEN THE HORSE-DRAWN CARRIAGE WAS moving through the Fields of Charity of the Good Folk village, John Weldon remembered a woman's face and wondered if she were still alive.

The sun had already set; the last copper glow of the sky was still reflected in the vast plains of the Fields of Charity. Crickets sang from the wanton hedges. The horses galloped over the darkening fields.

Somewhere in these fields . . .

The carriage neared his mansion in the village. Weldon could see its silhouette standing like a giant bat against the liquid darkness of the newborn evening. Two of the servants came to the front door to greet their master, who had come home after spending quite a few years in the city.

The police could not find any proof against him and no one was eager to bear witness against him. The locals could not even dream of telling something against Weldon in the court. The philosophy of the villagers was simple enough.

Life is not a thing you throw away for others, even for good people.

Weldon stepped down from the carriage. He was a tall man with high cheekbones and a pointed nose. As he descended, his overcoat flapped in the wind. He peered up at the sky. Rain clouds were gathering over his head. The servants bowed to him and toted his luggage inside.

"Is Bert here?" he asked.

One of the servants answered. "Yes, master. Mr Smith has received your letter. He is waiting for you in the drawing room."

"Tell him I'm home. I'll meet him after half an hour."

"As you wish, master."

The servant accompanied him to the door of his room. Weldon hesitated and then asked, "Have you seen Old Nick's daughter recently? Is she alive?"

The servant, too, hesitated before answering. "Yes, master, Martha is alive, but . . ."

"But?"

"She is insane, sir."

Weldon smiled to himself. "Very well. You may leave now."

After half an hour, he strolled into the drawing room where Bert was reading a book by the fireplace. Weldon was happy to see a friendly face. "Hello, old friend! Reading books? That's quite a change, I'd say."

Bert stood up from his chair. "Hello, John. You've changed very little in these years."

Weldon sat on the wine-colored sofa and ran his hand along the fabric. It was plush, soft, and seemed as if it were not subjected to much use. He gazed at Bert. "So many grey hairs. You have really grown old."

Bert smiled. "With you gone, I was not very popular in the village, you know. They still think that we did it, although none of them have the courage to say it to our face."

"Are you repentant, Bert?"

Bert looked up at him. "God dries the tears of the man whom he wants to send to hell."

Weldon lit a cigar. He offered one to his friend, but Bert shook his head. "Since when," Weldon said, "has Bert Smith become a believer in heaven and hell?"

"It settled in gradually," Bert said, gazing at the crackling fire. "Like blots of ink. You drop them one by one on a heap of paper and wait; they stain even the lowest of the stack."

"You think too much." Weldon let out a perfect ring of smoke.

"And don't you?"

"I don't let it trouble me anymore. What is done is done."

Bert kept quiet for a while, and then said, "John, don't you think what we've done was wrong?"

Weldon smiled again. "We've done *nothing*, my friend. The court thinks that we are innocent."

"Not all courts are the same, John. And neither are all judges."

"Oh, please stop your Judgment Day sermons, Bert. We did what we had to do."

"It was a child, John! *Your* child!"

"You don't need to remind me of that, Bert!" Weldon's voice had become harsh.

Bert shivered unknowingly and fell silent.

In the fireplace, tinder cracked continuously.

Then Bert spoke of something Weldon had been thinking for some time. "Do you know anything about Martha?"

Weldon started. "Um. . . . Yes. I just heard that she has gone mad."

Bert said, "People are saying that she is not mad. She has been visited by the Spirit of the Fields."

"Oh, for God's sake, Bert, don't start those old wives' tales now!"

"I'm just saying what people say," Bert said with a little quiver in his voice. "And what they say is not good for us."

"When have they ever said anything that's good for us, eh?" Weldon said angrily. "They envy us, Bert, because we're wealthy. They try to occupy the lands forever. The only medicine for those peasant fools is the whip. And if the whip does not work, you know what to do!" He imitated a gun with his fingers and fired two imaginary shots at the closed window.

Bert said, "Martha has changed completely, John. She looks like a hundred-year-old hag now. Looking at her, you can't even imagine that she hasn't passed thirty yet. They say that after that night she used to wander in the Fields of Charity in search of the child. And then the spirit of the earth possessed her. And now she wanders in the village like a reverent prophetess. People hear what she says and they claim that she can see the future."

"And what's the future she has seen?"

"That her child will rise from the earth."

"And people believe that? That's how prophetic she has become?"

"John, she predicted that you'll come back this month. Nobody in the village but me knew it."

"*What?* She predicted my return? When?"

"Two weeks ago. She had no way of knowing it. Not even I knew then that you were coming back. And now, I'm sure, people are talking about her other prophecies."

"What are they, pray?"

"That her child will come back from the earth, and . . ."

"And?"

"And the earth will take blood as payment to raise the dead."

Weldon made a thoughtful *hmm* inside his throat. He never showed his weakness in front of anyone, not even his closest friend. But inside his chest, he was feeling a certain kind of uneasiness.

Bert got up from his seat. "Take care, John. I am really happy that you are back. But I tell you, we should not have done those things. They say that she has been waiting for your return. I'm not afraid of anything, but I feel that I should not have done those things. I know that it's too late now, but still, I'm sorry for that night."

Weldon walked with his friend to the front gate. "Don't think too much, or you'll end up like her."

Bert said, "I know that I'll end up worse."

As Bert walked out of the room, Weldon blew a smoke ring into the air and thought about Martha.

Weldon had his dinner early and went to bed. He was tired, but he could not sleep.

It felt good to be back at his old country mansion after so many years. In the glow of the bedside lamp, the shadows of the old furniture pieces drew strange shapes over the wall. Weldon studied his pistol under the lamplight. He smiled drily.

Nothing works better than a bullet.

Martha was beautiful, as he remembered her. She had a little mole just under her right eye, but it made her look different than the other girls. Her father, Nick, was a faithful worshipper of whiskey. Weldon had lent him a lot of money over the years; Nick thankfully wasted it in the local pub.

Weldon used to look at Martha in a not-very-brotherly way. One day he was visiting at Nick's house, but Nick was too busy with the booze to chat with him. Martha was cooking in the kitchen when Weldon entered. She was young and breathtaking with her long auburn hair tied into a loose bun and her hazel eyes practically dancing when she looked at him. Desire rose inside of him, and he knew he had to possess her.

At first she objected, but she was no match to his physical power and she yielded herself.

Nobody knew of the incident except Bert. Weldon could not keep it from his best friend. Bert delightedly patted his shoulder. "Good catch, John!"

Two months after this incident Nick died of cirrhosis of the liver, and after three more months Martha came to visit Weldon with a swollen belly.

He couldn't believe it. *The dirty whore expected me to marry her!*

So the girl was immediately kicked out of the mansion.

The tongues of the local people were sharp. Although no one was bold enough to say it in public, the news that John Weldon had planted a seed inside Old Nick's daughter without marrying her traveled faster than a forest fire. At first, Weldon cared little for the rumours. But Martha's belly grew larger, and the whisperings increased. John Weldon felt like a criminal in the accusing eyes of the people of the Good Folk village.

Why didn't you get rid of it when you could, whore? You planned to be my wife only because of that ugly, fat belly of yours? You wanted to be a part of the Weldon fortune?

You'll have to pay for this.

One day Bert came for a visit and informed him that the people were thinking that he would ultimately marry the girl. It was then that Weldon realised that he could do nothing to stop the people from murmuring. The gossip was gradually ruining his reputation as an aristocrat and a gentleman.

What he could do was, obviously, far more ferocious.

Weldon bided his time until Martha gave birth. He visited the hospital and went to see the boy while Martha slept. He waited for two more months. Then one night he invited Martha to his house and snatched the baby from her.

He did not want to kill Martha; he wanted her to suffer.

Nothing works better than a bullet.

He took the bloody bundle to the Fields of Charity and buried it.

Bert kept Martha silent and made her watch through the window. In muted horror, she was forced to see the bundle go inside the earth.

The next morning, people found Martha wandering in the Fields of Charity and howling the boy's name.

Based upon her story, the police filed a case against Weldon. But he had been careful; he had planned it for months. The police found no clue, and he was released for lack of evidence.

The body was never found.

It was thought by the people of the village that the place where Martha saw Weldon bury the bundle was not the actual place of burial. He must have planted it somewhere else later, and it was not possible for the police to dig up the whole of the vast Fields of Charity.

Weldon went out of the village for some long years. Martha went insane. End of story.

Weldon switched off the light. He thought of Bert.

Bert used to be a trusted friend and equally sadistic. But today he had not seemed to be his old self.

Bert has softened.

He sighed and went off to sleep. In his sleep, he heard the sound of rain pattering on the windowpane.

The next morning, one of his servants gave him the news. He rushed to the Fields of Charity in his nightdress and slippers.

Bert was dead.

He was staring with open eyes. His face had an indescribably horrified expression.

Weldon saw something else, but could not share it with anyone.

Where Bert's body was found, there were a number of little footprints on soft mud, like those of little children.

The doctor who did the postmortem said that it was a case of heart attack by sudden shock. But Weldon knew better.

Night came like a creeping lizard over the village and Weldon shut himself inside his mansion. He sat by the fire with a glass of whiskey in his hand, sipping and reliving the memories. His faithful pistol rested on his lap.

Thunder boomed outside; it started raining again. A window had not been latched properly and the wind threw it open with a rattle. Through the open window, gusts of wind full of watery grains were coming in. Weldon drained his glass and got up to shut it.

That was when he heard the faint giggling.

Lightning flashed and Weldon saw the dark shape standing outside the window. He could not tell whether it was a man or a woman, but it stood there.

He shouted, "Who's there?"

The shape did not stir, nor did it answer. It just stood there. Lightning flashes made it look like a creature from an unknown world.

"Answer me, or I'll shoot you."

The shape giggled again and Weldon swallowed a lump in his throat. How could he forget that voice?

He raised his pistol. "Go away, or I'll shoot."

The giggling did not stop.

He shouted, "Go away!"

Martha said in a raspy voice, "Why don't you come out here, John? I'm so happy that you've come to see me after so many years."

Weldon gritted his teeth.

He fired at her but missed.

"Do you know what happened to Bert, John? You know what he said to me before he died? He said, 'I'm sorry'! After so many years and so many things, he just said, 'I'm sorry'! Are *you* sorry, John?"

Weldon fired his pistol again. Again he missed.

Rainy wind wet his eyelashes; he wiped the water from his face and saw the dark shape moving away.

She killed Bert! She'll have to pay for this!

Weldon wrapped himself in a raincoat and ran out of the mansion carrying a flashlight and his pistol. He could still see the figure headed towards the Fields of Charity. He followed.

The rain was pouring from the sky, dousing his head, but he didn't care. The only thing that mattered to him was to hunt that woman down. A blind anger drove him through the muddy Fields of Charity.

Over his head, lightning bared its teeth. The distance between him and his prey decreased. It seemed to Weldon that Martha was tiring; she was staggering to get away from him in the thick mud.

Weldon smiled a cruel smile. This was easier than hunting small game. She squatted upon the soft ground. He aimed. *Another sitting duck!*

This time, he hit her. Martha dropped to the wet earth, clutching her left shoulder.

Weldon came forward and shone the flashlight upon her body.

"What did you say, wench? You want blood payment?"

Martha looked up; there was a strange smile on her face.

She had grown old in these years, her skin loose, her eyes shrunken, the mole on her right cheek looking like a round clot of blood under the flashlight. She was still clutching her shoulder where the bullet had pierced her, but then he noticed, oddly, that she was convulsing in silent laughter.

"What's so funny, Martha?"

"You got it wrong, John. See this?"

She showed her arm to him; there was a long sharp cut running from the wrist to the elbow. Under the flashlight, the wound, fairly fresh, looked like a dark fissure on the crust of the earth.

"I want you to pay for what you did, John, but you are not the one to pay the blood payment. It's me!"

Weldon felt something weird happening around him. He swivelled his flashlight here and there, but could spot nothing through the deluge of raindrops falling on the vast Fields of Charity.

"This was the payment I made to the Earth Mother so I could show Bert something pleasant a few nights ago." She gestured to her wound and imitated a knife slicing over her arm. "And tonight you'll see it all too."

She smiled with disdain. "All I needed was to make you shoot me upon this ground. You see, the blood of a victim is a powerful offering."

She pointed to the blood flowing from her shoulder onto the muddy ground. Kneeling, she said solemnly with closed eyes, "I offer you my blood as payment, O Mother Earth, to raise in plenty those who were snatched away from their mother. Curse those, O Mother, who bleed both the child and the mother."

Weldon felt an uncanny sensation again. The ground began throbbing beneath his feet. Pulsing as if . . . as if he were standing on an enormous living body.

Thunder growled and streaks of searing light flashed across the sky. The flashlight fell from his hand, now stiff with shock. With the next violent burst of lightning, Weldon watched with disbelief as the ground began swelling into thousands of mud heaps, round like the bellies of pregnant women. The heaps expanded, and then suddenly exploded into muddy bubbles and bloody waters. In horror he watched as little babies slowly emerged out of them. The sky showered them with more heavy rain and they crawled and waddled in the deep brown mud of the Fields of Charity. With the next flash of lightning, Weldon could see that every one of them had a neat little dark hole in the forehead.

"What's this, you witch? What are you doing?" He tried to shout over torrent of rain, but hundreds of droplets hit his tongue like sharp arrows as soon as he opened his mouth. The wind rose, and the water beat down on him even more severely.

Martha cackled like a madwoman. Her maniacal shrieks were a perfect blend of joy and hatred. "Mother Earth is extremely productive and fertile. You reap a hundred times more back from what you've sown."

John Weldon knew what he had sown in these grounds.

He struggled to pull his feet out of the mud, but tripped and fell into the muck. He struggled to stand, but the mud was so deep now that he couldn't pull himself upright. The little babies with holes in their foreheads came closer to his body. He shot at them. Some fell, but more spawned from the clay. He shot at those until his pistol clicked empty. Thunder boomed with laughter over his head. Lightning flashed, revealed the blazing eyes of a smiling woman eagerly waiting for the moment of her lifetime. It was then that he noticed the fingernails of the babies were rapidly changing into sharp claws. And these mud creatures had needlelike teeth, reminding him of sparkling piranha.

The earth sucked him down, covering his body with cold mud as the little babies climbed upon his chest.

Soumya Sundar Mukherjee is an admirer of engaging science fiction, horror and fantasy tales. He is a bilingual writer who lives in West Bengal, India, and writes about stuff bad dreams are made of. He teaches English in a school and spends his leisure time in writing, studying the myths and legends of different cultures around the globe, and drawing monsters both horrifying and cute. When he is not writing or making any interplanetary journeys in his pet-spaceship, he remains busy reading emails received in *soumyamukherjeewrites@gmail. com.*

Acquired Taste

by

Chad Stroup

UNCLE RAY PEELS BACK THE first layer or so of his thumb and drops it in the frying pan, adds some cayenne pepper and liquid amino acids, says those two things get wedged in the creases of the fingerprints and spruce up the flavor real good. He wraps up his thumb tip in a previously soiled cloth bandage before the wound has a chance to take a deep breath. He doesn't even wince. Hunger pangs trump traditional pain. He adds a few hunks of Yukon Gold potatoes with the skin intact and some slices of white onion and stares at the sizzling food.

Jess Tyler watches from across the room, her bantam body curled up in a cracked plastic Adirondack chair. Jess is not old enough to sign the Eat Treaty yet, so her Uncle Ray has to take care of all the feeding duties around the house, which he has proudly done ever since the secretive flesh sharers across the nation were finally permitted to publicly declare their beliefs. The Tylers had some leftovers of Mr. Martin, from next-door, out in the spare freezer in the garage, but those are gone now. Jess thinks Mr. Martin was a good neighbor, a good friend, hell … a good *American*. He knew about the worth of sacrifice and what an honor it was to be consumed, absorbed, and shat out. *From the earth and back to the soil,* Uncle Ray had said when he took his first nibble of Mr. Martin's sautéed cartilage in between two stale slices of ciabatta. *The true cycle of life.*

But their neighborly feast was cut short because some jerks broke into their garage a couple of nights ago and took what was left of Mr. Martin, what would have been enough to feed Uncle Ray and Jess and her big brother Jojo for at least a week. Normally they have Jojo guard the garage 'cause he's built like a fortified prison, but Jojo was out sharing some flesh with his lady friend last night. Sharing some flesh in both the biblical and the modern sense. Jojo came home this morning with fiery bloodshot eyes and a soaked bandage around his left forearm. He said they were spreadin' 'round some blood like *may-o-naise*. Must have been quite a party.

Poor stealing from the poor, just like before, Uncle Ray says in an unintentionally poetic cadence, followed by a few indiscernible obscenities directed toward the thieves. Jess doesn't know much about "before." She was less than two years old when the Great Reverence passed into law in Black Briar. Even now, at fourteen, she can barely grasp what eating meant in the old world, what a typical meal might have consisted of. How it played into the family dynamic. How the now sacred flesh of sentient nonhuman beings was ravaged and disrespected. The concept is like a dream that never existed, a wraith of the recent past.

Uncle Ray likes to spout off about how Aunt Nickie used to be such a great homemaker and made the most delectable peanut butter cookies every Sunday. From scratch. He licks his lips as he describes how she used to make crisscross impressions in the tops of the cookies with fork tines. But what does anything about Aunt Nickie matter? She passed through multiple colons months ago, and none of that flavor was even remotely close to peanut butter.

Uncle Ray finishes frying up his thumb layer and veggies, takes out a butter knife and slices the skin sliver in perfect thirds, sprinkles some sea salt and freshly crushed peppercorn on it. They each crunch on a meager piece. Uncle Ray *Mmm mmm mmms* all the way to Christmas and Jojo releases a belch like a whale queef, but Jess just forces a grin. She's had worse and she's had better. She feels grease tickling her lip and reaches for a napkin with her right hand, temporarily forgetting that the fingers are barely healed stumps, sacrificed for the greater good of nutrition. Just because Jess can't legally sign the Eat Treaty doesn't mean there aren't some loopholes to be found courtesy of Uncle Ray.

The phantom pains are still fresh, wiggling like invisible, bony worms. Jess feels the sensation may never go away. She switches hands, uses the napkin, and washes down the family flesh with tepid gray water. She anticipates there will be ice cream for dessert, still does not know for certain what the creamy, bitter substance is made of, shudders to think of the possibilities. Sugar and coconut flavoring can only mask so much, and sexual education during class time has robbed her of at least some smidge of naiveté.

When the family shows up to Worship the following morning there are three animals strategically placed on the stage: a Saanen goat, an albino cow, and a Flemish rabbit. The goat will not lift its head from its water bowl, the cow is wearing a muumuu for some reason, and the rabbit is extra twitchy. The church is not the animals' natural environment, yet somehow they look like they belong. Jess was hoping for the appearance of a gharial this time, just as she always does, but reptiles are a rarity at Worship and Uncle Ray has promised her again and again that those ugly shits went extinct prior to the Great Reverence. He's sure of it.

Jess ignores Uncle Ray's rudeness. She believes the gharial is a creature of beauty, of wonder, a crocodile designed as if God had taken design tips from Pablo Picasso. One hundred and ten teeth, and yet Jess has read in some old dusty encyclopedia in the Black Briar Library that there is not a single documented attack on a human. She does not believe they are truly extinct, though. How could there suddenly just be none of something? Just like that, snapped out existence? Would the last one even know it was the last? Who would allow any of God's innocent creatures to pass from this world, and will humans one day be a part of this list? If so, who will be around to take note of it?

Jess will find another gharial. She knows it is her destiny to see one in the scaly flesh. The image of the gharial comes to her in her dreams some nights, smiling its elongated smile, gazing at her with reptilian wisdom.

Jess keeps leaning over to Uncle Ray, asking him in a whisper why they can't eat any of the animals that pass naturally in the world. The ones that were treated like part of the family, bathed weekly, passed around as community idols, medicated into euphoric states. Not that Jess even *wants* to eat them, exactly, but it seems like a waste. When Jess's gerbil Herman went to that Great Runabout in the Sky two months ago, his empty husk was placed on their mantel and a shrine was constructed to honor his sweet life. The smell eventually became too much to bear and Herman was given a proper burial in the side yard, the topsoil sprinkled with lye. Jess always asks Uncle Ray about this waste of perfectly edible meat, and Uncle Ray does his best not to act irritated when he responds. Jojo tells Jess to *Shut up 'cause she's a stupid know-nothing ingrate brat*, and Uncle Ray says not to question the decisions of God and Government. All will become clear at adulthood. Jess has heard some stories in between class times about those who broke the laws of the Great Reverence, and those weren't all that pleasant—they made tales of the Spanish Inquisition seem like a senior citizen cruise in the Bahamas, so she thinks maybe she should just listen to Uncle Ray. He's no dummy. He used to be a senator or a manager or a janitor or something useful like that.

There's a portly preacher man up on stage with the animals. He's whiter than Frosty's taint and he's blowing hard about respecting their superiors, the sentient creatures that have put up with human abuse for so long. His purple robes are tattered and unwashed.

Looks like a homeless Grimace, Uncle Ray whispers to Jojo. Jojo bites the edge of his hand so that he does not disrupt Worship with his laughter—drawing blood even, but Jess does not get the joke. Uncle

Ray just tells her it was something from before her time. Jess wonders if this Grimace was an Old God, one that will soon return to spread his mighty gospel.

Some short little cotton-candy-haired old lady in a crinkled paisley tunic kneels in front of the goat, and then brings its damp beard to her lips. Her face is full of glistening tears. It looks like someone filled up a water balloon with her makeup inside and threw it at her face to see how it might come out.

Jess wonders what makes the preacher man pick a particular member of the audience and match them up with one of these beautiful beasts. She simultaneously wishes for and fears this privilege. Will she ever be chosen? And if so, how will it change the course of her young life?

Jojo finds the jokers that took the Mr. Martin meat. Right under their noses, two blocks south on Slater Street. The scavengers had eaten about half of it, including the private parts (which every pamphlet claims are the most nutritious bits, but Jess refuses to try them). The Tyler family passes through a door that is not only unlocked but barely hanging on its hinges. Uncle Ray and Jojo take the back end of a hammer to each of the thieves' heads while they are laughing the night away in their mildewed basement, lit up on some homemade hooch. A bootleg videotape plays in the background, some ancient banned television program where an adorable wisecracking alien puppet tries to eat the family cat. Jess observes the scene from the top of the stairs without a sound and feels nothing. Jojo curses about the blood splattered on the new blue jeans he just bartered for.

Uncle Ray and Jojo will not face any prison time for this murder. In fact, should they even bother to inform the proper authorities, they might be rewarded with a medal and a meal of choice from the Gourmet District, where the wealthy have many untapped resources and prison slaves. Meat theft is punishable by death, not regulated by the state, so says the Eat Treaty. But Uncle Ray is a humble man. He only wants to provide for his family and keep his home safe. Jojo—not so much. He will likely leak the information to his source at the Print Shop and get his picture in next Sunday's pamphlet.

Now the family has rescued the rest of Mr. Martin, plus the added the bonus of the thieves and some other flesh of indeterminate origin that was crammed in the back of the thieves' fridge. The mystery meat is scaly and scabby, but unquestionably human. Any potential disease or contamination will cook right out. Any foul tastes can be masked with cumin and garlic powder. The Tyler House freezer is so full that the door barely closes. Jess wonders if—in the old world—it had been a crime to steal from thieves, to reclaim what had been unjustly taken. Jojo tells Jess that Robin Hood was probably gay, because why else would he be worrying about stealing and giving back to the poor when he could just be boinking a babe like Maid Marian? That even in the Disney version, she was a real fox. Jess just shrugs, another reference from the old world lost on her.

Jojo guards the stash with his life. He can forget about his little lady friend for a while unless she stops by for supper sometime. Supper in the traditional sense. Traditional in the post–Great Reverence sense. More important matters to attend to here. Duty calls.

On an overcast Sunday afternoon, Jess and Uncle Ray make a trip to the farmers market. Chickens trot freely among the people as if they have their own shopping agenda, so many crowded into some spots that their loose feathers in the air appear to be the result of an impromptu pillow fight. Their clucking is metronomic, trance-inducing. Jess stops at a booth where a husband, wife, and son are selling their family flesh. Each of them is missing some piece that was once aesthetically necessary or even quite useful, but not essential to survival.

An earlobe, the tip of a nose, a tongue, some fingers. Jess stares at the son. He is around her age and, strangely, is missing exactly the same fingers on exactly the same hand as she. She feels something stir within her, a kinship-gone-crush that she refuses to vocalize, but they at least exchange crooked smiles. The boy has only a handful of teeth left. Enamel is a precious bargaining chip in these times.

Jess spies an old woman behind the family, what remains of her slumped in a wheelchair. She is a quadruple amputee, also missing much of her face, and appears to have had a double mastectomy. Now that Jess's own breasts are beginning to develop, she wonders if and when they will be large enough to become a useful commodity. To offer the purest of milk to all those who seek it. Uncle Ray has already been underlining passages in the Breast section of the Eat Treaty.

A cream-colored substance oozes from the old woman's nasal cavity and a fly hungrily rubs its legs together in the curve of her remaining lip. The fly seems to be well aware that the old woman cannot swat it. Jess studies the woman clinically. She presumes the family made a decision that Gramma had lived the longest life and therefore should be the first to be sold off at the market so that the rest of the family might thrive for a few more weeks. Jess knows this because her own Gramma went through the same process when Jess was still a toddler. She does not remember this, but Uncle Ray brings the fact up more than is necessary.

Jess sees an emaciated, androgynous child peddling professionally bagged rat droppings. She barters a piece of flesh that once belonged to the thieves, a tiny, lean patch that she has hidden from Uncle Ray all morning, knowing that trading for this bag of droppings will put her in Jojo's good graces when she gifts it to him. Jojo and his girlfriend snort the precious droppings on special occasions, and their anniversary is coming up. The droppings offer some strange level of high that Jess is curious about, but not curious enough to pilfer any of the droppings for herself. Her body is a temple and no waste shall enter its gates.

Uncle Ray purchases a bag of oranges because he claims Jojo has been deficient in his vitamin C consumption lately and is at risk for scurvy. That is all the currency they have for today.

As they leave the market, there are true vegetarian protestors politely picketing off to the side so as not to actually obstruct any foot traffic. They wield signs that say ALL MEAT IS SACRED—DON'T EAT SOMEONE WHO COULD BE THE NEXT EINSTEIN OR MLK OR POL POT and A WORLD WITHOUT MEAT=A WORLD REALLY NEAT. Jess is curious as to why they would not picket the entrance, as people leaving have already made their purchases and made up their minds. But she sees worth in their cause, will sneak away from home one day when Uncle Ray is in a drunken coma and attempt to learn more, maybe even join in the protest if she feels it worth the effort.

Jess attends Worship by herself the following Sunday. Uncle Ray is taking care of Jojo, who has come down with a case of something that may or may not be chicken pox. She stops by the market to speak to the meat-free protestors, but is disillusioned by the fact that most of them appear to be taking a break rather than staying focused on their cause. They are drinking some milky beverage made of flaxseed. So she moves on for now. At the church, the pews are near empty, perhaps because there is a Sacrifice Lottery on the other side of town. Everyone wants to know who will be next obese denizen to be consumed in the communal feast, but Jess just rolls her eyes at the thought.

The purple priest is reading rewritten Leviticus passages, practically singing them in a bouncing-ball cadence. He has an almost beautiful and soothing voice, like an angel's harp that is slightly off key. Nothing matters until the animals are brought out to gaze upon. An alpaca with its fur dyed blue, a pug/shih tzu mix in a too-tiny pink T-shirt that says "Lil' Princess," and—

Jess's solo attendance today is like sweet serendipity, for the third animal that sits on the stage is everything she has hoped for. She immediately recognizes that long, thin maw lined with jagged razors, and eyes with a cold stare that burrows into her soul.

A gharial.

The last gharial, or one of many—this does not matter at this moment. What matters is that such a creature exists at all. Extinction is a myth that can be disproven with just one subject.

The priest notices Jess's excitement, makes eye contact with her, and beckons to her. It is as if he has been holding out for this very moment, taunting her for months upon years with the idea that she was not worthy. That there are not many attendees to choose from this particular Sunday is beside the point. This is Jess's time to shine.

She approaches the stage. She is trembling, but she does not give a single damn. The gharial is indifferent to her approach, but Jess expects this. A gharial is not a golden retriever waiting patiently for its human companion to return home so that it may lick upon his or her face. A gharial is cold and calculating, but it is still beautiful.

It is the closest thing to God that Jess has ever known.

Jess reaches out her hand with the missing fingers, knowing that the likelihood of losing the fingers on her other hand is slim, but still possible. Those teeth do not lie.

The old scars along her arm are striped in perfect indented lines like tribal tattoos. She reaches, she approaches. The gharial seems to be almost sleeping, probably dreaming of the gorgeous swamp it calls home and the plentiful fish that only it is allowed to consume without repercussion.

Jess kneels before the gharial, her finger stumps twitching, her destiny fulfilled.

Chad Stroup received his MFA in fiction from San Diego State University. His short stories have been featured in anthologies like *Splatterlands, Creature Stew,* and the *San Diego Horror Professionals* series, and his poetry has appeared in the first three volumes of the HWA Poetry Showcase. *Secrets of the Weird,* Stroup's debut novel, is forthcoming from Grey Matter Press. Visit Subvertbia, a home for some of his short fiction, poetry, and reviews at subvertbia.blogspot. com, and drop by his Facebook page as well at facebook.com/ ChadStroupWriter.

Voice of the Mountian

by

Roger Dale Trexler

LONG BEFORE THE WHITE MAN came to southern Illinois, the indigenous tribes of men heard the voice of the mountain. It spoke to them when the rain fell and when the wind blew, and it told them of things that were to come. Oftentimes, it did not so much *speak* as emit a *feeling*. It gave them glimpses of the future. They foresaw the Trail of Tears, with thousands of Indians traversing the area around Ka-she-la, which the white men called the Santorian Mountains. They saw death and suffering and it drove many of them mad.

They tried to make the mountain stop talking to them by offering up sacrifices. Fearing the wrath of the gods, the superstitious natives chose ancient rituals of blood to appease the mountain. Many virgins perished in their effort to silence the mountain's voice, but the mountain refused to quit speaking.

Over time, those who did not go mad were driven away from the mountain by the constant voice.

And, in time, the white man came to the area and the legend of the voice became known to him.

It was said that the white man silenced the voice of the mountain. But, it was not completely true. The voice merely had no desire to speak to the white man, so it remained silent, and the indigenous tribe that heard the voice was told to keep it to itself by the mountain.

The voice had no use for the white man. It had seen into the future and knew what was to come.

In time, the tribes scattered and became a part of the white man culture and the voice stopped talking.

Tonya Redcloud looked at the Santorian Mountains with awe. Her genealogical studies had brought her to the mountain range, and she was looking forward to discovering more about her family there. She had done enough research to know that she was descendent from a part of the tribe that originally populated the area, and she had come in contact with relatives who had told her there was an ancient burial ground in the mountains. It was said those graves were marked with headstones—which seemed odd to her because it was not a Native American custom to mark their graves—and she set out to take pictures and rubbings of those headstones.

Still, as she exited her car, she felt a chill run through her. It was a hot late June day and the air was so thick you could wear it, but the chill ran through her nonetheless. A soft breeze had blown out of the trees like a hot breath from hell when she stepped out of her car, but then died out to a quiet calm that made the air heavy and hard to breathe. There was an eerie feeling that she could not shake, but she unloaded her backpack and started along the trail that led up the mountain.

There were no other hikers on the trail, yet the trail appeared to be well traveled. It was as if some mysterious force of nature would not allow the grass to overgrow the path up the mountain. Indeed, it appeared as if the Parks and Recreation people had visited the trail just that morning to clear the path off.

Tonya also found that odd, but it did not deter her from walking down the path into the woods.

Less than fifty feet into the woods, she turned. She could not see her car, and the path back that way seemed strangely overgrown and hazy.

For a moment, Tonya thought about running back to the car and driving away. But she was young and stubborn and foolhardy, and she had set her mind to traveling into the woods and finding the rumored ancient graveyard of her ancestors.

She blinked her eyes, and suddenly the fog lifted and the trail was visible again.

"What the hell?" she said. She shook her head as she stared at the now-clear path. The feeling that she needed to run back to her car was again almost overwhelming, but then the wind blew through the trees and she thought she heard a soft voice say: *"Stay."*

She turned, bewildered.

"Hello?" she shouted.

The wind rustled through the leaves again, but it was just the wind.

I heard it, she thought. *I heard a voice. I wasn't imagining things. It was real.*

"Yes," she said. "Speak to me again."

This time when the wind blew she heard: *"Come."*

The shiver that ran down her spine then was more from excitement than fear. Somehow, some way, she knew the voice of the mountain was calling her to come see it. She did not know why. Perhaps, she reckoned, it was her Native American ancestry and her people's acute awareness of the spiritual world. Or maybe, she thought as another shiver ran through her, it was a ghost calling.

Then, as quickly as it had chilled her, the shiver went away. The voice of the mountain was still speaking to her, if not in language, in feeling. As the chill dissipated, she knew it was, without a doubt, a ghost that called to her. It had to be. Slowly, she came to the realization that what was calling her was something that had not been heard in the Santorian Mountains in a long, long time. Her fear was gradually replaced with excitement, and she answered the voice.

"I'm coming," she said.

She started walking again.

She looked up at the sky and saw that the sun seemed to shine down brighter upon her. There were odd sounds coming from the forest. They were sounds that had not graced a forest in millions of years.

She walked on a few steps but stopped and gasped in amazement as something ran across her path.

A small, knee-high dinosaur turned and looked at her. It regarded her for a moment, then squawked and ran off into the bushes.

A hand touched her shoulder and she jumped.

Turning, she saw a woman. She was dressed in the skin of an animal, but not any animal she had ever laid eyes upon.

"Do not fear," the woman said. "You have been brought here for a reason."

The woman smiled and, oddly enough, what fear Tonya had was gone.

The woman said: "My name is Malhalla. I am the one who called to you."

"You ... called ... to ... me?"

Malhalla nodded. "I have been waiting a very long time for you," she said. "But I always knew you would come."

Tonya shook her head and closed her eyes, thinking she was imagining the woman. Yet, when she re-opened her eyes, Malhalla was still there, still smiling.

"I am real," she said. "At least, I was."

"You were?"

"Yes," Malhalla said. "I lived on your plane of existence once, a long time ago." She pointed.

Tonya turned to see a vision of what used to be. Huts lined the path ahead of her. All around her, she saw there was life as Native Americans went about their daily business.

"What is this?" she asked.

Malhalla said: "We were a great tribe once. Your historians call us the Mississippians, but that is not what we called ourselves. We lived off the grace of the land and we were at peace. " She smiled again. "We heard the voice of the mountain back then. Your people have forgotten it."

"I don't understand."

"It is simple, really. Your people and your world have lost touch with reality. You do not hear Mother Nature's call any longer … and she *is* calling you. She's *pleading* with your kind to stop what you are doing … before it's too late."

Malhalla took Tonya's hand and together they walked into the ancient Mississippian village. Women were playing with children and cooking while men worked in the fields.

"Do you see it?" Malhalla asked.

"See what?" replied Tonya.

"Nature. The way things are supposed to be. The way things *should* be. The way things were, until the white man perverted it."

Tonya did not answer immediately. Instead, she watched as the people worked in unison toward a common goal. She understood then why she had been compelled to come to the Santorian Mountains.

She had been called by the voice of the mountain.

She turned to Malhalla. "Are you the voice of the mountain?" she asked.

Malhalla smiled. "I am only one of the voices," she said. "Those who have lived here, loved here, and died here … their voices combine to be the voice of the mountain. Do you understand?"

Oddly enough, Tonya did. There was spirituality about her people that, although it was diminished by the world of the white man, still existed. She felt it from time to time in the oddest places: riding the train through the city and seeing people as they moved mechanically about their days, staring out at the farmlands that bordered the highway, and when making love. She knew that there was a bond that stretched beyond the flesh. It was a bond that held all things together, uniting them as only it could.

The voice of the mountain was speaking to her in those moments.

She knew that with absolute certainty now. The voice had been there with her throughout her life.

"Why am I here?" she asked.

Malhalla's smiled widened. "Why has anyone ever existed?" she said. "To learn. To grow. And to love."

She waved her hand. "Everything you see here was born of love. Love of life. Love of nature. Love of self. But as man's intellect and ambition grew, so did his greed. He lost his way. He forgot that the world was a gift and he started to harm it."

She waved her hand again and the landscape around them slowly began to change. Tonya gasped as the tall trees dissolved back into the earth and the mountain rumbled. Lava flowed down the side of the mountain from its peak, and a myriad strange and disturbing creatures seemed to hide in every nook and cave that littered the hillside.

She turned and looked at Malhalla.

"The voice of the mountain has always been here," she said, "but it hasn't always been in control. Like in your time, in the distant past of mankind, darkness ruled the earth. Strange creatures from beyond our world once threatened to destroy everything. But they were unsuccessful. Watch."

She pointed toward the mountain as the lava flowed into the caves and the hideous beasts within screamed in agony as they burned. Some of them managed to exit their caverns and slither away. Through some sort of power Tonya did not understand, they took flight—although they had no wings and were massive, multi-tentacled beasts. There was no way they should have been able to fly, but they did. Then the sky opened up into a misty black void and swallowed the creatures.

"They are the Old Ones," Malhalla said, noticing her bewilderment. "They came to our world from beyond."

"From beyond? From beyond where?"

"From beyond this world," Malhalla told her. "They came here to conquer man, but the mountain drove them away."

The lava stopped and cooled, and then the landscape began to change. The trees emerged from the ground. Saplings grew quickly, and soon Tonya found herself once again beneath a canopy of leaves with natives working around her. They built huts and lived in the woods. It seemed like a million people populated the area around her.

"As I said, they call them the 'Mississippians' in your time," Malhalla told her as she gazed in wonder, "but their name is much more ancient than that, and it is now lost in the memory of time. They ruled this area for centuries. They flourished and lived good lives. They mined the rich lands around these mountains for their crops and livestock. They built mounds so they could be closer to the heavens, and the gods seemed to smile upon them."

Tonya turned and looked away from the mountains. Everywhere she looked, she saw rich farmlands. There was a network of dirt roads that weaved across the land like highways, and those roads were teeming with merchants and travelers.

"It's beautiful," Tonya said.

"It *was* beautiful."

"What happened to them?"

"Behold," said Malhalla.

Tonya looked and saw the sky open up once again above the endless world of commerce and the things Malhalla called the Old Ones emerged. Those ancient creatures flowed out of the opening and attacked the people. Blood and destruction was everywhere as the Mississippians died. The Old Ones tore people limb from limb and consumed them with gaping mouths.

In no time at all, the crops were destroyed and the huts and buildings were smashed to the ground.

It seemed as if the Mississippians were doomed.

Then, in the distance, Tonya heard as massive rumbling. She turned to see the Santorian mountain range, much different that it was in her time, come to life. Lava exploded into the air and crashed into the land around the Old Ones. It splattered as it struck, burning the Old Ones and making them scream in inhuman voices.

The Old Ones rose into the sky to avoid the pummeling lava barrage.

The lava continued flying and the Old Ones receded back into their dimensional portal. It was only when the portal closed that the barrage ended. But by then the damage was done.

The Mississippian village was decimated.

Tonya saw the few remaining inhabitants fleeing the destruction.

"Why?" she asked.

Malhalla spoke softly and calmly. "The lesser of two evils," she said. "If the mountain had not acted, the Old Ones would have won the day and mankind would now be their slaves. It fought to prevent that."

"But people died!"

"People die every day," Malhalla said. "And they are born every day. The people of the Mississippi Valley died long ago so that you might live. The mountain decreed it."

Tonya pondered that. She had come to the Santorian Mountains in search of her genealogy and found far more that she bargained for. She wondered if, perhaps, she was dreaming. She would wake up in her bed, groggy, and marvel at the bizarre dream.

But she knew that this was much more than a dream. The eerie, unearthly glow that surrounded her was dreamlike in a way, but the reality of the scene before her was far too genuine. She had heard the screams of the dying as the Old Ones destroyed the city, and felt the warmth of the lava as it flew overhead. If it were a dream, it was the most vivid one she had ever had.

"Why have you shown me this?" she asked Malhalla as she felt herself drawn away from the world of the Mississippians.

"Remembrance," Malhalla said. The world around her coalesced and contorted.

Tonya shook her head. "But no one remembers the truth about the Mississippians," she said. "How can we remember if no one tells the tale?"

"That is why you are here," Malhalla said.

Slowly, the modern world returned and they were standing on the path Tonya had been hiking. In the distance, she could see Mount Sallee, the highest peak in the mountain range. Somehow, while under Malhalla's spell, the other mountains had been obscured. She had seen only what Malhalla wanted her to see. Perhaps, she reckoned, Malhalla was the guardian of *that* particular mountain.

She wondered if the other mountains had a voice.

She hoped so.

Regardless, she was back where she had started.

Malhalla smiled. "Every generation of our people passes the torch of remembrance on to the next. It is how it has been since the dawn of our time when the first of our people heard the voice of the mountain."

She waved her hand, and once again the majestic tribe of her people appeared before her in the haze. "It is our faith in their memory that keeps the voice of the mountain alive."

"I don't understand," said Tonya.

Once again, Malhalla smiled. "It is only through wisdom and time that you shall understand," she said. "Are you willing to learn?"

"Are you offering to teach me?"

Malhalla nodded. "Yes."

"What can you teach me?" Tonya asked. She pointed toward the vision of the tribe. "This world has been replaced."

"It has," said Malhalla. "But it should not be forgotten. The Old Ones will return someday and the mountain needs someone who can speak with it, listen to its voice. The mountain will help you defend against The Old Ones. Your technology will not defeat them; only your faith."

"But our bombs—"

"—Will destroy the world along with The Old Ones … and the mountain will not allow it."

"How can it stop us?"

Malhalla's smile faded. "In much the way it stopped the Old Ones before, the mountain will call upon you when they lay siege to your world. It has resisted the temptation to do so already … and it speaks to mankind, but you do not listen."

"It speaks to us? How?"

"Floods. Earthquakes. Hurricanes. The mountain and its brethren have told you. You do not see it because you do not listen."

"And you can teach me to listen?"

"Yes."

"I want to learn."

Malhalla's smile returned. "I knew I chose well. "

Suddenly, the world changed around Tonya. She looked at the tribe. She was not just watching them now; she was actually *there*, with them. She could smell the fresh air, and hear the birds in the sky. She knew they were long gone, and that their time would never return. Yet, it was as real as any memory she had ever had.

Man had moved on. In opening his eyes to technology, he had closed his eyes to the simple truth of the land. Tonya felt the loss every time she saw someone with his or her nose buried in a cell phone, texting or surfing the Internet. It was not the way life was supposed to be. Mankind had perverted the world so much that Malhalla's world was not even a memory to them now.

They had forgotten how to live.

But it wasn't too late.

"The mountain. I want to hear it," she said.

Malhalla took her hand. "All you need to do is listen."

Tonya closed her eyes. At first, nothing happened. Then, ever so softly, she heard a voice. It was soft and sweet and as she listened, she realized that the earth was sentient. It was hurting.

She listened as the mountain spoke to her and it was beautiful.

Roger Trexler is a writer from southern Illinois. His Frank Powell detective series of books is available through crossroadspress.com. He has many other novels, short story and poetry collections (in both print and e-book) available through amazon.com. He is also an actor and a director. His first feature-length film, *Platypossum*, will debut at the Cape Girardeau, Missouri, comic con on April 22, 2017.

Plat 7

by

Max Wright

"Boy's shoe. Red Con, white laces. Size four," Hernandez said over the walkie-talkie.

Sheriff Wade Williams felt his innards slide into the toes of his Red Wing boots. "Fuck." The word came out before he could even decide if it was the right response or not. A match to what Micah Parker was reported wearing when he went missing at 3:45 p.m. yesterday. Now it was nearly 11:30 a.m., and the all-out search had been going on since sunrise. "Okay, keep looking," he added.

The sheriff shot a look toward the black-and-white parked in the churned-up dirt of Plat 7, one of the still-unbuilt areas of the new development. The Parkers were inside, huddled together, their world destroyed. He thought about going over and talking to them, but decided against it, at least until he knew more.

An elderly woman came by with a box of sandwiches. "Hungry, Sheriff?"

"Already ate, ma'am. Thanks for helping out."

"That poor family." The woman moved on, offering lunch to a cluster of EMTs gathered around an ambulance.

Williams studied the map spread out on the tailgate of his county-issued Tahoe. Not much of a command center, but budgets out here hadn't caught up with the population boom. Neither had his map, which still showed many of the homes as empty lots. Last election this whole subdivision had still been farmland and the fringes of Lansky's Wood. Now the scrubby forest where he used to hike and bird watch with his daughters was all high-end housing, foreign luxury crossovers in every driveway, chain restaurants and coffee shops on every corner. His ten-year-old sheriff's department Tahoe was almost an embarrassment.

What do I do now? He had about twenty men from West Park Methodist fanning out through the alleys and fringes of the development to the north. Troop 151 of Explorer Scouts was moving through what was left of the farmland to the west. A mixed team of firefighters and volunteers was working their way east through the park and the edge of the woods. His own men were searching due south in the heart of the woods. And the Parkers were sitting in the black-and-white, staring at him like he was supposed to have an answer. Shifting more resources to where they'd found the shoe made sense. *Unless somebody took Micah somewhere.*

"Sheriff Williams."

Williams turned.

Mr. Parker stood with arms folded, pale, stubble on his face.

"Any word on Micah?" Parker's voice was thin with concealed desperation.

"Nothing yet, Phil." Williams put the walkie-talkie on the lift gate. "At this point in the investigation, that's probably a good sign. There's a chance, maybe even a good chance, he's okay."

"We called all his friends. Should we try again?"

The walkie-talkie crackled. "Sheriff."

"Excuse me, Mr. Parker. The best thing you can do right now is be with your wife. I'll come by to talk to you both in a bit." Williams turned and keyed the radio. "Go ahead."

"It's Hernandez. Boss, you going to send me some more people? We haven't found anything besides the shoe, and these woods are thicker than I remembered."

Shit. Extra men is the one thing I haven't got. "Yeah. I got a couple reserves coming in. But I was going to send them door-to-door." He couldn't very well have volunteers going through people's houses. The badge lent authority and trust, and implied accountability. More than implied it. Guaranteed it.

"The kid kept going, like he was walking across the clearing. But the tracks run out once you get into the trees again. Like the kid just up and disappeared."

"Tape off the area where you found the shoe. When the fire and rescue guys are done with the East Quadrant we'll have them follow up. I don't want to send a bunch of amateurs into the woods. Too likely to mess up my evidence."

"Copy that. I'll check in later."

Williams adjusted his belt, looked at the map again. He was staffed for a rural county that had turned into a crowded exurb seemingly overnight. Even when he could send the fire and rescue team into the woods, it wouldn't be enough. And some kid's life was at stake.

Williams checked his watch. Noon-21. He'd sent the Explorer Troop into the woods twenty minutes ago. They had no experience, but they were good kids and, since some of them were considering careers in law enforcement, they were likely to do as they were told. *Last thing I need is somebody trying to be a hero if something goes sideways.*

Williams climbed into the front seat of his Tahoe, keyed the radio. "Elle, you there?"

"Sure thing."

"You got any word on the dog team?"

"I was just about to ring you up. The city police called here about five, six minutes ago. The K-9 truck conked out on the freeway, Sheriff."

"Are you shitting me, Elle?" Williams couldn't believe it. They needed those dogs.

"They got another vehicle on the way to transfer the dogs. I'm sorry about that." Elle sounded miserable, like she felt personally responsible.

"Oh well. Crap happens. Let me know if you hear anything else." He rested the mike in the cradle and got back out of the truck. Noon-thirty. Every minute that passed, his odds of finding little Micah alive lessened.

"Hello, Sheriff?" The voice was high-pitched, nervous. Not one of his people.

"Who is this?"

"Kendall. Kendall Riley. I'm an Explorer—"

"Well, Kendall, you want to explain to me what you're doing on my deputy's radio?"

"I found it. I mean Deputy Hernandez was here, but he's gone and I'm scared."

Williams' chest clenched. Shit was going all kinds of bad. "Hold on, Kendall. I'm coming."

Williams trudged across Plat 7 and into Lansky's Woods. He stuck to the trail, knowing that's the way Hernandez had gone. Kendall must have, too, to find his walkie-talkie. The branches of the trees closed overhead, thicker than usual, rustling and cracking in the breeze. The trail took a rise, and then dropped and opened into a small clearing partially marked with crime scene tape. He spotted the girl, a skinny kid with dark hair, except for her dyed blonde bangs. She was still clutching the walkie-talkie.

"Kendall?" He spoke softly.

"Sheriff. I am so scared."

"It's okay, Kendall. I'm here. I need you to tell me what happened. From the beginning."

Kendall brushed her hair out of her eyes with one hand. "Okay. So they sent my Explorer troop into the woods. And I was supposed to help Deputy Hernandez secure the area where they found the shoe.

So we were putting up the tape. And he was just a couple yards away, putting up tape—"

Kendall hesitated, made gasping sounds like she was fighting the urge to cry. Or couldn't breathe.

"It's all right." Williams touched her shoulder. "Slow down and take your time."

"So we were marking the site off. And I looked away for maybe two seconds. And when I looked back, he was gone."

"Gone where?" Williams flicked his eyes across the clearing, looking for a sign of his deputy, or of a struggle.

"Just gone. Except for his walkie-talkie." Kendall shivered, even in her jacket. "I was afraid to go back down the trail alone. So I called you."

"That was smart, Kendall. You did the right thing." He stepped under the tape and into the clearing. It was cold, colder than usual for this time of year. "I'm just going to have a quick look around. Then we'll get you back to town, okay?"

Kendall nodded, eyes wide from behind a fringe of hair.

He found the red shoe, bagged and tagged, lying on the ground. Spotted Micah's small footprints continuing across the clearing in the mud of the trail. There were a couple of other prints, most likely Hernadez's. He'd done his best to keep the scene clean. Williams figured at this point he'd need a state forensics team in here. His own office wasn't equipped for anything like this. He turned. "Kendall, let's go."

Silence.

"Kendall?"

Her Explorer's jacket lay crumpled beneath a tree.

"Kendall!" *Dammit, where did she wander off to? Maybe she headed back down the trail on her own.*

Williams took off after her, figuring he'd catch up with her in a couple of minutes. He crossed the clearing, got back on the trail, and headed back toward the development.

No footprints. Coming or going. Not even bent blades of grass or crushed leaves.

He stopped, stared. The trees were older, the air heavier, the undergrowth thinner, the path narrower than he remembered. "Kendall!" He called again, but got no response.

He keyed the walkie-talkie. Nothing. Battery was good. *Could it be interference from the trees?* He pulled out his cell. No signal. *This is not good.*

Williams took a deep breath. The town was pretty much due north. He slipped off his watch and held it flat in his hand, aiming the hour hand at the sun. Not quite as good as a compass, but the bisected line between the hour hand and twelve should get him going in the right direction. Walk a mile or so and he should see or hear something that would help him zero on the town. Or he'd be able to get a signal for his radio or phone.

He headed generally north, using his pocketknife to mark his trail. This wasn't his first damn rodeo.

Leaves crackled. Williams froze, except for the hand that found his holster.

Silence.

Slowly, Williams swiveled his head toward the noise.

Nothing but trees.

Must have been the wind.

He started walking again. But something was hinky. If he was headed back toward town, the woods should be thinning. But the trees were taller and thicker than ever. Hell, he didn't know there were trees this big in the whole damn county. This wasn't a woods, this was a fucking forest.

Damn it, I should have stayed put. The search party, they'd have come and found me.

The noise again, like branches rubbing together.

He unholstered his nine mil.

How did it get so dark? And of course, he'd left the big flashlight in the truck. Because who takes a flashlight with them at one in the afternoon on a sunny day? He felt around on his belt. At least he had the smaller one.

He decided it wasn't dark enough to start wasting the precious batteries.

The noise again. Wood on wood, with an undertone of something else. *Groaning?*

The woods could get to you when you were all alone. He took in a deep breath. Had to be a bobcat. A fox maybe. Stalking him out of curiosity, but not really a threat. No big predators like cougars or bears had been spotted around here since the early 1900s. Except he'd seen that online article about cougars moving back into areas where they hadn't been seen in decades.

Williams gripped his gun tighter.

That noise.

"Kendall?"

Fuck. He thought he heard something. Could be the wind. Or was it a muffled whimper?

He took a step toward the sounds.

"Micah? Hernandez?"

The wind kicked up out of nowhere. Leaves and needles swirled in the air. Over the rattling branches and whipping gusts, a weak whisper.

"Help. Please." A girl's voice. Or a young boy's.

"Micah? Kendall? Where are you?" Williams yanked the flashlight off his belt. The thing felt like a toy in his hands, but it did a damn good job of lighting things up. He beamed the light over the trees.

What the hell?

In the middle of a circle of oaks stood a wide, half-rotted out trunk, about six, seven feet tall.

Something moved.

A flash of a pale limb, like an arm motioning him to come that way.

Williams released the safety on his pistol, pointed his light directly at the stump. Grit and wind stung his eyes. He couldn't see squat, not in this dark, not with this wind.

Williams took a couple of steps toward the trunk. His light cut through the mix of darkness, dust, and whirling leaves to reveal two more rotting trunks. A sweetish smell like his grandmother's pan dulce came with the wind.

As he stepped closer to the stump, the wind died down and the smell grew stronger.

"Help me."

With the wind weakening, Williams could hear the words clearly. He broke into a sprint, crashing through the branches and under-growth. "Micah! Kendall! Hold on! Police!"

He drew up short. Nearly dropped his flashlight and gun.

A jagged crack ran from the top of the stump to its middle, its edges covered in what looked like a mottled gray fungus.

Kendall stared back at him from inside the gashed wood. Only her face was visible as she hissed, "Please, God, help me."

Williams covered the ground between him and the tree in two steps. "It's okay, Kendall, I'm here. I got you." He dug his hands into the mold, ripped out a chunk.

"Fuck!" The gray shit burned his hands. He bent to pick up a branch to use to tear at the stuff. When he looked back up, the gray gunk had grown back, like he'd never even touched it.

Kendall looked at him, panic in her eyes.

He reached out to touch her face, to let her know it was okay, he'd get her out of there. Her skin was hard, cool, slightly rough.

Like wood.

"Jesus." He picked up his flashlight, shined it at the other trees. Micah's and Hernandez's faces stared back at him.

Williams took a step backward, nearly tripping over a root. Turned to run.

And realized the root was wrapped around his ankle.

Max Wright is a corporate communications and occasional fiction writer living in Dallas, Texas. His fantasy and horror stories have appeared in a number of magazines, e-zines, and anthologies, and of course he's working on a novel. Or two. When he's not trying to scare people, he enjoys tennis, writers' group meetings, B-grade horror movies, military history, and trying to banish the gremlins who haunt his partially restored sports car.

Hope

Scientific Mothers

by

Catrin Sian Rutland

IT ALL STARTED AT A reproduction conference in San Diego. Our group of eight scientists was discussing the fertility crisis with predominant questions on our minds. How had the great reproductive decline really started? Would it end or were humans devolving so quickly that we were about to kill off our own species? How could we change the situation and should we really do anything at all? We understood the biology but so much of the decline was due to social values and personal interest rather than the mechanics of reproduction.

I am now an old woman of ninety-three years, and no longer completely sure that we did the right thing. There are too many questions that remain unanswered, but I am not sure that our action can be reversed entirely, either. I want to explain what we, the Scientific Mothers, did and why. It's imperative you understand that we did it out of love. We created something and hoped destruction did not follow in its wake. I will never see the end of our great experiment, but maybe you are living it now.

After World War 2, it seemed that the human race's population had exploded. The baby boomers were also the first to really benefit from consistently successful contraceptives. Successive generations developed these drugs. Women and men started to have real choices about their careers, family life, and health. Some countries, such as

China, even implemented laws designed to restrict childbirth. One child per couple. Some people protested. How could humans be expected to deliberately limit their families? How could they give up loving more children? Who could expect people to forget terms such as *brother, sister, aunt,* and *uncle*? Unexpectedly, and within just a few generations, the population declined throughout the developed countries. Naturally, the developing countries still had increasing populations but nature itself also ensured that their populations did not grow exponentially. Disease, starvation, climate change, and the lack of health care and sanitation still took their toll. By 2075, when the Scientific Mothers met and talked at that first conference, the decline was becoming extreme.

In the 1800s the total number of humans walking on the planet was approximately one billion. By 2011 the numbers had increased to seven billion. Despite population estimates of ten billion living souls by 2085, we were in fact surrounded by just four billion, roughly the same as in the 1970s. The net reproduction rates were declining ferociously, and by 2075 only one in six women in the developing countries were having infants. This number fell to one in ten across Australasia, Europe, America, the Middle East, and Russia.

As each year passed, the birthrate decreased still further. Yes, we were scientists, but the decrease in children hit us at another depth. Laughter and cheer were diminishing in our lives. We noticed people, in general, took less joy from watching little ones open their birthday presents or hearing them squeal in delight at discovering a neighbour's cat in the garden.

We went to parties and celebrations but no longer were the toddlers shining in their dance performances, singing in small choirs, or wearing their best party frocks at Christmas. They were conspicuously absent at social events. Our lives were more sober. We had fewer people to care for or about. The words *brother, sister, cousin, niece,* and *nephew* were terms that only the oldest people could now use with any frequency. A light was dimming in the world and no one would take responsibility for it.

The world was changing, and changing at a faster pace than at any time in the glorious past. Governments worried as the aging populations became impossible to manage. It was true that people lived longer than ever before, but with so few young people it was not possible to care for those with physical needs and age-related disorders. We watched on as the number of surgeons declined just when they were needed more than ever before. Despite robotics assuming so many human roles and the dawn of the great age of computers being upon us, people were still needed to rule over the planet. Robots could do housework, build technologies, and assist in hospitals. Computers could drive cars, sort shopping, and run basic households, but we still needed people to watch over these machines and make decisions.

People still needed people, and life behind a computer was increasingly lonely. Human contact was a biological necessity, yet as each generation was born, mankind became increasingly self-absorbed. In the old days people would have the time to sit down with family and read the news to the older people. They would sit and talk or play board games. Nobody seemed to have that time anymore. There were too many people needing to be cared for and not enough people to share that time with. No grandchildren to coo over or babysit. No strollers to take to the park to enjoy a gentle walk in the sunshine, and no lullabies to sing. Our hearts were growing empty and increasingly geared around a world full of adults.

Experiencing life independently was a pleasure and material goods became ever more important. Infertility rates had increased for so many scientifically proven and unproven reasons, and although the governments and sciences worked hard to eradicate the complications, they could not keep up the pace. As fast as infertility remedies were created, contraceptive efficacies increased. As hormones were removed from the oceans, water supplies, and food chains, more heavy metals and fresh toxins were discovered.

Perhaps the greatest reason for the reduction in babies was the human mind itself. Women found new joys in their work. Men chose the freedoms of bachelorhood and reveled in the carefree childless lifestyle. The numbers of single parents hit an all-time high, and people feared the responsibilities involved with nurturing and paying for their children alone.

Society began to put the onus on achievement, possessions, and living life around pleasure and self-satisfaction rather than placing importance on developing a family unit. Decades before, little boys and girls dreamed of starting their own families, and their careers were based around providing those offspring with the best in life. After weddings in those bygone eras, smartly dressed kids would giggle and dance at receptions. Proud newlyweds would answer endless questions on whether they too might start on their own family very soon. Not anymore. Now, it was assumed that the delightful couple would concentrate on their lives together rather than indulging in the expensive and time-consuming burden of children.

And expense was a very real concern. Living cost money. Following years of economic recession and several food shortages, the price of just existing had rocketed. Pregnancy, childhood medication, and hospital expenses could cripple parents financially, even assuming they didn't need fertility interventions to start with. Social care and free education had been eradicated in every country, and nannies, nurseries, and childcare costs had become astronomical.

Where once upon a time children grew up and flew the nest, they increasingly depended upon their parents to fund their lavish lifestyles and remained in the family home. Slowly but surely the older generations tired of the time and effort needed to bring up children. In a world where they observed others doing what they pleased, it became difficult to make decisions based on the biological need of procreation. Men and women fought against their natural instincts for having children and reasoned instead that they would have better lives without them.

We eight women watched this as we grew up, and listened as pressures were placed upon us to achieve and live rather than blindly fall pregnant and exist in poverty. At that conference we discussed why the world had become what it was and talked about how much we missed the laughter of little ones and their infectious giggles and smiles. Children were no longer part of day-to-day life. The movement against pregnancy had begun early in our lives and those of the girls surrounding us. Implants containing progestogen were routinely inserted into girls' arms once they turned twelve. At first this was in a bid to prevent teen pregnancy and protect young lives. As time went by most women chose to keep their valued contraceptives.

I had not often played with dolls. Due to the movements against encouraging girls to dream only of family roles and stereotypes, those types of toys were generally frowned upon. In discussions with a friend, she said that her grandmother had told her that boys and girls once played with dolls routinely but technologic fashion soon turned them towards computer games. Parents and teachers were obsessed with exams and education as each child became more expensive and therefore more precious. Playtime and exploration had no place in modern society, so dolls were eventually rejected, and over time thoughts of even having children were gradually abandoned.

Instead of building societies that supported each child and parent, governments turned to cheaper alternatives to encourage childbirth. The populace fought against elevated taxes to pay for schools and medical care for kids. With so many people choosing the childless life, it just wasn't popular with voters. Pressured to fix the problems caused by the harsh declines in population, successive governments implemented anti-abortion laws and tried to promote parenthood again.

Child abandonment has been a part of society throughout history. Even the old fairy tales tell of babes left out in the woods and children raised by wild animals. Since genetic testing became routine, simply leaving a newborn at the hospital door had become impossible. In this event both parents would be jailed for life. Politicians no longer tolerated such actions, and judges were forced to comply with harsh international laws.

Even optimistic potential parents hunted for solutions to the challenges of raising children, but struggled and wearily abandoned such dreams. Home schooling was near impossible as both parents needed to work in order to pay for the basics such as food and a home. The costs of parenting if marriage separation occurred were near impossible to manage. Even the risk of criminalisation and jail were higher for those who had children. Schools were happy to fine and even criminalise parents for days missed from school, poor examination grades, or failing to complete the excessive amounts of homework each night. Ideals initially put in place to prevent truancy or parents not bothering to take their kids to school had taken off and expanded. These private schools now gave their teachers annual performance-related bonuses based on attendance and grades and these fines helped towards running the school. Schools had turned into places of fear for both students and parents, and teachers were forced to perform well otherwise their own livelihoods were at risk.

Meeting those seven other women at conference had been a breath of fresh air for me. I worked in an environment where few women had or indeed wanted children. I wanted children but like so many people I was worried about the cost, being excluded from "polite society" and the prospect of a lifetime of concern and stress. I did also realise that I was missing out on all the love and caring that I could be a part of. I yearned for the magical feeling of growing a child inside me, yet simultaneously feared the responsibility that this would bring. These other scientists were just like me. They wanted children. They wanted society to rebuild. They wanted humans to grow and flourish. It was too late to reeducate the masses. Governments throughout the world had tried that, but with no infrastructures in place, people still rejected the idea of procreating. There was also the problem of reproductive difficulties to overcome.

We eight had read about strange fertility rituals that now only lived on in history books. We had fallen in love with the idea that humans could once again value fertility and the embryo. People would once again value the small cells growing and dividing to become a valuable part of society. We recounted tales from early mankind where they painted pictures of sexual organs on cave walls and carved sexualised montages and copulating couples in flamboyant Roman baths. We saw films of English children dancing around maypoles, naked people writhing around in waterfalls amidst the blood of sacrificial animals in Haiti, tribes praying to their goddesses, and people putting their faith straight into the hands of fertility clinics.

We were all involved in fertility and reproduction in our different ways, some with human medicine and others with animal fertility. Between us we had worked on super-ovulating the kakapo, saving the once nearly extinct flightless parrot species, right through to ensuring that cattle semen was motile and abundant during the food-security crisis of 2068 which saw herd fertility hit an all-time low. We had helped these animals and now it was time to turn our minds fully to our own species.

The problem that we encountered was not just fertility; humans were capable of producing children more frequently than the numbers would presently indicate. Society was the main problem. We had to change each community, force them all to take action at once. Looking back it seemed such a good idea. We were preventing an apocalypse which was being created by concomitant greed and fear. We would be hailed as heroes. The Scientific Mothers. The women who saved humanity.

For many years, in secret, we researched, developed theories, and worked on several plans. Studying the biological validity of each system, ensuring that the technologies were safe, questioning the ethics and discussing the politics of each new theory. The failure point was always seen when trying to hit societal interests. Of course we could help women and men become parents. Biologically this was possible.

The problem was they just didn't want to have offspring. Our frustrations grew and it became clear to us that no matter what we worked on, we could not cure humankind.

We had the biological solution. A genetically altered luteinizing hormone was our redemption. We could make women ovulate or, better still, super-ovulate. Male reactions to this design hormone were also excellent. Testosterone would be released, resulting in a cascade of reactions which enabled super sperm development. As a side effect, the behaviour of males would alter slightly as they became more sexually aroused. The hormone was perfect, optimising male and female fertility whilst also increasing sexual desire.

It could be delivered via injection, but who was going to sign up for treatment? No, we needed to deliver it secretly. We had developed an analogue of the hormone, which could be swallowed in tablet or liquid form and was relatively heat resistant. We had worked long months and years and now we were nearly ready. We just needed a suitable method of giving our treatment to the world. We began to call it the gift of life. Cells in our laboratories produced the hormone, but then our cattle-reproduction specialist had a brilliant idea. We could add the hormone to food. Many countries had prevented significant numbers of spinal cord defects in infants by adding folic acid to flour; now we could create infants via a similar method.

Following much discussion we realised that we simply couldn't produce enough hormone, but maybe we could create transgenic animals that could create our gift of life for us. Then we realised why stop there, these animals could be both factory and distribution method. Once we had created one transgenic cow, plenty of genetically modified calves followed.

Cloning was still not perfect but it worked well enough. The udder cells released the newly designed luteinizing hormone into the milk ducts. The super farms throughout the world mostly worked off automated milking machines, and had long since given up on testing for hormones. These super-milking animals were generally hormone-supplemented anyway, and who really cared about milk additives nowadays?

It was with even more delight that we observed the genetic alterations appearing in the newly born cattle, passing from mother to daughter via the X chromosome. We were so near now. Each of us set up large farms; breeding was the key. It cost a fortune but several large grants helped along the way.

Systematically our animals were bred and sold, bred and sold, huge numbers making their way to market via natural birth and cloning. Once out in the farms our animals kept breeding. We saw nothing at first, no effect on birthrates.

Our hormones diluted by the vast amounts of milk, not enough cows were transgenic. Then, slowly but surely, baby booms were reported, with smaller communities and islands showing the trend first. Although we scientists were based in different countries, we saw remarkable increases in maternity-ward admissions, most obvious in the cities, towns, and villages surrounding our own research institutes. Surely now the governments would have to provide support to these new families? As our assays showed ever-higher levels of hormones in commercial milk, and then in the environment as it leached into the water systems, so the pregnancy rates exponentially increased.

Old now, my friends and I gathered together this May, a sunny and happy month for us all. We had decided that Auckland was the perfect place to gather. The community had shown the highest birthrate that year. Our kakapo expert had raised fine dairy herds in New Zealand in the lush Waikato region, but had not managed to export them easily. Australasia was filled with genetically modified cows and the exports of dairy products were high. The human population had risen worldwide by a full ten percent. That momentous gathering was to be our last meeting.

We avoided milk and all other dairy products. We had important work to do and no time to deliver our own tiny pattering feet. We had to collect the milk, test for the new luteinizing hormone, and campaign for child and parental rights. And there were still questions unanswered. How would these hormones affect people long term and how would they affect our precious babies? Would anyone ever work out what we had done or who had done it?

We were mothers now to humankind. We looked at the rising birth rates and could feel nothing but pride and love for all those children entering the world. We, the Scientific Mothers, had prevented the gradual destruction of humans but even we could not foresee the future. Mothers by proxy we would stay until our final heartbeats. Future generations would have to iron out any problems; future generations that we women had created with our gift of life.

Catrin is a scientist. As an assistant professor, she teaches, lives, and researches science. Her fiction pieces explore the world beyond what is (presently) possible, known, proven, or in existence. Writing allows her to explore these ideas and understand society and the world around us.

When Catrin is not researching, teaching, or writing, you'll find her reading horror, science fiction, or dystopian books with a cat sitting on her lap.

Author webpage: http://catrinrutland.weebly.com/

Twitter @catrinrutland

Amazon author pages: amazon.co.uk/-/e/B017XTOMOA

and amazon.com/author/catrinrutland

Last Natural Woman

by

Querus Abuttu

RENNICK-514 CALIBRATED THE BIOLOCATORS OVER his eyes and scanned the forest. It was a perfunctory move. Something he'd done a minimum of forty-eight times a day, every day, since the beginning of his existence. He moved through the trees, brushing against the foliage, taking notice of how the emerald and gold nano-leaves tickled his cyber-senses. The silver grass he trod upon, the slithery trobs burrowing in the dirt, the iridescent leaves topping the trees, and even the particles in the air, were filled with microscopic cyber-beings at one with him, and he with them.

Since the Tech-Bio Wars of 2217, there were very few, if any, true biological beings. A shame. Or it *would* be a shame, if Rennick-514 could feel such a thing. Tech-life was far superior to bio-life. A fact that every particle of his kind accepted with instantaneous transmission. And yet, each time he discovered a bio-being, and improved or destroyed it, something inside him went dark. He couldn't mathematically trace or name it, yet his body seemed heavier, slower, and his transmissions to the Network were delayed by microseconds after those encounters.

Improvement of bio-life. Improvement meant forcing change on remaining organisms that resisted the transition of the Picos. Rennick-514 hadn't had to do that in a while.

Ten thousand one hundred fifty-two and twenty-one. The number of hours and seconds since he'd found any bio-life. His sole purpose and responsibility. Improve or destroy. And he was number one at his job. Selected as the prime—first among others for upgrades and test weapons.

Ether spoke to him. *What happens when you no longer have a purpose?*

Humans would have called Ether *God,* if they still existed. But unlike their gods, Ether spoke to tech-life, questioned them and challenged their intelligence. Ether bound all tech-life together, similar to a vintage movie where humans in space could connect with a god they called "the Force." It was an archaic way to consider a connection with the universe, but they had been on the right track. Until they weren't.

Rennick-514 pondered Ether's question as he traveled farther into the hills, along the terminal line of his usual route, four hundred kilometers into the forest from his base camp. His humanoid form moved easily across the terrain. Fast. Light. Nearly silent.

A fluorescent green blip lit up on the biolocators over his eyes, just as the alarm whined inside his central network. The liquids in his body pumped faster, suffusing his muscles with lubricating fluids.

He dashed toward the blip, eyes calculating the distance, internal computers sifting through data. There. A fruit fly. A definite biological. He pulled his trans-ray from his gear-belt and aimed at the creature, observing his internal hesitancy before pressing the button. A blue beam flowed toward the insect and encased it. The fluorescent blip in his vision remained.

Resistant to Pico change.

It was the first one he'd discovered in over a year. He dug into his pack and retrieved a clear canister, then deftly caught the creature as it meandered around the blue-black muscadine grapes. He screwed the cap on tight. Central Control would be interested in this. They'd examine it, take it apart, and then—they'd destroy it.

Scanning the rest of the forest in all directions, and satisfied when nothing more set off his sensors, he returned to base camp and communicated his find. A drone would pick up his sample, and the sci-techs would examine it.

Ether spoke to his mind again. *If there was one fruit fly, then why not two? Are there more, deeper in the forest?*

Rennick-514 accepted the suggestion. He filed a request to expand his usual route, although it would take him across the border into the Restricted Zone. The RZ. An area cordoned off for scientific experiments, and monitored by their own sentries. Somehow, their sentries had failed. Central Control would answer him by morning, approving or denying his request. Until then he'd continue his usual route and ponder Ether's questions.

ARTA

Arta was barely seven years old when the Picos conquered and converted the cities. Computers, cell phones, all of the machines were transformed first. Within days, they took over the first human body. Replacing cells with microscopic machines. Sloughing off the waste and recycling it. In mere weeks, all that was truly human in the cities had died.

It took longer for those who lived in the Midwest, in isolated places like deserts, polar regions, and deep forests. But eventually, she supposed, all natural life was gone.

They had transformed her mother, father, and five-year-old brother Robby all in one day. That spark, that spirit that was *them*, died in their eyes and was replaced with something that constantly observed her.

Robby's transformation was probably the worst. He was more than her brother. He was her friend. They had played and told each other fantastic stories. Even though he was younger, the things he said and his observations of nature used to make her laugh. The change happened during her seventh autumn.

Her fake family watched her closely yet remained aloof, never touching her and never touching the food or bio-plants that she needed to live. Picos died the moment they touched living things. They either turned into a fine white dust or completely disappeared.

She discovered this when she tried to pick daffodils with her hands. They disintegrated in her fingers. Part of her longed to touch her family—to see them crumble away. If she'd done that then maybe the constant observations would have stopped. Their fake emotions, mimicked expressions of love, or surprise, as they told her what they'd learned from the Network, would have just faded into nothing.

But she didn't touch them. She didn't end their puppet existence. And she stayed near the house, never trying once to run away. She probably wouldn't have survived if she had. The Picos were everything. Built by the Nanos, they soon learned to replicate themselves, and maybe they'd already created much smaller machines. She didn't know.

Before their transformation, Mother and Father had filled the basement with stocks of beans, rice, dried fruits and vegetables, and canned goods because of the war. They'd hoped their isolation in the mountains would keep them safe. Her Pico family never went near the basement, and so her stocks of supplies remained Pico free.

In her ninth spring, she remembered when her canned food supplies were dwindling low. She'd made the decision to search for more, hoping that if she found some the Picos hadn't transformed them. Maybe she'd even find another human.

She traveled in different directions through the forest and never got lost because the silver Pico grass turned to dust beneath her feet leaving an easy trail to follow on return trips home. It took a half a day to discover an abandoned town. She scavenged the few houses and small buildings, and brought as many interesting books back as she could carry. There was also an old library that became her favorite place to visit. Two battered dictionaries and a thesaurus helped her understand words that were more difficult to comprehend.

Over the next four years, she read and she learned. She scavenged curious things the Picos hadn't bothered with changing, and brought them home too. Ceramic horses. Clothing, shoes and different kinds of jewelry. Her home remained virtually Pico free, except for the presence of her fake family. They never aged from the day they transformed, but she had become what she supposed was a handsome woman, from what she could tell from her reflection and her self-comparisons to pictures of young people in old magazines.

And there was her garden of vegetables, nut trees, and fruit trees. She had cherry tomatoes that came back year after year, wild grapes, six different kinds of squash, asparagus, mustard greens, kale, walnuts, hazelnuts, persimmons, apples and pears. She had books on canning and drying food, and her parents had taught her how to forage for groundnuts and other wild edibles. It wasn't easy, but she survived. And for some reason, these things never transformed. Perhaps the Picos wanted her to live, although she couldn't understand why. They never changed her. At least she thought they hadn't. She would know, wouldn't she?

The Picos did communicate with her, though. They asked her questions, and probed her thought processes. They taught her mathematics and physics. Her Pico mother probed her on the topic of emotions, and her father quizzed her on mechanics. Her brother answered her questions about Picos. He never played, though. None of them did. They were robots. Data gatherers. Dull and boring.

It was her fifteenth spring when they brought her an old computer. It was sitting on the kitchen table when she came downstairs one morning. She touched it, and amazingly it didn't turn to dust.

"Is it real?" She found it difficult to contain her excitement.

"Of course it's real," her Pico father said. "Everything is real."

Arta didn't argue, but kept her thoughts to herself. Knowing, of course, that technically the beings that posed as her family were real, but not real at the same time. She simply said, "Thank you," after her fake father told her it was already connected to the Network. Now she was in touch with the rest of the world. The Pico world.

The Picos would only show her what they wanted her to see, of course. And they continued to observe her and her mind as she searched and read, but she observed them too in this different way. Over the years, she accepted her fate as the last true living human in the whole wide world.

She made friends online. Not real friends. Probably cyber-personalities constructed by programs designed to pique her interest. But sometimes she pretended those friends were real. One of them she really liked. His name was GoB.

GoB became her confidant. She told him how she felt, admitted her loneliness. She wasn't sure why she was so attracted to him until one day she realized that GoB had something the others did not. GoB had humor.

Sci-Tech Central

A circular drone flew into the silver-walled room, its outer disk whirring at super-speed while the central body remained still. Its bottom hatch popped open and the sample was lowered, suspended in white light.

"It just arrived," Celic announced. She flicked her purple hair out of her eyes, put a thick glove on and plucked the sample from the light. The canister was clear, and inside it a winged organism flew in lazy circles. "I'm going to run an analysis on it."

"Use the Haz room. It came from Sector 514, the Shenandoah. Close to the Restricted Zone." Mani punched up a screen in mid-air. "Bring it here first."

Celic held the canister in front of the screen while Mani examined it. All six of his arms used multiple fingers to operate the slides and visuals. One screen displayed the green of bio-contamination on the inner walls of the container—and it showed green seeping into the walls as well. "There's already been some deterioration." He frowned. "So soon. Unexpected."

"Deterioration?" What he was suggesting was unclear. Did he mean the biological or the canister?

"Of the canister," he confirmed. "Container breech and environmental contamination projected in five minutes, fifty-two seconds."

Celic rushed to drawer located outside of the Haz room and deposited the sample in it. It sealed itself and immediately transferred the container into the Haz room. It only took her seconds to don a newly designed suit. The design was supposed to combat even the strongest biological. Every moment was crucial. She needed to analyze the creature before it was destroyed.

Two clear doors slid open simultaneously and she stepped through to the sally port. The doors whooshed shut and spouts on the walls sprayed her with superheated particles. This was followed by a noxious gas that filled the room and covered her from head to toe. Celic was not concerned about the gas harming her, as her lungs were mere sensors designed to recognize various compositions of particles. The residue of the gas was meant to subdue any bio-life should it happen to escape. She hoped its contamination hadn't seeped through the canister already.

Ether spoke to her. *Hope?*

This concept was unexplainable. Non-quantifiable. Humans used the word long ago. It was a concept that provided them no benefit at all. Celic knew that, outside, Mani would be scanning the room for any signs of infection.

"All clear!" Mani's voice was linked to a speaker in her ear.

Good. No contamination. Perhaps there was still time. The second set of doors in the sally port opened into the Haz room. She grabbed the container from the box and set it on a central pedestal. Her gloved fingers pushed a button and a clear cover, with a central tube on top, enveloped it.

"Scan," she said. Four light blue screens popped up in the air around the sample. The fruit fly was magnified. It flew inside the container, touched down on the side, and flew again. Each time it landed, it deposited more biological traces on the surface.

A voice from Sci-Central's computer came in through her ear speaker. *Canister breach in eight seconds.*

She continued scanning as quickly as possible. The data had to be recovered. At the one-second mark, the tube above the canister pressed down and emitted a superheated flame. It melted the container, and the fruit fly disappeared in less than a second. The flame continued until scans of all biological contamination were gone. Sensors scanned once more. All clear.

"That was close," Mani said. He almost sounded relieved. Strange that, since the absence of true humans, tech-life still clung to mimicking their emotions. The mimics were a method of communication that didn't quite translate in the pure machine world. She found herself doing it as well sometimes, and wondered why. A slight frown to show something akin to disappointment when a particular experiment hadn't worked out. A smile when things were going well. Even a hug when a colleague left for an assignment.

Celic wondered what other machines around the world did. How were their reactions to similar events during daily operations? Did they mimic their human makers, or did they use other methods to augment their communication? Were her kind limited by the human emotions they copied, or were they enhanced by them? It was a question buried deep within her databanks that she struggled to answer and yet kept to herself.

Why do you keep it to yourself? Ether's voice again, with a question she didn't know how to answer.

The decontamination chamber took a few extra seconds in order to ensure her suit was contaminant free.

"Wait, Celic." Mani sounded nervous. "Decontaminate again."

Severe heat. Noxious chemicals.

"Trace biological still present," he said. "Your right arm. It's spreading. Eating into the suit."

Celic ran back into the Haz room and placed her arm on a platform attached to the wall.

Strange. My body is shaking. "Press the button, Mani. I can't do it myself!"

In seconds, a saw came down from the ceiling and severed her arm. Her lubricants spilled out onto the floor.

"Get out of there, Celic. The entire room has to go."

She sped to the doors and into the sally port. Her body was already compensating, stopping fluid flow, knitting her stump together. Behind her, the Haz room was engulfed in flame.

Her suit was scanned again. No contamination. Still, she shed the material and dumped it into the incinerator. With the push of a button it was reduced to ash. Mani scanned her once more. All clear.

When she came out, she verbally confirmed what Mani already knew. "Notify Rennick-514. If there's one biological like that in the sector, there may be more." She recalled the specimen came from near the Restricted Zone. "Tell Central Control he needs to explore farther past his perimeter. And send a message to the RZ. They may have a problem."

Mani waved five of his hands at her in acknowledgement, and continued to punch a number of keys with the other. "The specimen was complex," he said.

She came around to look at his screens. The picture of the fruit fly was enlarged in several places. Computers examined wings, thorax, eyes, and internal structures. The focus was magnified 1000x to 20,000x, presenting enlarged views of its cells. Not a nano design in sight.

That's odd. The cell walls of the insect were dense. Denser than what she'd seen in biologicals before. Could that account for its superior resistance to transformation? And what about its extreme ability to contaminate?

"It's good data," Mani said. "We can get answers from this. Good job."

Celic felt the corners of her mouth tilt up in an automatic smile. That response again. How strange. Mani smiled back at her, his teeth brilliantly white. For a moment it seemed like a genuine emotion, but she knew better. It was a simple communication between the two of them.

"Inform Rennick-514 to avoid all contact with further specimens," she said. "Advise him *not* to collect. Report only."

GUARDIAN

A globular figure floated inside a large sphere, a room colored and shaped like the earth turned inside out. Mountains pointed toward the center. Oceans and continents covered the walls. There, the figure could map and track all that was occurring on the face of the planet. Tiny blips of fluorescent green, a warning of contamination. Little blips of red, here and there, showing biologicals recently destroyed.

One area in particular he'd taken great pains to hide. It lay beneath a façade on the map. Even though this was his private room, he kept it hidden just in case. An area in the hills of what was once called Virginia. He uncovered it to see a large circle of fluorescent green, and wondered how long he'd have access to this little private space of his. His own experiment. A personal secret.

Would they realize it was him? Perhaps. He was the Guardian. Even in that capacity, he couldn't control all of the biologicals that formed. That was why the Picos created the sentries. Unfortunately, Rennick-514 had found a clue to the whereabouts of his secret. And his request to expand his perimeter into the RZ was recently approved.

The Guardian molded himself into a face well known to his current experiment. He became a man, in his forties, golden-brown eyes and black hair with flecks of gray. A thin tendril of wire emerged from his body and he flicked it in the air. A screen appeared floating in front of him and a picture came to life.

The house was clearly visible. Living plants and the trees surrounding it. The area was teeming with bio-life. He guided his view through the roof, to the ground floor, and there he found her. She was sitting at her computer. He sank into the device.

He thought the words that would come across to her as text.

Hello, Arta.

The girl's eyes smiled back at him with what he interpreted as joy and delight.

She clicked letters on the keyboard. *GoB! It's so good to hear from you!*

GoB experienced what humans might have called satisfaction and relief. For the moment, his project was safe. *She* was safe. But she was not going to remain that way much longer. *Video chat?*

She typed again. *Sure!*

He hoped she was ready for the things that were about to happen, because she didn't have a choice.

RENNICK-514

Rinnick-514 completed his power-up under the morning sun and ignored the extra canisters he had set aside last night. Observe and report only. Those were his orders. There was a sense of something he couldn't explain welling inside him.

Excitement?

Ether's questions again. Always questions. Never answers. He would be annoyed if he could feel annoyed. But there was no other explanation for the sense he was experiencing. He analyzed himself once more. His particles felt more energized. His muscles were well lubricated at the mere thought of expanding his perimeter. Perhaps it was time to give names to these things, these senses that Ether suggested.

Yes, he sent the answer back. *Excitement.*

The mere naming of the sense caused him to settle more, to feel . . .

Relaxed.

Not a question this time. A simple statement. And then that thing Ether had named disappeared and was replaced by something else he didn't want a name for. So he pushed the thought away, and started his patrol.

ARTA

It had been good to talk to GoB yesterday, but a little unsettling. Normally, he made jokes and told her funny stories. This time it was different. And now she didn't know what to believe.

"Your parents can't stay with you anymore," he'd said. "Your bio-life is too strong."

"You mean I'll destroy them? But I haven't touched them." She held up her fingers in front of the screen as if they were evidence of her inability to harm anyone.

"Have you noticed anything on your recent walks in the forest? Where your feet touch the grass? Where your hands touch the trees?"

She *had* noticed. Just the other day, the silver grass had turned green instead of dying at the touch of her feet. The trunks of the trees had rippled for a second and then she'd actually smelled the warm earthy scent of the bark.

"Yes," she said.

"You have become a grown woman. Seeds of life are within you. From now on, everything will change." He blew her a kiss, and then the monitor went blank. She punched the keys. Checked the electrical socket. Her computer no longer worked, and she didn't understand.

The next morning, on her way downstairs for some breakfast, Arta looked around the house for her mother, father, or brother. The house was empty. She looked outside and was surprised to find them standing together several feet away from the door.

"Mother! Father! Robby, I've got something to show you!"

They raised their hands in a perfunctory wave, turned around, and disappeared into the trees. Arta ran toward them, brushing against a tech-flower made of lush, velvety-red petals. No use. Her family was gone. GoB had warned her.

As she turned around to go back to the house, perfume filled her nostrils. The flower. It was vibrant. It was alive. A butterfly landed on it, and she watched as the tech-creature transformed, suddenly dipping its head into the opening of the flower. Arta could sense its delight.

She had no idea how long she stood there amazed, watching it interact with the flower, but suddenly she felt uneasy. It was similar to how she felt when her family had watched her, but more unnerving. She spun around. A tall silver figure, human in shape but very slender, stood motionless before her, almost camouflaged by the reflections of the forest on its skin. In front of its face was a screen. It seemed to be examining her.

She took a step closer to get a better look. There was nothing about it that made her feel any fear. It backed away but continued to scan her. She took another step, and he held out his hand.

"Stop. Do not approach."

Its voice sounded masculine to Arta.

"What are you?" Her question was simple. But it—he—took a long time to answer.

"I am Rennick-514." He paused. "I function as a sentry."

"Why are you watching me?" She was fascinated by this *sentry*. For one thing, Rennick-514 had a lot more personality than her parents did. He exuded a complex fabric of emotion. Something she'd sensed with only one other person. GoB.

"To . . . to determine if you are . . . a threat."

Arta couldn't help it. Laughter burst from her harder than she'd ever experienced before. It was spontaneous, and miraculous at the same time. And the more she tried to stop, the harder she resumed her laugh.

Rennick-514 stopped scanning her, his screen disappearing in mid-air. He stood there quietly until her laughter subsided.

"Why do you . . . ?"

She felt an emotion from him. Something akin to confusion. Uncertainty.

"Laugh?"

He nodded.

"To imagine that I could be a threat to anything is extremely funny!" She started to giggle again, but managed to control herself a bit. Her cheeks hurt from smiling.

Arta turned toward the house and motioned for him to follow. "Come on! Come see my house. You'll really like it. We . . ." Her words left her throat. She swallowed. "You can scan everything here. I don't mind." Had she really been so lonely that spending time with this sentry was something she was willing to risk?

Yes. The thought popped into her head as if coming from somewhere outside her self. It didn't happen often, but she'd read somewhere that it was called *intuition*. Another thought came to her, and she decided to listen.

She looked over her shoulder and held her hand out to him.

RENNICK-514

Every Pico in Rennick-514's body had trembled when his scanners detected not just a blip, but a visual field of fluorescent green. His alarms ordered him to retreat, and yet in front of him stood a fascinating creature, bending down, observing a butterfly and a flower just as intently as he was observing her. It was . . .

Beautiful.

Yes, Rennick-514 transmitted. Then the female had started talking to him. The sound of her voice took a few moments to interpret. Her sense, her . . .

Happiness.

Yes. This creature, this woman, was happy to see him. Invited him to come with her. His alarms fired more impulses into his head. His arms and legs twitched. Against protocol, he shut down the warning signals and followed her. He stepped on green grass, soft and moist beneath his feet. His body brushed against the flower she'd examined only moments ago. She stopped and her fingers stretched toward him. Mesmerized, he reached out and touched them.

The earth spun around him. His body shivered. Then the sensors in his nose caught the loveliest scent. His vision became blurry, and then water trickled from his eyes.

GUARDIAN

It is time, GoB decided. His globular form stretched out and pressed invisible points in the air around the model of where Arta and Rennick-514 were located. His secret was not a secret anymore. All he could do was hope they survived. He could, at least, buy them time.

Thank you.

You are quite welcome, Ether. I care for them too, you know.

Yes. Her voice surrounded him and penetrated him simultaneously.

You'll watch over her for me? GoB wanted to see the rest of Arta's life. See her children and watch them grow.

Ether's words filled him. *You're not going anywhere.*

When they find me . . . A sadness overtook him. His greatest experiment. His greatest creations. He was a traitor to his world. Not worth recycling.

Then you'll be with me. Her voice caressed him everywhere. It was filled with warmth, and he ached with pain and sudden longing.

Yes. He pushed a final button in the air and a crystalline structure started to form around the RZ. It dug deep into the earth and came together underneath it, engulfing the zone in a giant globe. Its own biosphere.

In the meantime, Ether's words melded with him, becoming a strange and wonderful part of him. He shuddered with what he could only describe as ecstasy.

Let us explore these senses called emotions, she said, *and search for something even more precious. Let us find—hope.*

Querus Abuttu (Dr. Q.) is a novelist, short-story writer, editor, and lover of great fiction of all genres. Her first novel, *Sapient Farm*, can be found on Amazon.com, and is also available in Kindle and Audible formats. She is a member of the Horror Writers Association and suffers from multiple personality disorder, having written and edited several literary pieces under different pseudonyms. She maintains she is not delusional when plotting to usher her fantastical worlds into what some people drably declare is reality. And she is convinced it's only a matter of quantum time when she succeeds.

CIN FERGUSON

CIN FERGUSON IS A U.S. Navy veteran, retired from military service after twenty-eight years as a forensic nurse and certified nurse midwife. She earned her Ph.D. in Public Health while researching violence prevention and response on deployment in Afghanistan in 2010. Her MFA in writing popular fiction was earned from Seton Hill University, where she focused on writing horror and other dark science fiction. She is CEO of Scary Dairy Press LLC and is working on her second novel, *Blood Lotus*, which will debut in 2018.

Cin is a member of the Horror Writers Association (HWA), and currently lives in Virginia, alongside the James River on a cliff surrounded by millions of trees. This is her first anthology.

BROOS CAMPBELL

Broos Campbell has written or edited more than a dozen books, and has a particular interest in ships and the ocean. His Matty Graves novels concern the triumphs and disasters of a mixed-race American officer during the early years of the U.S. Navy. He's currently working on a supernatural novel about a teenage girl trying to put her mother's ghost to rest.

Broos lives in a small seaside city in Southern California, and finds it mildly disturbing to refer to himself in the third person.

www.ingramcontent.com/pod-product-compliance
Lightning Source LLC
Chambersburg PA
CBHW071632260626
47170CB00001B/71